"I thought I knew Jenna's story. I know it i
dignity in the face of unimaginable difficult)
mom's words, and even in her own words, is t
different lens. This deeply moving book shows us the vulnerability of
a teenager facing her own mortality, the dogged passion of a mother
determined to give her child her best fighting chance, and the love of
a father and sister determined to create moments of joy even in the
face of their deepest fears. It is a lesson in resilience, and a real
tribute to the young woman they loved so much."

PIPPA HUDSON, TALK SHOW HOST – CAPE TALK

"This is the story of concentric waves of human connective
tissue, people who entered, with open, brave and broken hearts, the
kingdom of the sick, where Jenna dwelt in the last years of her short
comet-like life. It is an account of a battle against impossible odds:
disease, time, human error, the vagaries of medical insurance and, in
the end, death – that great absence. It is the story unadorned.
An account, from the heart, of a family confronted with multiple
grief and suffering, who somehow keep going, buoyed by the strength,
love and determination that blossomed in the wound."

MARIANNE THAMM, AUTHOR, JOURNALIST – DAILY MAVERICK

"This is an extraordinary book about a brave young woman's
fight to keep on living. The few hours I spent with Jenna, six months
before her death, left a lasting impact on me. Her story, told so
tenderly by her mom, Gabi, should be read by everyone. It will
make you appreciate every breath and every moment on this earth."

MELANIE VERWOERD, AMBASSADOR AND FORMER DIRECTOR –
UNICEF IRELAND

"Get Me to 21 is the beautifully written story of a mother's
epic struggle. This book will break your heart, as it simultaneously
teaches lessons of grit, determination and resilience in the face of
unthinkable loss. Gabi Lowe has the electrifying ability to pick you up
and slam you into her – and every parent's – worst nightmares, while
gracefully and powerfully demonstrating how to survive them."

VANESSA RAPHAELY, AUTHOR AND FORMER EDITOR – COSMOPOLITAN MAGAZINE

First published by MFBooks Joburg, an imprint of Jacana Media
(Pty) Ltd, in 2019
Second impression 2019

10 Orange Street
Sunnyside
Auckland Park 2092
South Africa
+2711 628 3200
www.jacana.co.za

© Gabi Lowe, 2019

ISBN 978-1-928420-53-8

Cover design and layout by Alexandra Turner
Editing by Alison Lowry
Proofreading by Megan Mance
Set in Sabon 11/15pt
Printed by ABC Press, Cape Town
Job no. 003597

See a complete list of MFBooks Joburg titles at www.jacana.co.za

May Jenna's grace and courage stay with you always... Gabi Lowe

Get Me to 21

The Jenna Lowe Story

Gabi Lowe

May Jesus's grace and courage stay with you always... Get well

Jenna: my beloved angel-child. So here it is. The heartbreaking truth as I remember it. I dedicate this book to you with deep love and every iota of my being. I am deeply grateful for the privilege of being your mother. You've left an indelible imprint on my heart, filled with your teachings and a void that will never be filled. I love you, Jenna. You have shaped the course of my life.

Kristi: my beloved earth-child. I am so proud of you. As I wrote Jen's story I felt I unearthed a part of yours. I hope that the losses, the disappointments, joy, pain and immense trauma you have had to deal with will enrich your life in ways you have yet to discover. I love you with all my heart and dedicate this book to you in the belief that a part of you will be set free by the telling of the story. Maybe you will write your own story one day.

Stuart: the love of my life, my rock. Your fierce love and support of me, of us all, your unfailing courage, your wisdom, humour and passion are a guiding light in my life. Thank you for helping to keep me on course, for holding me and loving me unwaveringly in the face of a parent's worst nightmare. I dedicate this book to you, with all my love and gratitude for your unquestionable belief in me and in us, for better, or worse, in sickness and in health. I love you.

Contents

PART 5

Foreword

This is the story of Jenna Lowe, her family – mom Gabi, dad Stuart and sister Kristi – and the concentric waves of human connective tissue – cousins, uncles, aunts, grandparents, friends, lovers and strangers – who entered, with open, brave and broken hearts, the kingdom of the sick, where Jenna dwelt in the last years of her short comet of a life.

It is an account of a battle against impossible odds: disease, time, human error, the vagaries of medical insurance and, in the end, death – that great absence.

It is the story unadorned.

It is an account, from the heart, of a family confronted with multiple grief and suffering, who somehow kept going, buoyed by the strength, love and determination that blossomed in the wound.

Jenna Lowe died on Monday, 8 June 2015, four months before her 21st birthday on 28 October. She had hoped to make it to the celebration with the help of a pair of donor lungs to replace her own, which were steadily being throttled by the then under-diagnosed, life-threatening pulmonary hypertension.

With truly superhuman powers, this family girded its loins against death and the challenges and impossible demands of rare disease.

In the years since Jenna's death much has been accomplished in raising awareness about PH, not only in South Africa but also in the US, the UK and Europe. The Jenna Lowe Trust and the boundaries it has succeeded in shifting – the provision of treatment and medication and other aids for those living with PH – is only one of Jenna's legacies.

She lives on also in the academic award that bears her name at Herschel Girls School, which she attended and where she excelled.

The lives of the Lowe family and that of my own are intertwined through a friendship spanning almost 30 years. As a young couple, Gabi and Stu, glamorous and successful, outgoing, intelligent, with a wide circle of friends, radiated a tangible lust for life. We called them our "Peter Stuyvesant" friends after the cigarette ads of the 1970s featuring healthy, tanned jet-setters living the life.

Theirs was a life built on poise, resolve and hard work.

We were introduced to Jenna in 1994 in Gabi and Stu's sunny cottage in Oranjezicht. A baby with curious, dark playful eyes, Jenna took it all in from the start. The world, for Jenna, was a wide open canvas. Later, when she found the language to articulate her investigations of the universe, she could mistakenly come across as precocious.

At eight, Jenna wrote a book, a story about a girl who falls ill after stepping on a poisoned thorn and who must find a magic cure. The story for the child in *The Magic Bissie Tree* ends happily, the sickness beaten back.

But in real life, not for Jenna and all who loved and came to know her.

It was philosopher Susan Sontag, in her now classic 1978 "inquiry", *Illness as Metaphor*, who defined the two kingdoms – that of the well and that of the sick – and reminded us that we all carry dual citizenship. It was Sontag who remarked that "the most truthful way of regarding illness – and the healthiest way of being ill – is one most purified of, most resistant to, metaphoric thinking".

Here it is then.

The story of a family and a community, an account of horror and triumph, exasperation and courage.

A real story, stripped of baubles and platitudes, purified of unnecessary metaphor, carried by tenderness, wisdom and love.

This is what it takes, blow by blow, to fight back.

And what it takes to get up again when you lose.

Jenna Lowe fought to live. Her remarkable courage and wit are revealed here in Gabi's account not only of her daughter's slow death, but also her full, busy and beautiful life, who Jenna was before PH, according to her lioness of a mom.

You will find here on these pages also the courage and the wisdom Jenna found between the fear, anxiety and the pain, while knowing and understanding all the while that she might not make it.

Death, be not proud.

Marianne Thamm
Cape Town, May 2019

Prologue

It's been three long excruciating years since you died, Jen. I know I have to tell your story, but it is overwhelming. I am immobilised by the enormity of it and cannot seem to start.

Help me, Jen. How can I ever do you justice? How can I find the courage to relive it? But how can I not? I have such a deep sense that your story needs to be told – to help me make sense of the suffering, to help integrate your loss into our lives, to honour your incredible legacy and celebrate the depth of the human spirit.

I'm on the beach, the sun is setting like a large red orb and my heart is aching. Warm air gently caresses my skin. I'm dizzy with the smell of salty air and my face is streaked with tears of grief.

I sway gently back and forth, hugging my body as I bury my toes deeper into the sand. I search the horizon, hoping to feel you, to hear you, when a single white feather floats to the sand.

"I am right here," you whisper. *"I am all around you. Simply tell the story."*

Here it is, the brutal truth, in all its terrible beauty.

The call – Wednesday, 10th December 2014

Keurboomstrand

I am in a restless, dream-filled sleep when my befuddled brain hears the distant sound of my cellphone ringing. It's unusual for me to sleep this late. Sleep-induced fog turns to high alert, nerve endings flash hot and my heart starts thumping. I grab for the phone before I've even remembered where I am.

For seven months I've been hot-wired to this phone, every cell in my body straining and waiting for it to ring. I take it with me to the toilet, to the kitchen, to do the grocery shopping … or simply to walk down the passage to check in on Jenna, my 20-year-old daughter. I listen for it constantly, awake or asleep, and I jump involuntarily every time it rings, my heart in my throat.

And while waiting, I barely leave Jenna's side. I barely leave our suburb. I have certainly not left Cape Town. But now, today, I am not at home. I am not there to sit on the edge of Jenna's bed, to check her pump, to mix fresh medication for the day; to stroke her hair, make her tea and calm her. I'm not there to check the colour of her lips and the nuances of her energy levels.

I am not there.

I am not at home when the call finally comes.

Instead I am six hours away up the east coast in Keur-boomstrand, a tiny village just outside Plettenberg Bay, with my younger daughter, Kristi. Yesterday I found my first-ever pansy shell in the shallow waters of Keurbooms beach and proclaimed with a hopeful heart that this might just be a sign. Last night I did something totally out of character: I ate half a weed brownie. Why? What was I thinking? There seemed to be such good reasons at the time and yet the minute I'd done it I couldn't remember any of them. I became paranoid and fearful. I'd had a strong feeling I should pack my bags. But I dismissed the idea. I was just being paranoid, right? Had I lost my mind? What on earth was I doing? Such a damn stupid thing to have eaten that cookie at such a vulnerable time. Feeling highly anxious, I had gone straight to bed so I could sleep it off.

Now half-awake, groggy, my head aching and wracked with nausea from the stupid brownie, I answer the phone.

"Hello? Gabs? Gabs, are you awake?" It's Stuart, but he sounds different, apprehensive, excited and afraid. A pause ... a deep breath. "Gabs, we've got lungs. Angela just phoned. It's happened, Gabs. We've got lungs for Jen."

Thick, hot, sticky adrenaline floods my body, my knees are weak, my heart squeezes, and my stomach turns to water. For 200 days we've planned, waited for and imagined this moment, right down to the last detail, but right now I can't think straight. My brain is exploding.

Stuart's voice cuts through my shock. "Gabs!" Then more gently and soothingly, "Gabs, get Kristi, pack and get on a plane to Johannesburg, now. We'll meet you there in about four hours. I must get off the phone to make the other calls we planned, but get on a plane ... fast. I'll stay in touch. I love you."

This is not how I imagined I'd feel, an all-consuming flood of elation and terrible dread at the same time. It's an unimaginable feeling. The realisation that this is it. Jenna's only hope, her chance at life has arrived. But it's not supposed to be like this. I am supposed to be with her, and with Stuart. We should all be at home together. I am supposed to be calm. But, no matter where I am, this is it. Operation O2 has kicked into action.

I throw open the bedroom door and run down the passage, cold tiles braising the soles of my feet, shouting breathlessly, "Kristi, Kristi! We got the call, we got the call … Kristi, we've got lungs!"

Hungover teenagers emerge from their bedrooms, staring at me wide-eyed. Kristi, my 17-year-old daughter, runs from her bedroom as pale as a ghost, eyes wide with shock. My inner lioness kicks into action. "Kristi, pack your stuff. We're leaving for the airport in 10 minutes; 10 minutes, that's all we've got, okay, my love? Go!"

I run back to my bedroom and call my lifelong friend Jillie. No two people are better equipped to get us on a flight to Johannesburg immediately than Ian and Jillie. They live in Plett, they know everyone, they have influence, they love us. More importantly, they love Jenna. Ian and Jillie are Jen's godparents. They will get us on a flight. My hands are shaking so much I can barely tap the numbers on my phone. I feel as if I'm hovering above my own body. I force myself to breathe large lungfuls of air. All signs of brain fog are gone.

"Jillie?" I can barely recognise my own voice. "Jillie, we got the call. We have lungs. I need your help. We have a donor for Jenna. Kristi and I have to get to Johannesburg, now."

Silence. And then, "I'll call you back."

I'm barefoot in my pyjamas, cupboard door wide open, scooping handfuls of clothing into my bag with one hand, my cellphone in the other. I stare at it in disbelief. Did Jillie really just put the phone down? Instantly it rings.

"Okay, I can breathe now. Gabs, we will get you on a plane. Don't worry, we will get you on a plane. I'm calling Ian. You and Kristi just pack. Ian will sort the flights and I will fetch you now. It will take me 10 minutes to get to you. Be ready, okay? Breathe, my friend, breathe."

Twelve minutes later Jillie's car crunches up the dirt road outside. I throw my car keys and the house keys at Kristi's stunned group of teenage friends. "Kids, I need you to pack up, clean up the house and lock up. And you're going to have to drive my car and the trailer back to Cape Town. I'm sorry. But we have to leave now. Be careful and be safe." Reggie, Kristi's boyfriend, and Dean have literally only just got their driver's licences. And all of them have just spent 10 days partying hard at Matric Rage. I'm concerned about whether they are up to the task, but there is no choice; they are going to have to step up and take charge.

Fifteen minutes after the first phone call from Stuart we are speeding along the Garden Route highway towards George airport, hazard lights flashing. Jillie is at the wheel, I am in the passenger seat, willing the car to go faster, and Kristi, now a whiter shade of pale, sits in shocked silence on the back seat.

Cape Town: Wednesday, 10th December 2014, 9:10 am

As usual for this time of day, Jenna is fast asleep. Stuart is in his office, which is on our property at home, outside the main house, going about his normal working day.

Jenna's cellphone rings but she doesn't take the call. Of course, she can't take the call. She is now at stage IV of her illness, and so oxygen deprived that she sleeps for a large part of the day and is hard to wake up. But on this day something makes her stir. The call cuts off before she gets to it, but almost immediately the landline down the passage starts to ring. Queen, as caring and regal as her name suggests, has been helping me as Jenna's nurse aide for nearly a year now. Close by in the kitchen, she picks up the call. It's Angela, regional transplant co-ordinator from Milpark Hospital in Johannesburg. Queen's pace quickens as she takes the phone outside to Stuart in his office. He is on a call to a client, but Queen thrusts the phone at him with an unusual sense of urgency.

"Hello, Stuart? It's Angela from Milpark Hospital. How fast can you get Jenna to Johannesburg? We've got lungs. We have a match. Stuart, we have lungs for Jenna."

Down the passage behind a closed door Jenna, our beautiful

20-year-old daughter, waits. Normally she never stirs much before lunchtime, but on this day something is different. She intuitively knows. She sits up slowly in her bed in the dark, bedroom blinds still drawn, and waits.

"We will make a plan. We will get there, Angela, we will get there. How long do we have?" Heart pounding, Stuart turns to Brandon, his business partner, and Queen, who is waiting expectantly. "Brandon, Queen … this is it. We have a green light for Operation O2, and Gabs isn't here. I need your help."

He picks up a stapled document sitting at the top of his in-tray. It is three pages long and marked boldly "Operation O2". Five days earlier, the day I left for Keurboomstrand with Kristi, I had printed out a fresh copy and Stuart and I had gone through it carefully together. When the call you have been waiting for so many months for finally comes, your mind can temporarily leave. He is grateful for our military preparedness and follows the instructions word for word. We have plotted it carefully and fastidiously:

"Operation O2"

	To do	Action	Status
1	New Discovery authorisation numbers	Gabi	Done
2	Copy of all IDs plus Lizzie's for Sue J	Gabi	Done
3	Create phone tree for Mary B and Sue J	Gabi	Done
4	Dry run to ExecuJet Cape Town	Stu/Steve	Done
5	Pack medication bag and spare meds	Gabs/ Lizzie	Done
6	Pack a hospital bag: PJs, toiletries etc.	Gabs	Done
7	Buy emergency car lights	Stu	

	When the call comes	
1	Call nurse Lizzie Brierley (Liz calls Queen)	Gabi
2	Where is Kristi? Find her, get her home	Stuart
3	Call Mary and Sue: airport lift to come to us	Gabi
4	Phone pilots: • Larry Beamish • Gunther Grobers • Garreth Gill • Ryan Dassonville • Ampie Steynberg • Jonathan Ackerman	Stuart
5	Discovery to activate authorisation numbers	Gabi
6	Call Raffaella Ruttell at Discovery Health	Gabi
7	Call Alison Paynter at Discovery	Gabi
8	Lanseria Helicopter: Disco 911 0860 999 911	Stu
9	Lanseria ground crew: Carlene Morrison	Stu
10	Call Prof. Wilcox	Stu
11	Call house-sitter for Bertha Ave to look after house and dogs	Stu
12	Pack Chase and battery for Chase	Stu
13	Pack Oxy-Jen and all portable oxygen, plus additional cylinders for plane	Gabi
14	Pack all bags and oral drugs (complete green bag 80% packed in drug den)	Gabi

15	Pack pesonal belongings, pyjamas, toiletries, clothes	Gabi/Stu/Kristi
16	Complete Jen packaging (80% done in bag in room)	Jen/Lizzie/Queen
17	Call Sarah at The Parkwood re accomm for first night	Mary/Sue
18	Call Sandy Harper if Parkwood full	Mary/Sue
19	Lift from Lanseria to Milpark – Richard Seegers?	Mary/Sue
20	No other calls to anyone until we are at Cape Town airport	All
21	Phone Granny, Grampa, Shirley and Ali	Gabs/Stu
22	Calls to other key family and friends and WhyFive (Brandon)	Mary/Sue
23	Call Abbotts and Stables re: Kristi	Gabi
24	GET TO AIRPORT AND FLY TO JHB	Jenna/Stu/Gabi/ Kristi/Lizzie

Stuart takes a deep breath and musters all the calm he can. The first call is of course to me and Kristi, then the very next to Nurse Lizzie and the third to my rock and neighbour, Mary Berry. After making the first few calls, he pads softly into Jenna's room to wake her and share the news. I don't think there can be a more significant moment for a parent. He is very surprised to see Jen sitting up in her bed in the dark, waiting, her soft brown eyes watching the door expectantly.

"Jen, my love, it was Angela from Milpark Hospital. We've got lungs, Jen. They found a match. This is it, my love. It's time to pack for Johannesburg."

She looks at him with those intelligent eyes and says, "I heard the landline and I knew, Dad, I just knew."

My stomach lurches when I imagine what was going on in Jenna's mind at that precise moment. She was under no illusions. This was her one and only chance at life ... but she also knew that lung transplants are extremely complex, and that she was desperately sick. The truth was that she might not survive the transplant – but she couldn't live without it. A terrible, gut-wrenching conundrum. For months she had been living in both expectant hope and terrible dread of this call. She had fought so hard for this miracle. Just a few weeks earlier, as we lay cuddled up together on her bed, she had turned to me and said, "Mom, one of the hardest parts is that I don't know if I am preparing to live or preparing to die."

And there it is, the ultimate gut-twisting paradox of hope and fear. She is 20, just 20 years old. This call is her ultimate chance at life, and yet it is so risky.

Getting Jenna safely to Johannesburg, within four hours, requires military precision. At this stage she is on high levels of supplemental oxygen and a 24-hour-a-day pump of volatile intra-venous medication. She is too weak and compromised to walk, never mind travel in a commercial aircraft cabin. But we have a clear and well-thought-out plan, with every detail documented.

Except I am not there. Barrier number one. Stuart continues executing Operation O2 without me. He has no choice.

With her golden-red hair, large light green eyes, friendly face and calm comforting manner, my trusted friend, confidante and neighbour of 15 years, Mary has become an essential and life-affirming support system for me. She lives directly opposite our driveway and is one of the first people on the list to call. I wouldn't have gone away with Kristi if Mary wasn't on hand and available for the time I was away. Within minutes she arrives at the house to help. Stu desperately needs to continue with phone calls as he has much to arrange (including the small matter of a plane! The city of Johannesburg is a two-hour flight from the city of Cape Town), and so it is the trusted Mary who goes into Jen's bedroom to be with her at a moment I always believed would be me. Jen, who in all the years Mary has known her to remain rational and full of smiles, is unusually anxious, but she keeps her tone calm.

"Jen," she says, "we can't control whatever is unfolding here today, but what we know for sure is that this is going to be one of the most interesting days of your life."

Even at the most challenging of times Jenna's intellect and curiosity are always at play, and this perspective appeals to her. Selfishly, I wish with all my heart that it had been me with Jen at that moment, but on reflection (apart from the fact that I can't change it) I think that the severity and significance of the moment would have been harder for her to cope with if I had been there, because Jenna would have felt responsible for the full weight of my fear and I would have felt responsible for the full weight of hers.

Stuart continues systematically executing Operation O2 without me. He hits a second barrier almost immediately. Months and months ago, Jonathan Ackerman and his family, out of the goodness of their hearts, had promised that when the moment came they would help get Jen to Johannesburg. He phones Jonathan, who picks up right away, and explains quickly what is unfolding. The Ackerman jet which has been on standby all those months is currently away in Europe. So is the head pilot. Stuart returns to methodically making his way down the list … every plane and every pilot is *not* on the ground in Cape Town. He phones option after option, getting more and more determined with each call. Meanwhile, unbeknown to him, Jonathan is activating his network, asking just one question. "What jets are on the ground in Cape Town?" Within 15 minutes Stuart's phone rings. The caller is the pilot of the owner of a jet, whose urgent call caught him in his swim-shorts just as he was about to get into the ocean at Bloubergstrand for a long paddle-ski with his co-pilot and best friend. This incredibly kind man – who we don't even know – is giving us his jet to take Jenna to Johannesburg.

"We are on our way to the runway," the pilot tells Stuart. "We will be ready and waiting in 20 minutes."

Stuart is still talking on the phone when Jonathan pulls up in our driveway. It is a colleague of his who has made this happen. His two pilots have quite literally dumped their paddle-ski, grabbed their car keys and are driving to the private runway at Cape Town International Airport. We have a plane.

Nurse Lizzie arrives at the house. She has her own gate-opener and lets herself in. Originally from the UK, blonde, blue-eyed lovely Lizzie is in her late 20s. She is a fully qualified nurse and has a youthful, wise soul. Serendipitously, she found her way to us through a long-standing former work colleague of mine from my magazine days. For the past year, Lizzie and I have spent every morning together mixing and administering the medication (an intravenous vaso-dilator called Eproprostenol) that goes into Jenna's right heart chamber via a medical pump and a port in her chest. The mixing – a precise 35-step sterile process – takes an hour and a half (well, we eventually got it down to an hour) and requires both of us to concentrate throughout and double-check accuracy for safety's sake. While I am away with Kristi, Lizzie has been doing the mixing either on her own or with Stuart at her side, both of them clad in their gloves and masks. Lizzie had been about to leave for our house to do the day's mixing when she got the call from Stuart to say we've got lungs. She now arrives packed, calm, ready to fly and help.

Lizzie busies herself immediately with the medical side of things, checking on Jen, closely watching her vitals, and cross-referencing our detailed lists to ensure that she and I have packed everything we need. We already have a bag packed and waiting in the drug den (Jen's affectionate name for our mixing room) on standby, but she triple-checks it anyway to make sure it includes extra medication for emergencies and that nothing is missing. What if the organs don't arrive in Johannesburg on time? What if Jen is all prepped and ready for surgery and it can't go ahead for some reason? These are valid and real possibilities that will require extra supplies of her daily intravenous and oral medications.

While Lizzie bustles and preps, Jenna tells Queen and Mary what to pack for her. She is physically weak, and her breathlessness doesn't allow for physical exertion of any kind, so she sits on her bed quietly while the team helps pack. The meds are one thing ... but the transplant also means we will be in Johannesburg not just for surgery but for recovery, rehabilitation and post-transplant care. Once Jen is out, we will have to remain close to the hospital for a minimum of six months, maybe even a year. All of this has to be packed for and thought about in just 20 minutes. Apart from complex medications and digital equipment such as her laptop, iPod, cellphone, Kindle and digital photo album, Jen's priorities are books, journals and soft comfortable clothing. She is also a stationery and toiletries junkie. Weeks and weeks later, when I unpack her belongings on the other side, it will be poignant to see what she thought she might need.

Sitting on her bed in her red dressing-gown and fluffy slippers, Jen is staring down the biggest moment of her life: massive surgery, a potentially lifesaving double lung transplant, and a move to Johannesburg away from everyone and everything she knows and loves. It will start in 15 minutes. She has time to send just one text, to her boyfriend James, and her two best friends Alex and Camilla. It says three words only …

"Lungs. Johannesburg. Now."

The bags are packed

The gate opposite our home slides quietly open and Steve Berry reverses his large red Toyota into our driveway so that Jenna's mobility scooter, additional oxygen cylinders for the flight, the fastidiously packed bulging bags of medication, plus all the luggage can be loaded into the back of his car. As the "Cape Town team" are mobilising, Jen's besties, Camilla and Alex, arrive wide-eyed to say goodbye. Emotion-filled hugs, some difficult words of support and hope-filled anticipation linger in the air as Jen is carried to the car. A last check … they have everything – it is a mere 35 minutes since the first phone call from Angela, the transplant co-ordinator. But where is James?

Filled to capacity, the red SUV starts making its way up Bertha Avenue in the direction of the airport. As Steve is about to turn left, a silver Polo comes speeding towards him and screeches to a halt. James throws open the car door, jumps out clad in his gym shorts, T-shirt and training shoes and runs towards Jen. They can't say goodbye, it is too loaded; impossible, they just can't say goodbye. "Come to the airport," says Stu. James gets back in his car and follows the red SUV, speeding behind them as they head purposefully towards the airport. He will say goodbye on the runway.

George airport

Back up the coast on the Garden Route we, too, are speeding along a highway, but to George airport. Jillie, my serene Mother-Earth, fun-loving, lifelong friend, has her hazard lights flashing. She is concentrating hard, focusing on keeping us safe and me calm. The intention is to make the 10:45 am flight to Johannesburg. It's going to be tight, but we can make it.

The phone rings. It's Ian. He asks me to pass the phone to Jillie – strange, because she is driving, but he insists. Jillie listens. "Oh, okay. Okay, we will do that," she says, slowing down. "I will call you from the airport." She ends the call and lifts her foot slightly off the gas. Then she switches off the hazards and slows down to a normal pace. My heart quickens. What is she doing? This is a matter of life and death, we have to get there!

"Gabs, my Gabs, you are going to have to take a deep breath," Jillie says. "There are currently no planes on the runway in George. A massive storm in Johannesburg has grounded them all. We will head to the airport anyway, but Ian says the next plane is only due in a few hours' time." I open my mouth, about to protest. "He's checked the private planes too. There is nothing on the ground, my friend." She reaches over with one hand to take mine. Kristi, sitting in the back, doesn't say a word. Neither do I ... there is too much to say. We drive the rest of the way to the airport in silence. Jillie is right – not a single plane in sight. If there had been, I might well have hijacked it. But there is not one single damn plane on that runway.

We make our way to the coffee shop and Jillie guides us to a table close to the window. She gently busies herself ordering tea to keep us calm. Jen loves tea ... she has a poster in her bedroom that reads "Where there is tea there is hope". We wait, and wait, and wait ... I buy a fluffy monkey at the airport shop, I have no idea why, and I cling to it. I phone my mom and my dad. I phone some close friends to tell them we have lungs. And we wait. And we wait. And we wait.

Cape Town airport

The packed red SUV pulls up on the private runway at Cape

Town International airport only 50 minutes after the first phone call has been made – a planning triumph – where a small jet and its two pilots, who are already preparing for take-off, are ready and waiting. The bags get loaded and James carries Jenna and her oxygen machine up the metal steps to settle her into her seat. Then he fetches the extra tanks and takes them on board. But he still can't say goodbye to Jen. Even the pilot is choked up. The strapping young man looks at James, this fresh-faced 20-year-old trying to say goodbye to his gorgeous young girlfriend and says: "Stay, stay with your girl. We are turning this baby straight back towards Cape Town once we've offloaded everyone at Lanseria airport. We will 'lift' you home afterwards."

And so, while Kristi and I desperately wait in George airport for a commercial plane, Stuart, Nurse Lizzie, Jenna and James take off in the small jet headed for Johannesburg, with Mary and Steve Berry and Jonathan Ackerman waving them goodbye from the runway.

Because it's a private jet, Stuart is able to phone and update me on how Jen is until they reach a certain height. He continues making some necessary logistical calls for as long as he can, including a very important call to Raffaella Ruttell at Discovery Health, our medical health insurance provider. Jenna will need a helicopter and paramedics to get her from the airport, which is north of the city, to Milpark Hospital so that they don't get stuck in the notorious Johannesburg traffic. Stu and Lizzie will follow in an ambulance. Raffaella and her team are on it, efficient and proactive. Operation O2 is not only operational, it is in full flight.

George airport

Phone calls ebb and flow between Stuart and me and still we wait. I am helpless, desperate, my stomach churns, adrenaline coursing. I just want to get to my child, but the mother of storms has other ideas. Kristi is still monosyllabic. One minute she was running with her pack, having a huge party with her boyfriend and her closest mates in Plett and the next she was plucked up and is now jetting her way to Johannesburg, where her sister (and best friend) is about to have massive and complex surgery. She also knows from all our research that the statistics for lung transplants with very sick pulmonary hypertension patients are not ideal.

I focus every bit of strength I have on staying calm and hopeful. This is our opportunity to save Jenna's life, to buy her more time. I need to stay present, but it's hard. It's so hard. There have been very few times in the past 365 days when I have been more than 10 minutes from Jenna's side. I have dedicated myself to taking care of her every need since the port was inserted into her chest on the 10th of December 2013 to start the 24-hour intravenous medication. And yet here I am, stuck at George airport as she wings her way towards a double lung transplant. I should be at her side! We have to get there, fast. I *have* to see her before surgery. I *have* to.

The first plane from George to OR Tambo leaves at 2:15 pm. 2:15 pm! We have been waiting for four hours, four of the longest, most conflicted and anxiety-filled hours of my life. Little do I know how many more of those waiting hours there are to come. Little do I know that this wait is just child's play.

Finally, we are about to board our flight. I won't be able to talk to anyone again while we are in the air, so I phone Stuart one last time.

"We've boarded, Stu, at last. We are on the plane, it's about to take off. How is Jen? What stage are you at?"

Stu is at Milpark Hospital. "Jen had a really difficult time on the jet, my love," he says. "Her oxygen saturation levels dropped dangerously low." James had apparently held her on his lap like a baby. "But the helicopter was ready and waiting to take her straight to the hospital and there was a full complement of doctors and hospital management waiting to receive her. We got here only half an hour later in the ambulance, with all the stuff."

We? Again, James and Jenna haven't been able to say goodbye ... he goes to the hospital with Lizzie and Stu, still dressed in his gym kit.

Soothingly Stuart urges me yet again not to worry. "I'm sure there is still time. They are doing all sorts of tests prepping her for surgery at a slow and leisurely pace and the organs haven't arrived in Johannesburg yet. Just get here safely, Gabs. We are waiting."

I settle in for the longest flight of my life. I spend the two hours thinking about the donor family. Somewhere in South Africa, as I fly towards hope, another mother, another family, is mourning the loss of their beloved while giving mine a chance at life. What is that poor family going through? Who are they? We will never find out. In South Africa the law prohibits you from knowing who your donor family is. The organs can come from anyone – male or female, child or adult – as long as the biology of the tissue, blood type and size are a match. Jen is petite, so the chances are that it had to be someone light in build, with the same blood and tissue type, but we will never know who. I spend the flight sending gratitude and love out into the universe in the hope that some of it will shower down into that mother's heart and ease some of her intense pain and loss.

While we are in flight, Jen is being stabilised and settled into the Isolation Ward, Section 7, where she will move once she is well enough to leave ICU post-surgery. James stays at her side all day, lying next to her on top of the hospital bedding (he's not really allowed, but everyone turns a blind eye), talking to her and keeping her distracted and entertained, chatting to friends on her mobile, while Stuart signs multiple forms, completes the paperwork, and has a tour of the hospital. Lizzie manages other medical logistics such as Jenna's pump and changing of medication and ice-packs. Even though Jen is now in a first-class hospital, there is still no one other than Lizzie and I who know how to mix and administer her meds. In 2014, Jenna is the first person in Africa to be on this medication.

Johannesburg airport

At 4:20 pm Kristi and I land at OR Tambo in Johannesburg. We have a plan – *run*. Forget the luggage and *run* to the first taxi. We stumble off the plane, stampede down the steps and start sprinting toward the exit, thundering down the escalator. As we run past the baggage reclaim conveyor belt towards the exit, I see a familiar and totally unexpected face. Shirley, Stuart's younger sister, is waiting there. The minute he heard about the call, our ridiculously generous, kind-hearted friend Gavin Levy had put Shirley on a plane from Cape Town to come and support us. There are many heartbreaking reasons (which I will share with you later) why Shirl is the perfect person to help guide and hold our family through this unfolding medical drama. I can't believe she is standing there! She can see how frantic I am. "Go, go, you go!" she says. "Get to the hospital! I will bring the luggage."

Kristi and I leave her waiting for our bags and tumble, wheezing (the altitude in Johannesburg is punishing when you first land), into the taxi. "Milpark Hospital," I say. "Take us to Milpark Hospital, fast!" I explain breathlessly that my eldest daughter is being prepped for a lung transplant and I have to get there, fast! The driver looks horrified.

It is 4:30 pm and the road from the airport is thick with bumper-to-bumper traffic. This is normal in Johannesburg for this time of day but made worse because of the large storm and dark moody skies overhead. The driver radios into his office. "Central, central, come in. Switch off the tracking system," he says. "I have an emergency." And just like that our taxi driver switches on his hazard lights, pulls across into the yellow emergency lane on the far left of the four-lane highway, puts his hand on the hooter and floors it.

I phone Stuart. He speaks gently and quietly. I can hear he is near Jenna and trying to keep the mood calm and low-key. "She is nearly ready, Gabs," he says, "but there is a minor delay with the delivery of organs. So that is good for you. Just get here safely. I think you'll make it."

Eight hours after the first phone call from Stuart, at about 5 pm, we skid to a stop in the drop-off zone right outside the Milpark Hospital entrance. Kristi and I scramble out of the taxi and run down the long passage that leads from the entrance hall towards the Surgical ICU. Down the stairs, to the left, through the double doors and down another passage right to the end and through the double no-entry glass doors at the back that read ISOLATION WARD. We push them open, there are nurses everywhere. Kristi reaches for my arm, we look each other straight in the eyes, stop for a moment, and take deep, deep breaths. In unspoken agreement we leave our frantic despair and fear in the passage and walk into Jen's room calm and steady.

We all fall into each other's arms. Relief at seeing Jen floods through me. I just want to hold her. Kristi and I perch on the edge of her hospital bed as she tells us in her gentle breathless voice all about the adventures of the day. But in true Jen fashion she wants to hear Kristi's Plett Rage stories too, not just talk about "the call". I am so grateful that James has been there for her. He makes her happy and he has taken a lot of the angst out of the day. Now he respectfully steps aside and allows Kristi and me our time with Jen. It is the first time I've heard Kristi talk for just about the entire day. I let the two sisters chat and giggle quietly, while I check in with Stuart and Lizzie on the side. They are ready, the medical team is ready. Her new lungs haven't arrived yet, but they are on a plane (from where we don't know) and on their way.

It is time. Time to get our Jen into surgery.

Everything we have been working so hard towards and waiting so hopefully for culminates in this moment. It is emotionally unfathomable, a moment in time so poignant and massive that you can't possibly know how to deal with it, so you just do.

Now it's time to say a pre-surgery goodbye. Stuart, Kristi, James, Lizzie and I walk next to Jen in her hospital bed, all holding her hands, as she is wheeled into the pre-surgery area. My heart is racing but my face is calm and encouraging, my voice gentle and considered. There is so much fear that can't be shown. We all have our brave faces on.

We kiss and hug one last time. Jenna is looking straight up at me, smiling, a smile full of courage and hope. I stroke her soft velvet cheek and kiss it one last time before the nurses pull her bed away from me towards the double doors that read THEATRE. The bed bumps the doors open.

I call out, "See you on the other side, my love."

Jenna calls back over her shoulder, "I'm not going to the other side, Mom." She is smiling encouragingly as the doors close behind her.

Part 1

CHAPTER 1

Profound joy

Nothing could have prepared me for the profound joy of becoming a mother.

I come from a long line of formidable women, who moulded my life in ways that I wasn't cognisant of until I became a mother myself. As a young girl, I remember visiting my great-grandmother and being grotesquely fascinated that anyone could live to be so old they literally looked like a walnut. She died of old age at 102, just one of many of the strong women in our lineage. Oma, my father's mother, was saintly, strong and fearless. She cooked large pots of nutritious soup to deliver to the South African townships during the riots in the mid-'80s, and allowed me to eat large spoonfuls of raw cake mixture out of the bowl when we baked. I loved her nurturing energy. Granny, my mother's mom, was a colourful character, in complete contrast to Oma. She ran a ballroom dancing studio and, in the 1950s, hosted a nightclub for "the ducktails" twice a week – to the horror of many at a time when most women didn't work. She was glamorous, bold and feisty, and undoubtedly a better grandmother to me than mother to my mom. I found her entertaining and interesting.

My mother had a significant impact on my life, but it was only when I became a mother myself that I started to understand and acknowledge just how significant the roles were that she and those other women played. Strong, bright, striking and outspoken, my mother Ann was a real go-getter, an independent working mother, well known as a consultant in her field of public relations and deeply admired by many. She had high standards and high expectations and she loved us fiercely.

I grew up, a much-loved child, in the leafy suburbs of Cape Town with my parents and my protective older brother Craig. My parents were gregarious and progressive in their thinking. My dad, Rein, was a social being who loved people and was loved in return. In his eyes I was "flawless". After school, I did a Bachelor of Arts at the University of Cape Town. At 20 years old I had a degree and I was ready and eager to explore the world.

In 1984 I travelled outside South Africa for the first time, an experience during which I gained a much-needed broader perspective of the world. It helped me become more aware of my privilege and the protected upbringing I had had. Growing up during the apartheid era meant I'd had little contact with anyone who was not similar to me. It was humbling and important to be exposed to international commentary for the first time. Two years later, when I went back to visit my beloved home town, I took nothing for granted. I noticed the beauty of Cape Town with a heightened appreciation.

I also noticed Stuart Lowe. We'd known each other for years, but now I looked at this young man with new eyes. At 25 he was intelligent, charming and attractive, comfortable in his own skin and yet humble. He had a sense of humour and an energy that was inspiring. He was great to be around, a self-assured combination of rule-breaker meets good guy. I thought he was damn gorgeous actually, and it wasn't long before we fell in love. I cancelled my plans to travel back overseas. Instead, I settled down in Cape Town and started working at *FairLady* magazine. Stuart was working in his dad's stationery and office equipment business at the time. Together we developed a vibrant circle of friends and forged ahead with our careers and our relationship. Nearly three years down the line everything was going well, but we weren't ready for marriage just yet.

I moved to Johannesburg, the City of Gold, to take up a promotion. The energy of Johannesburg was exhilarating, and I was committed to my work. It was hard to be away from Stu, but I felt I'd made the right decision. I needed to establish myself. However, whenever I returned to Cape Town on business, I saw him. The chemistry between us was still undeniable. I had a sense that this was unfinished business ...

But at that time we were both preoccupied with work and family. Stuart's family, like mine, was close and tight. He had two sisters: Alison, 18 months his senior, and Shirley, six years his junior, both of whom he adored. His mom, Jean, for whom he had the utmost respect, admiration and love, was caring and engaging, and Peter, his dad, was a charismatic, gregarious and sociable man. He was also the disciplinarian in the family. We had spent many a time with friends and family in their home over our years together, but those years were bittersweet. Jean was diagnosed with multiple myeloma, a rare bone cancer. In the year that I was living in Johannesburg her condition worsened and, aged 54, she passed away. Jean's loss was painful; she had made a difference in the lives of many. Stuart was devastated.

I'd been living in Johannesburg for just over a year when Stuart made a bold and creative move – an indescribably romantic proposal that was to ensure my return to Cape Town. The story of our engagement still takes my breath away. It was April, autumn, and I was going to my mom's 50th birthday celebration in Cape Town with Craig, my beloved brother. We arrived late that evening in the pouring rain. As Craig and I stood chatting together at the carousel waiting to pick up our luggage, I felt a sudden stirring in the people around us. Then a handsome young stranger wearing a tuxedo and clutching a bunch of white roses walked straight up to me. "Miss Badings," he said, smiling, "please will you follow me?" What was this? I quickly turned to speak to Craig, but he was no longer beside me. In fact he was being mysteriously whisked away by a tall person in a long coat and a hat. Mysterious indeed. "What's going on?" I asked, confused.

Somehow, this young chap convinced me to go with him

5

(this was before cellphones and Craig was no longer to be seen). I had recently had a rather unexpected and romantic reunion with Stuart at our friends Ian and Jillie's wedding, and so a small part of me imagined he might be behind this. Outside the airport a white stretch-limousine stood waiting, but now I was having doubts. The poor tuxedoed youth was agitated. Clearly his brief was to get me to accompany him, no matter what. "You *have* to get in, Miss Badings. Please." He held the limousine door open, leant inside and pushed Play on a cassette tape-recorder. Phil Collins. Phil Collins was symbolic for Stu and me. I took a deep breath and climbed in.

Nerves and excitement built as we drove towards the city, eased only by a glass of cold bubbles. What on earth was I doing? Forty minutes later we pulled up at the brand-new Bay Hotel in Camps Bay, rain still pouring down outside. The manager walked out. "Miss Badings, will you please come with me?" he said. It felt like a scene from a James Bond movie. Then I started to fret. What if Stuart was *not* on the other end of this plan? My heart pounded as we walked down the long passage towards a door. The door opened and there stood Stu.

Stuart had spent the entire day prepping this room. Roses, a fire, a ready-drawn bubble-bath, soft music … I fell into his arms all atwitter. That night Stu proposed. I knew we were meant to be together and within a month I had moved back to Cape Town. We were married six months later, in November 1990, at a large, happy and festive celebration for family and friends.

One year into our marriage Stu and I bought our first home, a gorgeous little Victorian cottage that we called Lilliput Lodge, after the Lilliputians in *Gulliver's Travels*. We poured our hearts and energy into renovating our little place on a shoe-string budget and loved every minute of it. We worked hard, played hard and contributed where we could to making a difference to the lives of others. Early into our marriage we joined forces with four other young couples and formed a group called Action For The Underprivileged (AFTU). We used our combined skills, networks and resources to raise funds for the homeless, for orphanages, shelters and other organisations that were in need of support.

The '90s were exhilarating times. South Africans were fired up with change and fuelled with hope. Stu and I grabbed all the opportunities life afforded us with enthusiasm and climbed our respective career ladders with gusto and determination. I left the world of magazines and moved into retail, working in the marketing department of Woolworths, one of South Africa's premium retailers. It was a busy and exciting time. By 1994 I was 30 years old and we'd been married for four years. It was time. Excited about the future of the country and our first democratic elections to be held in April that year, we were ready for children. By the time I stood in the queue with a long line of fellow South Africans to vote four months later, I was already pregnant. My child would be a child of the rainbow nation.

Like most pregnant mothers, my first trimester was punctuated with morning sickness and fatigue, but by 14 weeks I was feeling great. I will never forget the first time I felt my baby move, light bubbles floating across my tummy from the inside. I felt an overwhelming rush of love for this little being growing inside me. It was the beginning of an intense relationship.

I was due at the end of October. I needed an assistant to help out at work while I was on maternity leave. That was when Glynis arrived in my life. She was tall and commanding, with long red hair and light blue eyes, I didn't know it at the time, but this was to become a significant, cherished friendship, one that would sustain me through some very dark times in the future.

CHAPTER 2

When a child is born

Jenna Jean Lowe came into the world after 36 long hours of labour on the 28th of October 1994. Exhausted, elated and totally overcome with emotion, I pulled her out of my womb and cradled her slippery body on my chest, staring down into her velvet brown eyes. She was utterly focused and calm, gazing intently at me with an inquisitiveness that felt uncanny. In that life-changing moment time was suspended. I knew instantly I would give anything to protect this little being in my arms. I stared at her in wonder and awe. I never tired of that exquisite face with its creamy skin and rosebud lips. Her delicate little features were framed by arched eyebrows. She had tiny hands, the softest baby skin and smelled delicious. Jenna Jean Lowe was absolutely and utterly perfect.

Unconditional love is such a magnificent and all-consuming emotion, but let's face it, caring for an infant is demanding. As a driven, A-type personality, I expected myself to do everything "just right" and it came as a shock to discover that there is no such thing when it comes to parenting. Babies cry, they don't read the manual and initially it's hard to know what they need or want. To my own surprise I became anxious, and at the same time ashamed to feel that way. I found it impossible to leave Jenna's side and I barely let anyone touch her. I exhausted myself trying to perfect the amounts of breast milk, the amounts of sleep, the amounts of stimulation and a consistent routine. Poor Stuart. I don't think he knew what had hit him. At 4 am one morning, about three months in, he tip-toed through the darkness to find me in Jenna's nursery, cradling her, both of us crying inconsolably. He took Jen gently from my arms and said firmly, "Babies cry, my love, that's what they do. Now go back to bed, it's okay, I've got her." I slept and slept and slept, exhausted from trying to pre-empt my baby's every need.

In the morning, Stuart brought Jenna to me for a feed. We were cuddled in bed together, all three of us, when he hesitantly suggested we seek some help. As first-time parents, we were clueless as to what "normal" should look like, but he told me he didn't think it was "normal" for me to feel so exhausted and overwhelmed. I looked into his soft brown eyes and loving face and I knew it was a plea, not criticism. The only person judging me was me. I agreed.

I had post-natal depression. I felt vulnerable, I had trouble sleeping and I didn't want to leave the house, or Jenna, for a single second. My mood was often flat or blue, and I lost interest in the wider world. Many women who suffer from PND lose interest in their babies, but I became obsessive about mine. For the first three months, I didn't let anyone near Jen; even Stu had to fight to hold her.

On the recommendation of a close girlfriend, I started seeing a therapist, something that has become a regular and valuable practice in my life. My therapist has been a pillar of strength, guidance and wisdom during challenging phases, helping me to interrogate, integrate and make sense of my internal world.

Within a few months I found my feet as a much more confident mom. Jenna and I had a powerful connection, as if an invisible string joined us together. I learned to sense when she was tired, sore, hungry, sad or having a bad dream. For Stu and me, it was an adjustment having a third person in our relationship. We were no longer each other's "exclusive everything". But, like all new parents, we muddled our way through and along the way had many honest, brave conversations that brought us closer. Before long, Stuart and I were finding our groove as parents.

It was a pleasure to watch Stu step into his role as a father. Loving and playful, he was involved in every aspect of Jenna's life. He consistently broke my self-imposed, somewhat rigid rules about bedtime, bathtime and all the other routines that could drive me nuts. Stu was fun and spontaneous, the perfect antidote to my intensity.

My maternity leave drew to a close and I managed to negotiate a half-day contract rather than working full-time. My mornings were spent as an executive and my afternoons were spent witnessing Jenna reach her milestones. She was an ordinary baby in many ways, except for her extreme love of words. Her language skills were remarkable, and it soon became clear she was as bright as a button. She was talking by the age of one and by 18 months had an impressive vocabulary, happily reciting intricate rhymes and songs in her gentle voice while she played.

Jenna never tired of stories. Whenever we had a visitor, she would toddle off to find a book and present it with great enthusiasm, climbing up onto the person's lap before settling down to listen. Oh, and best you didn't try to shorten the story ... she knew every single word. We developed a nightly ritual of bedtime reading, which was a special bonding time for the three of us.

By the time Jenna was two years old, in 1996, Stu had moved away from his father's business and into the magazine world. He was part of a young, energetic team at Touchline Media who were busy launching magazine titles like *Men's Health* during the print industry's heyday. He worked long hours helping to grow the business, but he loved it.

It was December 1996, holiday time, and I was in Plett with Jenna, both of us looking forward to Stu's return from a business trip to New York. Sitting on a little balcony, we watched an unseasonal storm, thunder booming and lightning flashing across the skies. All of it, the wild stormy seas and seagulls swooping, had Jenna entranced. "Bunder, Mommy, bunder!" she said excitedly with wide eyes, enthralled with the world around her. "Big bunder!" she said at a particularly loud clap. With her silky smooth brunette locks with golden highlights framing her heart-shaped face, her big soft brown eyes and small but full little mouth, she was as cute as a cupcake. Cupping her little hand to her ear, she whispered conspiratorially, "Listen, Mommy, listen."

Stu arrived upbeat and enthusiastic and my heart skipped a beat when I saw him. He knelt down so that a very excited little Jen could run into her daddy's arms. She took him by the hand and pulled him towards the storm so that he, too, could enjoy it. We all sat on the balcony together, simultaneously soaking up the dramatic skies and his exciting stories from New York.

But I, too, had something exciting to share. Once Jen was asleep and we were alone, I pressed the small plastic tube I'd been hiding in the back pocket of my jeans into my husband's palms: two undeniable blue stripes. It took a few seconds for the reality to sink in. When it finally did, Stu threw his arms around me in sheer delight. We were elated. Our second baby was on the way!

CHAPTER 3

Sunshine and rare disease

Jenna loved to stroke and kiss my pregnant tummy. She would listen for the "baba" and ask, "When the baba coming, Mommy? What will it look like?" or "Where will the baba sleep? With me? Will it be a girl, Mommy? Can we choose a girl, Mommy?" Then she'd press her little cherub lips up against my skin and whisper loudly but in a secretive tone: "Hello? Hello, baba? It's Jenna here. I'm Jenna," and wave as if the little soul could see her.

Jen loved bathtime. Water, fun, toys, nursery rhymes, bubbles and the singing of songs. One of her favourite treats was when I climbed into the bath with her. These were such delicious moments. We would light candles and wallow in the warm water together, the water nymph and the pregnant hippo. It was on just such a night, seven months into my pregnancy, when we were at opposite ends of the bath, surrounded by floating plastic ducks and letters of the alphabet that Jenna watched my large tummy with fascination as the baby's tiny foot pushed against my skin, making a little bulge. I could see a thought forming in her mind. She took a deep breath.

"Mommy," she asked, "where will the baby come out?" Pause. She looked perplexed. "How will it get out, Mommy?"

I thought about it for a while and then decided the truth was the only option. "Out of Mommy's vagina, Jen," I said quietly.

She stared at me, eyes wide in total disbelief, then covered her mouth with her hands and started to giggle. Then, slowly, as it began to dawn on her that I wasn't joking, her little face crumpled. "Owie," she said. "Owie, Mommy." She clambered over my tummy and up onto my chest. She wrapped her little arms around my neck and rocked me gently. It was so damned cute and honest. I hugged her baby body into mine, breathing in her scent and holding her tight. "It will be okay, my angel," I said. "Mommy and the baby will be okay."

A few months later, on the 27th of August 1997, Kristin Ann Lowe, a robust blonde baby girl, arrived in the world. She'd been so active for the last four months of my pregnancy, I should have known we had a firecracker on the way. After a 16-hour labour, Kristi was born close to midnight. As I leaned forward to lift her out of my womb and onto my breast, I was completely overcome by the exquisite miracle that is new life. The depth of a mother's love has no limits. It is exponential. It grows more intense with the birth of each new child. We had a baby girl, a perfect baby girl.

Kristi was golden. Soft gold-brown eyes, soft gold hair, long but podgy baby limbs and a distinctive big, soft "squishy" mouth. From the moment she entered the world she was active and alert, with an inquisitive and adventurous spirit. She suckled almost immediately, holding onto me with one hand. She was a ray of sunshine.

We asked Stuart's sister Alison to be godmother to Kristi. Lovingly known as the "glitter glue" that holds our family together, Ali's energy, enthusiasm for life and positivity are infectious. Not only does she bring a sparkle to everything she does, but she constantly brings everyone together. That's the "glue" part. It is a gift of hers to ensure everyone in the immediate and extended family is loved, acknowledged and stays in touch with one another. Ali is a ray of pure sunshine who always knows how to find the good in life. She was the right fit for our new bundle of joy.

From day one Jenna was totally taken with Kristi. She held her, cuddled her, nurtured her and played with her constantly. She was always at her side.

It didn't take long for Stu and me to discover that Kristi was not a good sleeper, but, even so, coping with a newborn the second time round was a whole lot easier for me. I was far more relaxed and able to take everything in my stride. We did have a good giggle when, about five weeks after bringing Kristi home, Jen came through to the bedroom and asked politely, "Mommy, could we please take her back to the hospital now?" As cute as it was, it was also revealing. As much as she loved her baby sister, having to share her mom and dad was clearly an adjustment. Mostly, though, Jen would play happily with her books and toys while I breastfed or changed nappies.

Kristi was about six weeks old when I first noticed some deep red marks on her back and behind her knees. I was worried. I called Stu to come and have a look.

"What do you think this is, my love?" I asked. He took a close look.

"I've no idea," he said eventually. "A bite, or a rash maybe? Or an allergy?"

I looked at him.

"I don't know," he admitted. "Don't worry, but let's check it out."

Butterflies tickled my insides. I didn't have a good feeling.

I took Kristi to our paediatrician the next day. His reaction wasn't comforting.

"I've not seen this before, Gabi," he told me. "To be honest, I'm not sure what this is." He recommended a well-known dermatologist and arranged an appointment.

I was in her rooms two days later, cradling my new baby in my arms. Within moments the dermatologist was performing a biopsy and Kristi was crying from the pain. I did my best to calm her and then I sat down opposite the doctor.

"I don't know for sure yet," she said, looking straight at me, "but she could have juvenile xanthagranuloma or histiocytosis. Both are pretty rare, but I'm going to send this off to the lab now and I will let you know soon."

I was side-swiped. Histio-*what*? Rare? What on *earth* was she talking about? I drove home, tears pouring down my face. What did this mean? How could she just say that straight out with no explanation? I was in shock.

I phoned Stuart. "I'm on my way home," he said. "I'll see you in 20."

I managed to get Kristi and Jen down for an afternoon nap so that Stu and I could talk. We sat together, dazed, in the kitchen. And then we Googled ...

"Juvenile xanthagranuloma (JXG) is a benign histiocytosic disorder that primarily affects children under one year of age. Ocular JXG manifests in up to 10% of people with JXG and may affect their vision as the presence of JXG in the eye can cause spontaneous hyphema, secondary glaucoma or even blindness."

What the heck?

"In medicine histiocytosis is an excessive number of histiocytes (tissue macrophages) and the term is often used to refer to a group of rare diseases which share this sign as a characteristic. Occasionally and confusingly, the term 'histiocytosis' is sometimes used to refer to individual diseases."

You've got to be kidding me!

Waiting 48 hours for the results was unbearable. Stuart and I were shaken and confused. I was dreading how we would get through the weekend without knowing, but finally the dermatologist phoned, on Friday at 4 pm. I sat in our kitchen, shaking, as she explained that Kristi had mastocytosis urticaria pigmentosa, and we should come back to see her next week. Again, we Googled with dread ...

"Mastocytosis urticaria pigmentosa is a type of mast cell disease. A rare disorder affecting both children and adults caused by the accumulation of functionally defective mast cells (also called mastocytes) and CD34+ mast cell precursors. People affected by mastocytosis are susceptible to a variety of symptoms, including itching, hives, and anaphylactic shock, caused by the release of histamine and other pro-inflammatory substances from mast cells."

We were in a state of shock. Scared, we stayed up researching for hours and called anyone we knew with a medical background. In the days that followed my breast milk dried up from the anxiety and fear. Just about overnight I had to put Kristi on formula. I felt ashamed, but it was beyond my control.

We saw the dermatologist a few times. Kristi's condition was very rare and in many ways we were left floundering, searching for answers and someone to help. I threw myself into learning as much about mastocytosis as I could and discovered there was a chance that Kristi could outgrow it with the onset of puberty. That was our hope.

In the meantime, we had to find ways to manage her symptoms. She was at risk of anaphylactic shock, she had flushing attacks and an allergic response would be catastrophic. If Kristi *didn't* grow out of her condition, it could mean the onset of mast cell disease or mast cell leukaemia.

Looking for support, I joined the international Mastocytosis Society online, but found being part of the group very challenging. Many of the patients had more severe disease and symptoms, which was terrifying. I learned to filter the information that was relevant to Kristi. As the months passed, she developed more mastocytosis lesions all over her body. The flushing attacks were debilitating and became more regular. With no prior warning, her entire body would flush dark red and her lesions would become angry and raised. She became agitated for up to 30 minutes at a time. We worked to soothe her and mitigate whatever appeared to be inducing her attacks. Extreme heat or cold were triggers for her, as was crying. Over time I realised that if I kept her baths tepid, and ensured that she didn't over-heat or cry, I could reduce the attacks.

The risk of allergy meant I became meticulous about introducing foods, substances, creams and fabrics into Kristi's environment one at a time to limit the change of a negative response. Bites and stings, especially from bees, were also potentially very dangerous. Many over-the-counter medications are histamine-inducing: anti-inflammatories, codeine, anaesthetic and painkillers were among the many medicines we had to avoid. Anxiety and worry were ever present. I needed to be vigilant and to remain calm, when often I felt terrified and vulnerable, and very alone.

Help came out of the blue. One day while driving I heard on my car radio a professor of paediatrics being interviewed. His medical background and expertise made my ears prick up. This could be exactly who we needed. I tracked him down through the radio station and called his office the minute I got home.

"Yes," the receptionist said, "you are welcome to make an appointment. I have something in three months' time?"

"Please," I said, "just ask him if he has heard of a disease called mastocytosis?"

Perhaps she could hear the anxiety in my voice, but two minutes later Prof. Potter picked up the phone.

"Hello – Mrs Lowe?" he said to me. "Yes, I have dealt with mastocytosis before. In fact, I studied under someone in the UK who had a specific interest in it and I've had one or two patients through my practice with it over the years. Please come and see me this week. We will fit you in."

The man was a godsend. Prof. Potter guided and mentored us through the risks, the options, the do's and don'ts. He managed Kristi's case from then on and became our go-to person. I kept a very close eye on her and maintained records of her symptoms and responses. She started on a powerful anti-histamine, which I administered if she had a flushing attack. We expended a lot of energy making sure she didn't cry or over-heat. This made her already erratic sleeping patterns even more difficult and we got ourselves into a terrible loop, spending hours rocking her to sleep every night. Sometimes I was exhausted from the sheer effort of making sure Kristi never cried. Now, a couple of decades later, I wish my daughter could cry more freely.

CHAPTER 4

The younger years

Kristi appeared blissfully unaware of the fear surrounding her condition. She was sunny, energetic and positive. Her unruly blonde ringlets glowed like a halo and were a constant mess, no matter how often I tried to tame them. Constantly on the go, she was tactile, affectionate and curious. Her illness didn't slow her down. She crawled early and just about started running before she could walk. It was ironic that the child who couldn't have medication was so adventurous and fearless. Kristi rode her little black bike at speed, climbed trees and threw her arms around every stray dog she could find. I had to learn to sit on my hands so as not to wrap her up in cotton wool and stop her from engaging with the world around her. Ali soon discovered that the only way to keep her sitting at the table during family gatherings was with large bowls of ice that she would crunch and play with for a while before dashing off again. She was an active one and kept me fit!

It was time for me to leave the corporate world so that I had more flexibility to deal with Kristi's challenges. I resigned and started working from home. My "sabbatical" lasted a few weeks before I started a small PR and marketing consultancy called Upfront Marketing, which I ran for 18 happy years.

By now the girls had become inseparable. When Jen went

skipping off to playschool in the morning Kristi would wait at the front door every day, saying, "Jen go s'cool ... I wanna go s'cool too, Mommy. Kristi go s'cool too." At noon, when Jen eventually came home, Kristi would tumble into her arms, grab her by the hand and drag her off into the garden to make mud pies and potions. Their bond was extraordinary. They spent endless hours playing imaginary games, swimming, dressing up, dancing, rough-and-tumbling and giggling together.

Thankfully, just after Kristi's third birthday, new mastocytosis lesions stopped appearing. It was a massive relief and a good sign she might be starting to grow out of her condition. When her flushing attacks stopped shortly afterwards, Prof. Potter was delighted and optimistic. Things were looking up. We began to develop a more normal routine as a family and could now send Kristi to playschool. She was thrilled.

There is nothing better as a family with young kids than to have good relationships with other families experiencing similar life stages. Craig, my brother, was by now happily married to the wonderful Margo, whom he had met in Johannesburg while I was living with him. They, too, had two young kids and our families spent a lot of time together. The cousins adored each other. Tayla, a year younger, hero-worshipped Jen. She followed her around everywhere; it was too sweet to watch. Nic and Kristi, on the other hand, were born only 10 days apart, and soon the pair were dubbed "Double Trouble". They were mischievous and infuriatingly cute, particularly when together. Mud pies ended up in the washing machine, lipstick on the duvet cover and tadpoles in the bath, while Jenna and Tayla played "fairy, fairy" in the garden and Margo and I resorted to a glass of wine while we made supper. When Craig and Margo sat us down to tell us they were emigrating to Australia, it was devastating news.

I was so grateful that by then both Stuart's sisters had returned to Cape Town. Ali with her son Matt (six years older than Jen) had just moved back from Durban, and a few years later Shirley, with her daughter Natalie and son Kola, returned from Johannesburg. The entire Lowe family was now together in Cape Town. Three decades of marriage later I no longer call them "in-laws"; they are my siblings.

Jenna and Kristi spent loads of time with their cousins Matt, Kola and Natalie and family braais or large gatherings were regular events. Every day, when Stu came home from work, he played for hours with his girls. In summer the favourite game was "dolphins", which really just meant hours and hours spent swimming with Jen and Kristi riding Stu's back as he dived like a dolphin to the bottom of the pool. Sometimes they rode bikes until past sunset while the dinner turned cold on the table. Stu was the Pied Piper … all the kids, friends and cousins loved to spend time at our house and play with him. They still do!

Eating together as a family every night became an important ritual for us. We encouraged the girls to participate, to practise and develop the art of conversation. There was always open dialogue in our house about a wide range of topics; nothing was taboo.

Birthdays were a big deal in our home. I've always been a believer that if you don't celebrate life, it won't celebrate you. So, following on from my family's traditions, birthday mornings in our home began with singing and cuddles. I would carry a tea-tray, decorated with flowers and cards, to the birthday girl's room, where we would all jump onto the bed together singing "Happy Birthday" and then open prezzies together. Ali is also a big lover of birthdays, and so in the evenings there would always be a family gathering with an exquisitely set table, thanks to Ali, and time spent with all our loved ones. The girls loved it, but even so, it was an odd quirk of Jen's that she always seemed, for no apparent reason, to experience some sadness on her birthday. She didn't like getting older and had a sense of loss that another year had gone past. That didn't make any sense to me at the time, but remembering it now makes my heart ache.

Medically, Kristi was now far less at risk, and I started to slowly grow my business. I had a much larger office outside the house but was still able to be totally present for my girls. I worked hard to keep the balance between the two just right. Stuart, really focused and motivated, was approached by a much larger publishing house and started as their circulation marketing manager, before moving up the ranks to become publisher of their biggest title, *CAR Magazine*. A few years later, he was appointed CEO of the business. Stu was really flying. I was watching him tackle complex business challenges with great leadership and a strong strategic vision. He was stepping into his full potential both in business and as a husband and father.

Through the uncertainty of Kristi's condition, Stu and I had remained and become even more of a solid and loving team.

CHAPTER 5

The Magic Bissie Tree

One afternoon in 2002, when Jenna was eight years old and Kristi five, the girls spent the afternoon at Granny and Grampa's. One of their favourite things to do was swim in the pool with Gramps and then play in Granny's office. Driving home that day Jen turned to me and said excitedly, "Look, Mom, I started writing a book."

"A book, really?" I said distractedly. "That's lovely, darling."

I glanced at her. "Wait, hold on, what do you mean by 'a book', Jen?"

Jen explained that this particular day they had played a game called "author, author". With a smile she handed me a fistful of scrunched-up A4 pages. When we got home, I grabbed a coffee and sat down to read them. There it was, in Jen's small cursive handwriting, *The Magic Bissie Tree* by Jenna Lowe.

As I read, I got goose-flesh. This was the start of a children's story, already three chapters long.

"Wow, Jen, did you write all of this yourself?" I asked.

"Yes, Mommy," she said.

"It's really good. I mean it's *really* good."

"Ah, thanks, Mommy," she said, brushing off my comments.

"Are you going to finish it?" I asked slowly. I turned to look at her to get her full attention. "Jen, do you want to finish the story?" She looked up.

"I do, Mom," she said, "but it's really tiring." Jen had poor hand-eye co-ordination and so physical activities were not her greatest strength.

"You can finish it easily if you want, my love," I said. "I can type it up for you on my PC, you don't have to handwrite it." Her little face lit up.

"Really?" she said. "Okay, Mom – can we start now?"

Over the next six weeks Jen came into my office every afternoon for half an hour after school with her lunch and dictated while I typed. The story flowed out of her uninterrupted. I loved being part of the process. She would cock her head slightly to one side, and look upwards, then she'd take a deep breath and the story would pour out of her. Once we were done for the day, I would read it back to her and she would check carefully to make sure I hadn't changed one single word. Jenna was discovering a new passion: creative writing.

The story is about a little forest girl who steps on a magic thorn and becomes ill. The little forest girl seeks out the help and company of a witchdoctor, and together they set off to find the golden apple of the "the magic bissie tree" which holds a cure. The descriptions are magical. It is a mystical children's adventure story that describes their travels. For an eight-year-old, it is a remarkable piece of writing.

I showed *The Magic Bissie Tree* to Stu. "Shit, Gabs, this is really good!" he said. We were keen to publish it but believed she was far too young to cope with any publicity that might have come from that, so we left it. It took two years before Jen came to us and said, "Mom, Dad. Remember you said we could publish my book? Is that still an option? I think I am ready now." She was 10 years old at the time.

We approached Ashleigh, the 12-year-old daughter of Charles and Fran, who are long-standing friends of ours. Ashleigh was a talented artist and she and Jen spent hours together, with Ash working on the illustrations, drawing in pencil as Jenna described her characters in detail.

Initially we printed 200 books just for friends and family, but they were soon gone, and when a small article appeared in a local paper the story of this very young author erupted. As one of the youngest published authors in South Africa, Jen was suddenly being interviewed, visiting book fairs and speaking at breakfasts. We ordered another print run, this time of 2 000 books.

Jenna, always passionate about effecting social change, used the book as an opportunity to do just that. She first met Chaeli Mycroft at a shoot which was to be part of a feature on young girls making an impact. Chaeli, who was the same age as Jenna, was an active and effective South African disability activist. She had cerebral palsy and was wheelchair-bound. Her positivity, courage and passion had a huge impact on Jenna. Jenna decided to support her campaign, "Hope in Motion", and donated 25 per cent of her book sales to the cause. She also attended and spoke at some of Chaeli's awareness events.

Looking back now, it's crystal clear how community impacts children. Mine were lucky. They were surrounded by interesting, driven and intellectual people who brought different and important perspectives to their lives.

One such person was Jenna's godmother, Sandy. Sandy had been a close friend of mine for decades. Slightly built, with inquisitive blue eyes and dark hair, she and Jen developed a special bond. From a very young age Sandy engineered one-on-one time with Jen. She would read to her and they would chat for hours, debating all sorts of topics. Sandy's unique critical thinking skills were a formative influence for Jen. She stimulated her ability to think analytically. Whenever Jen came home having spent time with Sandy, she was always so inspired.

Stu and I understood the value of these kinds of conversations for our girls, so when friends visited, we encouraged them to join in. Some adults encouraged this more than others, but those who did were so loved by my girls. Genuine interest in their perspectives and opinions seemed to really feed their growth and confidence.

The success of *The Magic Bissie Tree* nurtured Jenna's social activism spirit. She learned that you can be an effective advocate no matter your age and her confidence grew daily.

We didn't know then that one day Jenna would use her illness to activate change.

CHAPTER 6

High tea and puppy love

By 2007, the age gap between Jenna and Kristi was more apparent. Jenna, now 13 and in Grade 7, was in her last year of junior school and Kristi, now 10, was in Grade 4. They still spent loads of time together, but they were also establishing themselves as different people. Kristi was besotted with horses and animals in general. She hung out at the stables as often as possible, fostered puppies and worked at the local vet in her spare time. While she tacked up horses and mucked out stables, Jen would tip-toe gingerly through the stables, ensuring that she didn't touch anything. Kristi wasn't a talker like Jen and found endless discussions tedious. They were different, but close.

Now that Jen's love of writing was piqued, she started to write more regularly – essays, poems, journal entries and notes. I love this poem she penned one day in class shortly after the Grade 7 "Moms and Daughters" school camp up the Breede River.

CAMP REFLECTIONS – Grade 7, Jenna

The wind blows softly
Caresses the checkerboard of blue and pink
Skims the gigantic crags that watch over the eager crowd

We step out into the pale sunlight, enthusiasm emanating
from our very pores
We are not disappointed
The watery rays of the sun giggle with us as we tumble into
the structured routine of camp
Organised chaos

Our very ears rejoice the experience
The quiet lap of the crystal, captured waters
The reassuring roar of waves upon shore
The shrieks and laughter that accompany us everywhere
we go.

The wind blows softly
Holding the camp leaders' sighs, trailing them over the left-
over pieces of
Inspiration, teamwork, leadership
Blowing them over the mist of the new green buds of
friendship
Breathing them over the shattered remains of prejudice lost
We are gone.

While Jen and I were away on that camp, there was a break-in at our home. Stuart and Kristi, sleeping, were woken by the sound of smashing windows. No one was physically harmed but the experience of seeing men in balaclavas and guns deeply affected Kristi. She no longer wanted to sleep out; she became a "homing pigeon", happy to explore during the day but needing to be at home at night. She noticed and was fearful of our safety for the first time. Some naivety was lost that night, and sleep became an issue for her again. For many years after the burglary we kept a mattress on the floor next to our bed so that she could creep through to us in the night if she was feeling scared. We took Kristi for two trauma counselling sessions and swiftly upgraded our security and alarm systems. It was a nasty fright.

Jen's 13th birthday was imminent and, as it was her first teen year, I'd promised we'd plan something special. Ali came up with the idea of going to the grand old Mount Nelson Hotel for high tea. It was such a Jen-like thing to do. She loved the idea! We had a gentle day on the lawns surrounded by close friends, family and cousins.

By now Jen was tall, long-legged, willowy and slim, with long brown hair that shone as she moved. She was a compelling beauty, with an even more compelling mind. Jen had a loyal and committed group of girlfriends and was becoming slightly less of a bookworm. She and her mates were just reaching the age of "movies at Cavendish Square", a popular shopping mall down the road. The group was also starting to show an interest in boys and spent many hours on the weekends socialising. Slowly, large groups of girls and boys started being invited to our home. Enter 13-year-old dark-haired Daniel, affectionately known to all as "Daffy". He was kind, affable, funny, cool and gorgeous; and coincidentally born on the same date as Stuart. Jenna and Daffy developed a whopping teenage crush on each other.

It was really cute. Encouraged by their mates, they started messaging each other constantly via BBM (it was the days of BlackBerry Messenger) and within a few months Daffy had asked Jen to be his girlfriend. They chatted daily and saw each other every weekend. They held hands, ate popcorn, went to movies and went ice-skating together. They dated happily for three months and then Daffy made a fatal error: he tried to kiss her! Poor Daffy. Jen was out of there like a scalded cat. She just wasn't ready and called the whole thing off. He cried behind his closed bedroom door and listened to sad music. Eventually, I am told, his mom sat him down in desperation and said, "Daffy, you are so young and there are many other fish in the sea, I promise." "No, Mom," he insisted, "you don't understand. This one is special." His mother took him seriously. "Okay," she said, "if she is that special, then

there is only one thing to do. My advice to you is to stay friends …
you never know what the future may bring."

It was nearing the end of Grade 7; Jen and her friends were all
so ready to leave junior school. One hot and peaceful summer's
day, a low buzz in the air, Jen sat at her school desk, staring out
of the window at the oak trees and chewing on her pencil. Double
English, her favourite class. The assignment was to write a poem
that finished with the words "It's Me".

Knowing what we know now makes this poem that she wrote
aged 13 even more powerful and poignant.

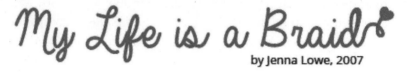

My Life is a Braid

by Jenna Lowe, 2007

My life is a braid
Some parts tightly woven
Some parts weakened in a way
The future lies before me
The threads are not yet sewn

They are lying in a pattern
One that I can't understand
Lying so uncertain
Like a wave upon the sand

My destiny is a blank page
The pen is writing as I speak
At some times I'll be strong and calm
At others scared and weak

All I know for sure
Is that nothing's yet complete
The world will carry on without me
Nonetheless, less sweet

I can make a difference
And a difference can make me
I am like a tiny seedling
Growing slowly to a tree

The future is still coming
Like a wild and restless sea
It's uncontained
I've tried in vain
But through me it will seep

I am shielded as I can be
As I stand I am prepared
I must admit though, just to you
That sometimes I am scared

The future is still coming
Surely that you see
My time has come
My will be done
Stand back world – IT'S ME!

Jen graduated from junior school top of her grade. The ground felt stable under our feet. Good. Solid. We were oblivious to the weirdly prophetic nature of this poem.

But then, nothing could have prepared us for what was coming our way.

CHAPTER 7

Sweet 16

In 2011 Jenna turned 16. Sweet 16. She was class captain and captain of the school's Debating team, and she had a wide circle of friends. All traces of early childhood shyness had dissipated. She was a high achiever but she also had humility, compassion and a good solid value system. One of the highlights of Jen's Grade 10 year was when she and her friend Lethu were chosen to attend the Archbishop Emeritus Desmond Tutu's Youth Peace Summit. Archbishop Emeritus Desmond Tutu, an Anglican archbishop, had been a well-known and much-loved activist for the rights of black people during and after apartheid. A key architect of the Truth and Reconciliation Commission, "the Arch", as he is affectionately called, was awarded the Nobel Peace Prize for opposing apartheid. He was one of Jen's heroes. The invitation to attend his summit was a great honour. It brought together a diverse group of young people from different geographic areas, youth institutions, economic and cultural backgrounds to inter-act, engage and learn to build peace in their own lives and communities as well as the world at large.

It was both an eye-opening and life-changing experience for Jen, one she treasured. Lethu told me (Jen wouldn't dream of it) that Jen was admired, respected and well liked within the group. I had just collected them from the summit, and they were chatting away in the back of the car, sharing stories of their workshop groups, when Lethu said, "Okay, Jen, that's it! We are going to run this country together one day. I will have to be president because I'm black [*giggle*], but you will be my right-hand lady. I'm simply not doing it without you." They certainly shared the passion, character and intelligence required of good leadership.

When she wasn't trying to save the world, Jenna was being a normal teenager. She had the same fears, insecurities and need to fit in as every other girl her age. She could be challenging, especially with me, and we had some spectacular spats (which I seldom won). We were very similar beings, Jen and I, and we could go around and around in circles, frustrating the hell out of everyone, Kristi in particular. And we were intensely close. There was nothing Jenna felt she couldn't tell me and nothing we didn't share.

By now her interest in boys was a bit more prevalent. As Stu said, "They just keep appearing out of the woodwork." Jen was both alluring and compelling, but she had very high standards. She was yet to have her first kiss. "I feel so stupid, Mom," she said one day. "Everyone else has done it already. Now they have that anxiety out of the way. I shouldn't have waited so long. Why did I do that?" In her slightly nerdy way she was making some sort of scientific experiment out of it. Cute. But in truth, she told me, she was concerned it might be awful ... I tried to tell her she needn't worry. Teenage hormones have a way of taking care of these things.

Plettenberg Bay – Plett – the little seaside town up the Garden Route was, and still is, our favourite place. Magnificent beaches, warm sea and an amphitheatre of mountains. I have visited Plett with my family for as long as I can remember. Stuart and I did the same once we were married. Every year we punctuated our lives with a family holiday in Plett, creating a lifetime's worth of memories. We developed close holiday friendships over the years, and it was a bonus for us that Ian and Jillie lived there. Family holidays were filled with boating, long lazy lunches, beach walks, mountain hikes, sunsets and body surfing in the warm salty ocean.

It was January 2011. Jenna strode out of the ocean in her black polka dot bikini, dark hair dripping, lithe body glistening in the sun. "But how did you know what to do?" She was chatting animatedly to her girlfriend Liv who was spending a few days with us. Their beach towels were laid out a few paces away from me, angled to face the surfers. "But can't you get it wrong?" Jen asked. They were talking about first kisses. It was the hot topic of the day. "Actually, I don't suppose it should matter," Jen sighed. "I just want him to be gorgeous." She was lusting the ultimate movie moment. It was one of the things I loved about our Jen … she was such a romantic.

It was an exquisite day at The Wedge. I could feel the sun beating down on my skin and pure joy coursing through my veins as I watched Stuart and Kristi body-surfing for hours in the rolling waves. They were bound to emerge ravenous eventually, so I sent Jen and her girlfriends wandering off down the beach, sarongs tied around their little hips, to the café to buy fried calamari, hot chips and granadilla ice creams for lunch. That was when she met them. The "Plett boys". One was an archetypically pretty tall blond surfer-boy called Nik with mischievous blue eyes, accompanied by his sexy dark-haired friend Josh, with his flashing white smile. They strolled back casually towards us in a large group, chatting, and I could tell from afar there was something different about Jenna's walk. Her gait was ever so slightly more self-aware and sensual than before. They were laden with hot food and cold drinks, the two boys walking with the group, all of them in lively conversation. Stuart came out of the water and saw me observing them. "Oh-oh," he said, as he towel-dried himself. "Here comes trouble."

The air was abuzz with flirtation. The gorgeous 16-year-old locals started appearing regularly at our social gatherings. They were in the prime of their lives and, somewhat unexpectedly, Nik and Josh were also really nice guys. It was fun to watch the dynamics unfold. Jen got her first glorious kiss with Nik the surfer-boy one night under the stars, and a light and lovely holiday romance ensued, with all the frissons of delight that go along with it. But, more importantly, a long and meaningful friendship developed. Surfer-boy Nik, his bestie Josh, and their families became good friends of ours.

Those were happy memories, but what I remember most about that holiday was that in the midst of all this frivolity, fun and flirtation a tidal wave of unimaginable tragedy struck our family.

CHAPTER 8

Natalie's Circle of Love

The 4th of January 2011 was one of our last long lazy summer days at Plett that year. I was lying mesmerised by the rhythmical sound of the ocean when, from inside a beach bag under our brolly, Stuart's cellphone rang loudly. He grabbed it and hopped up. "Hey, Shirl," he said, smiling broadly and wandering off up the beach to catch up with his sister's news. "How are you doing?" I could hear his voice fading as he strolled away.

Shirley and Stu had grown up together in Camps Bay. In true "big brother" fashion he would tease her, chase her, aggravate her and protect her. He was adventurous and mischievously naughty, but the siblings were very close. We saw the three of them regularly in Cape Town – Shirl and her daughter Natalie and son Kola.

"Hey, what's up, Shirl?" Stu asked warmly.

In her usual style Shirley first checked in to see how we were all doing, but by the time Stu walked back to us 10 minutes later his smile had gone. I knew immediately that something was horribly wrong. His tanned face was pale, and he looked shaken. He told me that 10-year-old Natalie was battling to breathe and had been slated for emergency surgery that night. No one knew what was going on, but X-rays had revealed a large tumour inside her chest that doctors believed needed to be operated on immediately. I thought I had heard wrong. I made him repeat it. How was this possible? We were together at Christmas lunch just a few weeks before and Natalie was fine.

We were in shock. We spent that evening processing the news and finding a flight to get Stu home fast. He flew home the next morning and I followed with the girls a few days later.

Jen had her last romantic kiss with her surfer-boy on the balcony in the soft rain just before we left, but the girls were silent on the way home in the car. There was no thumping music or carpool karaoke. We dreaded what we might get home to. Salty kisses and holiday romance faded quickly into the distance as we drove towards Cape Town.

That beach phone call was a lightning bolt of brutal reality, which changed our lives forever.

The results of the initial surgery were not good. The part of the tumour that had been pressing against Natalie's windpipe, which was why she was having trouble breathing, was just the tip of the iceberg. The real threat was to her thoracic spine. Six vertebrae were affected. The results of the biopsy were shocking. Natalie was diagnosed with a rare bone cancer called chordoma. There were no known cases of chordoma in South Africa and the local doctors offered little hope for a cure. The life of our beloved niece was in danger. None of us could get our heads around it.

Within hours of the diagnosis, Stu's cousin, Dr Greg Kew, offered to take on the role of family advisor. We needed him to help make sense of the medical language and understand the implications. Finding the global expertise that Natalie needed was an epic process. Ultimately, Natalie's unusual case gained the attention of global chordoma experts in Europe and America, who believed she could be saved.

Natalie's treatment would include a combination of proton beam radiation, not available in South Africa, and dangerous, outlier surgery. The tumour needed to be removed "en masse", which included removing seven affected vertebrae in her thoracic spine.

This had never been done before. Three different multi-disciplinary teams proposed three different approaches. Choosing the right team of doctors, the right hospital and the right city in the world was a minefield, but Shirley was unstoppable. She was a force of nature. Stuart would sit with her late at night through some long and emotionally tough phone calls talking to each team of doctors. It required grit to examine the facts and assess every detail of the various surgical approaches.

We didn't yet know where Natalie would go for treatment, but we did know that once she left South Africa there would be no medical aid cover and the cost of care as an international patient would be beyond any of our means. If Natalie was to have a chance, we would need help, not only raising money, but also with finding accommodation and support in a faraway place. We needed to reach out, to share the story and ask for help.

The family went into production mode. Within days we set up a trust and a website to launch Natalie's Circle of Love. I watched Shirley agonise over her first blogpost on the website. What do you say and not say when the truth is so brutal? How do you find the words to ask for help? It was hard, but the outpouring of love and support was overwhelming and deeply humbling.

Shirley sold her home to free up funds and I helped her find a rental flat close to Ali. It needed to be a lock-up-and-go, immediately available and all on one level. We had to factor in the likelihood that Natalie would be in a wheelchair when she returned from surgery and balance urgency, efficiency and the many practical arrangements that needed to be planned for, including our girls and nine-year-old Kola beginning the school year.

Within a few weeks we held our first fundraiser at the Baxter Theatre, an evening of theatre sports played by generous, talented friends to a full house. It was an emotional, laughter-filled event that provided a huge boost of love and support and some of the funds vital for those first expenses.

By early March it was decided that Natalie would be treated in Boston at Massachusetts General Hospital. Shirl and Nattie needed to get to the US as quickly as possible and would be away

37

from home for at least three months. Friends and family rallied around us, and people we didn't even know came forward to ensure that Shirley and Natalie would have the softest landing possible in Boston. In the days before they left we held a sunset picnic at the top of Table Mountain to say farewell. I have a pic of that night that I treasure. The evening sky is crimson red and Natalie, flanked by Jen and Kristi, is lying atop an ancient cannon, smiling to the camera, arms spread out wide as if she is flying. Shirley and Natalie boarded the plane the next day and we were left trying to hold the pieces of our family together.

Natalie's diagnosis changed me profoundly. I hadn't experienced anything this hectic in my lifetime. Helping to run the Circle of Love, advocating for Natalie, and raising funds became part of my life.

I was astounded at how our friends stepped up to support us during the tumultuous years that followed. There were so many acts of lovingkindness. My friend Nici conquered the icy open water swim from Robben Island to Green Point to raise funds for Natalie. Friends donated to her trust, hosted their own events, donated products, trips and paintings for auction, and helped sell tickets to our fundraisers. It was truly humbling.

Some profound connections developed during this difficult time. One such connection was with my neighbour, Mary. Over the years our families were friendly but not particularly close. When Mary had gone through chemo a few years earlier, I was glad to be able to bake her an apple crumble or take a casserole for the family on treatment days. I had so much respect for how she got through her battle with breast cancer. So when Mary suggested we start walking together more regularly as a healthy way for me to manage my stress, I jumped at it. What started out as walking became "wogging" – a rather pathetic combination of walking and jogging – and then after a while running. I never imagined I would become a runner, but I grew to love it. We went consistently three to four times a week and slowly Mary's friendship developed into a lifeline for me. Because she lived so close and our time together was so regular, she knew all about the complexities I was dealing with.

By then Glynis, who had covered for me at Woolworths when I went on maternity leave, had left the business world and was a qualified and practising clinical psychologist. She was another lifeline for me in a world turned upside down. Glynis knows how to listen in a way that few people can, without any shock or judgement, and gives astute and caring advice. I needed that. I also grew even closer to my beloved friend Vanessa, for whom nothing was, or ever is, too much to ask. She had a deep understanding of the challenges our family was facing as her stepdaughter had been seriously ill for many years.

There are so many significant relationships that carried me through that time and I really don't know how I would have coped without them. No one should have to walk alone.

By April, Natalie had completed proton radiation and she underwent two very long and dangerous surgeries one week apart. It was beyond intense, but the ground-breaking procedures were declared a success. Everyone was elated! After she stabilised, Natalie was fitted with a halo brace – a brutal experience in and of itself – and she began the long and extremely challenging road towards recovery. By May, she was transferred to a rehabilitation centre where she would re-learn to sit, stand and walk.

There were highs and lows, and complications, and it was challenging in the extreme. Shirley lived in the hospital with Natalie, constantly at her side. In the meantime, we worked hard to raise additional funds and sponsorship to ensure they had regular visitors in Boston. Being able to count down the days to see Kola and spend time with him, or be uplifted by visits from loved ones, made a big difference.

We had no idea at the time what further tragedy awaited us.

Part 2

CHAPTER 9

Breathlessness

In February 2011, four weeks after Natalie's initial surgery and diagnosis, Stuart and I were both back at work while also running Natalie's Circle of Love. Jenna and Kristi had started their school year.

It was around this time that Jenna first started to show signs of breathlessness.

At first it was subtle, barely noticeable. It was easy to assume this was anxiety related as we were all still in a state of shock over Natalie. When I questioned Jen about her breathing, she acknowledged that while Natalie was very much on her mind – "I am so worried about Natalie, Mom" – she didn't feel it was anxiety related.

"This feels like a physical thing, Mom," she confided, "a separate thing."

Jen may have been a sensitive soul, but she was also pretty sensible, and the truth was that she was more likely to be stoic than dramatic. I kept an eye on it.

Jen's breathlessness didn't subside. We became more and more aware of how loudly she was breathing. Initially it seemed exercise induced. Walking down the passage fast or moving pots around the kitchen, slowly and insidiously the breathlessness became more regular. I started to notice it when she leaned over me to read something, or if the girls were working quietly at the dining room table, I could hear her from the kitchen counter. We started calling her Darth Vader to make her more aware of it, thinking that maybe this had become an anxiety-related habit. That memory makes me want to cry now.

Then she started coughing. Immediately I took her to our GP, Kathy. There was a bad cough doing the rounds at the time and Jen was medicated appropriately. A few weeks later we were back at the GP again. The cough had not subsided, and her breathing was still loud. This time Kathy did blood tests as well as a full examination plus a lung function test. She gave us more cough meds and an inhaler pump just in case. We carried on as normal.

Jen was not a complainer. Sometimes I wonder, had she been more vocal about how she was feeling, would she have been diagnosed earlier? I was worried and paid close attention, watching her carefully. It became second nature to listen for the nuances in her breathing. Following Kathy's advice, we adjusted her diet to contain less wheat and dairy. These kinds of symptoms could indicate an allergy or food intolerance.

That first school term was hectic for both my girls as we tried to maintain their normal lives while dealing with getting Nattie and Shirl to Boston. But one of the things that was stressing Jen out most was a Grade 10 school event that was looming at the end of the first term – a five-day compulsory hike called "Step Out". It takes place every Grade 10 year and is seen by the school and the girls as a sort of rite of passage. The hike was set to take place in the scenic mountains of Greyton, a small rural town three hours outside Cape Town, in just three weeks' time.

"I'm really concerned, Mom," Jenna told me. "The way I am feeling right now I'm worried I won't be able to cope." Although Jen looked like a gym bunny, she was in fact the furthest thing from sporty. "Mom," she implored me, "I really need to get fit again, will you help me?" She had recently stopped swim-training due to her persistent cough, but now that it seemed to be getting better, we agreed we'd start walking together to get her hike ready.

On our very first walk together I got the fright of my life. Maybe, just maybe, something was seriously wrong. Could it be? Within a few blocks Jen was already breathless and when we turned the corner to walk up the first hill my alarm bells went off. She was really struggling. She had no breath. We turned back for home. "This is not anxiety or lack of fitness," I said to Stuart that night as we got ready for bed. "I am nearly 50 and I coped better than Jen. Something's not right, I can feel it in my gut."

The next day I took Jen back to see Kathy. Thorough, caring and as attentive as always, she asked Jen a long list of questions, after which she did another lung function test, blood tests and a complete "check and service". Again she found nothing. She was perplexed and concerned. Kathy knew Jen well and didn't take this breathlessness lightly. She sent us, letter in hand, to a well-known local physician, Dr VC.

There were only two weeks left before the hike and we were becoming increasingly concerned. Would she cope? Should she do it? What was going on? Dr VC spent a long time with Jenna and he, too, asked many questions, fleshing out a full medical history, examining the problem from every angle and feeling out whether Jenna was the anxious type. From her choice of language, how she approached the answers, her demeanour and attitude, it soon became clear to him that she wasn't; if anything, she was actually underplaying how she was feeling and a little embarrassed by her symptoms.

Dr VC did further tests: full bloods, lung function, a physical examination, chest X-ray, ECG and echo-cardiogram. He was thorough. Jen and I were both hurt when the echo-cardiogram technician implied that Jen was "air-hungry" and she should breathe into a brown paper bag. That wasn't helpful.

Still we found nothing. There was no apparent or clear explanation. Jen was starting to feel as if she was going mad. We discussed Step Out. "Mom," she said, "I *must* go, I can't not do it. It will be okay, I will just push through. I'm not going to be ridiculed for not doing it. And Dr VC didn't find anything." Nevertheless, the physician was concerned. "There is one more test we *could* do," he said, "but it's very expensive and highly unlikely. It's not a test I would normally do on a 16-year-old girl presenting this way."

The test, the one we didn't do, is called a VQ scan. This was the test that would put Jen into hospital six months later. It really is no one's fault, but I wish we had done it that day. We would have discovered her condition earlier.

Dr VC gave Jenna a pump to ease the breathlessness, and a letter for the school to say she should stop and pull out of the hike if she needed to. I should never have let her go on that hike, but Jenna was determined. I think she feared that teachers and friends would judge her and think she was faking it. Peer pressure is a powerful and dangerous thing. She explained that lots of kids faked injury to get out of the hike. I will always deeply regret the decision we made to allow her to go. I should have trusted my gut, but I overrode it.

Of course, as soon as you are part of a team, halfway to the top of a mountain, there is no turning back. When Jenna got home, she looked absolutely wiped out and exhausted ... and ill. She told us how day after day her lungs had literally felt on fire. She was left gasping for air, faint, weak and terrified. Letter or no letter, her group leader and group teacher did nothing about it; in fact, they subtly implied she was seeking attention. Not wanting to let anyone down, she pushed through. There was no cellphone coverage, only a walkie-talkie for emergencies, and the constant unspoken belief that this privileged bunch of girls had to toughen up. I had relied on Jenna and the school's good sense to make the right choices on our behalf during the hike. They didn't. I hadn't taken into account the fact that Jenna was someone who never gave up. It was one of her distinguishing features. But why on earth not a single adult thought to stop her hiking is still beyond me.

With hindsight I am still angry with myself. But at the time we didn't know about her illness. Nobody knew. We simply didn't know. This is significant. It is significant because exactly this kind of thing happens to so many pulmonary hypertension patients. They can go for months and often years either being misdiagnosed or undiagnosed, which leads to further damage. It is a difficult disease to diagnose, a rare and "invisible" illness.

Knowing and experiencing this so dramatically, as Jen did on that hike, later became one of the driving forces behind her campaign for early diagnosis.

CHAPTER 10

Asthma, the mad Aussie and a secret talent revealed

Straight after the hike we were back at our GP, and this time we agreed Jen should go to a specialised asthma clinic. Off we went, detailed doctor's letter in hand, and a thorough history for our first appointment. On paper it looked like asthma, but yet again Jenna's lung function test was good. It didn't make any sense. This "red herring" that kept throwing everyone off track is something that happens with pulmonary hypertension. It was obvious that Jen was battling for breath, but it did not reflect in her lung function tests. How did that make any sense? The asthma clinic armed us with a flow chart and blow machine so that Jen could track her lung function twice a day for a month. We needed to see if there was a trend emerging. Meantime, she now had two pumps to ease the symptoms.

It was June 2011 when a bundle of chaotic energy came tumbling into our lives. "Aniko the Australian" had landed. Blonde, busty, with big blue eyes and a distinctive gravelly voice, Aniko fitted perfectly between our two girls in age and personality. "Koko Pops" or "Ko-Ko", as we affectionately called her, was Jenna's Grade 10 exchange student from Sydney. She was to live with us for three months. Natalie and Shirl were in rehabilitation in Boston, and Jenna was supposedly on the right medication. The timing was perfect. Aniko was exactly the delightful distraction our family needed. Uncomplicated, boisterous, messy and fun-loving, she had the alter ego of a golden retriever. She moved effortlessly between Kristi and Jen. When Jen needed some downtime the boisterous Aniko could be found giggling with Kristi in her bedroom. They couldn't have been more different and yet the three of them became firm friends, a tight trio.

The sadness that had been in the house since Natalie's diagnosis shifted a bit and Jen appeared to have stabilised, or was seemingly not getting any worse. The intensity of watching, listening and being on constant alert had lessened, and we settled into a new routine with our "third child" in the house. Within weeks Aniko had a black eye from a stray hockey ball and had turned my house upside down, but she was a constant source of entertainment, joy and laughter.

Determined to make sure that Aniko loved Cape Town, Jen introduced her to all her friends, and we hosted heaps of get-togethers in between the ordinary business of school and homework. Despite her "asthma", academically Jenna was shooting the lights out. A valuable member of the school Debating team and top of her class, she took school work seriously but very much in her stride. Our weekends were jam-packed with social arrangements and "touristy" outings as we showed Aniko the Mother City. Signal Hill, Clifton, Table Mountain, The Waterfront, Kalk Bay Harbour, Hout Bay, Chapman's Peak, Cape Point, the West Coast flowers, Kirstenbosch Garden, markets and restaurants, and even shark-cage diving outside Hermanus. You name it, we did it. And we loved being tourists in our own city. On Aniko's 16th birthday, Kristi and I baked a huge cake in the shape of Table Mountain. We decorated it with the Australian and South African flags. If Jen was too tired to participate, Kristi and Aniko would fill the gap. There was so much going on that it was easy for Jenna to hide the fact that she didn't have the same levels of energy as everyone else.

In mid-July Jen and I returned to the asthma clinic, taking with us her carefully completed lung function chart. "Ah," they said, "this makes slightly more sense now." Her lung function was surprisingly good, but her lung capacity appeared different at different times of the day. A confusing picture, but one that implied the possibility of asthma. We were so relieved to have a diagnosis at last … something that could be treated. Pumps, cortisone and meds were prescribed, together with a detailed description of how to manage the asthma and her meds. She would feel better soon, we were assured. What a relief. Jen started her routine and stuck to it. She was desperate to get her energy back. Her breath back.

Meanwhile, Shirley and Natalie were having a rough time in Boston. Stuart planned a trip so that he could help them transition from rehabilitation to housing near the hospital, but instead when he arrived, Natalie was admitted back into Mass General. It was a gruelling visit and he came home quite shattered by what he'd witnessed. Natalie's halo brace was made up of a plastic vest that immobilised her spine and head. The metal ring surrounding her head was attached by pins to her skull, and though this was not painful for her, wearing the brace was hard. It resulted in complications that made her proton radiation treatment an extremely dangerous exercise. This was the time Natalie reported as the darkest of her journey. I would lie awake at night willing relief for her through the days and weeks of relentless vomiting she endured, praying for protection against the very real risk of choking because of the halo. I tried not to imagine the terror that Natalie and Shirley were going through. I felt useless.

Running with Mary helped me. She suggested we train for the Knysna half-marathon. It was good to have a goal, and we used it as an additional way to raise funds for Natalie. If Natalie could overcome the extremes of pain she was in, then I (a useless runner) could push myself to run a half-marathon. Helping with fundraising and managing admin for Natalie's Circle of Love was now a normal part of my working day. It helped to know that my efforts and the kindness of others were chipping away the hospital costs, and making a difference to Natalie, Shirley and our whole family.

In July we needed to start finalising the details for Jenna's scholar exchange to Australia. Aniko was leaving at the end of August and then it would be Jen's turn to fly to Australia and live with Aniko's family for three months. It would be Jen's first trip away from home alone, and she was really excited. The girls planned a farewell picnic for Aniko in Kirstenbosch Garden.

Two weeks later we were packing Jen off to join Ko-Ko in Australia. The flight to Sydney was hideous and long. Up at altitude Jenna began to feel sicker and sicker. Her chest hurt; sharp shooting pains. She arrived 24 hours later filled with flu-like symptoms and a full-blown chest infection. Margo phoned me from Sydney.

"We've got Jen," she said. "It's so wonderful to see her, Gabs, but she got off the plane feeling really sick. Don't worry, though, she seems to be getting better, slowly. She'd like to chat to you."

It was so good to hear Jen's voice, but I was worried. Asthma and a chest infection are not a good combo. "Don't worry, Mom," Jen reassured me. "I think I just caught a bug on the plane. Margo is looking after me." I was disappointed that her arrival in Sydney was marred by flu and I could tell she was being brave. I was glad she was staying with family for the first week.

A week later she moved in with Aniko. She had her own room – "Mom, it's the best room in the house, I love it here" – and took the train in to school every day. She was loving her first taste of real independence away from home, but in a safe environment and with reliable public transport. It brought a freedom she hadn't experienced before.

Back home it was Kristi's last term of Grade 7 and she was really coming into her own. She missed the laughter of Jen and Aniko, but she had many diverse groups of friends, and her beloved horses and dogs. At home we had Prince and Sahara and she was fostering puppies every weekend. Plus she had the full attention of Stu and me with no distractions. Kristi blossomed. She had an impressive growth spurt, in every way. She literally grew about four inches taller in the 12 weeks that Jen was away. It made me cognisant of just how big a shadow Jenna cast. Kristi needed her time in the sun and we gently found a different rhythm, just the three of us at home.

In October 2011, halfway through Jenna's three-month exchange, I decided to book a flight to Sydney to visit. I wanted to spend Jen's 17th birthday with her, to visit Craig and the family, and, truth be told, I also wanted to check on Jen's health. I was so looking forward to seeing them all.

I was shocked. The severity of Jenna's breathlessness was noticeable. A short burst of running for a train or bus wasn't possible; in fact, even a fast, flat walk was a challenge. Jen was worse, not better. I phoned home and spoke to the asthma clinic. We discussed it and upped the dosage of her meds and her pumps.

Jen insisted that the increase in meds made her feel a little better and I tried to put the anxiety about her health to one side. We had a happy two weeks together, taking the ferry to visit Manly, exploring the city of Sydney, visiting the zoo, having lunch at the Hardrock Café in Sydney Harbour, and visiting the aquarium and the Sydney Opera House. Jen took me to Ko-Ko's school and showed me with pride her tidy bedroom and her favourite spot to buy red velvet cupcakes and fudge.

Jen was happy, she was so happy, fulfilled and confident and loving being independent, finding her way in the big wide world. I realised she was growing up, that things would be different when she got home. She would need more independence. We also discussed what she wanted to do with her life, what she wanted to study and projects she could be involved in. At the time that I booked my trip to Sydney it was an expensive extravagance but, looking back, I am so glad I went. I cherish those memories.

Back in Cape Town, Stuart, Kristi and I worked hard for the three months that Jen was away. Stuart now had seven print media titles under his watchful eye, including some of the biggest niche-market titles in the country, and the business was simultaneously launching many other exciting projects and websites. He worked long and demanding hours, but he loved it. Upfront Marketing still had a good line-up of clients and of course my efforts raising funds for Natalie's Circle of Love were ongoing.

After months of uncertainty and delays, we got the best news from Shirley. Natalie had managed to complete treatment and, mercifully, the halo brace could now be removed. Based on the final scans, her doctors declared the sweetest four words in the world: "No evidence of disease". She still had a lot of recovery and recuperation to do, but after nine hectic months away, she was coming home, chordoma-free. Their homecoming was a huge moment and it was an indescribable joy to be reunited.

Kristi, about to finish her Grade 7 exams, was itching to get to senior school. While Jen was on the other side of the world, Kristi was finding her mojo as a young teen, going to parties, spending hours on the phone, planning movies and having friends over. She was growing into a tall teenager with a fun-loving easy manner. Her long blonde hair and legs reminded me of a gangly palomino horse. She was 14 going on 20, or so she thought.

It was nearing the end of the school year, and time for the school fair. The fair marked the end of the year and the start of the summer holidays and held the promise of the much anticipated Grade 7 disco. Even more exciting was the opportunity for those Grade 6 and 7 pupils who could sing to perform live on the main stage, complete with microphones, backing tracks and a professionally rigged sound system. Kristi had been asked to sing and we were thrilled. During all the years of "carpool karaoke" it had become obvious that Kristi was talented, but this was the first time she was brave enough to sing in public.

It was a balmy summer's evening, with hundreds of proud parents quaffing beers and gin and tonics in the marquee on the field. We couldn't quite believe that our "baby" was about to graduate from junior school. It was at this fair that a good friend of ours, well-known South African rugby commentator Matt Pearce, first heard Kristi sing and it made a lasting impression on him. It was Matt's belief in Kristi's talent that would lead to the release of her first single 18 months later.

Matt and I had a special connection around live music. Shortly after I turned 40, I joined a rock band as a lead vocalist with my talented counterpart Jules. We joke that it was the optimal way to have a mid-life crisis! But it probably doesn't count because Stuart and the girls were my biggest fans and supporters. Matt was one of many friends who used to support us. When he was there, we would summon him up on stage to sing "Summer of 69" or "Mustang Sally". His gravelly voice would bellow forth while Jules and I belted out the harmonies. Jen and Kristi begged to be allowed to come and watch. If there was a Friday or Saturday gig, they were sometimes allowed. They would come with Granny and Grampa, who would then take them home early for a sleepover.

The night of the school fair was one of those perfect nights, complete with a full moon, warm air and gentle breeze. The atmosphere was festive, with the youngsters dancing and cheering each other on as each new performer took the stage. Matt and I were right up there at the front of the audience, enjoying the show and reminiscing about our old band days, when Kristi stepped up to the microphone. Holding the mic in her hand, eyes closed, a soft breeze blowing her golden hair, she began to sing. She had chosen Adele's "Someone Like You" and as this hauntingly beautiful young female voice echoed across the field, slowly it went quiet. People stopped, turned and walked towards the stage. Everyone was captivated.

Matt turned to me. "Wow, Gabs," he said. "She is really good. She is properly good."

We had just witnessed what had until then been a secret talent.

CHAPTER 11

Something is seriously wrong

In late December 2011 Jen finally arrived back from Aussie, brimming with tales of her travels. At the airport she fell into Kristi's arms and then looked up. "Oh my God," she said, "what have they been feeding you? You're all tall and grown up!" She was as thrilled to be home as we were to have her back, excited to be in her bedroom and see her family.

Amidst the joy of being back I sensed that Jenna was not entirely herself. She was tired, very tired. For her first night home I'd made her favourite supper – roast chicken with gravy, crispy roast potatoes and broccoli with cheese sauce – but she wasn't hungry. We blamed the long flight and decided to let her "sleep it off". But after a few solid days of rest, Jen still wasn't rushing out to socialise. Other than seeing some close girlfriends and her family she just wanted to chill at home, sleep or hang with Kristi.

Grade 11 was around the corner and she'd missed a whole term of school because of the exchange. With Kristi now moving up into Grade 8, the girls would be on the same campus for the first time in three years. They chatted animatedly about the best place to sit during break, which subjects to take, the dynamics of the school playgrounds, and which teachers to hope for.

Having seen how much independence Jen had enjoyed in Sydney, I imagined she would be champing at the bit to spread her wings and carve out new boundaries. In fact, it was just the opposite. She turned down invitation after invitation. "I'd rather stay home with you guys, I just need to catch up on some rest," she'd say. "Next time."

A week after Jen got home, we set off to spend Christmas in Greyton. Ali and her husband Les (they had married in 2009) had been planning this holiday carefully for months so that the whole family could be together for Christmas and we had been looking forward to this special time for a while. There was so much to celebrate now that both Natalie and Jen were home. But Jen was not her usual engaging and open self. It came as a shock to notice just how much she was struggling to breathe. The heat in Greyton was oppressive and it seemed to knock the wind right out of her sails. It struck all of us that Jenna appeared to have less stamina than Natalie, who had worked for many months to be able to walk short distances. This was not right. Although there were also plenty of fun, happy times, the undercurrents of anxiety were undeniable.

It was also a Christmas filled with so much love. It was that Christmas that Kristi met her first real love – a magnificent black Friesian stallion called Riaan. The instant bond between Kristi and this horse was magical and the farmer in the village who owned him was so taken by their special connection that he kindly allowed Kristi to ride his stallion on the mountains every day. He even let Riaan sleep over in our garden, which provided much entertainment. It was striking to see this magnificent animal on the lawn outside the window, and a delight to watch Kristi attend to his every need, brushing him, feeding him or washing him down. She took him everywhere with her and was clearly in her happy place. It was perhaps inevitable that Riaan would relocate in due course ...

Jen joined in the activities, but only for short periods. She would excuse herself to go and have a nap or lie down in a cool, dark spot to read. She wasn't well, we could see that, and Stuart and I were worried. Could her asthma be more severe than we thought? Was there something else going on? Jen thought she might have pulled her intercostal muscles when swimming in the cold water, but it didn't seem likely.

We returned to Cape Town, but only briefly. It was time to pack for our annual Plett holiday. Jen's breathing was laboured, to the extent that she was unable to help with the packing. It was alarming that simple things, normal daily tasks, were becoming too much for her. I sent her to lie down while we finished up.

The asthma clinic was closed until January, but I hoped that once we got to Plett everything would settle down. Jen would be happy, and we would be with our wonderful friends. Plett was our safe and happy place.

Plettenberg Bay

Fine white sand, blue skies, the smell of indigenous bush unique to the area and spectacular beaches. Plett was warm and balmy, and the ocean inviting, just the right temperature for hours of swimming and playing in the waves. Although we were thrilled to be there for the summer holidays, this year was simply not the same. Jenna had lost her love of the beach. Once her favourite playground, it had become a brutal environment for her. The heat made her asthma worse and being in the sea quite literally took her breath away. She couldn't cope in the waves, she couldn't swim, and she couldn't get comfortable sitting under the umbrella. Walking through soft sand was impossible. She couldn't even get from the carpark to the beach without stopping to pant. This was a stark and shocking contrast to the healthy, robust 16-year-old brimming with vitality the year before.

We were now desperately worried. Jenna and I visited the emergency rooms in Plett many times that holiday. Nebulising can be very relieving for those with severe asthma, but for Jen nothing was helping. I contacted the asthma clinic in Cape Town for advice via their emergency line and made the soonest possible appointment available in January. We would be back in Cape Town by the time they reopened. As Jenna continued battling to breathe, nothing made sense. Stuart and I tried to hide our anxiety from Jen and Kristi, but it was difficult. By the third visit to the local emergency rooms the nurse was suggesting that maybe Jen's struggle was psychological. In another child perhaps attention-seeking behaviour might have been a plausible explanation, but Jen was no drama queen. Everyone was grasping at straws. Later Jen would tell us that trying to breathe was like breathing through a straw. The heat and any exertion made it much, much worse. But there was nothing more to do until the New Year and, knowing this, we tried to enjoy the time together; just at a more measured pace than the jam-packed holiday we had planned.

We balanced out Jen's need for rest and Kristi's need for normal teenage high-action fun, and I spent time alone with Jen when Stu and Kristi did activities like body-surfing or beaching. Jen would spend many afternoons lying on her bed, where it was cooler, Skyping Aniko and Tayla in Australia. Sometimes, when Jen was feeling quite well, we would see family friends and her Plett gang of friends. She did much better when it was cooler but, watching her carefully, I could see how quickly she tired. She had already become adept at hiding her struggle when other people were around.

Ian and Jillie's serene home became a safe haven for us, and Jen and I were grateful we could seek refuge from the crowds, to sit quietly on their big comfy couches next to their pool and listen to the birds. Ian and Jillie were Jenna's godparents and are our closest friends, so they were acutely aware of what was going on and were as confounded and worried as we were. They took good care of us, pampered us with love and tried to soothe our fears. We spent New Year's Eve at their home, enjoying a braai and the company of the adults Jen loved so much. Just before midnight we kissed everyone Happy New Year and departed to scoop Kristi up from a party before heading off, all four of us, for our traditional "pop in" at the Valentines' house. The Valentines throw the best ever New Year's Eve parties and it's tradition for us to pop in at midnight. The party was thumping when we arrived. My first instinct was to bundle Jen up and take her home immediately, but she surprised me. She became swept up in the moment, beaming and joyful, feeling 17 and carefree.

At 1:30 am, when Stu, Kristi and I were leaving, Jen begged us to let her stay. All her mates were going to another party and she wanted to join them. Stu and I debated it, heatedly; I didn't want to let her go but she was happy and having a good night for the first time in weeks. It was a hopeful night. Maybe this was a good sign? We agreed to let her go as long as she stayed in touch.

She went off cheerfully, asthma pump in hand. I couldn't sleep. I checked my cellphone every half hour.

"Don't be a worry-whale, Mom, I'm having a great time."

"Moving to another venue – Dyl's place with the Plett boys."

This last text had me concerned. "Jen, how the hell are you getting there? I will lift you guys, give me two minutes to throw on some clothes and come get you."

"Don't worry, Mom, we're walking."

"Walking! What!? How? Jen, you can't walk … your asthma … I'm coming to get you. Leaving now!"

"Mom, please don't do that, it's embarrassing. I am good … I'm getting a piggy-back … Jillie just pulled up, she says she will lift us."

I sat up waiting until Jenna called me to collect her and Liv at 5 am. It took two full days of sleep for her to recover, but she was so animated and full of stories that it felt worth it. Over time we learned to grab those moments with both hands and be grateful for them. We learned to take the good days and moments as they presented themselves, no matter the circumstances.

We got a glimpse of healthy Jen again. But it didn't last long. Within three days she was in deep trouble, battling to breathe. We rushed back to the emergency rooms. I vacillated constantly between convincing myself she would be fine and feeling overcome with absolute dread. I couldn't wait to get home to Cape Town.

Jenna's journal
Monday, 2nd January 2012
Plettenberg Bay

I had to be nebulised today! It was flippin scary – turns out I should have been taking prednisone for about a week already. I have never been this bad before, I have such a tight and sore chest. I felt as if a giant fist was in the centre of my chest and squeezing hard.

I feel better now – it's been about six hours since I have been on the nebuliser and that feeling has eased – although I must say I'm nowhere near optimum or even vaguely normal breath levels. The asthma has been awful this past year, worse in the last three months and definitely at its worst these last two weeks. Hopefully my new medication combo – Nasonex, prednisone, still two puffs twice daily of Sereflo, Fexo and Ventolin as necessary will bring me back to normal. We are going to bed now, I am sleeping in Mom and Dad's room so that they can monitor my breathing ... Tomorrow night we are going to a bonfire at Solar Beach! For now, sleep! It's 12:06 am, night xxx

Tuesday, 3rd January (noon) 2012

I just re-awoke, and we sit debating what to do with my day. It's windy. There is going to be an excellent swell today – Nik mentioned it last week – so Kristi is champing at the bit to get to the beach. We have eight days left. Liv and I are going to get in as much jolling as possible. I'm getting nervous for the bonfire tonight, which is a bit silly, but I don't feel great. I could go to the beach today, but I was hoping for a Grand Caesar salad and to wander around town a little bit. I should go get ready ... seriously. I can hardly be bothered standing up though. Sigh ... I'm going to do that.

Monday, 9th January 2012
Plett, doctors' rooms

We are sitting in a very air-conditioned waiting room between appointments. Anyway, yesterday we went up the river. I sat on the beach in the shade. It was boiling hot and I got out of breath if I tried to tan so I'm starting to think that perhaps extreme heat/extreme cold could trigger or exacerbate it. A troop of vervet monkeys descended from the forested river banks to join us on our tiny beach. They were absolutely adorable. The male silverback-looking one gave us an unasked-for display of his bright blue balls. The boys and Kristi went knee-boarding and we headed home at around 4 pm with the boat weighed down by all of us to a point where its top speed only just rivalled that of a snail. Anyways, at present I sit in the car outside Robberg Pharmacy waiting for Mom.

Tuesday, 10th January 2012
Last night in Plett

I'm sitting on my bed mourning the loss of my holiday. OK that's a little dramatic ... but it is our last night.

CHAPTER 12

The slow road to diagnosis

On Wednesday, the 11th of January we drove home, uneasy and apprehensive, to Cape Town. The next morning Kristi and I bustled about sorting through school uniforms and getting her ready for the term. Jen and I had an appointment at the asthma clinic later that morning. We walked up the clinic stairs, slowly, and pushed open the doors. Jen flopped onto a chair in reception, gasping for air, clearly struggling. She also had chest pain. Her lung function test, though, showed up as normal. How could that be? The doctor was perplexed.

"This is not asthma," she said. "There is no way this can be asthma. You need a physician."

"We were at the physician nine months ago," I said. "We saw Dr VC. We have already been."

"I think you need to go back, Gabi. It's good that Dr VC already has all Jenna's baseline tests. It's advisable to go back." She phoned Kathy, our GP, and requested that she get us an appointment with the physician. "It is urgent," I heard her say.

We secured an appointment with Dr VC for 11 am on Monday morning, so it would be a weekend of apprehension. When I look at Jen's journal, she was more worried about her school work than her health.

Jenna's Journal
Saturday, 14th January 2012

School on Wednesday! I need to revise my maths and read my AP books.

On Sunday night I barely slept. I tried to stay calm, to convince myself that everything would be OK, but I didn't have a good feeling.

Dr VC's forehead puckered with concern. He asked Jenna to describe what she was feeling.

"It feels like someone is sitting on my chest and I just can't get enough air in," Jen explained. "It can really hurt. Not a 'burny' sore, more like a deep ache from inside. And sometimes there are sharp pains. I can't run, or walk fast, or far, without getting completely out of breath. Sometimes I'm out of breath just standing still."

Dr VC then asked Jen a lot of questions, beginning with "How are you when you wake up in the morning?" and persisting until he had a full and detailed history of the last nine months. Then he sent us downstairs for more chest X-rays and full bloods. He did a thorough physical examination and another ECG in his rooms. Jen described her extreme fatigue and the different kinds of fatigue, the light-headedness and severity of her breathlessness. Listening to it all in one sitting was hectic for me, but Jen was so matter-of-fact about it. These hideous symptoms had quietly and insidiously just become part of her life.

Jenna was presenting with the same problem we had been having for a year now, but still Dr VC could find nothing definitive. We had been in his rooms now for nearly two hours.

"Please just walk down the passage with Jenna," I said to him. "That's all you need to do. Just walk down the passage with her and you'll see."

Dr VC was an older man, with decades of experience, a mature face, and a kind, no-nonsense sort of manner. "C'mon then, Jen," he said, "let's go for a little stroll."

They were back within moments. Jen was panting. Dr VC picked up the phone and made a call. "Yes, please, Sister," he said. "An oximeter. Will you send someone up with it?"

The small blue and white oximeter was duly brought up from the hospital ward below his office. Dr VC placed it onto Jenna's thumb and checked her oxygen (O2) saturation levels. Then they walked down the passage again, stopping every couple of paces so that he could check the levels. Dr VC didn't look happy. "Jenna's oxygen levels are dropping as she walks," he said. I could hear from his voice this was significant, but I didn't understand why. I would later find out that whether one walks up a hill, runs a marathon or takes part in the Olympics, one's oxygen saturation levels (the levels of O2 present in your blood) will remain stable. Even when we get out of breath, our oxygen saturation levels will remain relatively the same. This was not the case with Jenna. It was not a good sign. It was serious.

Dr VC spoke gently but firmly and carefully. "So," he said, "that test that we didn't think was necessary last year? I am going to send you to do it now. It's a sophisticated and expensive assessment, but the indication is that we should go ahead. In fact, we are definitely going ahead."

"Now?" said Jen. "I have things to do before school tomorrow."

"Yes, now," he replied.

He picked up the phone again and called his colleague. "Right," he said, turning towards us. "He will be ready for you in half an hour. It is just around the corner. I suggest you get something to eat and then go straight there. He will tell you what to do when he has the results. Okay, Jen?"

"Yes, Dr VC," Jen said. Jen was no rebel, she would do exactly what the doctor suggested. So would I.

We chatted cheerfully in the car, relieved that at least something was being done to finally get to the bottom of this. "I can't wait to see everyone at school, Mom, and hear everyone's exchange stories. I've missed them all so much! Also, I want to do some past papers tomorrow, it's been a whole term of no maths, and I'm a bit worried about that."

"You'll be fine, Jen," I said, "I know you will. Rather rest and get completely ready for the term. There will be lots of time to catch up."

We sat and shared a cheese and ham sandwich in reception while we waited, Jen scrolling through her phone.

"Jenna Lowe?" the technician called out.

"Here," she said, smiling, putting her phone away instantly.

"Right, so I am going to have to give you a little injection before we can do the test," he said. Jen was a co-operative patient.

"No problem," she said, smiling brightly.

I was asked to wait in reception. I phoned Stuart. "She's gone inside," I said. "I'll keep you updated."

Fifteen minutes later Jen joined me. I looked at her quizzically. "And?"

"It was no big deal," she said. We sat quietly together and waited for the results. Half an hour went past. I was not comfortable.

"Mrs Lowe? Are you Mrs Lowe?" The tone of the technician's voice was far too caring. And he was looking straight at me, no longer making eye contact with Jen. "Um, here are the test results," he said, adjusting his glasses as he handed me a large brown envelope. "I need you both to go straight back to Dr VC. I just spoke with him – he is expecting you."

"What's going on?" I said. "What did you find?"

He looked at Jen and then back at me. "Her ventilation perfusion is not normal," he said.

"What does that mean?" I asked, confused.

"It looks as though there are clots in her lungs," he said deadpan. He didn't move. Neither did I. A weird feeling crawled up my spine.

"Clots?" I said carefully. "I don't know what that means?"

"I'm sure the doctor will explain everything," he said.

I took the envelope, took Jen's hand and we walked to the car. Subdued, we drove back to Dr VC's rooms. Inside, my mind was racing. Clots?! Why would a young girl have clots? What did this mean?

"So, Jen," Dr VC said, looking at her directly, "your VQ scan shows multiple areas of ventilation perfusion mismatch indicative of multiple pulmonary emboli – blood clots – which would explain why you are finding it hard to breathe." He took a deep breath and then said, "I need to hospitalise you for more tests and monitor you. You will go onto blood thinners immediately and then we will take it from there, okay?"

Hospital? Blood thinners? I thought only older people took blood thinners. Questions were racing through my head, but I forced myself to stay calm. I reached over and took Jen's hand. She squeezed mine and then looked at him.

"Thank you, Dr VC," she said, "but please can I go in on Saturday? I start school on Wednesday, and I really don't want to miss any. Can we do the tests on Saturday?"

He talked slowly and deliberately. "No, Jenna, I'm sorry, there will be no delay. You and Mom are going to go straight back home, collect some pyjamas, a toothbrush and a few things, and I will meet you at the hospital in 20 minutes, okay?"

"Okay," I said, taking over and gathering Jenna up. "Come, my love, let's get you sorted."

We drove home, stunned, and called Stu on the way. Within half an hour we were all at the hospital.

Kristi was calm and contained, chatting lightly to Jen and laying out her stuff for her while Jen lay tentatively under the crisp white hospital sheets. She set out Jen's toiletries, moved a few chairs around and improved the room, and plugged in Jen's cellphone charger and laptop. She kept Jen company while Stu and I met with Dr VC at a small table in the passage. I remember every mark on the wall, the uncomfortable chair, the body language and looks on the faces of visiting families. The foot rug was skew. Our meeting would be a long one so Stu phoned Ali. She came to sit with Jen and then take Kristi for supper. She did that a few times that week. Stuart and I were in shock. On auto-pilot. Dr VC was concerned. That was clear.

It was hard to leave Jen at the hospital that night. I wanted to stay. She looked so little in that blue gown. Stuart and I barely slept. I played the last three weeks over and over again in my mind. Images of the VQ scan haunted me. This was clearly something Dr VC had not seen before. He explained there could be many causes for the emboli, but for now all we knew was that Jenna was in trouble and she had to be monitored closely.

There were many more tests to come, but that night she started oral blood thinners. Warfarin, an anticoagulant, was originally intended as rat poison when, in 1983, scientists unexpectedly discovered its magical ability to thin the blood. How peculiar. As soon as we'd settled her into the ward the pathology lab technician took bloods.

"We are checking your INR," she explained.

"What's that?" asked Jen.

"It stands for Internationally Normalised Ratio, and is a measurement of how long it takes for your blood to coagulate. Mostly one's INR level is at around 1.1. But the doctor wants yours at around 2.2, so we need to monitor you regularly. You will see me again tomorrow. Okay, Jenna?"

"Okay." Jen smiled at her. She didn't flinch as the needle went in. She wanted to make this poor woman's job easier. It was the first of many ongoing blood tests.

Turns out it's quite a thing to keep your INR levels stable. If your INR becomes too high, it greatly increases your risk of internal bleeding. And, in Jenna's case, if her levels were too low, it greatly increased her risk of clotting and creating more thromboembolisms. What you eat, drink or digest in any way (such as medication, painkillers or supplements) will interfere with your levels. As a blood thinner Warfarin is highly effective, but it has to be managed carefully with consistent diet and blood tests.

"How long will she be on this?" I asked Dr VC.

"I'm hopeful that once we have thinned her blood sufficiently, the clots may start to dissipate," he said encouragingly. How long would that take, I wondered. A few days, a week, a month? And what did he mean "may"? "For now, I encourage you both to go home so Jen can get some rest. We will talk again tomorrow – I have arranged further testing."

My eyes snapped open at 5 am. Jen was in the hospital. It was the first day of school – and for those, like Kristi, starting high school at Herschel, it was Orientation Day. What should have been an exciting first day for Kristi now had a different taste to it. She wanted to go via the hospital so that she could say good morning to Jen, so I hurriedly made her lunch-box and we set off. Jen was so loving. She wished Kristi luck and waved her off encouragingly.

As Kristi headed into her first day of high school, I made my way to the headmaster's office. The office was bustling but he made a plan to see me. He was shocked by Jenna's news. "Gabi, please stay in touch," he said. "I will tell Jenna's teachers and keep an eye out for Kristi. If there is anything you need, absolutely anything, please let me know."

By day three in hospital Jen was still just as breathless. She was sent for another chest X-ray. I was standing in her hospital room waiting, looking out the window in a daze, when she was wheeled back in by the nurse. She smiled up at me radiantly. It hit me in the chest like a mule kick. My child was in hospital and in a wheelchair, and no one really appeared to know what was going on. I wanted to cry. "Hello, my darling. How was that?" I said instead.

The doctors were more befuddled; it was a confusing medical picture. "I'm thinking of calling in a specialist professor and pulmonologist from UCT Academic Hospital," Dr VC said to Stuart and me in the passage outside Jen's room. "He may be the right man to help us towards a diagnosis."

"Let's do it," Stu said. "Why wait?"

Prof. Wilcox from the UCT Academic Hospital was about to become a regular fixture in our lives.

Word got out about Jen fast. Friends began visiting and the phone started ringing off the hook. We didn't know what to tell people. Kristi took homework to the hospital at night and then Granny Annie or Ali would take her for a meal. Stuart and I stayed with Jen until lights out.

On day four or five, having examined all Jenna's test results, Prof. Wilcox arrived. He saw Dr VC for a thorough debrief before seeing Jenna. That day was the first time I ever heard the words "pulmonary hypertension". In my ignorance I believed it sounded better than thromboembolisms.

Prof. Wilcox was a smallish man with light green eyes, glasses, greying hair and scruffy eyebrows – if you were to cast a professor in a movie, he would be awarded the role. He spoke in a quiet and considered manner.

After a long while examining Jen, Prof. Wilcox looked at us intently. "I can't be sure, but I think this could be pulmonary hypertension," he said. I was trying so hard to listen, to take it all in, but the words were slippery and foreign. "Or," he continued, "maybe pulmonary hypertension with an element of chronic thromboembolic disease." What language was he speaking, I wondered, as he turned his attention to Jen. "We will carry on with your blood thinners, Jenna, but I want to keep your INR at around at least 3 just to be safe. I might also put you on something called Sildenafil, but we will explain that later. Meanwhile, I'm going to move you across to the UCT Academic Hospital for further tests. Is that okay?"

Another hospital? I thought we were about to take her home.

Prof. Wilcox ordered an ambulance the next morning to do the transfer. Wow. It was hard to absorb. "I will see you there tomorrow. But Jenna," he said in parting, "don't Google. We don't know for sure what we are dealing with and there is a lot of misinformation on the internet. Pulmonary hypertension is a complex condition."

Jen was given a ward on her own in UCT Academic Hospital with the nurses' station right outside her door. Because of that we were able to be at her side most of the time. Prof. Wilcox had thoughtfully arranged it that way. Friends and family took turns to visit. And delicious meals miraculously arrived at the ward thanks to Andrea, a generous friend and renowned caterer. It was a real gift – there was no time for cooking. I spent barely a minute at home.

Prof. Wilcox did another whole battery of tests, the same and more. Included was a much more targeted echo-cardiogram conducted by a specialist technician who knew exactly what she was looking for. He also did the dreaded "six-minute walk test" with Jen. Her first of many. This is a standard assessment tool for PH patients to clock their exercise tolerance, desaturation and chest pain when walking. Jenna came to dread this test over the years. The hospital's specialist cardiologist and haematologist also got involved. Jenna's case was quite a novelty for these academic doctors, but they handled her, and us, with care.

When visitors came Jen would "hold court" from her bed, gracious and dignified, and somehow managing to rock that hospital gown. She often had us in stitches with her dark humour. She was hungry for news of the outside world and for friends. There was no mention of her chest pains, injections, blood tests or nasty side-effects. And no mention of her fear. That she kept to herself. In the hours between visitors and tests she slept while Stu or I sat by her side. In the evenings Kristi balanced her books on the bed to do homework and we sat around chatting as if this was our regular dining room table. I got so used to driving to the hospital that, one day, I drove right to the doorstep of the hospital before realising I was meant to be somewhere else entirely. Some nights, when we got home late, there would be a meal and a note from my friend Mary. If there had been no cars in our driveway all day, she knew we would arrive home hungry and weary. Her thoughtfulness went way beyond the norm.

The echo-cardiogram, among other things, showed that Jenna's pulmonary pressures were up.

"It's possible," Prof. Wilcox said, "that Jenna does have pulmonary hypertension. There is a test, a catheterised angiogram, which is considered the gold standard test for PH, but we will not do that right now."

"Why not?" I asked.

"It's a more invasive test," he said. He wanted to wait for Jen to stabilise before ordering it.

So, for now the diagnosis, as we understood it, was that Jen had chronic pulmonary emboli. There was hope that they would be contained and dissipated with the regular treatment of blood thinners. She was still breathless and fatigued, and had chest pain, but it was far less severe. It was time to take her home. We were delighted.

"But, Jen," said Prof., "you have to take it easy. Absolutely no exercise. And regular blood tests. You need to be consistent with your medication and have lots of rest. You will come to me for an appointment next week." He knew he could rely on her to be compliant. We packed up Jen's things fast and took her home before he changed his mind.

Jenna stayed in bed for a while, and we monitored her symptoms carefully. She was coughing a lot and complaining of what she said felt like pulled intercostal muscles, at the back of her lungs. We seemed to be managing it until after a few days she coughed up blood. We went straight back to Prof. He was concerned that despite her INR levels being between 2.4 and 3.2 this may be another embolic episode. It was decided to keep her INR levels even higher. Around 4, if we could. He further increased the dose of Warfarin and monitored her INR very carefully with blood tests. The coughing started to settle down.

Jen could not wait to get back to school. She was concerned about the amount of work she was missing and really wanted to see her friends. She started with half-days, taking work home in the afternoons. Kristi was so happy to have Jen on campus; at last they were together, albeit in much different circumstances than expected. They spent breaktimes chilling under the trees with Jen's mates.

I was on top of the medical regime, at times deeply worried and at others optimistically hopeful that this would pass. Even though her diagnosis was not yet finalised, Prof. Wilcox had spoken often enough of suspected pulmonary hypertension for me to know it was time to get to grips with what PH was and do some in-depth research. I started Googling and reading through medical journals. PH sounds pretty innocuous, right? Well, it's not. In fact, what I came face to face with was pretty horrifying.

Pulmonary hypertension is a complex and commonly misunderstood disease.

A rare and life-threatening lung disease, pulmonary arterial hypertension (PAH) is when the small veins and arteries of the lungs become damaged and constrict, making it very difficult for a patient to oxygenate their body.

A quick biology lesson in case you have forgotten:

"The heart and lungs work together to carry oxygen throughout the body. The heart is a muscle made up of two halves that pumps the blood. As deoxygenated blood returns from the rest of the body, it first goes into the right side of the heart, which pumps it into the lungs. The lungs take carbon dioxide from the blood – which the body releases as you exhale – and replace it with oxygen that you have inhaled. After the blood picks up the oxygen, it is considered 'oxygenated' again and is ready to go to other areas of the body. The blood then travels from the lungs into the left side of the heart. The left side of the heart then pumps the blood to the rest of the body. This process starts over again with each heart beat."[1]

I scoured through the material, sharing it with Stuart. The information was always carefully worded – "It is complex ..." "There are treatments available ..." "Each case is unique ..." – and densely populated with medical terminology. I was looking for the bottom-line. Some of the words that kept jumping out at me over and over again were the following: "can live for many years with the right treatment"; "medication and multiple treatments can extend life span"; "can improve quality of life"; "there are many different causes"; "average age from 35 onwards"; "many different categories"; "find the right doctor"; and "triple therapy required and early treatment critical".

Chronic thromboembolic disease was a sub-section or category of pulmonary hypertension, and there were many others. It was so complicated, but everywhere I searched and whatever I read contained the real kickers, the phrases that, as a mother, you never ever want to read: "average prognosis from diagnosis to death 3–5 years ..."; "survival can be increased with the possibility of a double lung transplant ..."

---

1   PH Association of the USA www.phassociation.org

I was reeling. We were reeling. There must be a mistake. Did Prof. Wilcox really think Jenna could have this awful life-threatening disease? Stuart phoned him. We needed to talk. It was time to ask the hard questions.

Prof. Wilcox saw us on a Saturday morning. I had printed out all the medical articles and we had a list of questions ready. There were no absolute answers, Prof. said, but yes, it was highly likely that Jen had pulmonary hypertension. She had no evidence of an underlying condition so understanding the cause was difficult. At this point it was what one would call "idiopathic" or "primary" pulmonary hypertension. Even though we pushed him, he wouldn't give an absolute prognosis. He was careful to manage our fear and horror. What was clear to us was that this was not going to be an easy road.

Stuart was the first to ask about a lung transplant. I found the concept brutal. But yes, Prof. said, the chances were that Jen would need a double lung transplant at some stage in the future. If a double lung transplant was a solution, Stu persisted, why didn't we just do it now? Because, Prof. explained, lung transplants are extremely difficult surgeries and they don't buy you a lifetime. We would have to wait until it was absolutely necessary. I wanted to vomit.

Stuart and I stood for a long time in the carpark after that meeting, weeping. We couldn't go home and face our girls like that. We had to pull ourselves together.

CHAPTER 13

Reality dawns

One of the curses of PH is that it's a curiously "invisible" illness. Unless you knew Jen really well, it was impossible to tell how sick she was. She appeared so normal and calm and had become adept at hiding her breathlessness. It was easy to misunderstand why she didn't hop up when an adult walked into the room, or rush to help stack a dishwasher or clear the table. If you didn't know any better, you could assume laziness. She hid her struggle and so it was easy to not notice a slight change in her pallor, the leisurely and seemingly casual pace of her walk, or the fact that her lips were darker than normal. Dark lips are the mark of low oxygen saturation, a look that our Western society deems "pretty".

Mornings were tough and getting to school on time impossible. I would take Kristi, then go back to wake Jen and help her get dressed. She was dizzy and oxygen deprived in the mornings, but wanted no pity. She arrived at school all smiles. It was hard for those who were not in the know to understand what was going on. To some it appeared as if Jen had special privileges, sometimes attending class and sometimes not, sometimes attending social events and sometimes not. I understand it was confusing, but it is also true that teenage girls can be cruel and judgemental. There was some petty politics and doubt as to the "authenticity" of her illness. It was hard to manage, knowing what we did, but luckily

Jen's close inner circle knew just how much she was battling to function and were incredibly supportive. And, of course, she had Kristi at her side, her fierce protector.

On days when Jen had enough energy (her days were highly variable) we encouraged her to see her friends, go to Debating and find ways to remain connected with her social groups and her passions. If we'd based our daily decisions on medical data only, I would probably never have let her leave the house. Thank heavens neither Stu nor Jen would allow that. Regardless of the massive adjustments she had to make, at no stage did Jen play the role of victim or display one iota of self-pity. Where others might have asked "Why me?", she would ask "Why *not* me?"

Teenage socialising moved to our home, where it was safer. Kristi spent a lot of time with Jen and her friends and became integrated into her group. We also spent an inordinate amount of time with family, which was comforting. We came to know every inch and corner of the winding road to Shirl's house, where we all spent many evenings together with Ali, Les and Matt, all supporting each other. Natalie was at this stage being tutored at home; she was able to attend school for a few hours on some days, but recovery from surgery was hard and slow.

Between the heaviness of our medical challenges and the mundanity of endless blood tests, logistics and doctors' appointments, it would lift my spirits so much to walk down the passage at home and hear Jen and her friend Cami giggling loudly as they played a ridiculous game they called "marry one, date one, kill one". Between school projects and maths homework they wrote silly lists of boys' names on pieces of paper, which they then drew out of a container. They would then double over guffawing at the results, sometimes inviting me to join in the silliness as I brought tea and shortbread biscuits. It was so good to see Jen having some adolescent, carefree moments.

But mostly, while friends played hockey, danced or swam, Jen sat quietly and watched, with a graciousness that made me both proud and sad. Sometimes, cuddled up in her bed together, she would tell me how isolating it felt to be physically incapable of joining in. Sometimes I'd notice her watching Kristi in a way that made me wonder if she had moments of fleeting envy, just as there were times, I think, Kristi felt guilty for her health and vitality. It was a complex dynamic to balance. Roles and rules easily confused.

There was a lot going on for our family and we had learned and developed black humour, which, though shocking to outsiders, became an important and powerful coping mechanism for all of us. As Freud said in his essay *Humour*: "Humour is not resigned; it is rebellious." Natalie and Jenna were particularly observant, quick-witted, wry and funny – they truly led the way when it came to dark humour – and I think this is exactly the point: black humour has the ability to "assert itself against the unkindness of real circumstances".

It helped us deal with the terrible uncertainty. Jen was clearly very sick, although her diagnosis was not yet confirmed, and Natalie's recovery was uncertain. Just as we were forced, in a very real way, to stay in the moment and squeeze out all the joy that we could, it also felt as though the Sword of Damocles was hanging over the heads of two of our much-loved children.

On the 12th of April we were dealt a heavy blow. A follow-up PET scan revealed a recurrence of Natalie's tumours. It was devastating. Shirley knew all too well what this meant and moved quickly to get Natalie back to her doctors in Boston.

By mid-April Jen had been on Warfarin for a while. There were some hopeful moments of improvement, but they didn't last. She came down with a chest infection and within days her severe chest pains returned. Her breathlessness was extreme. We went directly to see Prof.

A chest X-ray showed significant deterioration since January and "blunting" on either side of her lungs (mosaic perfusion and bilateral peripheral pruning in the small vessels). Prof. arranged a Doppler – a non-invasive ultrasound – of Jen's legs, pelvis, abdomen, neck and upper limbs. A Doppler is done by bouncing high-frequency sound waves (ultrasound) off circulating red blood cells to estimate the blood flow through one's blood vessels. A regular ultrasound uses sound waves to produce images but can't show blood flow. A Doppler can. The idea – and, weirdly, our great hope – was that we would find a thrombosis somewhere that could explain the cause of the emboli. If so, then we would insert an IVC, an interior vena-cava filter. The Doppler checked Jenna's entire body. Nothing. There was no thrombosis and the CTPA had shown no evidence of a proximal clot amenable to surgery. Small-vessel pulmonary emboli in children or adolescents normally have a predisposing cause or evidence of thrombosis. Not so in Jenna's case. It was a confusing picture.

Jenna's bilateral chest pains were becoming increasingly frequent, despite anti-coagulation, and Prof. felt it was time to do the catheterised angiogram. On physical examination there was still evidence of a loud P2 and clinical pulmonary hypertension, but a right and left heart catheterisation needed to be done to be sure. A catheterised angiogram is a dye test used to check the pressures in the lungs and heart. A long tube, a catheter, with a camera on the end is inserted into the femoral artery located in the groin and guided all the way up into the heart to X-ray the veins and arteries measuring the pressures.

Jen was re-admitted to UCT Academic Hospital on the 23rd of April 2012. The procedure, in and of itself not dangerous, would be invasive but quick, but the fact that she was on high doses of blood thinners made things a little more complex. Despite her risk of clotting, she needed to come off the blood thinners to decrease the risk of a bleed-out in surgery.

Jen was prepped and ready, smiling at me as she was wheeled in. She was awake for the procedure, having elected to skip sedation because of the effect it had on her breathing. It was only a 30- to 45-minute procedure, but I paced outside the theatre door. An hour went by. I was still pacing. This was taking much longer than expected.

It was another half an hour before Jenna came out. She was strained, blue lipped, cold and miserable. She was shivering and her blood pressure was low. We got her to the ward quickly.

"Mom, I could feel a warm flush as the dye went in," she said breathlessly. "It wasn't easy lying still for so long. The stainless-steel table was so cold, and I needed to pant. I tried very hard to stay totally still, Mommy."

She was hungry. I calmed her and fed her small bits of crumbed chicken schnitzel from home. We piled her high with blankets, found hot water bottles and brought warm tea. Her blood pressure stabilised but her back ached and all she wanted was to curl up and pull her knees into her tummy to relieve the pain. But it was high risk, the catheter had been inserted into her femoral artery in her groin and she needed to stay straight-legged. For six hours. I read to her as she dozed in and out of sleep.

Later that evening the cardiologist checked in on us and Jenna asked him if he had got what he needed. "Yes," he said. "We could see that your pressures are way up." My heart skipped a beat. This was not good. "We took extra time to check if your pressures responded to nitrates, but they didn't. Prof. Wilcox will explain." I went cold. Skin crawling. I knew this meant that our worst fears had been confirmed. Jen's pulmonary pressures were way up. Every awful medical detail I had ever read came at me. I was nauseous. I felt outside of my body. An altered state of time.

"May I curl up now, Doctor?" Jen's sweet little voice brought me back to the room. "I just want to bend my legs."

"Yes," he said. "It should be safe to move now, Jen."

After the doctor left, Jen needed the toilet. I helped her out of bed and she walked gingerly to the bathroom. I was standing right outside the door when I heard her shout. "Mom!" I could hear panic in her voice. I threw open the door. She stood, wide-eyed with fright, blood literally pumping from her femoral artery. I screamed. A nurse came running, immediately jamming her thumb into Jen's artery. Together we got her onto the bed and the nurse applied pressure to stop the bleeding. "Get the doctor!" she instructed. I ran down the passage, my heart pounding, but I caught him, and we raced back to the ward. "You're not going anywhere," he said to Jen, and to the nurse, "Don't let up on that pressure." Jen's eyes were wide, but she was quiet.

There was blood everywhere. While I talked calmly to Jen, the nurse bore down, applying maximum pressure. It must have been so sore. Jen held my hand and looked out the window, focused on her breath. Eventually the bleeding slowed, and the nurse could reduce the pressure.

At that moment Granny, Grampa and Kristi strolled unsuspectingly around the corner into the ward, smiling and chatting. It was visiting hour. I ran to block their view and hustled them outside into the passage while we stopped the bleed, changed the sheets and tidied Jen up. Jen and I hugged. "Call them in," she said calmly. She was remarkable, chatting lightly to her grandparents and putting her wide-eyed sister at ease.

Later that night I climbed into bed next to Stu. In the stillness of the night I started to shake. There was no more doubt. No matter which way you looked at it, we could not suspend the truth. Jenna had PH. The full weight of her diagnosis hit me hard.

Two days later Jen came out of hospital. She was limping slightly and had a bruise that spread from above her groin to halfway down her thigh.

There was a school function in the sports hall that evening that she wanted to attend. I remember, with absolute clarity, the moment that the school choir began their opening song. Their emotive voices echoed round the hall with familiar lyrics from "I Hope You Dance" by Lee Ann Womack. It was a singular moment. The music, the words, the sight of all those fresh-faced healthy young girls singing their hearts out. Jen would never dance, she would never take one single breath for granted and she probably didn't have a fighting chance … and yet no one knew. Seated in the middle of the huge hall, packed with robust children and their hope-filled parents, I felt utterly alone. I held on tightly to Stuart's hand, scanning the mob of blue school dresses frantically searching for my girls. I needed to see they were okay. I saw Kristi, hair pulled back into a tight high pony, leaning playfully into a friend, chatting animatedly. I scanned the crowd again and found Jen. Her head was lifted high, she was smiling, standing, shoulders back, next to Camilla as if nothing was wrong. She was the ultimate picture of poise, grace and courage. Stu and I held tightly onto each other, our palms sweaty with emotion, battling to contain ourselves.

It was a glimpse of what lay ahead ... the constant struggle to cope in the normal world, while holding the knowledge that Jen was fighting for her life. Nothing for us was normal. It was the ultimate paradox, to hold both fear and hope.

With no more room for denial, Stu and I talked at length about finding ways to consciously create joy. It was tempting to withdraw and batten down the hatches but, having learned the value of staying connected, we made sure our loved ones were always welcome in our home, no matter how sick Jen was. Our friends and family flocked to support her.

Daffy started to visit more regularly – he and Jen had remained friends over the years – and he had become a much-loved part of our family. They grew incredibly close. They played chess, chatted for hours and watched movies. It was a joy to hear them laugh, easily and often. When Daffy visited, Jen was her most natural, relaxed and happy self. She was loved by Daffy for exactly who she was. It didn't matter how tired or challenged she might be feeling that day. With him she didn't need to pretend.

There were also regular visits from a gorgeous tall boy called Max, who lived just a few blocks away from us. This friendship was a lot more charged and complicated, as both Jen and Kristi perked up when he arrived ... mmm ... two young teenage girls with a crush on the same boy. This was a potential recipe for disaster.

On Natalie's 12th birthday, the 28th of April, we went to the revolving restaurant, the Top of the Ritz, to celebrate a long-held tradition to mark the children's first "double digit" birthdays. This would have happened for Natalie's 10th birthday, but she was in surgery at the time. With Natalie and Shirl about to head back to Boston, we knew this was the time to mark the milestone.

Ahead of their departure, Ali and Les kindly arranged to rent the same country house in Greyton where we'd spent Christmas, so that we could insulate from the world and spend a weekend together as a family. The weekend was bittersweet and saying goodbye again was painful.

En route to the airport Shirley stopped in Somerset West to say goodbye to her dad. Peter's health was deteriorating and she knew it was possible that Natalie would not see her Pop again. He had been diagnosed with multiple myeloma, the same rare bone cancer that had claimed the life of his wife Jean.

We were facing assault from all sides. The harsh reality of Jen's illness was that even though she had been on a vaso-dilator, Revatio, since the angiogram, we were yet to see any improvement.

CHAPTER 14

Jenna's journal

Jenna was stoic. No one saw, or knew, the depth of what she was grappling with inside. She saw her therapist regularly, and spoke to me, but mostly she protected everyone around her from her darkest fears. Writing became a constructive way for her to cope and she journalled a lot. There were some exquisitely painful and precious late-night moments when she would share some of it with me.

Jenna's journal
Sunday, 6th May 2012
In bed, Julia's house

I am stressed and should be working for exams, but I want to clear my head. I've realised, when skimming through my journal, that I have minimal descriptions of my actual condition – because they are unnecessary as I am writing for myself.

So right now, I have deteriorated to a similar state I was in in January. I struggle to breathe if I talk too fast, stand too long or walk even a couple of metres. Stairs pose a massive challenge for me. I am as weak as a kitten and have dropped to 45 kg. The other night I realised that I cannot lift a pile of three plates with one hand – cannot. I struggled for ages and simply could not lift them.

With my breathlessness comes, of course, the exhaustion. On my best days I wake up feeling as though I have slept for five hours after doing a massive hike the day before. On other days I can't wake up. Of course, I can't spend my whole life in bed, but often by the end of the day I am so fatigued I can barely string a sentence together. Because my oxygen saturation is so low concentration is a nightmare. Where I could work steadily for a straight four to six hours before, I now struggle to focus and stay awake for one. So that's the breathing and energy description.

The chest pain is another aspect. The last three days it has been pretty much constant. On Thursday I couldn't get out of bed for hours. The pain manifests in a number of ways:

- Short severe stabbing chest pains that make me hold my breath and double over.
- Prolonged severe sharp pains which stop me from breathing properly. These pains usually fade slowly but are immediately worsened if I breathe in and out deeply. I take shallow breaths until I am so desperate that I have to breathe in deeply and then it usually makes me gasp or cry.
- Pains that last for hours or days. These pains are also affected by breathing and thus usually confine me to bed, lest I move and get more out of breath. These pains normally trigger corresponding pains in my back, neck and shoulders.
- Back "rubbing" pain occurs usually on my left side by my spine. It happens when the lung engorged with blood rubs against my back muscles. The "rub" sensation can actually be heard and felt – it feels as though a rough, textured surface is being moved back and forth in my back as I breathe; and it sounds like a crackling noise.

- Streaking pains are like "stabbing" pains, different chiefly in location. They "streak" across my chest suddenly.
- Corresponding pains – my back, shoulders and sometimes neck often develop pains in perfect unison with my chest. For example, my lower lung on the left often triggers pain in a specific point on my left shoulder. Massage helps my shoulders, but not my chest.

Now onto the medication. Warfarin, of course, causes bleeding and bruising. It also dries out your hair and skin and for some reason I am always cold. I am also now on Revatio/Sildenafil which causes nausea, dizziness, headaches and hot flushing. But I have become resistant, after two horrible weeks, to the initial Revatio side-effects now.

Jenna's journal
Tuesday, 15th May 2012

I had a lovely weekend at Julia last weekend, though with bad chest pains. This past weekend was better, though. The pains have improved, and I'm not sure if I'm imagining it, but my breathing seems better too.

Nothing has happened yet with Daffy … but we have been chatting a lot. He's so sweet. I really enjoy being around him.

Exams start next Thursday! Stress!

Jenna's journal
Friday, 18th May 2012
School – English office 11:30 am

I am insanely tired. I still have to get through Afrikaans, biology, history, debating and then we are going to Stardust tonight. An afternoon sleep is without doubt going to be necessary.

It is six days to exams. I have no idea how I'm going to do this. I'm not concentrating well at all.

Jenna's journal
Saturday, 19th May 2012
Home 9:05 am

Last night we went to Stardust. It was such fun! There was definitely a vibe between Daffy and me but nothing major happened. It was great, though. Kristi definitely needs to work there! I only got a little bit bleak when I had to sit, not dance. But oh well, we still had a great night. I definitely want to go more often.

Jenna's journal
Sunday, 20th May 2012
1:30 pm home

I just read up about lung transplants, because if I have idiopathic pulmonary hypertension or pulmonary veno-occlusive disease ...
Survival rates look like this:
One year – 75%
Five years – 50%
Oh. My. God.

On Monday, the 21st of May, I was sitting in my office poring over medical journals when my cellphone rang. It was Jen, phoning from school. Immediately I was on high alert.

"Jen?" I asked. "Is everything all right?"

Silence.

"Jen?"

Silence.

"Jen?!"

"Mom?" I heard a crumpled, crushed little voice crying breathlessly into the phone. My heart was pounding. She was panting and crying but eventually managed to say three little words: "Mom … I Googled."

Horror flooded my body. She knew. I took a deep breath. "I'm coming," I said quietly. "I'll be there in three minutes."

Jenna was waiting in the school carpark, hiding behind a tree so that no one would see her crying. We drove home clutching each other's hands across the gear-box, tears streaming down our faces. The silence was heavy. I knew I couldn't take the pain away and I was nauseous. Once home I helped Jen gingerly out of the car and up the steps to the front door. We stood there hugging, clutching each other for the longest time. Her face was buried in my chest, her fragile body shaking against mine. *Oh God. Oh God. Please help me to take this pain away.*

We stood for a long time before she pulled away. She looked up at me, huge brown eyes brimming with unanswerable questions. Then she nodded imperceptibly, turned away and slowly walked down the passage, closing the bedroom door softly behind her. In the privacy of my bedroom I doubled over, clutching my stomach, and wept and wept. There was no way to make sense of this. My head ached. An hour passed and I couldn't stay away from my baby any longer. I crept into her bedroom with warm, sweet tea and climbed into bed beside her. I wrapped my arms around her and rocked her gently back and forth. For a long time, we cried together. Jen was so sad I thought she might break in two.

That day I promised we would do everything we could. That we would never give up. We would fight. I promised she would never be alone.

That heartbreaking day, when she was alone in her bedroom, this is what Jen wrote:

Jenna's journal
Monday, 21st May 2012
Home; my bedroom

I'm lucky if I have 10 years left. No long life for me.

No career, no opportunity to change things or be

promoted. No kids. No kids! Because even if I last double that, 20 years, then at 37 I would still die while my kids are young. It's not fair to them. And who wants a mother who can't take them hiking, or play ball, or even prepare them dinner?

I will not get better before I get worse. Never again will I run, jump or swim in the ocean. I'll never learn to surf, ski or scuba-dive.

I have to cling to the hope that the medical experts will develop a cure.

What a pathetic hope!

I'm 17 and yesterday I basically found out that I have either:

Two years left (pulmonary veno-occlusive disease)

Seven years left (pulmonary veno-occlusive disease with successful lung transplant)

10 years left (idiopathic pulmonary hypertension/CTEPH with good meds, all the right treatments and maybe a successful lung transplant)

And my quality of life isn't exactly going to be the best considering I can barely walk.

So now it's 11:38 am at school and I'm meant to be studying for exams. I'm meant to be learning Afrikaans. How am I supposed to deal with this? I don't know. I have to alternate between being immersed in life-or-death issues and being distracted by the petty considerations of everyday life. I need to try and make every day the best it can be if I'm going to die soon.

But I'm so scared.

This isn't fair. I was always going to help people – be a politician, fix people's lives. Something. How can I die?

It's not meant to happen.

I want to go to UCT, do a PPE and then study at Oxford. Get a high-paid job doing something I love, like helping others. Design my dream house. Become famous. Write. Meet the right man. Have children. Be a good mother. Retire and travel the world with my husband. Set up a charity. See my children often. Help raise my grandkids. Die peacefully in my bed.

I wanted to swim with dolphins, hike Kilimanjaro, cycle around the neighbourhood. Do the Otter Trail and Table Mountain. Be a prefect. Party hard at varsity. Drink and dance at Plett Rage. Go to lots of matric dances. Enjoy going wild on the dance floor at my matric dance and after-party. Make brilliant public speeches. Star in house plays and help direct them. Be helpful to others. Be the dependable (not dependent) friend. Canoe on the Orange River. Travel. Be a waitress or work at the movie-shop. Model.

Have boyfriends who I can kiss without getting tired. Go out with them and dance all night. Be able to be attractive to people without them having to be nice to/careful with "the sick girl".

Not be cold all the time. Be able to walk to my friend's house. Be able to concentrate properly. Be able to go to gym. Get muscle back. Have rosy cheeks sometimes. Go to the Swartberg farm and be able to join in the "boys'" games and throw a ball around.

Be able to have kids. Be pregnant. Then be able to look after them. To live. To watch them grow. Have my mom and dad be proud of me for being a vibrant, empowered woman, not a virtuous invalid.

"If I die young, bury me in satin, lay me down in a bed of roses.

Sink me in the river at dawn, send me away with the words of a love song."

11 pm – can't sleep …

When I look back at the beginning of this journal, some of the things I wrote about seem so trivial. It's amazing how they still bother me, though. It's like I'm operating on two levels – one where I am trying to handle the fact that I'm never going to be healthy again and I'm going to die young, and the other is concerned about everyday trivial things. Not that everyday things get to me that much, but if I don't have a great deal of time left then each day needs to count. I'm worried about exams and studying, and I am finding it so hard to concentrate. Partly because I have other things on my mind, but partly because I'm just being lazy. And I'm so out of practice. I haven't written an Afrikaans essay in over six months!

So that's exams. Then there are boys, and friends. Friendship. I just feel isolated. I want to be there every break time. I want to sob and have people help me. I would never, though. What would be ideal is to have a giant girls'-night sleepover, which will have to be after exams.

… I don't know who to tell …

The thing is … how do people cope? How do they treat you? …

I don't want to burden them. But I also know that if I don't tell anyone and I keep it bottled up inside and try to protect everyone then I'm going to cause myself more hurt, and distance and alienate my friends.

I have already had to act, put on a show, and I only found this out yesterday. It makes me feel fake. It scares me that I have to put on a good front for everyone, adults even. To some extent, even my parents. So scary watching your mother sob. I am not a child anymore. I am a full-grown woman.

I know this sounds weird, but I don't think I want to die a virgin. And not even for the sex, more for the relationship. I don't want to die never having experienced that kind of love, or intimacy or trust.

I've always thought I would never be in a rush to marry. My career came first. But now, what about it? Am I ever going to hear a proposal? And even if I do, would it be fair?

Who deserves to know their wife will soon die? And how could I do that to a man I loved? Let him nurse me? Watch me fade away?

It is killing me (ha-ha) that I won't be able to have kids. I want to be a mommy. But even if I had a baby tomorrow, I couldn't look after it. And actually, a pregnancy would probably kill me anyway. I so wanted to be a parent. I wanted to do it right. I was going to be the best mother ever.

My only hope is that things develop fast enough that a cure turns up. I'm seriously clinging to it. It has to happen. I don't want to die. It's not fair.

I really need to sleep now. I'm going to try soon …

"Every day is so wonderful
But suddenly, it's hard to breathe."

I'm going to have to live life in the moment. Speak my truth. Take what I want.

Things I want to do:

Diving lessons. Stardust. Get scooter. Mani. Haircut. Buy Clinique "Happy". Watch *Burlesque* and *Titanic*. Do a family photo-shoot. Do a shoot with Kita. Do a test shoot … if I'm too sick to do proper modelling work, I definitely want to do a test-shoot with mom's photographer friend. Ace my exams! Write. Read. See Maike and Chaeli.

Jenna's journal
Tuesday, 22nd May 2012
11 am; English office

I should be studying. I am not, though. I just Googled "dealing with a terminal illness". Never thought I would have to. To think that I used to worry about getting cancer when I reached middle-age. Or was stressing about skin cancer. I'm not going to live long enough for any of that to take its toll. Neither is walking on my toes going to be an issue. It's most likely that my hips and back will suffer from this immobility. All that work to get me fit. To never have a filling. To stretch me out. What was the point?

Although I suppose the fact that we were planning for the future was a privilege in and of itself.

I've had an incredible life, I really have. Maybe I have used up my share of happiness? Maybe that's why ... like I need an expiry date or something.

So apparently the stages I will probably go through work something like this:

Shock; Denial; Anger; Grief; and Acceptance.

I could probably have made that up myself. Will I write people letters? What will my last words be?

"A penny for my thoughts?
I'll sell them for a dollar.
They're worth so much more
After I'm a goner."

"... Funny when you are dead how people start listening."

I think I need to work now. It might be a nice distraction.

Still Tuesday
School: 3:08 pm
Waiting to be collected
English office

I just wrote the start of an autobiographical piece, on my laptop, about finding out I was going to die.

I seriously can't handle this. I've never been so scared in my (unfairly short) life. This can't be happening. It's so not right. Not fair. Clearly, I'm still in shock 'cos this feels like a bad dream.

How do I act at school? Partly it's a nice distraction being here, but partly it feels so fake. If I were being real, I'd be sobbing constantly. Incessantly.

Mom's fetching me.

In rare moments Jenna would share her vulnerability and pain with me and Stu, but mostly she was private and inordinately strong. She chose to respond with dignity, grace and courage. She imagined her sadness would drive a wedge between her and her friends and believed they shouldn't have to cope with her fear. So Jen chose to make it easy for people to be around her.

CHAPTER 15

Going to war

News from Boston wasn't easy. Natalie needed to gain weight for surgery and was having a rough time. This made it especially hard to share the impossible truth of Jenna's prognosis with Kristi. It was a lot for our family to deal with and we needed help. I searched for a therapist who would be the right fit to help guide us through the multiple ongoing trauma.

And on a practical level, now that we had clarity we needed a treatment plan for Jenna.

The lioness in me had awoken and I wasn't going to stop. I drowned myself in medical journals. How could we extend and improve Jenna's quality of life? What therapies were available and where could we find them? What did her prognosis really look like and what *could* it look like? How could I access the right treatments? Did we need to supplement our local team of doctors with the best expertise in the world? The literature described three pathways to treatment but on the southernmost tip of Africa we had only one, Sildenafil/Revatio. That was not good enough. We needed to find and fund the treatments she needed.

We saw Prof. Wilcox every two or three weeks and Jen kept a meticulous record of her symptoms. It showed us she was systematically and consistently getting worse. We needed additional treatment, fast. I'd started speaking to people around the world, and one particular woman in the UK, who'd been a PH patient for many years, gave me incredible hope. Multiple treatment had successfully extended her life. She was on a drug called Bosentan and had been on it (as well as Sildenafil and Warfarin) for more than a decade. I wanted to get my hands on it.

Prof. Wilcox's office was small, messy and piled high with stacks of paper files. It always came as a surprise to me when he found Jenna's file. I kept copies of just about everything I could just in case we couldn't find something. We had developed a good relationship but at times it was also exasperating.

"But *why*?" I said, when I raised the possibility of Bosentan. "*Why* is it not possible?"

Bosentan (or Tracleer) was an expensive drug, and not registered in South Africa. In fact, many of the drugs freely available elsewhere for PH patients are not registered in SA. I explained to Prof. that I'd been reading up about triple pathways to treatment. I felt he wasn't fighting to help us get our hands on the right treatments, that he was almost encouraging me to accept the status quo. Perhaps the state medical system had tired him out over the years, or maybe it just felt that way to a desperate mother. It is a particular added layer of cruelty for *all* mothers of children with rare diseases that they find themselves with the additional challenge of fighting every step of the way to source what their children need. It is all-consuming. At this stage I had the benefit of naivety and belief, plus the promise I had made to Jen. I would go to war if I had to.

"But, Prof, what *can* be done? What can *I* do? There must be *something*. There must be a way around," I asked, again and again.

"There is one way," he acknowledged eventually. "We can apply for Section 21A approval to import a registered and FDA-approved drug into the country. It requires stringent paperwork, motivated by a medical doctor and valid reasons to believe that the drug may be effective for the patient. Then it needs to be approved by the Medicines Controls Council of South Africa."

"Okay," I said. "How do we get started?"

The Medicines Control Council (MCC) is a statutory body that oversees the regulation of medicines in South Africa. Appointed by the Minister of Health, it protects the public by making sure that all medicines used in South Africa are safe, effective and meet acceptable standards of quality. The protocol Prof. Wilcox had outlined would have to be repeated every six months. In order to get approval for such a drug, one must prove a credible, reliable, legal source of the medication, the ability to fund it and a registered pharmaceutical company to ship, receive and navigate customs with all the correct accompanying documentation.

Prof. looked weary at the thought but he was willing to help. He cautioned me. "Gabi, you and Stuart need to be sure you can fund this consistently." Once Jen was on treatment, she would need to stay on it. It is detrimental to be inconsistent. This required a long-term commitment. Well, of course. There was no choice and no question.

"We're sure," I said. "We will make it happen." I had learned how to do what needed to be done.

The cold reality was that it wouldn't be easy. Having less time to work, I therefore had less time to earn. Since Jen needed me more as her physical strength lessened, Upfront Marketing had taken a back seat. My assistant was trying to keep everything together for my existing clients, but my priorities had changed. I was becoming a momcologist. Yes, there is such a thing ... if you Google it you'll find: "A *momcologist* means that in the blink of an eye, your entire life changes. You become an advocate. You become your child's voice, and sometimes, their strength."[2]

Stuart was earning well, but the print industry was under siege from the digital media sector. Gone were the high days of great magazine sales and advertisers banging down the doors to book ad space. The publishing empire in South Africa was floundering. He was under huge pressure and of course his priorities had changed too. As the pressure of a sick child at home ratcheted up, so did the pressure at work. It was an ever more hostile environment to work in and the long hours were proving really tough. Stuart

---

2   https://www.roswellpark.org/cancertalk/201605/day-life-momcologist

wanted to spend as much time as he could with Jen and with us. His heart was no longer in the business and he had lost faith in the magazine industry. Even though he had introduced digital and research divisions into the thinking, this felt like a large tanker that was slow to turn.

Naturally we had approached Discovery medical aid a few times to help fund Jen's current medication, but back in 2012 pulmonary hypertension was one of the many rare diseases not yet recognised by medical insurances. It was an "orphan" disease. We didn't know where we would find the money, but we started the paperwork anyway, and the search for a pharmaceutical company to help with shipment and customs.

Sometimes the world has a serendipitous way of working. A few things happened to help turn the tide. At a wine tasting we were attending with friends, we unexpectedly met a couple who were dear friends of someone who worked at Discovery head office with the ex-gratia committee. We explained our difficulties with accessing treatment for Jen and they insisted on making introductions to Raffaella Ruttell, who was about to become a beacon of light and hope in our future. It was thanks to the relationship we developed over the years that we were able to get pulmonary hypertension onto the radar screen for other patients.

A few days later Stu was in Johannesburg on business. His colleagues were about to go out for drinks but he wasn't feeling up to it. "I think you should join them, my love," I told him when he called. "It might help to have company." Jen's illness was taking its toll. As I got ready for bed later that evening, Stu phoned. He sounded excited. "You won't believe what happened," he said. "I ended up having an honest heart-to-heart with someone I'd never met. You won't believe it ... he works for Equity Pharmaceuticals. Gabs, they are going to help us bring Bosentan into South Africa. They are perfectly placed to help." The pieces were falling together.

We filled in the Section 21A paperwork and found a source in Switzerland for the medication. Equity helped us with the correct procedures and legal paperwork required for customs, and Stu and I made a plan to increase our access bond to fund the first six months. We were close. Just the actual MCC approval was outstanding. That was the part I thought would be a slam dunk; this was a registered FDA-approved medication elsewhere in the world. But getting the phone answered, a fax responded to or an email replied to took some doing. We attempted to reach the MCC just about every day for many, many weeks. Eventually they responded and Jen's first six-months supply was approved.

It was time to push "go", but nothing was simple. Prof. Wilcox was away at a medical conference and there was a big potential complication. If there was a possibility that Jenna had pulmonary veno-occlusive disease (PVOD) rather than idiopathic pulmonary hypertension, then Bosentan was not the right drug for her and could in fact be damaging. We tracked down a cardiologist, with experience in PH, in the northern suburbs of Cape Town who agreed to give us an opinion in Prof.'s absence.

Chronic thromboembolic disease (CTEPH) and pulmonary veno-occlusive disease (PVOD) are both scary and complex sub-groups of pulmonary hypertension. "CTEPH is caused by the blood clots in the lungs that create scarring that blocks the arteries in the lungs. Certain conditions, like cancer, blood diseases, or inflammatory diseases, are linked to a higher risk of CTEPH. Other risk factors for CTEPH include: unprovoked large pulmonary embolisms, or Pes."[3]

Pulmonary veno-occlusive disease looked even worse: "(PVOD) is a rare form of pulmonary hypertension caused by progressive blockage of the small veins in the lungs ... The disease is progressive and fatal, with median survival of about 2 years from the time of diagnosis to death."[4]

---

3 https://my.clevelandclinic.org/health/diseases/17635-chronic-thromboembolic-pulmonary-hypertension-cteph

4 https://www.google.com/search?client=safari&rls=en&q=what+is+pulmonary+veno+occlusive+disease&ie=UTF-8&oe=UTF-8"

Jenna's journal
Tuesday, 5th June 2012
Home 10:20 am

Today we are meant to get a firm diagnosis. If it's pulmonary veno-occlusive disease, then we will fly up to Johannesburg next week to get listed for transplant. So, if it is, things will need to start moving very quickly.

I still haven't told anyone. I am so scared. It can't be veno-occlusive! But anyway, no matter what the diagnosis, I'm going to have to start telling people. I've sat down with the family and we have made a list of who to tell first. There's some relief because Kristi knows now that I won't recover, I'll deteriorate, and she knows I will live a shorter life ... she doesn't know how much, though ... and we haven't told her about the possibility of pulmonary veno-occlusive in the hopes that we won't need to.

Anyway, I'm trying not to think about it too much.

Stuart, myself and Jen drove out to the northern suburbs. Sick people streamed in and out of the waiting room. Most of them older, a lot older. One went outside in between tests to smoke. It really upset Jenna. Here she was, young, had eaten healthily her whole life, didn't drink and certainly didn't smoke, with a potentially fatal lung disease while elderly patients who smoked were taking life for granted. It didn't make any sense. The doctor was extremely thorough. He showed us Jen's enlarged right heart chamber on the screen. I was alert to any small sign, change in his voice or body language. It became clear to me that he believed there could be a chance this was PVOD. He had extensive knowledge and offered to share Jenna's scans, X-rays and reports with his international colleagues and specialists around the globe. We would get feedback ASAP.

We left his rooms quiet and depressed. The three of us were shell-shocked. From the back seat came a single comment from Jen. "So this would probably be a good time for me to turn to religion, but I'm just not feeling it." She never had the benefit of believing in heaven and angels. Jen believed firmly that nothing is actually known, or can be definitively known, about the existence or nature of God. She erred on the path of science rather than faith.

CHAPTER 16

Sharing the news, reaching out

Being alone in Jenna's diagnosis was becoming unbearable. Other than immediate family, it was still common understanding that she had pulmonary embolisms and an excellent chance of getting better. We decided as a family that it was time to reach out to our friends and share what was really going on.

Jenna decided to speak to her close friends before we spoke to ours. That may sound weird, but it made perfect sense. This was her illness and her body. It is easy to feel you have no control when you are ill. Taking ownership of her illness gave Jenna a sense of agency. It was empowering. We arranged appointments to visit Camilla, Julia, Lisa, Celeste, Nikita, Alex, Jo, Giulz, Daffy, Max and other of her closest friends. It was surreal. They were impossible conversations to have but we became adept at delivering Jenna's awful news with hope, determination and love.

Then it was our turn. For Kristi, Stuart and me to talk to our loved ones. It was confronting and painful on many levels, and yet the sharing also brought some relief. It doesn't help to carry pain alone; isolation is not the answer. But reaching out is also hard and leaves you vulnerable. People deal with difficult news in many ways. Telling the truth opened us up to a full array of responses and often left me feeling like we were holding the emotions and fear of others. "Are you sure?" "But she looks so well." "I just *know* she will be okay." "You just need to be positive." These were the most common responses. Then there was anger and disbelief: "It's so unfair." "What did you do in a previous life?" "You are only given what you can deal with." And: "It's all part of God's plan." In sharing the truth, we opened ourselves up, but overall it was compassion and care that came flooding in. "How can we help?" "What can we do?" "What do you need?" "What can I do to make this easier?" "I am here for you."

Two weeks later we received news that it might *not* be veno-occlusive disease. Two of the international experts said "no" and one said "maybe". We would take whatever small reprieve we could get. We decided to push the green light on ordering the Bosentan. This was the beginning of a long road of fighting for the treatments readily available for PH patients elsewhere in the world.

With the additon of Bosentan, Jen's medical regime now consisted of a maximum dose of vaso-dilators, blood thinners, loads of sleep, no exercise, a consistent diet, additional shakes to keep her weight steady, and regular blood tests.

Jenna's academic track record was impeccable, but she was now managing less than half a day at school before needing to go home to sleep and then work on her own. I decided it was time to call a meeting with the principal and vice-principal of Jenna's school and her teachers. I needed to keep them informed. Jen was much loved by her teachers and they were gutted to hear the extent of her illness, but they were hopeful, as we all were, that the right treatments would enable improved quality of life. They made sure I knew they would do anything to help.

We had ordered a mobility scooter for Jen, which was on its way, and this, I explained, would make it easier for her to get around to her classes. So the principal and I walked around the school campus together plotting where to place wooden ramps so that the main areas wouldn't be inaccessible to her. They built the ramps within a couple of weeks. They were incredibly supportive and compassionate.

PH is a complex disease and so misinformation is easy, confusing and destructive. But now that there was support on the ground and the broader community had a better basic understanding of her illness, it was easier for Jenna. Adjusting to being less and less physically able was emotionally difficult but she had much more empathy and support.

Kristi's experience at this time was different. She wanted to spend every spare minute with her sister … she'd help carry her things, meet her between classes in the passage and sit with her at break. She was constantly on the lookout for what Jenna might need. She no longer sat with her grade and so, while everyone else was forming the usual groups and alliances, she was absent and separated from her peers. Her own school buddies were oblivious of the impact that Jen's illness was having on Kristi and so they couldn't necessarily have been blamed for reading her choices as rejection. I think they believed she was being "cool" by spending so much time with the older girls. Apart from one close girlfriend, Kristi was pretty much joined-at-the-hip with Jenna and her friends, which had both its upsides and its downsides.

By June 2012 the exams were over. Still pretty shell-shocked, we planned some precious time away with Granny and Grampa at Eastford Country Estate in Knysna, where we'd spent many happy family times together over the years. The girls really loved Eastford and it would be good to get away. Or so I thought. The reality was that once we were away from our busy lives and the myriad medical appointments, the uninterrupted downtime meant there was now plenty of time to reflect on the severity of Jen's diagnosis. She grew sad and quiet, and it was heartbreaking to watch. No exams, no projects, no distractions and no reasons to pretend … just the silence of the forest and her difficult thoughts and conflicting feelings.

After a few days we made our way further up the coast to spend time with Stuart's cousins and extended family in the Eastern Cape. We explored the farmlands, caught up and sang songs around the fire together. Then we were off to the Addo game reserve and a few glorious days at Gorah Elephant Camp, gifted to us by Ian and Jillie. It was an extraordinary and healing time for the four of us, experiencing the bush together. Magnificent, great big herds of elephant are quite something to experience up close. On one particularly close encounter we were literally surrounded by a herd. Two "teenage" ellies were babysitting a youngster and needed to guide it past our vehicle. The matriarch of the herd, a massive creature, emerged from the bush and stood at the front left wheel of our vehicle to ensure the babies and their "sitters" safe passage. They were so close we could have reached out and touched them. Everyone sat dead still. As I stared up at this massive gentle creature in wonder, she looked me straight in the eye and a huge rumble emanated from her belly – a message of solidarity and knowing from one mother to another. I wept silently.

While on our trip Jen and Max had started messaging each other constantly. Their romantic interest in each other was growing and Kristi was unimpressed. Because she and Jen were both interested in Max and had spent a lot of time with him, she believed Max should be out of bounds. I didn't know how to handle it. All things being equal I may have agreed with her, but with Jen's prognosis looking as it did, I was unashamedly delighted at all opportunities for happiness, so I didn't discourage it. By the time we got back to Cape Town, Max and Jenna's relationship had taken on a life of its own.

It was mid-June. In Boston, Natalie went into further surgery to remove the tumours that had re-seeded. But the surgery was not successful and left her severely compromised. It was touch and go for a while. Shirley knew that Natalie was not getting better and the focus became about getting Natalie home to South Africa and her family. It took two agonising months of rehabilitation for her to learn to walk again and stable enough to make the trip home.

CHAPTER 17

Chase

Just before our trip away Stuart had made a project of researching, sourcing and ordering a "cool" three-wheeled mobility scooter that would be light enough for me to lift and pack into the boot of our car. We worked out it would need a rechargeable battery, good speed and distance capacity and to not look like an old lady's shopping cart. We finally found the right one and placed an order. It was being shipped from the States and would arrive any day. Jen's godmother, Sandy, and her partner Bruce very kindly offered to fund it.

We headed home and threw ourselves back into work. Stuart was snowed under with preparations for board meetings and I was behind on client work. It was the start of the third term for the girls and within a few days Jen was voted director of her school house play at the Grade 11 cultural dinner. She was excited and determined to take the project on, despite my obvious concerns about extra workload. She said it was an honour and she intended to write the script and direct the play. Her new drug, Bosentan, was just starting to have an effect. She had far fewer chest pains and was visibly less breathless than the previous months. Motivated by the improvements, we agreed to let her take it on.

The arrival of Chase, which was what Jen christened her mobility scooter, was significant on two levels. Chase brought her a new-found freedom and much-needed mobility, but it was also the first time her illness became visible. At first Jen was a truly terrible driver and Kristi, a natural behind any wheel, was desperate to take Chase for spins around the block at high speed. But the novelty soon wore off. For Kristi it was a choice. It was fun. For Jen there was no choice. She no longer went anywhere without Chase and soon started mastering tight turns and difficult steering. I became adept at folding and unfolding Chase into the back of my car and my arms quickly grew strong.

Midday, a few weeks after Chase arrived, I was waiting in the school carpark as Jen came tearing around the corner, hair flying out behind her in the wind, school books on her lap, pale-lipped but smiling. The full realisation hit me in that moment. Jenna could no longer walk. She was what society would label "disabled". It was an excruciating and singular moment. She screeched playfully to a halt just millimetres in front of me.

"Hey, Mom," she said. "What's up? You okay?" I whipped up a smile.

"All good, my love," I said cheerfully. "I'm just distracted. Let's get you home to bed to rest, you look pale."

Stuart's dad, Peter, known to the grandchildren as "Pop", had been steadily getting worse and in between everything that was going on, Stu was driving out to Somerset West to visit him. Ali, too, was a huge support system for her dad. We were hoping and praying that Shirley and Natalie would get back in time to see him.

Jenna and Max started dating officially at the end of July. Kristi and Jen started spending less time together. Aged 17 and 14, it was natural for there to be some separation between the girls by now, but any normal competitiveness or sibling rivalry went "shamefully" underground. Unspoken and difficult dynamics muddied the waters. What do you do with envy when your sibling has a terminal illness? What do you do with envy when your sibling has a right to health? They loved each other deeply and were navigating some difficult subconscious stuff. Kristi started spending more time with her best friend. They went off to socials together every weekend and spent hours getting ready in her room, loud music thumping, the inevitable pile of discarded outfits left in their wake. It seemed appropriate. We were delighted she had found a "partner in crime", so we encouraged the friendship.

Jen and Max were spending more time together. It was a normal teenage romance and a blessing to see Jen's spirits lifted and a twinkle in her eye. Max visited every other day. She helped him with his English and Afrikaans essays; he helped her with maths. They chatted, they laughed, they made out, they watched movies and sometimes she even had enough energy to go out with him and his mates for short periods. When she did, they left Chase at home and Max would carry her. It was a poignant and emotive sight, this tall gorgeous young man carrying his love.

Life seemed normal for a brief while. Then, at the end of July, Peter Lowe passed away. It was the end of a generation for Stuart, Shirley and Alison, both their parents now gone.

In the midst of their sadness and grief, neither of us had given any thought to the fact that Stuart's 50th birthday was just a few days away. But Ian and Jillie, and other of Stuart's friends, wanted, more than ever, to honour Stu and so they rallied together and organised a surprise celebration. Some of our most special people were there. Overwhelmed with emotion, Stu gave an incredibly moving impromptu speech. Jen and Kristi, who had been in on the surprise all along, were beaming. Jenna's tribute to her dad broke my heart. I have yet to find the strength to listen to it again. And when Kristi sang to him there was not a dry eye in the place. Stuart had been carrying us through the most heinous of times with integrity, strength and humour and there wasn't a person in the room who didn't know it.

Three days later we attended Peter's funeral, one short week before Shirl and Natalie managed to get home to South Africa. Pete's funeral was tough and emotionally loaded. There were so many layers of pain to hold and bear all around us. Somehow Stu managed in his usual fashion to have the oldies laughing and remembering his dad the way he would have wanted to be remembered.

But there was more. Stu was fast becoming progressively

unhappier at work. Differences in opinion about the future of the business had become a major issue between him and the board and he wanted out, but we just didn't know how we could afford to do that. Especially considering our escalating medical costs. We talked late into the night about the challenges we were facing and clung to each other for support. A few things were becoming crystal clear: 1) Stu needed more hours in the week to spend with us and Jen. He had no interest in wasting precious time on corporate politics. 2) Logistically, financially and emotionally we knew we had to stay on top of Jen's medical needs and the children's needs, no matter what it took. 3) Stu longed for a career he believed in, that he had equity in, and that was sustainable. A business that could offer financial stability, but potential for growth, and flexibility. 4) We required medical funds and it was becoming clear that down the line this need would only increase. It was time for some strategic thinking and a creative plan. 5) I could no longer work full time. My life had changed dramatically.

Stu and I knew how to be a team. It is one of our strengths as a couple. It was time to employ our skills and do what we do best. We have decades of media and marketing experience between us, and meaningful relationships with influential people in the media industry. Now that Jenna's difficult medical journey was public knowledge, we had started talking about the challenges we, and other PH patients in SA, were facing. It didn't take long before journalists and writers started showing an interest in Jenna's story. What was PH? How was she coping? How were we coping? How many other patients in South Africa were undiagnosed? It was a compelling story and Jen's intellect, wit and command of the English language made her a dream to interview. She had a growing public profile, and, with each new feature or article, more PH patients came out of the woodwork and sought us out for guidance and support. This extremely rare disease appeared to have more cases in the country than we thought, and Jenna's story was starting to bring them all together. To give this awful disease a voice.

CHAPTER 18

Up for debate

Between writing the script for her house play, directing rehearsals, school work, her romance and adjusting to the side-effects of her increased medication regime, Jen appeared, somehow, to be coping. We were hopeful the new meds had a role to play in this. I kept a very watchful eye on her and stayed on top of my quantities of stock. I would need sufficient time for the MCC approval process when re-ordering. I had settled into some sort of everyday life routine that consisted of juggling blood tests, check-ups, meds, lifts to and from school, Kristi's extramurals, medical research, nursing Jen, managing my business ... all the while dealing with the internal fear that we may lose our child.

By the end of August, it was time for the inter-house school plays. The excitement was palpable and the competition fierce. Performances took place two nights in a row to full houses in the school theatre. Jen was both exhausted and exhilarated. It had been physically taxing, even though she had shared the additional hours with her team. Only we could quite understand the monumental effort it had taken for her to pull this off. The standard was exceptional, the level of creativity and talent quite astounding. What bright young women they were. On the second night the judging panel gave their detailed critique and announced the winner. It was close, but Jen's play won! I will never forget how she came flying down the ramp on Chase from the back of the theatre with a large bunch of yellow helium balloons floating out behind her. She wheelied onto the ramp and up onto the stage and came skidding to a halt in the centre with a huge grin on her face to receive their award. There was a standing ovation. Stuart and I fought back the tears.

The next day we discovered that Natalie was coming home! The hospital was sponsoring a medical escort for her back to South Africa. It was a long journey with two paramedics at her side. She went straight into hospital for one night to be monitored before they made their way home to their little cottage in Hout Bay to be reunited with Kola. Oh joy! But it was a shock to see how fragile and severely compromised she was. Shirley had known since the first time she saw the final PET scan, but only now did it dawn on me that Natalie was not going to live long. Shirley put an experienced palliative care team together. Her mission was to nurse Natalie at home and make whatever time she had left on this earth comfortable and pain free. We didn't know how long that would be, maybe even years, but one thing was for sure – Natalie would be surrounded by her loved ones in the comfort of her home with her beloved brother by her side. We were going to make each moment count. We were going to track down some joy.

Three weeks later Jen was voted by the scholars for a prefect interview – she was thrilled. I hadn't realised how much it meant to her to have this leadership opportunity. She was also invited to travel to Durban with the Bishops Debating team for the 2012 Debating and Public Speaking National Championships. With all these opportunities presenting themselves to her it would be easy to think she was a normal, healthy teenager.

I worried constantly about her taking on too much, balanced by the desire for her to live her best life possible. Throughout her high school career Stuart had encouraged and supported Jenna's love of debating, as well as her interest in philosophy. He believed that debating would develop her critical thinking skills and increase her confidence, poise and self-esteem. Jen was good at it; she was the team's "secret weapon". Why secret? Because her gentle feminine manner belied the sharpness of her mind and could unexpectedly topple unsuspecting competing teams.

Whether I would let her go to Durban was the question ... That in itself was a debate. I knew Jen was immensely sensible, but I also knew that she ran the risk of pushing herself too much. How to draw the line? I wasn't keen but she was elated and enlivened by the idea and turned her debating skills on me. There was no chance of her not going. The Bishops teacher, Mr Holtman, who was taking the team, met with us to get to grips with the challenges and logistics he would be taking on. Not only was he wholeheartedly up for the task, he told us he thought it would be good for the boys to have to care for someone other than themselves. He, Jenna and Stuart convinced me to let it happen.

On Friday, the 27th of September the team boarded the plane for the two-hour flight to Durban. My heart was in my mouth, but I waved Jen goodbye and resisted the urge to shout "Wait! I've changed my mind!" While Jenna was in the air, Kristi messaged me to say the prefect shortlist had just been announced in assembly and Jen was on it. She couldn't wait to tell her sister.

They arrived safely in Durban and went straight to the competition venue. Friday was a full day of competing and prepping. Jenna was tired, but it went well, and she had managed to stay the distance. Then the team checked into their guest house, had a quick pizza and decided on an early night. Jen's room was separate from everyone else's so that she didn't have any stairs to contend with. She and I talked on the phone just before bed. I was relieved she was coping and reminded her to set an alarm for the next morning. I wouldn't be there to help her with physical tasks and she would need extra time so as not to become too breathless and dizzy.

Early on Saturday morning my phone rang. It was Jen. She sounded very shaken, breathless and panicked.

"Jen? Jen? Talk to me! What's going on?"

"Mom, I've been burgled. Someone broke into my room while I was sleeping. I've been robbed." Oh. My. God. Someone had been in her room while she was asleep. Anything could have happened.

"Are you all right? Jen! Are you all right?"

She assured me she was and then handed the phone to Mr Holtman. He was with her and the police were on their way but, yes, someone had broken into her room during the night and stolen Jen's Kindle, iPod, money and cellphone. They had rifled through all her personal stuff, including her meds and purse, and taken everything they could find.

All I could think was thank heavens she hadn't woken. The panic and shock would have been dangerous for her. And thank heavens they had left her meds – and Chase. Everything else was gone. What Jen was saddest about was the loss of her cellphone. It was full of treasured memories and heartfelt messages of support from friends that she had stored and which she read when she was feeling down. "If they could just have left me my memory card, Mom," she said.

The mere thought that Jen had been in danger was overwhelming. Stuart and I were so upset. First I demanded she get put on a plane and come straight home; then I offered to fly to Durban ... but Jenna was having none of it. She wouldn't even entertain the idea. She wasn't going to let the team down. It was done now, and she was fine, she told me. Upset and shaken, but fine. Eventually we agreed she could complete the competition but only if the guest house stationed a security guard right outside her bedroom door. They agreed readily, partly due to mortification that this had happened to Jen and partly because Max's enraged mother had got hold of them too!

The team was late for the start of the competition due to the burglary, but the judges moved their allotted time slots by an hour or so to give Jen time to calm down. She had lost all her prepared speech notes, all her team debating notes, her interpretive reading, and hours of prep work that was on her Kindle. She went ahead with the competition anyway. Her memory would have to suffice.

In fact, Jenna's memory more than sufficed. On Saturday she made it to the finals for the Persuasive Speech section of the championships – a tough and coveted part of the competition. Unlike Debating, the Persuasive Speech section consists of a

12-minute prepared speech, which is delivered to an external panel of judges and a full audience. Each entrant chooses and prepares their subject well in advance.

Sunday was the final day. Jen had prepared and chosen the topic "Marginalisation of the physically disabled in society". She deliberately discarded Chase before entering the room so that the judges would not know she had any impairment at all. She walked slowly down the centre aisle toward the stage and found her place in front of the podium. We have been told by many that it was mesmerising and astounding. She was word-perfect, graceful and utterly persuasive. The judges assumed her breathlessness was anxiety related until the end of the speech. This is the speech she prepared and delivered that day:

Jenna's prepared speech
Debating Nationals 2012

Everyone is born into a certain situation. People are born into poor families, rich families. All manner of colours, shapes and sizes. But no matter which situation they find themselves in, we value people. We value their human contribution. There is only one group in society to which this doesn't apply ... in any form. And it's one of the most neglected issues today – the marginalisation of the physically disabled. They are constantly excluded from mainstream participation in the community.

If I told you that disabled individuals globally fall into the lowest possible economic bracket, you probably wouldn't be surprised.

Herein lies a major problem; we assume that because they are physically impaired, disabled people are incapable first of all of supporting themselves, and secondly of contributing to society. In the USA, a major Western power, 75% of disabled people are unable to find employment. They are seen as charity cases. In reality, however, these individuals are not the victims of their own inadequacy but rather of constant and systematic exclusion from society.

In South Africa, when we think of discrimination, we think immediately of race, or perhaps gender. Disability is just not something which we associate with injustice. We think of things that are wrong with people's bodies, not things which are wrong with society. But actually, to become disabled is to experience a crash course in the realities of social inequality.

The default way of thinking places all the blame on the disabled individual. It's a Medical Model way of thinking, and it's how you would have been conditioned to view disabled people – they are physically less, and just not able – I mean, it's in the very word! We're all terribly sorry about it, but that's just how it is.

This is an incredibly ignorant way of approaching the issue – but it is a view which has been around for centuries. In the Middle Ages, having a child with a congenital disease was seen as punishment from God. In some traditional African societies, a sick child could only mean the ancestors' displeasure.

The perception of physically handicapped individuals as objects of pity, and not subjects in their own right, was first challenged in the '70s, when the world was presented with "The Social Model of Disability". This is a new frame of reference, based on two terms, which completely redefine the entire issue of disability in society.

The first new definition is impairment; defined as a structural or functional difference of the body. If you were to ask a quadriplegic what her impairment is, you would probably receive a factual, medical answer. "My third cervical vertebra is damaged."

The much more interesting change lies in how disability is defined. "The loss or limitation of opportunities that prevents people that have impairments from taking part in the normal life of the community on an equal level with others due to physical and social barriers."

Think about it: society – its physicality, architecture, procedures – is designed for able-bodied people. Disabled people are denied access to their most basic human rights. Rights such as transportation, education, healthcare, and housing. Some hospitals don't have wheelchair ramps. It's ridiculous! It's simply unacceptable.

Physically handicapped individuals' experiences of the way society runs leaves them with the overwhelming message: "I don't belong here." It's not a very big leap from "I don't have a place here" to "I don't *deserve* a place here." In the most basic principle of oppression, this minority group is being taught, as they have been throughout history, that they do not deserve basic citizenship rights. They have been brainwashed into agreeing with their own disadvantage, because we all agree with it.

The underlying issue is psychological. Disability is an evocative/emotive thing for people, an uncomfortable thing. We look at, for example, a quadriplegic, and our immediate thought is: "What if that were me?" Disability reminds us of our mortality, and of the frailty of our own bodies. Each of us understands how easily we could end up in that situation, and it's not a pleasant reminder.

On a psycho-analytical level, this falls in with what Freud called "The Uncanny" – in other words, things that make us uncomfortable, not because they are alien, but because they are too close. It's the same reason we don't like having cemeteries in the centre of a city – it's depressing! It reminds us that we're all going to die!

We have the same reaction to disability. We want two things – control and distance. We as humans have been trying desperately to fool ourselves into thinking we have control over everything, including our bodies – I can fix my hair, change my face, my breasts, even attempt to stop the ageing process. It seems we can fix anything. The disabled person is evidence that this is an illusion ... It shatters our collective denial, and that's just unpleasant.

Between 8 and 14% of the world's population are disabled at any one time – not so small a minority. But in reality, the overwhelming majority of human beings will experience disability for a substantial part of their lives – it's called old age. We don't call frail old people disabled, though they are. We call them elderly. It's a form of mass denial – of the fact that most of us will eventually be completely incapacitated.

So, although it's clearly in our best interests to allow for disabled participation in society, there is a resistance, on the part of institutions, business, government and on an individual level, to really, candidly begin any kind of conversation about improving the conditions of disabled people.

Ladies and gentlemen, these are conditions that need improvement. In true South African style, we have absolutely fabulous legislation on this issue ... which is completely and utterly ignored by every single body of society.

South Africa has ratified the UN Convention on the Rights of Persons with Disabilities, so technically our government is legally bound to honour and enforce the stipulated rights. We even have a Ministry for Women, Children and People with Disabilities, and an Integrated National Disability Strategy. According to all this documentation, disabled people cannot be disadvantaged in any way – in employment, education or access to public facilities.

But Andrew, my paraplegic friend, still cannot go to the beach, to a club, a restaurant or even a friend's house. He cannot use public transport. He could not attend his cousin's eighth birthday because his wheelchair can't fit under the tables at a restaurant.

Changing all that sounds expensive. Actually, it's not. Commonly accepted in Europe and the US, there is a style of architecture called "universal design". There has been extensive research on the expense of this style – it costs not a single cent more, and caters for, among others, the sight-impaired and the wheelchair-bound. Buildings compliant with universal design have small, unobtrusive modifications

– such as a slightly ridged tile on the bathroom wall which allows paraplegic individuals to lift themselves to use the bathroom facilities, or an attractive pattern on the taps, which reads "hot" or "cold" in Braille. These modifications do not affect able-bodied people, but for someone with a physical handicap, they could make an incredible difference.

It's all about shifting our paradigms. I ask that you be aware of the way you view those who suffer from physical impairments, and to demand that South African institutions honour the law in allowing for disabled individuals to participate equally in our community. I ask you to make a noise, to raise a fuss; to challenge people and to hold them accountable.

But most importantly, never assume ... For example, you assume that competitors in Public Speaking Nationals would be non-disabled.

You think that I sound out of breath because I am anxious in front of an audience.

I'm not.

My disability, or rather, my impairment, is a lung condition. Never assume that the impaired are incapable.

Jenna won.

In the worst of circumstances, she became the Junior National Persuasive Speech Champion of South Africa. The team flew home that evening filled with celebration and joy. I was very proud of her but there was little chance I would be allowing her out of my sight again.

A few days later it was announced that Jenna would be deputy head girl for 2013. Lethu was head girl. It looked like those two just might run the country after all!

CHAPTER 19

True colours

The school was thrilled that Jenna was deputy head girl but, believe it or not, one or two of the parents were horrified. Sadly, their comments filtered down to me. It was deeply upsetting. How could a disabled child be given such enormous responsibility, they asked. Would she be up to the task? Surely their (healthy) child was better equipped? It was painful to hear such a closed-minded view of leadership. Such envy. No, Jenna couldn't hand out brochures or decorate a hall, but clearly she had purpose, strong values, integrity, self-discipline, grit and strategic vision. Lethu knew that, the girls and staff knew that, and we knew that. I was so glad the school had not fallen into the trap of marginalising her because of her disease. It would have devastated Jen, and us, not to mention undermining everything they stood for as a school.

Meanwhile, behind the scenes Stuart and I were grappling with serious issues. Stu's work environment was becoming more hostile, but we needed his income and we needed financial stability; it was a difficult and complex situation. The realities confronting us and the choices we needed to make had both fundamental and strategic implications.

Firstly, were Jenna's meds working? Could we see an improve-ment? We had started treatment so late into her illness, maybe it was too late? Was the regime she was on progressive and aggressive enough? Research talked about treatments that were way more expensive than what she was currently on. Funding, where we were now but also looking to the future, we knew was going to be an ongoing challenge. What did the future look like for Jen and how could we prepare for her needs?

By now Jenna was successfully spreading awareness of pulmonary hypertension through regular radio and television interviews. Although her prognosis was ever present, there was also hope that we could save her. Many international patients were responding well to their treatment programmes. There was the promise that therapies and medical interventions available elsewhere could *really* make a difference to her. That her breathing would improve. That her oxygen saturation levels would rise. That the fog of the debilitating fatigue she had to deal with on a daily basis would lift and that tolerance for normal everyday physical tasks would improve.

While I was constantly concerned about Jen, I was also concerned about Kristi. Jenna's condition was demanding the lion's share of my time and attention. How was this for Kristi? I tried hard to keep her needs top-of-mind too, but the boundaries were blurred. I found no handbook, no A–Z of how to deal with this.

One thing Stuart and I were totally sure of was the need to facilitate moments of joy. Friends came over on school nights, we ate chocolate and fudge (Jen adored fudge) whenever we felt like it, we swam in the rain and played card games when the girls should have been doing homework. We also allowed Kristi freedom that we would never have afforded Jen at her age. We tried to pack a lifetime into every day.

One of the things that helped the most with this was therapy. I was seeing my therapist again regularly and Jenna had developed and maintained a solid relationship with hers since the beginning of the year. I believed it was time for Kristi to do the same because she appeared to have gone silent about the things that mattered. Her adventurous spirit was taking a beating and I felt sure that psychotherapy would help her unbury the difficult conflicting feelings and learn the emotional language and coping skills to bear whatever was buffeting around deep inside her.

Jen's 18th birthday was coming up. We discussed and planned it right down to the last detail. Twenty-first birthdays are a big deal in our culture, normally acknowledged with a large gathering, speeches and tributes. They're seen as a rite of passage, celebrated as a gateway into adulthood and independence. Jenna's 18th was going to be treated like a 21st for obvious but unspoken reasons.

Strangely enough, for someone who couldn't dance, Jen chose a "salsa" theme in keeping with her love of all things red. We printed thick glossy invitations with a pic of Jen and Max on them, Max with a red rose between his teeth and Jen in a sexy red and black lace dress. For the kids, receiving a printed invitation was a total novelty. Word was out that this would be a special party. Ali, the queen of event planning, helped us with the creative planning and also introduced us to Paul, a capable and generous man who ran a large events business (and who has supported us unstintingly over the years). At nominal cost Paul supplied a stretch-tent, bar, sound and everything else required to make this a celebration to remember. Jen invited many of her close friends but she wouldn't allow me to invite Granny and Grampa. It was the strangest thing. They were so close and yet it became a symbolic battle for her.

"No one has their grandparents at their 18th birthday, Mom. If I wasn't sick, we wouldn't even think of inviting them. Grandparents go to 21sts, not 18ths. I don't want to be the only person who has her grandparents at her 18th. They will come to my 21st."

She wouldn't budge. I know her decision hurt my parents terribly. Grampa made that very clear. I felt torn but decided to protect Jenna. Intuitively, I understood that in some way, inviting them to her birthday felt like an admission to the world that she may not make it to her 21st. We decided as a solution that we would host a very special family dinner on the actual date of her 18th birthday, the 28th of October, to coincide with my brother Craig visiting from Sydney.

The party was a raging success, complete with heartfelt, funny speeches. Jenna's friends placed a bar stool in the centre of the dance floor and danced around her. At one stage she slipped away, no fuss, for a short sleep before joining the party again. I'm glad we went ahead with a special celebration. It was a happy night for her.

One of the first things I did when Jenna's diagnosis finally hit home was phone Craig in Australia. He immediately started planning a trip for late October. It was so good to have him with us and for me to be able to share, face to face with him, the pain and angst we were going through – and for Craig to witness first-hand exactly where we were at. There is nothing like a sibling for unconditional love, support and a shoulder to cry on. We talked for hours. Craig was determined to get involved somehow back in Australia. He was also a great support to Stu. They talked into the night about Stu's work and options for the future. The decision had finally been made that Stuart would leave the corporate publishing world in December and he was busy strategising ideas for our future – a scary but necessary change of tack.

It was also becoming clear that we needed to fundraise. We thought long and hard about how best to do this, knowing that whatever we did needed to a) help pay for Jen's medication and b) make a difference for other PH patients in South Africa. And so The Jenna Lowe Trust was born. We were determined to set it up professionally and transparently from the start, and so we gathered together a small group of executive advisors who would sit on our board. We wanted people with accounting, financial, administrative and strategic skills; and, because this was pro bono work only, they needed to be people with the integrity and intention to help and to make a difference. Together we agreed on the objectives, intention and mandate of The Jenna Lowe Trust before starting a legal entity. We now had an appropriate vehicle through which to raise funds and much-needed national awareness for pulmonary hypertension. The awareness Jen and her journey were generating meant that more and more patients, potential patients, doctors, experts and associations were finding their way to us. A community was being built around Jen and PH patients.

When it came to Jenna's medical progress, Prof. Wilcox was concerned. Her six-minute walk tests showed minimal improvement from the Bosentan. He advised us it was time to travel to Johannesburg to meet and consult with Dr Paul Williams at Milpark Hospital. At the time Milpark was one of the few institutions in South Africa with a lung transplant programme. Not only was Dr Williams one of South Africa's top pulmonologists, and more experienced than most in the treatment of PH, but he was also the critical care expert for lung transplants at Milpark.

Our visit took place in November, in between exams. The altitude in Johannesburg was punishing for Jen, but she warmed to Dr Williams and his team. He, in turn, was very taken with Jen. They had a good rapport from day one. I didn't know it at the time, but he had a daughter exactly Jenna's age. We needed to establish a relationship with him and get Jen on his radar, but the visit was also a harsh reminder of the possible need for a lung transplant in future. It was becoming clearer that, long term, this would be the only potential solution available to Jenna.

Back at school Jen started preparing for her duties as deputy head girl. She attended the prefects' leadership camp, which took place in Simon's Town, a little naval-base harbour town on the outskirts of Cape Town. She came home from the camp tired, but elated and inspired by the intense group work and meaningful leadership discussions they'd had. This was an astonishing bunch of girls, diverse, bright, open-minded and committed. They were full of integrity and fresh-faced belief in their futures.

All the while Jen and Max were still behaving like the quintessential teenagers in love ... they appeared intoxicated with each other. It was time for the conversation that could no longer be avoided. Jen could not afford to fall pregnant, it would put her life at risk. She also couldn't take contraceptive pills because they would interact negatively with her medication. It was a conundrum, but one that needed to be addressed. "Mmm, we're not at that stage just yet," she said when I broached the subject, "but I suppose we're getting there. What do you think I should do, Mom?" I had to be sure that Jen was safe. I did my research and we discussed it with Prof. Wilcox. The reality was that pregnancy could be fatal for Jen; we would have to find a way to keep her safe. Rare disease doesn't just rob you of your health, but of so many things. In this instance it was Jen's privacy. She dealt with our discussions with the calm maturity of an adult, but it broke her heart, absolutely broke her heart, to discover that PH patients cannot fall pregnant, ever. Understanding that she could never carry her own children was a cruel realisation for Jen.

As 2012 was drawing to an end it was time to prep for exams. Grade 11 results are important as they are generally used to secure provisional entry into universities and colleges. But luckily exams were never a major stress in our house. Both my girls took them in their stride with little anxiety. I was the supplier of copious cups of tea, chocolate biscuits and an environment conducive to studying while they worked. Mostly I would encourage Jen to take breaks between her studies and Kristi to study between her breaks!

Prof. Wilcox was right to be concerned. Disappointingly, November's blood tests and the six-minute walk test showed the earlier improvement in Jen's O2 saturation levels had been short lived. The signs weren't good. It was time to get her onto supplemental oxygen. We researched, found and ordered a small portable oxygen concentrator that would be light enough for her to carry, but strong enough to supply up to at least three litres of O2 per minute. It needed two rechargeable batteries so that it could be functional 24 hours a day if needed. I also continued to add supplementary modalities to support Jen's medical regime such as optimum nutrition, homeopathy, massage, physio, reiki, meditation, gentle private yoga, supplements of many sorts, cell food, protein shakes and more. My aim was to keep her weight and strength up to give her body the best chance of the treatment working.

For myself yoga, walks and jogs around the neighbourhood with Mary and my friend Sue were a lifeline. We would go at first light before the household awoke. We talked, a lot, about everything going on in each other's lives and I discovered the power of walking in nature. The movement, being mobile, soothed my body, which was often sore and stiff from tension. The friendship healed my heart and nature soothed my soul, reminding me of the ever-changing cycles of life. In my heightened state I started to really notice things to be grateful for – like the way the light falls, the fragrance of a breeze, where the owls nest or the form of a tree.

Year-end prize-giving was the final event of the school year and the hall was full of blue uniforms and youthful faces. Kristi was on stage with the choir. It was also Jen's first formal school function as deputy head girl. She always managed to pull off looking so damn well when she needed to. Her shoulders were back and she had a wide smile on her face.

And Chase was kept very busy that day … whizzing up and down, to and from the stage …

In all Jenna collected nine academic prizes and her academic colours. It was a massive achievement for anyone, but considering the inordinate challenges she'd been dealt in 2012, it was nothing short of extraordinary.

Our family of equipment was growing. Chase now had a sibling in the shape of a small black portable oxygen concentrator complete with cannulas (two see-through tubes that feed the oxygen into your nostrils), batteries and a car charger. Jen named the new acquisition Oxy-Jen. It is an understatement to say it was becoming quite the mission to leave home!

Oxy-Jen arrived in mid-December, just in time for our annual Plett holiday. This year we would be meeting up there with Max and his family.

December heralded Stuart's last few working weeks. He was stressed, very stressed, and I couldn't wait for him to get out of there. I could also see just how difficult leaving actually was for him. Stuart really loved the people and the teams he worked with and they loved him. It was an emotional wrench and the end of a long and significant chapter in his life. On his last day at work, with our car all packed and ready, the girls and I collected him from the office just after lunch. He was waiting on the pavement for us, briefcase and laptop in hand, company car left parked in the parking lot. What a bittersweet moment. We headed straight up the N2 towards Plett and I held Stu's hand tightly as we drove away. I was so proud of this man, this rock of mine.

Despite the anticipation, it wasn't the happiest of summer

holidays that year. What we as a family had very slowly become acclimatised to over the past months of 2012, the depth and breadth of Jenna's illness, came as a shock to Max and his family. It's one thing to see someone once a day when they present their best selves, and altogether another to live with them and come face to face with the reality of illness. In that situation I came to realise just how confronting our "normal" was for other people. As a family we had learned to take our challenges and Jen's needs in our stride seamlessly without even realising we were doing it.

I had with me the names and numbers of all the local doctors, hospitals and clinics close at hand and, just as we did at home, we made weekly visits to the local Pathcare to do bloods to check Jen's INR and liver function. Jenna really battled with the heat and she slept long hours while everyone else was off fishing, boating, beaching and body-surfing. By then Chase was a fixture but Oxy-Jen was new. Jen was now wearing her illness on her face.

It was a heartbreaking time, experiencing how big the gap had grown between what she was able to do and what "normal" healthy kids could do. Sometimes she'd attempt the beach with us, but her breathing would become too laboured. It was all too apparent that she couldn't keep up. She would sit under the umbrella, battling but not wanting to leave.

Max treated Jen differently from the first day we arrived. It was excruciating to watch.

Kristi was in the prime of her life, with the health and dynamism of a normal young teen. She was in search of action, adventure and excitement. Stuart was battling the demons of having left a long corporate career and distracted by what on earth to do with his future. Jenna was realising just how drastic the impact of her illness was, not only on her but on those around her. Me? I found it so hard to witness Max's subtle rejection of my daughter, her pain, her ailing health and the slow breaking of her 18-year-old heart.

On the 22nd of December we went to spend five days in Greyton, where Ali, Les and Matt were staying. Shirley joined us for Christmas too, with Natalie and Kola, and Granny and Grampa drove up from Cape Town. It was wonderful to be with family.

Neither Jenna nor Natalie was doing well, though. Not only was Jen sad, but away from the coast the midsummer heat in Greyton was oppressive, which made her breathing and fatigue really bad.

The family bustled gently around the girls, cooking, chatting, swimming and relaxing. I have a poignant memory of Kola riding his bicycle with Kristi next to him on Riaan, the black stallion, heading off down a leafy green country lane together. That was how they found release while their respective siblings lay quietly together in consolidation with each other. Each one of them braving the unthinkable.

After Christmas we drove back to Plett to finish our holiday as planned. We managed to carve out some happy times, but it wasn't easy. I knew in my gut that something wasn't right. My heart bled for Jen. I could see Max had moved on.

Early in January we headed home to face 2013. It was a big year ahead, our minds were proccupied and our hearts were heavy.

Part 3

Jenna models for *Cosmopolitan SA* magazine

Top: Kristi (2) and Jenna (5) with dad Stuart
Bottom left: Jen with her godmother, Sandy
Bottom right: Jen (7) doing yoga on the beach

Top left: *The Magic Bissie Tree* by Jenna Lowe
Top right: Jenna the bookworm
Bottom left: Sweet 16 – Jen with surfer boy Nik in Plett

Top: The Lowe family with their faithful hounds, Sahara and Prince
Bottom left: Jenna Lowe, deputy head girl, 2013
Bottom right: Jen and Kristi – as close as two sisters can be

Top: Herschel Valedictory Day with Granny and Grampa
Bottom: Cousins Natalie and Jen – oxygen buddies

Top: Shooting the #GetMeTo21 campaign from Jen's bed
Bottom left: Jen on her way to the prefects' dance
Bottom right: Alex – friend and Jen's matric dance partner

Top left: Jen and Daffy
Top right: Kristi and the love of her life … Riaan!
Bottom: Jenna and Camilla

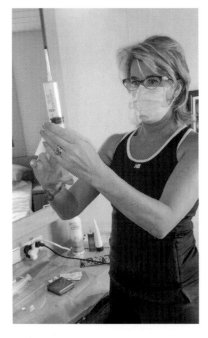

Top: Kristi sings 'I Need More Time' at Newlands rugby stadium before the Stormers match and (**bottom left**) Jen thanks the crowd for their support

Bottom right: Gabi mixing Flolan in her cabin on Reach For A Dream cruise

CHAPTER 20

Matric

This new year, 2013, was Jenna's final year of school. Matric – a time that even the most robust of kids find stressful. I was concerned it would be a taxing year for her. I knew it would be for Stu, who had returned to Cape Town to face the significant challenge of starting a new business. The pressure was on.

The first thing I arranged when we arrived back in Cape Town was a visit to Prof. Wilcox at UCT Academic Hospital. Jen's six-minute walk test revealed her lowest desaturation ever. On the upside, her liver function was good so we could push up her doses of medication. In keeping with a schedule that had become our new normal, we drove from that appointment straight to a dressmaker in Rondebosch.

There were two dances coming up – the prefects' dance and the all-important matric dance – and Jen needed to look fabulous. We had had enormous fun doing the fabric shopping. After much walking around the mall (Jen zooming along on Chase), Jen had settled on a deep red satin, after which we rewarded ourselves with a special lunch. There was much excitement in the build-up to the dances and it made me very happy to see her so animated. Now it was time to make the dress …

Max was still around, but on a more ad hoc basis after our rather strained holiday. Two weeks later, he popped in to visit. He seemed tense. He went down the passage to visit Jen. He left within half an hour. As Jen let him out the front door, she uncharacteristically tossed the keys down on the table in the entrance hall and turned abruptly to walk back to her room. Something was wrong. I hopped up to go check on her. Max had ended their relationship. Jen was devastated, but also filled with dignity. We spoke late into the night. She fully understood the depth and complexity that her illness brought to an otherwise ordinary teenage romance. She got it, but she was really hurting, feeling vulnerable and scared. She didn't want to die young without having experienced the joy of passionate romance in her life. Would her illness preclude her from having a relationship again, she asked me. Would anyone be able to deal with the different lens she had on the world at such a young age? I assured her they would, that any young man would be blessed to have her at his side.

In reality I knew it would take a strong and rather special young man to handle Jenna's reality, but I hid my concern.

Jen was fragile, pale and wistful in the days following her break-up. She had no appetite, was sleeping more than normal and had lost something of her fighting spirit. Her emotional vulnerability was tangible and showing physically. I needed to do something.

Jen's very best girlfriend – they had been friends since junior school – was Camilla. She had huge green eyes, a quick acerbic wit, and a canny ability for lateral thinking, qualities she and Jen shared and probably what drew them to each other (Cami also had a weird love of maths). They had a special friendship that had withstood the dynamics of changing friendship groups, jealousies and the complex challenges of Jen's illness. In addition, Cami was fiercely loyal and protective.

Whether it was pride or a sense that she should be able to cope on her own, I didn't know, but I knew Jen would not reach out on her own. Hoping she wouldn't be angry with me, I phoned Camilla. Just a short message. I shouldn't have second-guessed myself. Jenna's friends came flooding through in support of her in the most unexpected ways. They literally fetched her out of the darkness. As did Kristi. Kristi and Jen found their way back to each other quickly. I was so relieved they did.

It was time to order more meds. It was also time to get approval for home oxygen. Oxy-Jen was great for outings, but didn't provide enough oxygen flow for the long hours Jenna spent at home. What was needed now was a large home oxygen concentrator. A much bigger and stronger machine that plugged into the wall and was the size of a medium-sized suitcase, but heavier. When it arrived a few months into the year, Jen named it Thunder. Thunder made a huge noise, which initially I found intrusive. Soon it became soothing – it was a way to monitor Jen from the other side of the house and know she was okay. Thunder became comforting white sound.

I also ensured that our travel documents and passports were up to date. We might need to travel to collect medication. Maybe lung transplants elsewhere in the world had better results than ours? It was also time to apply for a disabled disc for our little blue Honda Jazz. Medical admin and logistics had become a time-consuming part of my new normal.

By early 2013 Jenna had been interviewed quite a few times by KFM, one of our biggest radio stations in the Western Cape. Every time we left an interviewer's studio, they had tears in their eyes … I think it was Jen's courage and humility that did them in the most. It was after one of these interviews that Matt Pearce phoned Stuart. He had heard Jen being interviewed by Ryan O'Connor. He had an idea … a great idea. Kristi must launch a song for Jenna. Matt set up a meeting with the KFM team. Jen described her illness and the battle we were having with medication, and how so many people in South Africa were most likely undiagnosed. This orphan illness needed awareness and education. The team were incredibly supportive and suggested the girls think about writing an original song – perhaps Jenna could write it and Kristi could sing it? If the song was professional enough, they promised to support it on KFM. Any proceeds from the song could go to The Jenna Lowe Trust.

It was such a great idea. We set off enthusiastically to make it happen. First we needed professionals to help produce and record the song. Serendipitously, I bumped into old friends Iain and Kim

Banner about a week later. I had known Iain since my childhood, and his wife – as Kim Kallie – was one of South Africa's most talented and experienced singers (and daughter of the famous Judy Page). Kim was excited about the project and willing to help us. She agreed to come and meet the girls and listen to Kristi sing. Maybe she could offer some training and help with the process of sourcing the right musicians to produce a song. Kim cautioned us that a song would not raise tonnes of money (music seldom does), but it would help raise vital awareness for the disease and provide a good media platform for The Jenna Lowe Trust. Also, and for me most importantly, it would give Kristi a voice and a significant role to play in our unfolding and difficult journey.

Jen's mood and health had taken a knock. She was doing what she could in terms of school and her deputy head girl duties, but she was still uncharacteristically down. It impacted everyone in the family. Stuart and I realised that, apart from individual therapy, which we were doing regularly, as a family unit we needed further emotional support. We faced uncertainty every day and each of us dealt with it differently. This was a marathon of epic proportions. We were not a religious family, so without the comfort that religious faith can often bring, we needed to find other ways to navigate our way through, to stay hopeful and hold our family together. This was when we sought out and found Sue Cooper to teach us the healing art of meditation. A skilled clinical psychologist and teacher of meditation, Sue had experienced a lot of pain and loss in her own life. She spent an hour alone with each of us before starting guided family meditation in our home (logistically this was much easier for Jen) every two or three weeks.

We developed a routine. Sue would arrive at about 7 pm and we would settle down in the lounge with our three dogs at our feet. First Sue would lead us in a guided meditation for 45–60 minutes, after which we would do a "listening meditation". Each of us would share how we were at the time, what was consuming us, what was scaring us, what was helping us. No one could interrupt, criticise or even comment. We simply listened without judgement. Active and empathetic listening is extraordinarily powerful. It was painful, at times even brutal, to hear how each member of the family was feeling and exactly what they were dealing with at the time, but it gave us a sacred window into each other's hearts and minds. We continued this practice as a family for two years. It helped us bear it and stay in touch with each other. Initially, it surprised me to discover just how different our perspectives were, but then I came to understand that of course they were. It was a powerful way to stay in touch with each other's needs and see our challenges through each other's eyes. It took enormous emotional maturity and commitment on everyone's part. It allowed each one of us a safe place in which to be honest and real. Sue was a gift.

CHAPTER 21

Love will find a way

Jen and Kristi had both plunged headlong into the new school year, Jen conscientiously trying to keep up with the demands. Stu and I were constantly concerned that Jen might be getting worse, not better, and we persisted with our research. Kristi was now enjoying weekly voice training with Kim, who had become a second mother figure to her. Progress was being made on ideas of how, and with whom, to produce the song.

Daffy was a regular visitor in our home. While we could all see there was a vibe between him and Jen, they'd been friends for so long that it was difficult to "cross the great divide" and put their friendship at risk. Jen's matric dance was almost upon us, and she was unsure about who to ask. Originally, she was taking Max, but now she had to make another plan. There was no shortage of male friends, but most of the girls had long since confirmed their dates for the dance. I was adamant that asking someone Jen didn't know well was out of the question. Chase, Oxy-Jen and all the other logistics made that too difficult. The most important consideration was that she was safe, with someone she knew well, and someone she could have fun with.

Alex was the perfect solution. A long-standing friend of Jen's, since Grade 8, Alex was tall, blond, with blue eyes and an angelic face. He was also loyal and kind, a devoted friend. I had long suspected that he had a bit of thing for her and he was delighted to be asked. With that settled, Stu took on the task of finding a car they could borrow for the "arrival moment" – of course it had to be red to match the red dress! It was all very exciting but it worried me how Jen was going to manage. Between the car, the bus and three changes of venue, it was logistically too difficult to take Chase. Plus, Oxy-Jen's battery wouldn't last for 12 straight hours, so we would need a second fully charged battery. The dance started with pre-drinks at 5 pm and it only finished at midnight; and then there was an after-party … I didn't think Jen would last that long, to be honest. How on earth was this going to work?

There was no way she could do a normal school day and then manage the dance, so I kept her home without formal permission and allowed her to sleep until lunchtime. Then, instead of rushing from pillar to post, my close friend Vanessa (who was director of Associated Media at the time) arranged to have a professional come to the house to do Jen's hair and make-up. She had just finished making Jen look like a supermodel when a deep, throaty sound heralded the arrival of the red Cobra in our driveway. Stuart had borrowed a beast of a car for their arrival. A few minutes later Alex arrived, looking gorgeous if a tad nervous in his dark suit, clutching a bunch of red roses. As I helped Jen slip into her red satin dress – the fabric rippled like water on her slight frame – she told me firmly that she wouldn't be wearing Oxy-Jen, not until much later. I chose to let it go and packed up Oxy-Jen and all her batteries in a separate bag for Alex to carry. Tonight, Jenna would spend a few hours equipment free. She looked radiant, like a normal, healthy teenage girl.

I fought back the tears as I watched her alight like a princess from that red car and walk slowly, with Alex proudly at her side, up the pathway to greet her headmaster. The crowd didn't understand the physical effort that it took to carry that off with such elegance. That night Alex was her prince. He carried her from place to place and looked after her so thoughtfully.

Apparently, she had a really bad spell at around midnight when she nearly passed out, but she refused to let him call me. She was going to that after-party come hell or high water. It was with much relief that I collected them from the bus at 3 am.

Jen slept solidly for two days. Her oxygen sats were low and she was battling with nausea, but she told me adamantly that she didn't regret staying out for one single second.

At the start of the second term Prof. Wilcox recommended another echo-cardiogram and further X-rays to compare to previous ones. Jen wasn't showing much improvement.

We were also confronted with the brutal reality that Natalie was not doing well; her tumours were growing again. The Lowe family was spending a lot of time together. We visited Natalie in Hout Bay many times a week, Jen on her oxygen and Natalie on hers. It was tough bearing witness to Shirley, Kola and Natalie's excruciating journey. It motivated me to keep searching for medical solutions for Jenna. Shirl encouraged and supported me, teaching me not to settle, not to accept what was right in front of us but to keep looking further afield. PH patients in South Africa may not have access to the latest medical therapies, but that didn't mean they weren't available elsewhere in the world.

We needed more stocks of Bosentan, but funds were tight. Stuart hadn't had a salary in four months, and I had fewer and fewer available hours for marketing consulting. We began to plan our first Jenna Lowe Trust fundraiser for the end of May. It was a big step for us, but a necessary one. We were reaching out for funding help, reaching out for medical help and reaching out for emotional support. Learning to ask for what we needed was very humbling for me.

My continual efforts and searching for new treatments we might try for Jenna were probably exhausting for Prof., but he was in agreement that if there was any chance that Jen had chronic thromboembolic disease (CTEPH) then we should be completely sure that she wasn't a candidate for a procedure called a thrombo-endarterectomy. This is a procedure whereby large central:sed clots are removed from the lungs and my understanding was that certain CTEPH patients benefited hugely from it. If it could work for Jen, then it was a ray of hope. I was determined to chase down every ray I identified, no matter how small the chances.

I spoke to everyone I knew who had any kind of global pulmonary medical connection, and everyone they knew, and everyone they knew. I was looking for the best expertise and the most experienced PH centres in the world that did this procedure. I followed my leads to an experienced physician at the National Pulmonary Hypertension Service at Hammersmith Hospital in England and contacted him. He suggested that Jen's imaging should be reviewed by a pulmonary endarterectomy surgeon in a high-volume PEA centre to agree with the diagnosis and advise whether there was any chance of a surgical intervention. His return email read: *"Although I entirely accept PEA surgery seems an unlikely option, it is always my practice to have every thromboembolic case reviewed for operability since there are no clear criteria by which I can judge this with certainty."* He gave me a suggested list of the best PEA surgeons in the world, all of whom worked at high-volume centres of excellence.

As the UK would be the closest and easiest to get to if need be, I wrote to the secretary of their top cardio-thoracic surgeon on the 19th of March, asking if the surgeon would be prepared to review Jenna's case, and examine her data and imaging (which I was sending directly to him) to see if she would be a candidate for this surgery. On the 2nd of April I received a response to acknowledge receipt of the letters and imaging and to say: *"... Our meeting will be held this Thursday afternoon 4 April and Jenna's case will be discussed."*

I wondered if they realised how much it meant to us to even get a response. How incredible to know there were specialists out there willing to help out of the goodness of their hearts. We held our breath and waited. Three days later came an email directly from the cardio-thoracic surgeon.

... we discussed your daughter's case at our meeting yesterday. My colleague Dr X has also been in contact with Dr Williams. We could not be certain, because of the imaging quality, but there is a chance she might benefit from pulmonary endarterectomy surgery. I will send a full report

next week. She needs an up-to-date CTPA with thin slices (1 mm), and ideally an MRI PA gram (our radiologists would be able to inform the local team re best protocol) for us to make a final decision on operability. If it is not possible to get these performed locally, then she could have them performed at Papworth, but that would involve a lot of travel and expense, and therefore it would be best to try locally in first instance so we can give an opinion remotely.

We have now performed nearly 1 000 pulmonary endarterectomy operations and we will provide the full experience of our team to make sure she has the best available advice.

I re-read his email many times and looked up all the medical terminology to ensure I understood it entirely. There was a chance, a small chance, that Jenna might benefit from surgical intervention! We had work to do. We had to get the right imaging and fast. I sent motivations to Discovery to ask them to cover the costs of the imaging required and then set about finding the best radiologists for the job in Cape Town. They would need to speak to the radiology specialists in the UK about best protocols for the MRI pulmonary angiogram (PA). I turned to our friend Mike, Max's dad, for help. Mike was involved in medical IT and he kindly guided us to finding the right people and getting their buy-in.

Jenna's journal
Tuesday, 23rd April
9:16 pm; home

Alex left for the UK tonight. I don't have the emotional reserves to delve into how I feel about that. After spending so much time together and him living with us for a while, it doesn't feel right without him here. He wrote me the most beautiful letter ever. Alex loved even my most unattractive self. When I am less exhausted, I will write how I feel about him leaving.

I feel emotionally exhausted. Natalie is so much worse lately and I haven't even written about that. I just don't have the will to even properly think about it. It's too painful.

I have so much school work that delving into my emotions just doesn't feel practical right now, but I don't think I can maintain composure for that long.

I think I'll try connecting with and leaning on my friends this week. I feel that will help me through. Maybe it's time to let Daffy in to more of the sad stuff I'm facing with Natalie. But also, to share with him that sometimes in order to make up for being sick I feel everything else about me needs to be perfect. He should know that sometimes, however, I feel insecure and unsure of my worth. I don't want to scare him off, but if that is gonna scare him off then it should happen sooner rather than later.

The unconditional acceptance and love I feel from my friendship with Alex has taught me that it is possible for someone to want and love me and not let me down because of my illness. Alex has consistently and constantly seen me at my worst (greasy bun, zero make-up and pink nose from crying), but when he looks at me, I can still see all the reasons why I'm loveable.

It's not like I need anyone to fix my problems, they just need to be OK with me being sad every now and then. I think that despite his easy-going personality, Daffy has pretty good emotional capacity and maturity. He has been a solid and trustworthy friend to me, and he is always honest with me. I love dating Daffy. I think I love Daffy but my friendship with Alex has upped my standards. I am used to that kind of unconditional love from my family and I am starting to realise it is possible from friends and boyfriends.

Perhaps after years of trying to be a perfect, fun, attractive friend and girlfriend I can relax and realise that my true friends will love me anyway, that I am enough. It's an epiphany I am having. Slowly. I still feel self-indulgent writing that "I'm enough" but my therapy and other intense conversations and experiences are showing me that it's OK to just be, and not to have to do things to prove my value to myself and others.

I should sleep now. Got lotsa work to do tomorrow. Juggling.

Jenna's journal
Friday, 26th April
9ish; School Sports Centre

I am waiting at the Sports Centre to have all my photos done, then I have an MRI. I'm not looking forward to it. I have to lie still for like two hours. I just want to make sure I'm warm and comfortable.

After weeks of medical logistics, on the 26th of April, Jen had an MRI pulmonary angiogram, the first of its kind at Constantiaberg Hospital. She lay totally still in the MRI chamber for just short of two hours so they could capture the quality of imaging they required. Technicians pored over their books and the protocols to get it right. Thankfully Mike helped us get the extremely high-res images onto a disk and sent back to Papworth. Then we waited. And while we waited we continued with "normal" life.

Stuart had had an excellent idea for our first fundraiser. *WINE* magazine had been one of the many titles his company published, and Stuart had a long-standing association with South Africa's most widely consulted wine authority and respected international wine writer, Michael Fridjhon. With over 40 years of experience, Michael would be a major drawcard for wine lovers. He kindly agreed not only to host a spectacular wine tasting master-class, but to supply the finest of South Africa's award-winning wines as well. A close friend, Sue, offered her spectacular venue, the Grand Café and Beach. When I eventually pushed "send" on our first piece of marketing to sell tickets, I put my head on my desk and wept. This was a public admission that we needed help. I found it very hard. And it marked a moment from which there was no going back.

Reaching out can be humbling in the extreme, but it is a virtuous circle. Giving and receiving lead us to compassion and empathy because we start to recognise our need for each other. That is how it works. Maybe it is easier to give than to receive because our ego gets in the way, but what I realised is that giving and receiving are in fact the same thing; there cannot be one without the other. We vowed as a family that our fundraisers would always be a worthwhile and meaningful experience for those attending. There would be total transparency regarding funds raised, and we would always advocate for others with pulmonary hypertension.

I read over my diaries now as I write this book and I am astounded by what we as a family did, or had to do, each day. Where did we find the energy it took, on an ongoing basis, to do what we did for so long? But now, I recognise that same limitless drive and determination in the faces of many families who are fighting rare disease. Daily fear for your child's life will galvanise and drive you in ways you didn't know were possible.

At the very same time, and far more conscious and heightened, was fear for Natalie's life. Her tumours were growing rapidly and there was nothing medical left to be done. She was being nursed at home by Shirley, and as a family we rallied together to help, support and spend as much time with Natalie as we could. Her stoicism and wicked sense of humour were astonishing. It was also devastating, painful and ironic to witness Jen and Natalie sitting together on the couch sharing their oxygen.

Between our visits to Natalie, planning our first fundraiser, facilitating Jen's school commitments and leadership duties, the weekly blood tests and medical check-ups, lifting Kristi to and from extramurals, running my consultancy, therapy appointments, medical research and holding our family together, there was also constant discussion in our home about "the song".

Kristi was loving her singing training, and nothing gave me more joy (or made me cry quite as much) as listening to her sing. Her voice has a hauntingly lyrical quality, especially when she sings emotive songs. Kristi, Kim and Jen had been chatting to some fabulous local musicians and, ultimately, we found our way to Ben Peters and Juliet

Harding from the talented local South African band GoodLuck. When they heard Jen's story, they kindly agreed to help us.

The major work took place in the GoodLuck studio on the weekend of the 4th and 5th of May ... significantly, it was also World PH Day. What an incredible experience for us all, and especially the girls, to work with these young professionals. We "camped" with our snacks and meds in their studio for the day – Stu, myself, Kristi, Jen and Kim. Jen had written way too many lyrics and had to edit, adjust and rewrite on the fly while Kristi, just 15 and totally inexperienced, behaved like a pro, unflustered and calm but open to the learning. She has a natural ear and was note-perfect, taking direction from Ben and Juliet with gratitude. She laid down the majority of her tracks and harmonies in one session. Then it was over to Ben to work on the production and complete the backing tracks. Soon we would be ready for KFM. Their song was called "I Need More Time".

We were dealing with so much and yet to the outside world we "wore it" with bravery. Even our closest circles didn't necessarily understand the harsh reality of our daily life.

For Jen and Kristi this phenomenon was exaggerated by the fact that what the world saw was the very best of Jen, the "presented" Jen, for short periods when she was in public. Jenna and Kristi's teachers and friends had shown so much support, but there was some petty politics that went on for the girls from those who weren't close to us and didn't understand. They felt Jen had too much leeway, or that it wasn't fair that she could "pick and choose" what she felt like doing. Why didn't the rules apply to her? These comments were never said near Jen, but were sometimes strategically said within earshot of Kristi and they stung. Kristi's response was to withdraw. She knew Jen would have been devastated by some of those comments. My girls understood the power of words all too well. Once something is said, you cannot take it back. Words have the power to heal and the power to destroy.

There were some days that were harder than others. On one such day Kristi was in tears at school. She went to find Jenna sitting on the matric lawn for comfort. She'd been there for a few minutes when one of the seniors approached and ordered Kristi to get off the lawn as the rules were clear. You couldn't sit on that lawn if you weren't a matric. It was a small thing, but the cruelty of it (Jen couldn't hop up and go to where Kristi was) impacted Kristi hugely. It became a metaphor for her of how rules sometimes have no value in times of crisis. It was one of many incidents that came at a critical time for Kristi in her development and contributed to her wanting to leave Herschel. She was starting to feel quite alienated from her peers.

I, too, sometimes experienced feelings of isolation. Harmless comments could be like water off a duck's back or cut to the quick, depending on how vulnerable I was feeling. I learned to smile and wave and avoid conversations in the school carpark or the supermarket shopping aisle. Sometimes it was just too hard and superficial banter could really make my heart ache.

I also had to deal with the fact that some people were critical of the fact that we had made our journey public. I told myself it didn't matter to me, but in truth it did. In a time of crisis families need kindness and support. None of us knows how we will respond until we are actually dealing with something. A saying like "never judge a man until you have walked in his shoes" is a cliché for a reason. Understanding or no understanding, I had to do what I had to do, and the public side of the journey took huge courage. Every time one of us was interviewed, we came face to face with a little more of our terror. And every time we did an interview, we surfaced more possibilities and options for Jen and other sufferers. Talking to media may have appeared glamorous on the surface, but in reality it was severely humbling and made us vulnerable in ways people could not imagine. But it was necessary. It was the only way to get what we needed to help Jen.

Kristi retreated into herself and hid her hurt by appearing more and more "contained", outwardly confident and unreachable in public. In reality I knew she felt just the opposite. She reverted to spending every waking moment with Jen, her animals or singing … but the cracks of pain and daily stress were real. All three of us were now on mild antidepressants.

On the 28th of May, in the middle of mid-year exams, we got disappointing news from Papworth.

> *I am sorry to have to inform you that, based on the new imaging, we felt that [Jenna] would not benefit from pulmonary endarterectomy surgery.*
>
> *I realise that this is not the answer you were hoping for …*

My small ray of hope had been snuffed out. Even though I hadn't placed much faith in it, I was still very disappointed. I comforted myself with the knowledge that at least we were sure, sure that no stone had been left unturned. I had to keep moving forward. Our first fundraiser was taking place in three days' time. We needed to raise enough funds to continue with Jen's meds for the foreseeable future.

The fundraiser tickets were sold out two weeks in advance and the loving support from our friends and community blew us away. I felt as if they had been waiting to find a way to help. We were both elated and overwhelmed by the generosity and kindness of our community. Thank heavens I had had the foresight to ask Mary and Steve, our neighbours, to video the evening for us. They had a very successful television production business, Berry Productions, which shot, produced and edited video footage and inserts, and had done so professionally for decades. Our first fundraiser was the starting point of the Lowes and the Berrys documenting Jenna's journey and I don't think we could have done it with anyone else. The intimacy and closeness of our relationship, the trust they already had with Jen, gave them a unique window into her world, and the footage we have as a result is a treasure.

The night of our first fundraiser was an incredible evening filled with emotion and love. The room was full to the brim with people whose only intention for being there was to help us, to help Jenna, as much as they could. The wines, venue and food were spectacular, and Michael Fridjhon held the room with his charisma and expertise. When Jenna spoke and Kristi sang you could have heard a pin drop. The auction, swiftly executed by Michael, fetched enough money to cover six months' worth of medication.

The night we invited our community into Jenna's journey with us, there was magic in the air. It was the night Jenna became everyone's child.

CHAPTER 22

#I Need More Time

"I Need More Time" was ready. At 15 years old, with only a few months of vocal training, Kristi recorded her first single. KFM were ready to interview the girls to launch the song the day before school closed for the mid-year holidays. They had heard and approved the rough master which we'd submitted for their input and approval and they'd loved it! Now GoodLuck could produce the final master tracks.

In my naivety I'd assumed this was all that was needed. Of course, KFM then pointed out that in fact the song needed to be legally published on digital platforms such as iTunes and Spotify so that listeners and supporters could actually download and purchase it. Plus, we needed a way to promote it, preferably via an SMS code. Yikes. I was in over my head.

I reached out to an old contact from my modelling years three decades before, Martin Myers from Triple M Music. He would know what to do. He in turn put me in touch with Next Music, NORM (National Organisation for Reproduction Rights in Music) and Exact Mobile, all of whom came willingly and swiftly on board to help us. On Thursday, the 20th of June there we were, the whole family, in studio with Ryan O'Connor at KFM at peak time, 7:15 am. Oh my heavens, there was so much excitement! Steve and Mary came with us to capture the moment, and the headmaster at Herschel gathered the school together to listen in just before assembly started. Matthew Pearce had been working tirelessly in the background to make sure it all went ahead smoothly. Straight after the on-air launch he called to tell us that, thanks to his campaigning of our cause, the Western Province Rugby Union were inviting Kristi to sing the song live at the Newlands rugby stadium three weeks later at an important local Stormers-Bulls match.

It was such an exciting time, watching our girls work together with a shared purpose. They were literally beaming as they were interviewed by Ryan in the recording studio, with Stu and me standing right behind them. The response of the Western Cape was extraordinary. Comments streamed in via WhatsApp, Twitter, text and email. Listeners were deeply touched by these two sisters. Pulmonary hypertension was no longer an unheard of condition. The way Jen explained her physical challenges and her future, with absolutely no self-pity, was deeply moving.

Not only that, but the song was a hit. "I Need More Time" went to No. 3 on the iTunes chart overnight.

I Need More Time
(written by Jenna Lowe; sung by Kristi Lowe)

Standing alone in a crowd
Puppet-smile on, voice too loud
Good isn't always enough
Pain isn't fair; life plays rough
Trying to shove this aside
Savour the moment, discover the sky

Chorus:
You only live once they say
 Imagine that you knew the day your time was up
And think about it, envy every single stranger 'cuz they have
what you will never –
time enough
I need more time

145

I promise I could shine
'Cause I wouldn't waste what's rightfully mine

Recklessly spinning around
These empty thrills run you to ground
Feeling your life speeding up
Savour the moment; just know when to stop
Struggling to open my heart
Too much to bear, hard to start
Wanting to trust those I love
So much I can't give; just hope it's enough

As we were driving to school the next day, the radio on, suddenly Kristi's voice filled the car … We turned up the volume, opened the windows and shrieked with delight. It was thrilling. Then the phone calls and emails started coming through from listeners seeking help. More and more people found their way to us to share their fears that maybe they, or a member of their family, had PH. It was so rewarding to be in a position to help, to be able to send other patients to the right doctors. The fact that people were being diagnosed and treated as a direct result of Jenna's awareness campaign gave us all a sense that what we were doing really mattered, it was making a difference. It spurred us on and made this all worthwhile. It gave us hope.

National newspapers, magazines, other radio stations, television talk show hosts, bloggers and digital platforms and websites woke up and started sharing Jenna's story, and the plight of all PH sufferers in South Africa. We had no idea how many people our girls would touch.

Their appearance at Newlands rugby stadium was coming up. Matt arranged for the girls to meet some of the players at their practice the day before the big game. This visit gave Kristi an opportunity to see and map out where she would be performing. Wow … until you stand in the middle of a rugby stadium you don't realise just how vast it is! I was nervous, but Kristi seemed fearless. Ryan O'Connor asked her live on air how she felt about being the youngest person ever to sing at Newlands and she answered, "As long as I have Jenna by my side, I can do anything."

Saturday, the 13th of July dawned. It was a big game and the atmosphere was electric. Tens of thousands of people streamed into Newlands as our little group parked and found our way to the unassuming side entrance that led us deep into the hallowed underbelly of the stadium. The girls looked so composed, I don't know how they did it. While they appeared to be taking it all in their stride, my stomach was churning.

We'd made sure they had their "support teams" in place. Jenna had Daffy and Camilla with her, and Kristi had Kim and her girlfriend. Stu and I had Steve and Mary for emotional support and to capture the magic. Plus, we had Kola, who was only 10 at the time, with us. He was wide-eyed at the sight of all these famous rugby players limbering up and getting ready to run onto the field. What an honour and a privilege it was to be there!

By the time Jen and Kristi made their way up through the tunnel and onto the field there were about 20 000 people in the stadium. The noise was deafening. Kristi helped Chase pick up enough speed to hurtle up the incline and as they hit the grass instinctively the girls held hands. We stood on the side of the field, hearts in our mouths, as they came to a stop in the middle of the field and turned to face the commentator's box and television cameras. Jen got up off Chase and, taking the mic, she stood and looked up at the crowds. She thanked them for the opportunity and she thanked them for listening. Then she handed the mic to Kristi … It was an unforgettable moment, seeing my daughters there together and hearing Kristi sing her heart out. The stadium was alive!

The headlines in the Sunday newspapers said it all: "Young girl sings from the heart for her sister" and "Brave teen won't let rare illness kill joy of living".

Halfway across the world, in Sydney, Australia, Craig shared Jenna's story and "I Need More Time" with the Australian pulmonary hypertension community, for whom he was now doing pro bono work. The link he sent out found its way to 300 HP specialist doctors in Australia. Prof. Anne Keogh from St Vincent's Hospital was one of them.

We started to receive messages of solidarity and care from PH associations around the world. The mother of a young teen in France contacted me directly to request that Jen mentor her daughter, who had the same condition but was so depressed that she couldn't leave the house. This was the start of quite a few digital dialogues that Jen had with other sufferers around the world. She became known in PH circles globally, which gave me much greater access to information and expertise. People were contacting me with names of doctors all over the world who might be able to help.

This was how we found our way, just a few days after the launch, to David Badesch, Professor of Medicine, Divisions of Pulmonary Sciences and Critical Care Medicine, and Cardiology Director, Pulmonary Hypertension Program, University of Colorado, Denver. Quite a mouthful, I know, but Prof. Badesch turned out to be one of the kindest, most humble and committed doctors I have ever known. He was about to become an extremely important man in our lives. The first email I ever wrote him read like this:

Hello Prof. Badesch and thank you for being happy to assist via email with advice regarding our daughter, Jenna Lowe. I am Gabi Lowe, the mother of 18-year-old Jenna Lowe, who was diagnosed with either idiopathic pulmonary hypertension OR chronic thromboembolic disease with PH in early 2012. I am attaching the following Word documents for you:

1) Medical report from 26th Jan 2012
2) Medical report from 25th April 2012
3) Medical report from Nov 2012
4) 4 March report of ALL 6MWTs
5) Also please visit Jenna's website at www.jennalowe.org <http://www.jennalowe.org> to find out more.

These documents should give you a brief overview of her history and where we are at currently … she has two doctors looking after her now, namely Prof. Paul Wilcox (pulmonologist), who is based at UCT Academic Hospital in Cape Town and Dr Paul Williams, who is based at the Milpark Hospital in Johannesburg (two hours' flight away from where we live in Cape Town), who is the "gateway" to lung transplants in SA. If you would like to review any of her visual data, we can either send it to you via drop box or courier a disk.

Jenna's current regime is as follows:
07:00: 80 mg Revatio (Sildenafil), 125 mg Bosentas by Cipla (Bosentan)
13:30: 80 mg Revatio (Sildenafil)
19:00: 125 mg Bosentas by Cipla and between 6–7.5 mg Warfarin
20:30pm: 80 mg Revatio (Sildenafil) and 10 mg Cipralex for depression

NOTE: We aim to keep her INR levels between 3 and 3.5 and do regular blood tests to monitor this. Oxygen therapy – 5 litres per minute on home machine throughout the night plus a portable oxygen concentrator that she uses while at school (max 3 litres per minute).

Jenna has pretty much been getting worse and worse and so at the end of January this year we increased her Sildenafil to the maximum dose of 80 mg 3x a day while keeping her on the full dose of Bosentas and adding night-time oxygen.

You will see from the record of 6MWTs that Jenna's latest walk test shows an increase in distance, but she de-saturated to 89% and pushed her heart rate up to 160 so it's hard to know how much of this is actual improvement and how much is sheer determination and will, which she has bucketloads of. However, it is also good to note that she didn't have severe chest pain at the end of the latest walk test like she normally does.

We have excellent doctors here who are giving her the best care they know how; however, due to the fact that most of the drugs available for pulmonary hypertension are NOT registered in South Africa and the fact that it is such a rare condition, they do not have much previous experience to draw on. All my reading and research indicate that she is currently on the right mix of medications BUT I am not a doctor and my husband and I have many questions that I am hoping you can help all of us with – our whole medical team is open to collaboration.

My questions are numerous, but the most pressing are as follows:

1. *In your opinion, are we on the right track with her current medication regime?*
2. *Is Dr Paul Williams right in saying that if there isn't significant improvement on this regime she should move onto Prostanoids ... is there not an interim step before this? Also, what would constitute "significant improvement"? And in your experience, at what stage does one progress onto Prostanoids? What are the exact indicators/precursors to making that decision, bearing in mind that we would need to import the drugs at great cost and our doctors here have no experience with them?*
3. *How successful are bilateral transplants in your opinion for someone of her young age – when do we contemplate this and surely the timing is critical?*
4. *Would you have any idea why Jenna has lost weight – she now weighs only 45 kg (down from 51 kg) when most patients I see on the internet with PH are quite overweight?*
5. *Lastly – seeing that we have SO little experience of this*

condition in SA, do you think it is worth our while to raise the funds for a trip to the US to see you for some tests and collaboration? Bearing in mind that this is a VERY long trip that will have quite an impact on her, is it worthwhile?

I did make contact with Dr David Jenkins at Papworth who is an expert in endarterectomy surgery and he has had us do extensive tests here and send the data over – unfortunately Jenna is NOT a candidate for endarterectomy surgery.

We really appreciate your willingness to help and SO look forward to hearing from you.

Within 36 hours Prof. Badesch responded to tell me he had heard of Jen and was willing to review her records and discuss her case with me. He gave me his direct mobile number in the United States. I couldn't believe it. We had a direct line to some of the best expertise in the world. This is the strength of social media; it gives direct access to our global village. How we use this access is what matters.

A week after the launch we headed off together as a family with all the oxygen machines, meds and Chase, to have some rest time in Keurboomstrand just outside Plett. Jen brought Liv and Daffy, and Kristi brought a school friend. It was a happy, easy-going and comfortable time together.

Something important had shifted for Jenna at the matric dance. Seeing Daffy with someone else made her realise properly for the first time that she may just have romantic feelings for him. It was a turning point for both of them. I wasn't sure how they were going to make the change from five years of friendship into romance, but I needn't have worried about that. Daffy started visiting more and more and very soon they were together (Jenna's journal says they officially became boyfriend and girlfriend on the 13th of April). It happened naturally, easily and comfortably. It was just meant to be. Truth be told, they had loved each other for a very long time.

Love always finds a way. Daffy was caring and open, and nothing about Jenna's condition scared him. He saw her, he was in love with her. The oxygen tubes, Chase and challenges of her illness were irrelevant to him. He simply saw the powerful and beautiful human that she was.

Daffy and Jenna brought each other so much joy. They were a pivotal part of each other's lives by now and very much in love. Openly affectionate, playful and kind, but honest and easy-going. One of Jen's happiest memories, and I know Daffy's too, was when Ian and Jillie treated the two of them to a night at Tsala Treetop Lodge. Ten minutes outside Plett, Tsala is a magical place nestled in lush forests with beautiful views extending across rolling valleys and distant hills. Each suite extends off a wooden ramp and has its own rimflow pool. The two of them were entranced! I remember them saying how they felt like adults who had taken off on a romantic getaway. They often reminisced about it.

Kristi was also happy. The song-launch under her belt and her best girlfriend at her side, she was in a good place. It was a special 10 days together, one of our happiest and most relaxed holidays in a while.

Amidst all this, our girls had both done well in their mid-year exams and we planned a launch party of the song for the youngsters at the Grand Café and Beach on Saturday, the 3rd of August. It would be a special night, a way for the youngsters to have fun, dance and support the cause. Ryan O'Connor from KFM agreed to be master of ceremonies and a large sound system was donated free of charge. Yet again Sue, who owned the venue, supported Jen's cause and it was astounding how the kids got behind it. All the local schools put up posters and we sold just under 1 000 tickets. Matt and his friends agreed to man the door and Ali organised a ticket sales system for us and helped manage the set-up. We arranged bouncers, and had Stu and the older guys of course, to ensure no one got out of hand.

Jenna's journal
Tuesday, 30th July
10 am: my bedroom

I am about to head off to school. Things are feeling more manageable which is good. Last week was tough. The launch party is coming up this Saturday night, and Kristi just got a horrible cough ... not good! Fortunately, it's only Tuesday and hopefully we can kick it before this weekend.

By the night of the launch, fortunately Kristi was well enough to sing. A few frantic phone calls to a friend of ours in London, singer Suanne Braun, for her advice on recovery fast enough for live performance (steaming is a singer's best friend!) had Kristi on the mend in no time. It was a great night. I have never seen such a large crowd of teens all in one place! All the cash raised went towards Jen's medication.

Whenever we did a public event, I was always acutely aware how, in any one moment, we could simultaneously experience the highest of highs and the lowest of lows. "I Need More Time" was an incredible initiative. It created huge awareness and was downloaded all over the world. It has since been used as the theme song at the Sixth World Symposium on Pulmonary Hypertension in 2018. It was without a doubt a massive success, one that turned out to be a double-edged sword for Kristi in many ways. Emotionally it is a very tough song to sing, and I believe a small part of her shut down every time she sang it. Kristi is young and talented with the gift of an amazing voice, but delivering a painful message on behalf of her sister may just have taken the joy out of singing for her. Well, for a while anyway. It is easy to look back and see that now with hindsight.

With a successful launch behind us, we headed towards a much more challenging time with Natalie and with Jen. Jen was getting worse. No amount of media coverage slowed down her illness.

I was in regular contact now with Prof. Badesch in the US and making use of the direct line he'd so generously given me. I followed up a telephone conversation with an email:

... My family and I are seriously discussing and looking into the possibility of coming over to you in the September school holidays ... so quite a few questions arise:

1. *Are you there and available to assess Jenna at this time (say from 24/25/26/27 Sept – or longer)?*

2. *How long do you think we would need to be with you and will we hospitalise her for a few days for tests? I know you wanted to repeat the catheterised angiogram, amongst other things.*

3. *Is the hospital prepared to come on board and help us financially? What can I do to help you facilitate and negotiate this with them? I wouldn't be able to afford the airfares, accommodation and hefty hospital bills.*

4. *Stuart (my husband, Jen's dad, copied on this mail) is wondering if it is more cost effective to bring you and a nurse here – or do you have facilities, equipment, tests, expertise, etc. there that we don't have here? We are all very open to being immersed in a centre of excellence and experience with PH, but as the exchange rate is NOT in our favour and the intravenous therapies are so expensive (and not available here), we need to be absolutely sure that the money spent on making this trip wouldn't be better used on a month or two of intravenous therapy if that is what our Jenna needs.*

5. *Who are the key suppliers of Flolan/Eproprostenol, and do you have contacts in the US or elsewhere? Maybe we could set up meetings with key suppliers while we are with you to try and negotiate a compassionate programme and supply chain. Are there any generics available?*

6. *If after assessment you believe that intravenous therapy is what she needs, we would need to get permission from the Medical Control Council here; get a supply chain of the drugs sorted out and find a way to finance it ... all difficult and fraught with problems, but not impossible.*

7. *From what I understand it would also be imperative for*

training here – so maybe we would then need to bring yourself and a nurse to SA for that reason. I understand that intravenous therapy can mean many years of good quality of life, but is a burden as well as there is a pump and risk of infection.

Have I understood everything correctly, David? From our discussion it became clear to me that you feel waiting till next year June/July [this is when a PH conference was due to be held in SA] is not in Jenna's best interests and that the sooner you see her the better. I also understand that you are concerned about the difference between how symptomatic she is (cannot walk around the block) and her walk test results and that cardio pulmonary rehabilitation should be considered, but cannot be recommended unless you have seen her. It also seemed to me that you believe that the oral therapies she is currently on are not going to make much difference to the progression of the disease and that aggressive treatment in an 18-year-old who is presenting like Jen is (therefore intravenous therapies) are the only option to prolong her life. Did I understand this correctly? Also, I'm not sure if I understood this part correctly – whether she has PH with heterogeneous perfusion or chronic thromboembolic disease with PH makes a big difference to the risk of intravenous therapy?

I am copying Prof. Paul Wilcox and Dr Paul Williams in on this email as they are Jenna's doctors here on the ground in SA and will need to be involved in her care every step of the way. I also welcome their opinion and comment on any of this discussion.

I pushed "send" on the email and one day later boarded a flight with Kristi to Johannesburg. She'd been asked by the Reach For A Dream Foundation to sing with a young "Dreamer" named Robyn at their annual gala dinner. A "Dreamer" is a child who is fighting for their life and has been identified by this amazing organisation to have a dream fulfilled. Robyn's dream was to sing live for an audience, but she was too nervous to do it alone and needed support. Kristi would be that support. Kim had got involved and had been coaching the girls through "My African Dream" together. She even arranged a surprise visit by the original artist, Vicky Sampson, to one of their rehearsals. You should have seen the girls faces! Sheer delight.

It was a rare privilege to spend time alone with Kristi and I loved our weekend together, sharing a hotel room and chatting like teenagers. There were 800 people at the gala dinner. Kristi had been catapulted into a new world by her singing, that was for sure. She behaved, as always, like an absolute pro. Kim had taught her well, including how to manage a proper technical sound check. Always, no matter how much pressure she was under, every time Kristi sang she would deliver a note-perfect performance. It was astounding really, her big-match temperament. It's a skill that has been useful over the years, but at what cost? To what extent is this incredible ability also a well-developed defence mechanism against difficult and conflicting emotions? I have to wonder how else an empathetic 15-year-old could have coped with all that was going on around her and inside her. She had to find a way, and her way was to shine, to always appear calm and contained and to be resourceful. I think we expected too much from her, that life expected too much from her. There were some incredible highs, though ... moments that will live with us forever.

Shortly after we returned from the gala dinner Shirley arranged a Greek evening at her cottage with immediate family and friends who might as well be family. We dressed up in white sheets we turned into togas and went laden with platters full of delectable Greek treats. Ali sourced some unglazed Greek plates and we started the evening by writing messages on the plates and then smashing them enthusiastically on the floor. It was liberating.

Natalie looked up mischievously at Shirley, koki in hand and asked, "Are we allowed to swear, Mom?"

"Oh God, yes!" we all chimed.

Natalie wrote carefully: "Stupid Fucking Chordoma". And then we helped her hold the plate up high above her head and smash it down onto the hard tiled floor.

A few days later, Natalie, in her wisdom (and no, I'm not being facetious), decided Kola needed a dog. She decided it was time for unconditional love of a furry friend who could go everywhere with him. Kola, Kristi and I were dispatched to DARG, the local animal rescue shelter, to choose one. Banjo, medium sized with silky soft reddish-brown fur and handsome white markings, had a gentle energy and took to Kola immediately. We looked at all the rescue pups, many much younger than him, but he was the one. We were still "umming and ahing", trying to make a final decision, when Shirley's car pulled up in the drive. How was that possible? Shirl couldn't leave Natalie! Well, she hadn't. Natalie was in the car with her. Apparently, she had insisted. The dog was her gift to Kola, and she was determined to make the final choice. She stayed in the car while we brought the puppies to her one by one, making sure they didn't rough-house her in any way. Last to be introduced was Banjo. He looked up at her with his large brown eyes and then gently placed his head on her lap. It was done … It was Banjo who had actually done the choosing.

CHAPTER 23

Upping the ante

I heard back from Prof. Badesch. He said my summary was "pretty accurate", and he was happy to make contact with some of the big pharma companies on our behalf. However, he wouldn't be in the States during Jenna's upcoming September school holidays, so that couldn't work.

By mid-August Jen was having a reccurrence of bad chest pains on a regular basis. She was asking for a shower chair. Standing in the shower for long enough to wash her hair was too exhausting. My tone in my next email was slightly more desperate.

> *... Stuart and I have been hard at work doing our research. We are totally committed to doing a trip to a centre of excellence around PAH to get Jenna assessed for intravenous therapy and to pave the way forward. In order to make sure we take steps that are sustainable I have a few queries:*
>
> 1. *Do you know of Prof. Ann Keogh? She works in Sydney Australia – which is slightly closer and less expensive for us as I have family who live there AND Jen and Kristi have just been introduced to the PH community in Australia through the song that Jenna has written that her sister Kristi sings. My brother, due to Jenna's diagnosis, is currently doing some pro bono PR work*

for the PH Association of Australia and so we have good introductions to Dr Keogh through the CEO Dr Geoff Strange. If Prof. Ann Keogh is as willing to get on board as you have been (I haven't even been able to talk to her yet), then it may make more sense for us to go Aussie ... Your thoughts on this?

2. *If we are looking at Aussie as a potential source of expertise, then maybe we should look at the UK as well, as that is the closest? Dr David Jenkins has already been very involved and assessed Jenna to see if she was a candidate for endarterectomy surgery, which she is not. Should I ask Dr Jenkins if he has a colleague who could assess Jenna for intravenous therapy? I already have a relationship with him, which is a start!*

3. *To help us cost and assess this exercise thoroughly are you able to give me a list of the tests you think you would do in hospital with Jenna and what those costs are likely to be? I can then get the same from the UK and Australia.*

Jen had awful chest pain yesterday and is now asking for a chair in the shower. She really isn't doing too well.

Prof. Badesch responded within 24 hours in a calm and soothing way. He explained it was premature to make plans for a visit by Jenna to the University of Colorado Hospital, but he agreed that Jenna's worsening symptoms would suggest she needed advanced care in a PH centre soon. Yes, he knew Prof. Keogh. She was very knowledgeable in the disease, among the world's leading experts. "I'm sure that she would provide excellent care, if you were able to establish contact and make arrangements for Jenna to be seen in Australia." He also said he was trying to contact one of the companies involved in intravenous Prostanoids "to get a sense for where things stand with respect to access in South Africa".

I emailed him straight back.

Was he still prepared to come to South Africa? If so, what timing could work? I asked him to email me a letter of motivation for our medical insurance (I had to try) as to why Jen needed Flolan, how soon it was required, how much it could improve her health and what the benefits would be of either bringing expertise here OR visiting a PH centre of excellence.

I was well aware how busy he was and that I was asking a lot, but I had no choice. I would ask anything for my child. The very next day – the same day Jenna started writing her matric prelims – I received this letter from him:

University of Colorado Denver
Pulmonary Hypertension Program
21st August, 2013

Medical aid, or the appropriate medical authorities for South Africa

Dear Madam or Sir,

I am writing as a pulmonary hypertension physician who has reviewed the medical records of Ms Jenna Lowe, at the request of her mother, Ms Gabi Lowe. Due to the geographic distance between us, I've unfortunately not had the opportunity to personally examine the patient, or to view the actual images from her diagnostic studies. My opinions are therefore based on the reports and records that I have had the opportunity to review.

Jenna is an 18-year-old woman with pulmonary hypertension that appears to be idiopathic in nature. It is difficult to completely exclude the possibility of small vessel chronic thromboembolic pulmonary hypertension (CTEPH), but this appears to be less likely. She has previously been deemed, by an expert centre, not to be a candidate for pulmonary endarterectomy (PEA) surgery and should probably be treated as though she has idiopathic pulmonary arterial hypertension (IPAH). She is currently receiving treatment with two oral agents, an endothelin receptor antagonist and a phosphodiesterase inhibitor, and is symptomatically worsening despite this.

In an ideal situation, Jenna would be evaluated in a centre expert in the care of patients with pulmonary hypertension, and capable of offering the full range of advanced therapies, including intravenous prostanoids. I understand that access to such therapies is restricted in South Africa. Jenna's mother, Gabi, is attempting to ensure that her daughter has access to the best available medical care. I would support her efforts to ensure a thorough re-evaluation of Jenna, likely including a current right heart catheterization, and then appropriate adjustment of her therapeutic regimen, which might include the addition of chronic intravenous prostanoid therapy.

I would be happy to discuss this situation by teleconference, if this would be helpful. I have indicated to the patient's mother, Gabi Lowe, my willingness to travel to South Africa, if necessary, to assist in professional education and the establishment of an expert pulmonary hypertension centre, capable of providing comprehensive evaluation and advanced therapies to patients with this potentially fatal disease.

Thanks very much for your consideration, and best regards,

Everyone in our family had their own fight going on. While I was dogmatically working to find, source and secure medical therapies, Jen was writing exams. The school had arranged a separate room with a dedicated external examination invigilator so that the noise of Thunder didn't disturb the other students.

Exams took their toll on her physically. The strain of sitting and writing for hours at a time meant she required long periods of sleep between exams. While the other students crammed, she would come home and fall into a deep sleep before I would reluctantly wake her and take her back to write another exam. She was both fragile and determined.

161

A conscientious lover of learning, it upset her that she was no longer able to study for long periods. She knew she was in trouble physically. Jen's beloved drama teacher, Tessa, and other students had created a space for her at school where she could rest during the day. They decorated it with a screen on which they wrote messages of love and support. It was such a kind thing to do and Jen often used to visit it, but by now it was easier for her to come home to her air-conditioned bedroom with access to meds, a comfortable bed and my constant care.

We devised convenient systems at home. For instance, Thunder had a seven-metre-long cannula so that she could walk anywhere in the house still attached to her machine at maximum levels. We cut small squares out the bottom of most of our doors, so that she could have privacy but still be connected. Stuart built shelves next to her bed, at exactly the right level, for her tea, medication, books, reading light and a bell. When she was really bad, and it was too hard for her to call me – shouting loudly uses a lot of breath – we devised a bell system. She would ring the bell if she needed help.

Jenna still got up, went to school and wrote her exams. She still smiled and found ways for it to be easy to be around her. She still laughed and chatted to her friends. She was totally engaged in life but at the same time she needed constant help and rest. I was on call to facilitate her life.

At school there was deep and caring support from her teachers. Nothing was too much trouble. Clearly her track record of consistent conscientious work for the past 10 years helped enormously, but the teachers willingly gave of their personal time for one-on-one tutorials at home to help Jen catch up on whole sections of work that she'd missed. They often remarked how she needed to hear something only once to understand it, absorb it and remember it. Stuart called it a "sticky brain". Information would literally go in and stick there in the annals of her mind forever. I don't know how she did that with so much going on. I was the opposite. I made copious lists because the consistent stress was playing havoc with my memory and I was terrified of forgetting something important.

CHAPTER 24

Oxygen buddies

Over the months Natalie's condition had worsened. Her tiny body was ravaged by tumours, the main one protruding substantially from her chest. By now we were visiting every night because we knew the end was near. Kristi would take her homework with her, and Jen and Natalie would sit on the couch together. It was relentless and yet Shirley never lost sight of the fact that meaningful time spent with friends and family was the most important thing for Natalie.

Our times together brought us face to face with the reality of death every day. Apart from being "oxygen buddies", Jen and Natalie's wicked sense of humour kept us laughing in ways you could only understand if you were there.

Out of the blue one day I was contacted by the mother of a Herschel scholar I didn't know well. She put me in touch with a man who was to become vital to me. This was a professor of medical ethics who sat on the board of the MCC but was based in Cape Town. He was an important link in the chain of people who made the dream of intravenous therapy for Jenna a possibility.

I had emailed Prof. Anne Keogh in Australia with Jen's medical reports and current regime. I explained that I had been in recent contact with Prof. Badesch, who was concerned that Jen should have been on aggressive IV therapy already due to the fact that she wasn't responding to oral therapy. Prof. Keogh. said she knew exactly who Jen was. She went to sleep at night with the words of Jenna's song going around in her head. Her response to my medical questions was quick and unequivocal:

Jenna sounds very ill, breathless moving around the office, getting onto examination bunk = Class IV. Inhaled Iloprost is probably too weak. Intravenous Iloprost, Intravenous Flolan and Subcutaneous treprostinil are all possible. Almost everyone would recommend Flolan IVI first, except Germany would go to IVI Iloprost.

The thing about Flolan is that anyone could start it for Jenna. A peripheral line can be used to start at a dose of 2ng/kg/min, then a day later, up to 4ng/kg/min and then sneaking the dose up to about 10ng/kg/min by about Day 10 but according to side-effects (so simply back off with dosing if jaw pain, diarrhea, abdominal pain, etc.).

The ultimate dose should be about 28+ng/kg/min!

The central line would be whatever line the hospital uses – a tunneled line, a Hickman's (care with the Warfarin, of course).

The pump is CADD pump with occlusion alarm, 17.5 inch pressure tubing, cold pouch, etc. and a backup second pump spare.

This is all we do. There is not really any special trick to Flolan – it just somehow frightens everyone!! The only scary bit is if the diagnosis is PVOD pulmonary veno-occlusive disease and they go into pulmonary oedema. But this diagnosis seems to have been excluded.

If the blood pressure falls at all when Flolan has started, I ease off on the dose of Sildenafil (especially as Jenna is on such a high dose).

If the Flolan drug supply was yours, pumps, disposables, and pumps, etc., it may be that one of your docs is prepared to get going with the Flolan in Cape Town? We have protocols we can send along.

Work-up for transplant should be performed now and

be in place, since an infection or similar could destabilize Jenna, i.e. do not wait any longer to have transplant testing completed.

Sounds like Latin, right? It did to me too, but I had to make sense of it. I had no choice. I combed my way through the email again and again, referencing medical terms on Google. It didn't take long before the Latin become abundantly clear – Jen was in a whole lot of trouble and something drastic had to happen, fast.

While Jenna finished her mid-year exams, I rounded up the local team to discuss our options. Prof. Wilcox, Dr Paul Williams, our ethics professor on the MCC, our team at Equity Pharmaceuticals and our health insurance, Discovery. We all agreed on the urgency of getting Jen to Johannesburg within two weeks for a full evaluation for the introduction of Flolan and to list her for transplant.

If Flolan, with all its complexities and complications, was what Jenna needed, I would do whatever was necessary: find it, fund it, bring it to South Africa and learn to administer it. While trying to keep things calm and constructive at home, at the same time Stuart and I worked, relentlessly, to make this happen.

On the 7th of September Natalie came to us for a visit. It was a huge deal. This was the first time she had left the sanctuary and safety of the Hout Bay cottage in months. It took careful planning and organising of the logistics. First, I dropped off Oxy-Jen, for Natalie to use in the car to our house. Then we planned the timing between her four-hourly medication administration. Shirl and Kola made a bed in the back of the car to reduce Natalie's nausea and increase her comfort for the trip. Natalie really needed a change of scenery. A small adventure. But it had to be somewhere safe with, among other things, access to oxygen. Really it was a trip from one home hospital ward to another.

The visit went so well. Sitting upright and cross-legged, her favourite position, on Jen's day-bed in the lounge, facing the garden, and sipping what she called "Gabi-Tea", Natalie rapid-fired questions. Her voice by this stage was very small; you had to really pay attention not to miss anything.

Daffy's matric dance was coming up in a few weeks' time and Natalie quizzed Jen on every detail. What dress? What shoes? What jewellery? How would Jenna wear her hair? She also quizzed me on what plans I had in place so that Jen could cope. Had I thought of everything? She may have been 13, but you knew not to mess with Nattie. Her spirit was indomitable. Inside that fragile little body was a warrior princess with the maturity of a young adult. She could barely walk by this stage of her illness, but here she was in my home holding court as if this was an ordinary tea party. Every now and then she would get up and start walking somewhere in a wobbly sort of way and Shirl and I would jump up instinctively. Natalie stared us down as if to say: "Really? Back off, you two ... I will decide if and when I can walk." That feisty independent twinkle in her eye made everything okay. Tea at our house was her last-ever outing.

It was nearly the end of the third term of matric, which heralded the onset of myriad school-leaver functions for Jen in her capacity as deputy head girl. There was a prefects' tea, a teachers' tea, a sports dinner, a cultural dinner and more. Leaving school is a huge deal in any student's life ... but for us it was particularly poignant.

For most school-leavers this "end" is also the beginning. It's the beginning of independence and for making any number of choices. But Jen and I saw life through a different lens now, and it made these school-leaving functions challenging. Every activity, speech, quote, poem, song, tradition, ritual or performance delivered at these functions revolves around the same theme – setting off on the adventure of your life and finding your way in the world. True for most, but for me every speech stung like acid poured onto a raw wound. Jenna was the epitome of potential, and yet her future looked so different from the picture these speeches were painting. We were determined to cultivate hope, but we were also under no illusion as to just how brutally the statistics were stacked against her. It took discipline and determination on my part to bear everyone else's obvious joy and anticipation for their daughters' bright futures. I had known and loved many of these girls for so long, but I'm not going to lie, it was still hard. However, in some ways the experience of sitting through those functions made me more determined than ever. Maybe, just maybe, we could beat the odds. I, too, had a choice. I chose to believe that we could. I chose to push on, regardless of the fear. I chose to keep fighting, even though all I really wanted to do was sob and sob and sob.

The 19th of September was a big day for Jen. It was the date of her final drama practical exam, an hour-long performance in the Herschel school theatre. A pair of twins, two extremely talented drama students, would be sharing the stage with her. Jen had to perform on Chase and on oxygen and her difficulty with breath meant that she couldn't project her voice very far, and so her drama teacher, very cleverly, arranged it so that the audience (which included an external examiner, her school colleagues, some teachers, Stuart, myself and Kristi, and Steve and Mary, who videoed it for us) sat in a semi-circle right on the stage. The topic was pulmonary hypertension. Jen hadn't shared the script with me at all.

As we walked into the darkened theatre, we were all handed a straw. We were given an instruction to block our noses and breathe through the straw, for as long as we could cope, during the performance. This way, Jen explained to us, we might get an inkling of how pulmonary hypertension patients feel at any one time. The script was written, crafted and powerfully performed by Jenna and the twins. What followed was a combination of parody, narration, poetry, visual aids, verse, song, fiction, humour, real-life experiences, existential questions and some bald harsh facts, all cleverly threaded together and performed with bucketloads of intellect, passion, humour and heart. It stopped us all in our tracks. It was brilliant.

When the performance ended the entire grade of girls sat stunned, in utter silence, deeply moved and exhausted from the experience. I think the full extent of Jenna's prognosis was only now becoming clear to them; the school counsellor had to be called to come in and be with them. I was in the carpark in the disabled parking bay packing Jenna's stuff away into the car when I saw the external examiner leaving the school grounds. She didn't see me, but when I looked at her I could see that she, too, was emotionally wiped out.

The drama exam gave Jenna permission to express the truth. She and the twins were awarded 100%.

Jenna came home and slept deeply for three hours, but her day wasn't over yet. It was the day of Daffy's matric dance. By now not only was Daffy part of our family, but Jenna was part of his too. His parents Karen and Bob adored her and were lovingly determined to find ways for Jenna to enjoy as much of the evening as she could. They arranged the logistics right down to the last detail. First, they signed up for parent duty at the after-party so they would be present in case of an emergency. Then they collected Thunder hours in advance to set up at the after-party venue. Then they came back again to collect Chase and extra batteries for Oxy-Jen. Jen would be collected by Daffy and taken to the pre-drinks (the "pre's") at a close friend's house (we were going too) and then he would drive her in a fancy borrowed car to school for the grand arrival, where Chase would be waiting for her.

The night was a highlight for Jen, for all of us, one of the gloriously happy memories that really stood out in the last few years of her life. We'd had a long dress designed for her in dark red trimmed with black lace. It was made with care by the same dressmaker who'd created Jen's own matric dance dress. Julie is a kind woman who won my heart when she made no fuss about the fact that Jenna couldn't actually make it up the stairs to her sewing room, or that I had to help her try on the dress during fittings because she was too breathless to do it herself. She dealt with Jen's physical limitations in a deeply respectful and undramatic way, something we'd found to be a rare quality with people we didn't know.

When Jen made her way down the passage, she looked like a movie star. She wore her hair up with a few glossy ringlets framing her heart-shaped face, and her brown eyes were sparkling. She wore red heels (Jen always said no heel or goal was too high) and diamanté jewels. Tall, dark and handsome Daniel (it seems more appropriate for this special night to use Daffy's real name) arrived, looking smart and dashing in his dark suit. It was a great joy for Stuart and me to witness this love affair. I treasure the magnificent pics we took of Jenna and Daffy that night, and I'm reminded of the "face" of Jen that the world saw ... she looked 100% well and radiant. They had such a fun night, and I was able to relax knowing she was safe in the hands of Daffy and his friends. They would look out for her, carry her and Oxy-Jen when needed, and be just the right amount of attentive. Daffy knew exactly when, where and how to watch out for Jenna without it being a big deal, without any drama.

CHAPTER 25

In this case, "no" is not an answer

Three days later, at the end of September 2013, Kristi, Jen, Stu and I flew to Johannesburg for Jen's big check-up with Dr Paul Williams and his full transplant team. Even though we had been in the thick of the reading and research about lung transplants for some time, this meeting was the first time the reality of just how difficult this might be began to crystallise for Stuart and me. Other transplants are a lot simpler, we realised.

Lung transplant surgery is cutting-edge, high-risk and difficult – and the recovery is exceptionally challenging. Even then, you are buying yourself, on average, about five to 10 extra years of life – if you are lucky.

What we also learned is that there is a long waiting list of those in need and just being listed for a transplant – for any organ – is a process in itself. It is merely the beginning of a long agonising wait. An agonising wait for the right donor, for a match ...

The situation for organ donation in South Africa is dire.

For starters, a donor and recipient for a double lung transplant need to be a blood type match, a tissue type match, and size match. On top of that a minute percentage of our population are registered organ donors – only 0.03% to be exact – and we are desperately short of transplant co-ordinators in hospitals around the country. In the country of the first heart transplant, this was the last thing I expected. I had imagined that the lung transplant surgery was what would be the biggest challenge, but I was wrong. I didn't expect that finding a donor and being lucky enough to receive a transplant in the first place would be such a major struggle. Add to this the fact that lungs specifically are the most difficult organs of all to come by.

For us, just having the conversation about a transplant felt brutal, never mind the additional challenges on top of that, and yet there we were, all four of us, now hoping for something that a few years back seemed like the worst possible outcome, the very last resort.

Half of the day with the transplant team was spent doing interviews, psychometric and physical testing for Jenna and it all took much longer than I had expected. We had to go straight from there to a meeting with the clinical review board at Discovery Health. The whole day was a great big dose of reality, served up in one giant helping. The review board agreed to help us with Flolan. They wouldn't pay for the drug, but they would help us with all the additional expenses for disposables, lines, pumps and more. They were also open to discussing the possibility of sponsoring a symposium in South Africa for other doctors if Prof. David Badesch agreed to come. It was a win, not just for us but for pulmonary hypertension as a whole. This cruel disease was now on Discovery's radar.

We had been invited as a family to spend the following day at the Rare Diseases of SA Association's family picnic. The invitation came directly from Kelly, who headed up the association, because she wanted Jenna to be their ambassador for pulmonary hypertension. None of us was at our best. We were drained and tired. But as I stood watching all the families of children with rare diseases gather together a strange feeling came over me. It was the first time I think I realised that we weren't just guests in this environent. We were a part of this community now, a powerful, beautiful and in some ways emotionally broken community of families who face and deal with inordinate challenges, and the risk of losing their children, daily. These families, like us, were at war to save their loved ones, with all the collateral damage that goes with war. The trip was both harsh and hopeful.

As always, the altitude in Johannesburg was punishing for Jen. She was whacked by the time we got home; we all were. There was no more hiding. There are only four WHO categories of severity with pulmonary hypertension and Jen was officially now category IV. This was the end of the line. The time had come for her to go onto Flolan, immediately. She should have done so a long time ago and would have if we'd lived in a country with access to First World centres of excellence for PH patients.

Back in Cape Town Jen picked up her school life once more. The end of her time on a relatively sheltered school campus was drawing near. That week Jen had to attend her prefects' dinner and a Debating team dinner. When it came to school events, there was always the option for Jenna not to attend and to stay in bed, but that was never going to happen. She seemed more determined than ever to grab every minute of life as and when she could. She would chat, giggle and behave just like a normal teenager, even immediately after those two gruelling days she had just endured in Joburg. Her spirit was infectious. She never let on about any of it. Outside of the immediately family, only Daniel, Aniko and Tayla in Australia, Camilla and a few other of her very closest girlfriends knew the implications of the trip. Even then, she packaged it in a way she knew would help them cope.

How did she do it? How did any of us do it? Where did the horror go? Mostly we took our lead from Jenna. The one thing that struck me most was her inordinate grace and poise, no matter how grim the circumstances. It is a bittersweet gift and skill to have, one that I both admired and wished I could take away because it was born out of adversity.

I was thankful that we had had the foresight to introduce valuable and much-needed coping mechanisms into our upside-down lives. The therapy, the family-led meditation, the evening ritual of family supper and honest conversations, a tight-knit circle of support of family and friends, and some chemical help with mild antidepressants were all things that helped keep us going. I know many a traditional man (sorry if that sounds sexist) who may have shrunk or run from a situation like ours, but Stuart was not one of them. He and I were completely united in our fight, our struggle and our pain as parents. I could not have faced it without him, and he could not have faced it without me.

Although what we had been forced to confront during the Joburg trip was a lot to process, this was not the time to become immobilised by fear. In fact, fear needed to have the opposite effect. I hit the ground running. First off, I got back in touch with Prof. Badesch. He had positive news. He confirmed that Dr Frank Gray at GlaxoSmithKline in the UK had agreed to supply Flolan to Jenna for as long as she needed it and that he, Prof Badesch, would come to South Africa in December to help us start the titration of the drug. It was a coup, an absolute coup. I wrote to Dr Gray immediately to thank him wholeheartedly and I received the most heart-warming response:

"To be honest, I am happy to have been able to help. It is a great reminder and motivator of what the job is really all about. Plus, this is an exceptional case, and family! I have really been struck with your positive attitude and how you have pulled everything together. Also, Jenna and the strength she is showing. All the best with her exams. It is not easy considering her PH, I would equate it to someone running a competitive 100m sprint with a 50kg kitbag on their back."

These amazing humans were giving us hope, a way to bridge Jenna to transplant. Securing the Flolan was a massive step forward. However, Stu and I knew we would need everybody on all sides to make this work. We would need the full and consistent co-operation and support of Dr Paul Williams and his team in Johannesburg, Prof. Wilcox and his team in Cape Town, the Medical Control Council, Equity Pharmaceuticals as the responsible pharmacist to help with importation, papers and customs, Discovery Health to help with local costs and funding of education/symposiums for local doctors, Smiths Medicals for local disposable supplies, Prof. Anne Keogh for help with cartridges and pumps from Australia, and GlaxoSmithKline in the UK and in SA. It was going to be a mammoth undertaking, and a high-risk one on many levels. I was under no illusion that once Jenna was on the drug, she could never come off it ... not until transplant, so there could never be a break in the supply chain. Flolan would help "bridge" Jen to transplant, but as the first person in Africa to be on this drug, it presented not insignificant challenges.

It was imperative that I nailed down the approvals. Thanks, in part, to Jenna's media profile, my new contact at the MCC and Jen's extreme need for this therapy, *within two weeks* I had in hand all the necessary paperwork and Section 18A approval for the first six-month period. The wheels were turning.

It was time to start shipping the stock from the UK to South Africa and the pressure was on ... the clock was ticking. Jen would have her central line put in after exams, just a short six weeks away. One of the next steps was to get a full and detailed list of all the disposables and medical equipment needed to go with the Flolan so that I could source it in South Africa and cost it. I knew we needed two CADD Legacy pumps complete with batteries, cassettes (a square plastic container that gets filled with the medication once mixed and clips onto the pump), lines and I wasn't sure what else. I had recently watched a few YouTube videos of patients in other parts of the globe mixing their medication and I have to say I was apprehensive. It looked very technical and scary, and these patients had the back-up of clinics and specialist pharmacies and nurses to help them, which we wouldn't have. It was becoming abundantly clear that I would need to be meticulously organised because once Jenna was on the drug, the buck would stop with me.

In my efforts to really understand Flolan this was what I found out, and I would be lying if I didn't tell you that some of it kept me awake at night!

Flolan (Epoprostenol), the first medication approved by the FDA for the treatment of pulmonary arterial hypertension, is a prostacyclin only available as a continuous infusion requiring a central line to be placed and maintained for the duration of treatment. It is known as the gold standard of treatments for pulmonary hypertension because it has been used for an extended period and has been researched extensively. The scary bit for me was that it has a very short half-life, meaning that if the medication is stopped for any reason at all the levels in the blood diminish rapidly and therefore any interruption in therapy from a pump or line malfunction, or human error, is considered a life-threatening emergency. The medication is not stable at room temperature and so ice-packs have to be used at all times to keep the medication cold. Mostly it is provided by a speciality pharmacy (focused on providing therapies to pulmonary hypertension patients) – there is no such thing in SA – and normally the patient is educated either by a pulmonary hypertension nurse co-ordinator from the PH clinic, or by a nurse specialising in PH with the speciality pharmacies (again, we had neither in SA).

This medication requires sterile mixing vials of the medicine with diluent daily, programming a small infusion pump, and maintaining a central line. It is a complicated 35-step process. Patients are permanently attached to the pump via their central line (a line inserted during surgery directly into the right heart chamber) and carry it over their shoulder like a purse or around their waist like a belt. It is initiated at a very low dose and slowly increased over time. A dosing sheet provides outlines of how to mix the medication and how to programme the pump and should be kept in the carrying case with the pump at all times, as this is the only way to know what dose of Flolan you are currently on. This medication, like all medications used to treat pulmonary hypertension, has side-effects. Common side-effects reported by patients using Flolan are headache, nausea, vomiting, diarrhoea, first-bite jaw pain, leg pain and flushing.

Wow, this was not going to be an easy ride for me or for Jen.

It was scary, but there was no choice. We had to get our heads around it.

Dr Williams and Prof. Wilcox were in contact discussing potential formats for a symposium. They were delighted at the opportunity to discuss their other difficult PH cases with Prof. Badesch. At the time I had my head down fighting for Jenna but now, with a different lens, it is incredible to look back and see where the first big shift in the landscape of pulmonary hypertension in South Africa began. It began here, with Jenna.

I didn't yet have a commitment from Discovery Health to help with any costs, but we were going ahead regardless and so I called a meeting with my "angels" to plan our next fundraiser. Just as effective and gorgeous as the famous *Charlie's Angels*, mine are three special girlfriends – Karen, Melissa and Carlie – who became affectionately known as "Jen's Angels". They threw themselves into helping me organise many of our Jenna Lowe Trust fundraisers. Kind, generous, well-networked and highly effective, they had already held a fundraising breakfast at the Vineyard Hotel (one of Jenna's favourite places) and now we were planning a magnificent Valentine's picnic for February 2014. The intention was that it would bring in enough money to cover the financial shortfall for the large medical expenses looming ahead.

It was around this time that I heard back from Discovery Health. It was good news. They were going to assist us with flying Prof. Badesch and his nurse practitioner to South Africa from the United States; and they'd also get involved in managing the PH symposiums for GPs, specialists, pulmonologists and cardiologists in Johannesburg and Cape Town. Not only would this be an enormous help, but it also meant that many more doctors and patients would be educated about pulmonary hypertension. They were so impressed by Jenna that they also requested an in-depth interview with her for a three-page spread in their Discovery Health magazine, which gets distributed to literally millions. We knew this could greatly increase the awareness of, and understanding of, pulmonary hypertension, which would in turn help earlier diagnosis. A separate Discovery Health department had also heard about Jen and was keen to print 1 000 copies of *The Magic Bissie Tree*. This, complete with a personal letter from Jen, was distributed to sick children in hospitals around the country on Christmas Day as a way to inspire them. Jen was elated. It was such affirmation for her that she could really make a difference for others.

In between the highs and the lows, normal life has a sneaky way of simply carrying on, no matter what. Every day was still a struggle – to feed Jen, to get enough weight on her, with additional protein shakes between each meal, and to ensure she got enough rest and sleep. There were still the weekly blood tests at Pathcare, where the staff in the Claremont branch had become like family; they knew all Jen's codes off by heart and had all her media cuttings pasted up on the wall.

The end of the third term was imminent. It marked the end of an era for Jenna and her friends, it was definitely time for us to think about what 2014 could hold for her. If she responded well to Flolan, then there was no doubt that she would be able to attend university. We decide to plan for the best-case scenario. Sandy, Jen's godmother, worked in the Environmental Department at UCT, so she knew and understood the lie of the land. She offered to set up a meeting for us with the UCT Disability Department. Jen had already been accepted on the basis of her Grade 11 results, but how was it going to work? What support was there for her on campus? Did all the buildings have lifts? Would all her lecture halls have wheelchair access? Where could she rest and charge her oxygen machines? Students find university life a big adjustment under normal conditions. Can you imagine how daunting it might be for someone with special needs? We had to get started with the process of finding out how to make this manageable, do-able.

There were only two functions left for the matric students to attend before school life, other than final exams, came to a close. Senior school prize-giving was on a Wednesday night and the weekend before Jenna had a dramatic and very scary collapse at Daffy's house. It happened on Sunday night.

Stuart, myself and Kristi were sitting having dinner when Daffy's sister, Demi, called us in a total panic. "Gabi, Gabi, come quick!" she screamed down the phone. "Jenna can't breathe."

Usually a 10-minute drive minimum, we got from our house to Rondebosch in a matter of minutes. Stuart was driving and my hands were shaking so much I was unable to punch the numbers into my phone. Kristi took over. She phoned the ambulance, following my instructions to make sure they had a paramedic with them. While we were on our way, Daffy was on the bathroom floor with Jenna. It was terrifying, he said. Her chest was literally heaving trying to get oxygen and her face turned blue. He was shouting at her, "Don't leave me, don't leave me!" when he rememberd CPR. He had completed a first aid course just two weeks before. By the time we got there Jenna was starting to come round, but she looked blue and dazed and was struggling to breathe. Immediately I managed to overcome my panic and dropped to the floor next to her, talking calmly and helping her draw slower, deeper breaths and upping the oxygen flow on her machine. Three ambulances and a paramedic car arrived within minutes (Demi had also pushed the panic button).

Jen was stabilised and then rushed to UCT Academic Hospital in an ambulance where Prof. Wilcox was waiting for us. She spent two days being monitored and having further tests done. It was a terrible shock to all of us, especially Daffy and Demi, who had witnessed Jen's collapse. Kristi's ability to stay calm in such a scary crisis was remarkable. Jen slowly recovered. For me it felt like a punch in the stomach. A reminder of just how close to the edge we were all the time. I was running on adrenaline daily and sleeping at night with one ear open, constantly listening for the soothing sound of Thunder hissing and bubbling loudly in and out. If the rhythm changed just slightly, I was fully awake in seconds.

We'd had a big shock that had rocked everybody, not least Craig, Margo and the family in Australia. Tayla, Jen's beloved cousin, decided she was visiting us in December for Christmas. We were SO delighted and excited. It was good for all of us to have something special to look forward to.

Jen was still weak but she made it out of hospital in time for year-end prize-giving. The headmaster had implored us to make a special effort to attend. Her oxygen saturation levels and blood pressure were still very low, and she was fragile, but she was there – head held high, hair scraped back in a thick pony tail, dark purple-red lips and clear pale skin, sitting up straight and smiling. There is a certain way in which Jen's full bottom lip dropped ever so slightly lower on the right-hand side of her mouth when she smiled a smile of pure joy. It was a small and beautiful imperfection that I loved. She smiled so much that night, a wide, proud and uninhibited smile, as she was called up again and again to collect 10 different academic prizes. Watching her zoom back and forth on Chase, breathlessly collecting her prizes and smiling at everyone, made my heart squeeze with an excruciating combination of joy and pain. That night she won Top of the Grade subject prizes for English, drama, history and business. She was also awarded a certificate for academic excellence (awarded to pupils who had an over 85 per cent aggregate in all subjects non-stop for two years), the Bilingual Oral Proficiency Award (for English and Afrikaans), the Ethel Hill Cup for Spoken English, and the Jennifer Sale Drama Trophy for Outstanding Performance.

She came third overall in the entire grade and won the Schonborn Trophy for exceptional achievement in the face of extreme adversity. When her final award was announced, the entire hall of high school girls leapt up clapping, screaming and whooping while thundering their feet on the wooden floor. It was deafening and emotionally overwhelming. At the very same time every teacher spontaneously rose to their feet, many with tears in their eyes, applauding enthusiastically. It was an unforgettable moment filled with so many extreme and mixed emotions. How could Jen be facing what she was facing? It made no sense. It made no sense at all. I wanted to scream with the unfairness of it all and yet there was no place for my rage, for our rage. No place to put it and no way to deal with it. I wondered how Kristi must have felt, watching her sister win so many awards in these ridiculous circumstances. Did it put her under pressure? Did Kristi feel she had to live up to this? Was she allowed to envy or resent her sister in some small way? How could anyone? Stuart and I were bursting with pride and with pain. For Jen it felt like important affirmation. She appeared humble and grateful, and slightly embarrassed by the massive applause, but she was also delighted. Later she told me how stupid she felt; that on some level winning all those awards had affirmed for her that her physical illness had not taken away from her who she was. It had not taken her mind. I assured her that that was in no way stupid.

The next morning at the final matric breakfast, the girls and two senior librarians presented Jenna with a giant paper mobile that had been painstakingly constructed out of 1 000 handmade paper cranes. For weeks and weeks girls across all grades and ages had voluntarily popped into the library during their breaktimes to make paper cranes in secret to add to the mobile. It is a magnificent and fragile piece of art, made with love, that hangs as a testament to one of the many ways in which Jenna's journey brought people together.

Fighting back the tears, I looked around at this lifetime's worth of friends and families around us. This community had, sometimes literally, "carried" Jenna through her final two years of school during the degeneration of her health. Their support had been nothing short of exceptional. They had built ramps, bent rules, and given additional support in any way they could, recognising and allowing Jen's contribution, no matter what her physical challenges. And she had had an indelible impact on them. How would it be for her without this supportive community? How would it be for all of us? It was hard to leave the walls of the school, hard to venture forth ... into what? How would it feel when all these healthy young women strode off into their futures and we were left fighting alone for Jen's? Her school years had been Jen's happiest. There was a massive sense of loss and fear at leaving.

Meanwhile Daffy had been accepted to "stooge" for a year at a school in New Zealand the following year. He'd put his name down months and months before. He phoned Jen, excited that he'd been accepted, but distraught at the thought of leaving her. He didn't know what to do. Daffy was having doubts. Sad though Jen was at the prospect of him going, there was no way she was going to hold him back. "He must go, Mom," she said. "We will always love each other, but I can't hold him back. He must go."

She was right, of course, but as her mom, a large part of me wished that Daffy would stay. I just wanted Jen to be happy. I also knew she was very good at hiding her disappointment and she would never put herself first in that situation, but there must have been a big part of her that wanted to scream: "STAY! This is not fair, please stay." Jen would never have done that. Besides, it would mean showing and getting in touch with her vulnerability, which was tucked neatly away in order to cope with the enormity of her battle. This was going to be a tough hurdle for her.

I put my head down. I had to get on with the business of ensuring all the logistics were taken care of for the importation and initiation of Flolan. I had been receiving some rather scary emails, complete with order sets, dose tracking sheets and breakdowns of what we would be needing. One of them came from nurse practitioner Debra Zupancic, who would be accompanying Prof. Badesch on his trip from the States. It read:

I have been gathering information regarding daily needs for Flolan.

When our patients are started on IV therapy, they are discharged with what we call a "seven-day supply". This consists of what the patient needs to safely mix their medication on a daily basis. One question I have is: will you be supplied with what is known as a "needless system"? It is what is used here in the States as opposed to a system where needles are necessary to draw up the medication and diluent. Based on a "needless" system, it consists of the following:

For daily mixing:
Vials of Flolan 0.5 mg ("blue top" in the beginning)
Flolan 1.5 mg ("red top" as drug is titrated up)
2 vials of sterile diluent for Flolan
2 60 cc syringes
2 small syringes – typically 5 cc, but when first up titrating, it may be of benefit to have access to 3 cc as well
2 vial adapters (for the needless system; if not needless, this

would have to be needles)
1 set of tubing
14 alcohol pads
1 roll of tape
1 cassette
1 drape
1 tray to be used as a "clean area" to mix daily
Masks and gloves

The cassettes used are 100 cc. There is no need for 50 cc cassettes.

The CADD pumps run on 2 AA batteries. These batteries are to be changed every Monday (always) in both pumps; so, a minimum of four new batteries every week.
Dressing change kits are necessary as well.

A supply of small ice packs (I will find out the actual size). Ice-packs must be changed every six hours, or more frequent in hot climates. This is VERY important to keep the medication cold. NEVER freeze Flolan.

Dr Badesch and I will keep in touch.

I hope all is going well, and this helps.

It was more than just a little intimidating! I was starting to realise two things. Firstly, I was going to need some help; it was time to find a part-time nurse who could be trained with me when the medical team came to South Africa.

Secondly, we had to create a dedicated medical room in our home. Stu and I found the perfect spot: the girls' old playroom, which was a small narrow room conveniently situated directly opposite Jen's bedroom. We stripped it, painted it, laid hospital flooring and plumbed in a basin with "hands-free" taps, sanitising dispensers, plug points for charging batteries and pumps, a small medication fridge to keep meds and ice-packs cold, sterile storage space, an air-con, single bed and medicine mixing desk. It became wryly referred to as "the drug den". Stu looked after the small renovation while I handled the logistics of getting medical supplies into the country.

On the 8th of October my first parcel arrived, a large box containing two CADD Legacy pumps, pouches, cassettes and some tubing – an incredibly generous gift from St Vincent's Hospital in Sydney, supplies that were not needed by the hospital but would make an inordinate difference to us. It was a strange combination of both exciting and very daunting opening that first box of supplies. As more and more scary-looking medical equipment emerged from the box, I have to admit thinking: "OMG. What on earth have I done?" I unpacked it all onto the shelves we'd prepared and took a deep breath. I told Jen how excited I was that the first signs of help had arrived.

I called the Vineyard Hotel in Cape Town and The Parkwood Guest House in Johannesburg to make the necessary accommodation bookings for our medical team. Both were more than willing to help out and gave us their rock-bottom, absolutely no-profit, rate. Prof. Wilcox booked The Lung Institute in which to host the Cape Town symposium. Discovery Health had booked the international flights. It was confirmed. Prof. David Badesch and his nurse practitioner would arrive in Cape Town on Saturday, the 7th of December. He would meet the family and have dinner with us that evening. Sunday, the 8th, Prof. Wilcox and Prof. Badesch would meet to discuss and go over Jenna's case and Jen would have a full session with Prof. Badesch; and on Monday, the 9th, she would go into hospital to have the Hickman line procedure done. This was the insertion of a central line directly into her chest so that the medication, delivered by the CADD Legacy pump, could go straight into her right heart chamber on a permanent basis. The idea was to initiate treatment of the Flolan in the afternoon of Monday, the 9th and titrate for a few days. Then they would fly up to Johannesburg to meet Dr Williams, visit his clinic and hold a symposium there.

We were slowly putting all the pieces of the puzzle together, but where was the stock of Flolan? None of this could happen without the actual medication landing on South African soil. I was starting to get very anxious.

19th October 2013 (Gabi Lowe to Dr Gray at GlaxoSmithKline UK and Carl at Equity Pharma)

I am wondering where we stand with regard to getting Jenna's supplies of Flolan to SA? I sent this message with the SA Medical Control Council documentation to you 10 days ago.

Are we on track? Have you been speaking to each other and getting the documentation done to ship it here?

20th October 2013 (Dr Gray to Prof. Wilcox)

I believe we still need an official request for the amount of supplies you require, unless you have already sent this? Request just needs to state why you want to use Flolan for Jenna, and the amount you want to request (strengths plus number of vials for reconstitution) for initial shipment.

21st October 2013 (Prof. Wilcox to Dr Gray, GSK UK)

I am requesting Flolan for [Ms Jenna Lowe] as she has severe pulmonary hypertension due to chronic distal thromboembolic disease. She has been on Sildenafil 80 mg tds plus Bosentan 125 mg bd and Warfarin for some time, but despite this she continues to deteriorate. She has dropped from WHO Functional Class 3 to an advanced 3 bordering on 4. Hopefully she will respond to Flolan, which will then postpone sequential lung transplantation.

I understand you have received the South African Medicines Control Council approval for Flolan.

In the first instance she will require the following:

21 vials of the 0.5 mg Flolan plus 2 vials of diluent PLUS 200 vials of the 1.5 mg Flolan and 2 vials of diluent.

This should cover her for the first six months.

Dr Gray sent a large pile of forms for Jenna to sign (because she was 18, she needed to give consent) which I saw to that she immediately did.

22nd October 2013 (GSK SA to Gabi Lowe and Prof. Wilcox)

Thank you for your request to obtain FLOLAN for a patient. Apart from the logistics of obtaining Section 21 approval from the Medicines Control Council, also find attached the GSK application forms.

Once you have received MCC approval, please forward a copy of the relevant approval certificate to me together with a signed prescription so that we can finalise approval with our parent company to allow us to import stock. (I already have a copy of the MCC certificate; we need a signed prescription for the Flolan.)

1. *Once we have received notification of approval, we will order stock from our parent company; this may take some time to arrive, possibly up to a month.*
2. *Please note that it is your responsibility to comply with all the requirements of the Section 21 process, that is; once you have used FLOLAN.*
3. *The Section 21 application form must be completed for this specific patient and sent to GlaxoSmithKline. The six-month follow-up report must also be sent to the MCC and GlaxoSmithKline will require a copy for our records.*
4. *ALL adverse events (serious and non-serious) are to be reported to GlaxoSmithKline, as soon as possible after becoming aware of them.*
5. *In order that stock be replaced it will be necessary to repeat this process each time stock is used.*

The 23rd and 24th of October were spent sending all the required forms back and forth, figuring out a few fax issues as we went along. We were all starting to get jittery about the Flolan arriving in time for the beginning of December. Imagine if we had problems at customs? It was starting to get pretty nerve-wracking. I also then discovered that once the medication was shipped, it could not come directly to me. Once it had cleared customs it had to go to our responsible importing pharmacist, Equity Pharmaceuticals, before being sent to us.

Wow, there were so many things that could go wrong and there was no room for human error. I was starting to get a deeper understanding of what we had let ourselves in for.

That same week I had a business meeting with an old colleague from my magazine days. As fate would have it, her son was newly engaged to a young woman from England named Lizzie. Lizzie, it turned out, was a qualified nurse who was looking for part-time work in Cape Town. Lizzie was about to become an essential part of "Team Jenna".

A very brief update; Jenna Lowe
Blogpost 22nd October 2013
Jenna Lowe Trust Website

So, I haven't blogged in a while. Partly because I've been busy and tired, but honestly the chief reason is because there is much going on that I still need to wrap my head around. I guess it's hard to write about things that you haven't come to terms with yourself, so I will keep this post short and informative.

I start a new treatment in December, and I have asked my mom to write a news update regarding that. She will explain how it is going to work and so forth, but the short story is that I will be having a small procedure and from then onwards will have a tube under my clavicle which will give me a continuous infusion of drugs from a pump which I will carry with me.

My focus at the moment though is the NSC finals, which I write in a week or so; the first exam being on my 19th birthday. I am not completely freaked out because I know

I have time for studying, but I do certainly have hours of work ahead. Over the last two years I have missed a solid amount of school time and so have a bit more revision to do than most people. As the majority of my subjects are content-based, this shouldn't be an issue. My only concern is maths, as it is the one subject that really truly requires both teaching and practice. So, I shall be buried in practice exams for the foreseeable future.

There was a rather scary incident about two weeks ago. Without dwelling on the details, I collapsed briefly and spent two nights recovering in hospital until my blood pressure rose to an acceptable level. It is very unlikely to ever happen again and I'm glad it's over.

We had a beautiful valedictory and prize-giving, a wonderful send-off, shortly after that. Unfortunately, I was weak and dizzy for both ceremonies, having just been discharged from hospital, but the school and my friends took care of me, so it wasn't too hectic. It feels incredibly odd to be at this stage already. I don't think it has truly hit me yet that school really is over. At least I will still see teachers and friends as I will be returning there to write finals.

Wish me luck!
Jen

Between Valedictory and the matric exams, we managed to fit in another quick fundraiser. A live performance of *The Rocky Horror Show*, a brilliant musical, was wowing audiences in Cape Town at the Athol Fugard Theatre. The lead artist, Brendon, was a friend of a long-term friend of mine from my youth, Luanna. He, his cast, and the theatre, generously agreed to donate one of their performances to The Jenna Lowe Trust as a fundraiser. It was an incredible evening. Everyone dressed up in *Rocky Horror* kit and Cape Town's finest came out to support us. Tickets were sold out, for an ordinary old Tuesday night, within a week. All funds would go toward Jen's medical costs.

It felt surreal, but at the same time I was also finalising arrangements for Jenna's Matric Rage. Matric Rage is an institution in South Africa (as with many other countries in the world – in Australia they call their equivalent "Schoolies"). This is a one-week to 10-day period at the end of the year when rowdy matric students from all over the country converge on various coastal towns (for us this was Plettenberg Bay) in late November/ early December after their final exams, to celebrate. Basically, it's just one party after another. The organisers try and plan it down to the last detail to ensure that the teens are safe, but it is certainly not the ideal environment for someone who is not well. That being said, Jen was determined for us to find a way for her not to miss it. The idea terrified me, but all things considered, Stuart and I agreed to put our heads together and find a way. It was so difficult for Jen to be on the cusp of independence and yet have none at all. Her total lack of self-pity spurred us on daily to find ways for her to live each day to its fullest, regardless of the challenges. We needed to make each day count. As Jenna said in one of the interviews she gave: "I may have made sacrifices, but I have decided that the way I want to live is with positivity, with joy and love."

Jenna's journal
Sunday, 27th October
7:10 pm; home

I start finals tomorrow. It is hot and muggy, and I have a bad headache. I am filled with restless tension and nervous energy. It is also my 19th birthday tomorrow – so a bittersweet day all in all. But Daffy is coming to have supper with me. I love him so much. I don't know what I'm gonna do when he leaves for New Zealand at the end of Jan.

CHAPTER 26

Farewell, beautiful dragonfly

Jenna started her final matric exams on the 28th of October, her 19th birthday. Between studies, sleep, medication and blood tests, she would have massage therapy, psychotherapy, maths tutoring and probably a media interview or two on the phone plus a chat to Daffy ... not quite your regular routine for a matric student!

At the end of her first week of finals we had a special event planned, a Halloween evening for Natalie. Natalie wanted everyone to dress up and she asked Kristi to sing for her. The fabulous Greek evening still fresh in our minds, we donned our black capes, purchased some witch hats and arrived laden with sweet delicious goodies for the table. The entire cottage was dressed up with pumpkins, lights, bats, streamers and handmade décor. Kola, his friends, and Nattie, when she could, had been making décor for weeks. Ali, Les and Matt arrived laden with gifts and adventure stories from the outside world. Stuart amused us with fabulous stories. Kristi cuddled up to the dogs, played with her cousins and then serenaded us all. And Jen and Natalie were lovingly looked after in their dressing-gowns by our tight-knit family circle where dis-ease was held with ease. There was so much joy that night. I think of Natalie so often, but always at Halloween when I remember that night 10 short days before she passed away.

I'm not quite sure how this works, or even *if* it works, but I have to fess-up to a terrible weakness. Whenever Kristi is in dire need of comfort, we somehow end up with yet another furry animal in the family. When things are bad she fosters small puppies until we can find them a home, and when things are *really* bad, we end up adopting or visiting the pet shop ("just to look"), which inevitably ends up in a soft and fluffy acquisition of some description. This time it was two adorably cute, snow-white baby bunnies. Kristi had somehow convinced me it was a brilliant idea and she ended up telling Natalie all about them that night. Of course, Nattie then begged us to bring them for a visit.

As both girls were writing exams, it would have to wait for a short while, but we said we'd make a plan. Although we had known it for a while, it was now abundantly clear that Natalie was close to the end. Shirley was astoundingly calm.

The 10th of November was the weekend of Stu and my 23rd wedding anniversary. We asked Lizzie to sit with the girls that night so Stu and I could go out for dinner.

Jenna's journal
Sunday, 10th November
6:40 pm; home

I spent the last week cleaning, re-sorting and refreshing my room. It's so nice to have my space the way I want it. I'm totally on a mission to feel in control, though. I think that's what this is about, considering that my future is so uncertain. I have no idea what is going to happen after I start Flolan on the 9th of December. Last night Daffy came over. He noticed I was crying. He was so sweet and loving and he said he loved me. He's something special, that boy (heart).

Nothing in my life is certain. I have no idea how I am going to be next year – the same, better, at UCT or worse and having a transplant.

Three days later, Wednesday the 13th of November, was the day we decided that Kristi and I would take the bunnies with us to visit Natalie. Kristi did an extra-special clean of their cage, ensuring it was full of fresh straw and clean water. Kristi had an appointment in Hout Bay so we arranged that I would drop her off, go to visit Natalie with the bunnies and then pop out to collect Kristi once she was done and bring her to Natalie for a visit. Stu and Jenna would join us later and bring supper.

I arrived at the garden gate carrying the bunny cage. There was a secret way to open the door without having to ring the doorbell so that the sound didn't disturb Natalie every time a family member visited. As I closed it behind me, I could instantly feel something was wrong. I stood outside the front door, not wanting to go in. Shirl's best friend came out and fetched me into the lounge with her. I set the bunny cage down softly in the centre of the floor. Natalie was in her favourite cross-legged position on the couch, but slumped over slightly and her breathing was laboured. I could see she wasn't completely conscious. It was quiet and calm. She was surrounded by her nearest and dearest. Her mom, her dad, her brother, her carers and best friend, her godmother and the palliative care team. I joined the circle, making tea for those who needed it and talking quietly. An hour later I collected Kristi and made a call to Stuart to tell him that this was it … he would gather Jen up out of bed and come through right away.

Kristi was sitting on the floor at Natalie's feet and I was on the couch opposite her when she died. Stu and Jen had not arrived yet. Shirley gently took the oxygen mask off Natalie's face and kissed her, telling her what a brave and beautiful warrior girl she was. It was utterly devastating. Then Shirley laid Natalie's body gently down on her bed in her bedroom. That was where she was, lying peacefully, gone from this world, when Stuart, Jenna, Ali, Matt and Les arrived.

Jenna's journal
13th November 2013
8:30 pm, Natalie's bedroom

Natalie is gone. She passed away at about 6:45 pm this evening. I am at her house now. It is 8:30 pm. Daffy was at our house when I heard the news. I didn't cry at all until I walked into Natalie's room. She was laid out on the bed, under the duvet. There were flowers on her pillow. She is pale and at first, I was shocked, but the more you look, the more you see she still looks beautiful.

I think I am still in shock. It doesn't feel real. Our bunnies are here; it helps. We will have many, many rituals Shirl says. I'm glad. I'd like to have many ceremonies to commemorate Natalie.

Dad rubbed oil on Natalie's feet. It's so beautiful. He always rubs – rubbed – her feet. She would have wanted beautiful feet.

I found Natalie's death and Shirley's loss unbearable. In so many ways it held up a mirror that I didn't want to look in. Shirley had never left her daughter's side. She was there for her warrior princess through the most horrific of challenges. I vowed that, no matter what came our way, I would never leave Jenna's side either.

It took me a long time to mourn Natalie. At the time I was still "at war" for my own child. I was armoured and defended against Natalie's loss because I had to be in order to cope. Not any more. I miss you, baby girl. Wise, strong, funny, beautiful Nattie-Noo. I miss you so very much.

The week after Natalie died, Kristi wrote 11 Grade 9 exams: Afrikaans 1 and 2, mathematics 1 and 2, technology, economic management sciences, geography, history, English, biology and science; and she did her drama practical.

Jenna was in the middle of her final run of matric exams, the most important exams of her life so far. In the weeks after Natalie died she wrote life sciences 1 and 2, business studies, English paper

3, history paper 2, and her drama theory paper.

It felt insane, like a world gone mad.

In the months leading up to Natalie's death Shirley had commissioned the construction of a huge papier-maché dragonfly. It was being built in the garage of their home and while it was being crafted, she filled its belly with notes to Natalie from everyone who knew and loved her. It hung in the centre of the room at her memorial one week later, suspended like a magnanimous spirit watching over us.

Metaphorically, dragonflies symbolise change in perspective, self-realisation and awareness. Elegant and agile, they can fly upwards of 70 kilometres an hour, hover like a helicopter, fly backwards like a humming bird, fly straight up, or down or sideways. They navigate life's storms with confidence and ease, adaptability and lightness. The dragonfly was the perfect symbol for our Natalie.

Dragonflies also have a fairy-like quality about them and they visit us in meaningful ways. Perhaps one of the most significant lessons learned from the dragonfly lies in its short life-span. They live for only four to six months, reminding us to live life fully present and search out the gifts and beauty we encounter every day no matter what. Natalie taught me that more than many lifetimes could have done.

We held a memorable memorial for Natalie 10 days later at the Rotunda in Camps Bay. Hundreds and hundreds of people arrived from all over the world with decorated cupcakes in celebration of her life. Kristi sang for her cousin so bravely and Jen shared her deep respect for Natalie's courage, grace and humour. It was excruciating.

With broken hearts we gave Natalie an exceptional send-off … I hope she hovered for a while to witness it.

CHAPTER 27

Plett Rage

For 10 days of the year, at the end of November or beginning
of December, the little seaside town of Plettenberg Bay becomes
transformed. Residents and infrastructure alike are set up for it
and ready for the sprawling mass of matric school-leavers who
descend. Massive parties and music festivals, with the best of the
country's bands, are hosted every night, and beach parties in the
day. The safety of the kids is taken very seriously. Official transport
to supplement private cars is provided, and additional hospital and
nursing staff brought in, police and security on standby, and Red
Frog volunteers and life guards are on duty. It is the equivalent of
a large festival where matriculants are bussed in in their droves to
celebrate leaving school.

It is hardly a gentle environment for a very sick young girl, but
Jen was not prepared to miss it. Daffy would be there, Camilla,
all their friends – everyone she knew would be there. Jen couldn't
drink and she couldn't really party, but we set about finding a way
to make it work so she could participate somehow.

Months earlier friends of Jenna's had organised the shared
rental of a cottage. The cottage was inside The River Club, a
security estate conveniently situated in the middle of Plett. Jenna
would share with Camilla, Giulietta, Kirsten, Shaaz and Abi. Jen
was determined, totally determined, to go. It was tight but we

could fit it in just before the American doctors arrived. One of the edgy sides to Jen, which stood her in really good stead through her tough journey, was a steely will when she set her mind to something. She could be very persuasive – those debating skills of hers came in handy when she needed them.

Stu and I discussed the trip at length. It would have been so much easier to just say "no", but in the end we arrived at a compromise. We agreed that I would drive Jen up and stay a few blocks down the road with Ian and Jillie so I could be available 24/7 if she needed me. We agreed to keep the trip just short of a week and Jenna promised she would listen to what her body needed. She was due to start Flolan on Monday, the 9th of December. With only one more week of not being permanently attached to a pump, she wanted to make the most of it.

There was so much she couldn't participate in at Plett Rage and yet, even so, she had some fabulously fun and mad times just being in the house with the gang and hearing all their wild stories. She watched everyone get ready and called me whenever someone needed to be collected in the middle of the night because they "weren't doing well" (what goes on tour stays on tour). Jen managed to go out for a few hours once or twice in the week with Daffy and her girlfriends carrying her and shielding her; and Daffy came over to the cottage on the nights she simply didn't have the energy to push through.

I watched my phone every second, but it was also good to have a break and spend quality time with Ian and Jillie. I did some energising walks on the beach and caught up on much-needed sleep. Sometimes Jillie would guard the phone for me while I had an afternoon nap so that I could sleep without having to listen at the same time. Those were the deepest, most restful sleeps. Some days, when she needed a break from the hungover kids and the "student" house, I would collect Jen and whisk her off happily to Ian and Jillie's peaceful home for some hours of serenity and calm, when we would chat softly and revel in each other's company. Sometimes all the kids would go out and only Cami, always loyal, loving Cami, would stay with her.

Sometimes Jen and Daffy had the cottage all to themselves, which I knew they loved. Jen's illness meant I probably knew more than I should about her private romantic life. This was definitely not first choice for a 19-year-old, but it had to be like that. In order for me to keep her safe, I had to get my head around playing a role that was outside of the ordinary. I knew how in love Daffy and Jen were, and actually it gave me inordinate joy to know that she was able to have a healthy and happy sex life in spite of her illness. At least there wasn't yet another significant life experience she would have to miss out on. We talked about it sometimes; I needed to make sure she was okay.

"Are you sure you don't get too breathless, my love?" I asked her.

"It's fine, Mom," she said, "I really am fine … and careful, and happy. It makes me happy."

Stuart and I had been so nervous about Matric Rage, but actually it was the right choice to let her attend, even though there were moments when it made her really, really sad. She mourned the loss of the beach, partying all night, dancing, swimming or just staying up late; but even so she managed to have fun. Watching her manage those internal dynamics, witnessing her courage was hard. It made me deeply sad.

After a week Jen, myself and Daffy drove home safe and sound. It was becoming more intense between the two of them as the time got closer to Daffy leaving for New Zealand at the end of January. We talked openly about it in the car on the way home. How difficult it felt for them to leave each other, but how necessary it was for Daffy to go off and travel the world. Daffy teased Jen about her probing questions and ability to get him to talk about virtually anything. He still says he's never had more honest and meaningful conversations with anyone in his life. He is convinced that was why Jen could form such strong and deep relationships so quickly.

They shared lots of funny Plett stories with me and we giggled and listened to music, the two of them draped all over each other in the back seat. Only as we got close to Cape Town did we discuss how it felt to know that there were only three days left to go before Prof. Badesch and Debra Zupancic arrived from America. I can't pretend Jen was looking forward to it, but she was mentally and emotionally ready and prepared.

I was also ready ... ready and nervous and hopeful all at the same time. I was far more steeped in the medical details and aware of the potential dangers than anyone else. We arrived home delighted to see Kristi and Stu and share Rage stories around the dinner table before Jen collapsed in her bed and slept for two whole days.

CHAPTER 28

New hope: Flolan and the Americans

On Saturday, the 7th December we collected Prof. David Badesch and nurse practitioner Debra Zupancic from Cape Town International Airport. They had flown all this way, from Denver, Colorado, for no financial reward, to help us. Prof. Badesch insisted we call him David from the first time we met. Fit and elegant, quietly spoken, with the kindest blue eyes, David turned out to be an incredibly erudite, bright, experienced and yet humble and compassionate human being. He and Jen warmed to each other from the very start. Over dinner that Saturday night at our home he talked a lot to Jen, getting the measure of her, and us, in an informal setting. I could tell he appreciated Jen's intellect and her calm demeanour. In turn Jen asked him about his history, about Denver and his family, about other patients he'd treated, and how he had ended up specialising in pulmonary hypertension. There are whole centres of excellence dedicated just to PH all over the world and how they work was fascinating to us. David took care to interact with both the girls, asking Kristi about her singing, the song she and Jenna had written together, and how it had felt to launch it. She answered all his questions happily. It was such a relief to have him in our home. He must have been exhausted from the long flight, but he didn't show it and he wasn't in a hurry to get to his hotel. Simply meeting David and Debra made us feel confident that we'd made the right decision bringing them to South Africa. Stu and I were positively upbeat when we went to bed that night, filled with hope.

On Sunday, the 8th, the next day, after David had walked Table Mountain, Stuart drove him through to meet Prof. Wilcox to go through Jenna's entire case history in detail. Jen and I joined the meeting a few hours later so that David could do a thorough physical examination and ask us further questions. While they met, Debra, Nurse Lizzie and I met in the drug den to check our stock and the layout of the room. Debra was impressed. I had a large white bookcase stacked full of Flolan blue tops and red tops, hundreds of bottles of sterile diluent (the solution or carrier that the Flolan gets mixed into), syringes, masks, sterile gloves and drapes, a mixing desk, alcohol swabs, cartridges or cassettes, three pumps, lines and tubing, literally hundreds of AA batteries, and dressing change kits. There was a mini-fridge in the drug den to keep the medication cold and ice-packs in the freezer section. We were ready for lift-off.

"Mom." It was Sunday night and I was helping Jen get ready for bed and preparing a small suitcase for the hospital. "Thank you for doing all this." A pause. "Mom, do you think it will work?" Another pause. "Do you think the Flolan will work?"

I stopped packing and turned to face Jenna. Sitting down on the bed, I took her hand, and, looking into her eyes, I said, "I hope so, my darling, I hope so. What I think is that Prof. Badesch would not have come this far if he didn't think it would." She nodded.

"I know," she said. "You're right. I'm just nervous. What will it feel like to constantly be attached to a pump? Will it look okay? Do you think I'll be able to hide it with clothes?" I thought for a while.

"I imagine so," I said, "but you are so beautiful, Jen, that I don't suppose it matters either way. As long as you feel better, that's what matters. As long as your quality of life improves, my love, that's all we want." We hugged for a long time.

"Night, Mom," Jen said. "I don't know what I would do without you. I love you."

"Sleep tight, my love," I said. "I'll see you in the morning." I smiled and closed the door behind me, switching off her bedroom light as I went.

At 6 am on Monday, the 9th of December Stu, Kristi, myself and Nurse Lizzie drove Jen to the hospital. She would go into surgery first thing to have a central line and port inserted into her chest to carry the Flolan infusion directly to her right heart chamber. The surgery to have the port for the central line inserted really was not expected to be a big deal; it was simply Jen's weak condition and the same complication of blood thinners as before that made it riskier.

Jen's Angels – Karen, Carlie, Melissa – had arranged a one-hour meditation led by Sue Cooper to be held in the Bishops Prep School Hall so that we could all hold Jen in our thoughts and hearts while she was in surgery. The procedure had gone smoothly and by mid-morning Jenna was sitting up in bed in her blue hospital gown, a little red and sore at the site of the line, but otherwise nothing untoward at all. It was time to start the Flolan treatment.

Prof. Badesch and Nurse Debra had set up a mixing area in Jen's hospital ward. As the drug is so potent, they would start Jen on a minute dose that would slowly be titrated up over a period of five to six months. Her body would need to get used to the drug and adjust slowly to the side-effects. A big dose could be life-threatening; so could quick withdrawal. We – Stuart, myself, Lizzie and Kristi – gathered around Jenna and Nurse Debra as she started to mix the first dose. As she went about it she carefully explained exactly what she was doing and why. It was terrifying. It took a full hour and was absolutely precise every step of the way. What the hell had I got myself into? In just three days' time this responsibility would rest with me. Thank God my therapist had had the foresight to suggest I find someone like Lizzie. Sharing the load with Lizzie and Stu made it feel more manageable, but hell, this was really quite a challenge.

After Nurse Debra had mixed the first dose (the amount of

diluent always stayed the same but the amount of Flolan changed), she showed us how to attach the cartridge or cassette (now filled with medication) to a line, then prime the line, and then attach it to the CADD Legacy pump, cleaning everything with alcohol swabs three times, every step of the way. Once the line was successfully primed, meaning simply that you had to run some medication through it and ensure there were no air bubbles, the pump needed to be programmed to dispense precise quantities of medication at exactly the right speed over a continual 24-hour period. Oh my God. It was so complex. There was a chart to help work out the quantities of medication versus diluent required every day as we titrated the dose very slowly upwards. Once the pump was operational and set correctly, the primed line (from the newly mixed medication cartridge that was now connected to the pump) needed to be connected, after carefully cleaning the wound and wearing sterile gloves and mask, onto Jen's central line, which had just been inserted into the port in Jen's chest. This would then dispense the medication directly into her right heart chamber.

When the pump was successfully attached, without tightening the stat locks too much (we had that problem once and had to resort to sterilising a pair of pliers to get it open), then the pump needed to be switched on and hey presto! If an alarm went off, then you knew you had a problem – a big problem. Either there was air in the line, the pump had a problem or the central line did. But you had to hope like crazy that this never happened. In case of such an emergency, though, the protocol was always to mix a second cartridge of medication (tomorrow's dose), label it and put it in the fridge. That way tomorrow's dose was always available as a back-up, and a second pump was also always ready and waiting. There were just a few minutes to make a successful change-over every morning, as it should be done at much the same time every day.

Once everything was up and running, then you could insert the pump and its cartridge into a pouch that Jen wore over her shoulder with pockets in it for ice-packs on either side of the medication to keep it cold. It would run 24 hours a day, every day, for the rest of her life ... until transplant. "Oh," said Nurse Debra, "and don't forget to change the pump batteries every week on a Monday and the lines every Monday, Wednesday and Friday."

That was day one. Stuart and I caught each other's eye over our blue masks. He looked as terrified and wide-eyed as I felt. So did Nurse Lizzie. Wow. Jen, on the other hand, looked serene. From her vantage point she had quite literally been handed a lifeline. Nothing was going to dampen her spirit, and her faith in us was absolute.

Jen was staying in hospital for the first few days to be monitored and Prof. Badesch was worried that someone could unknowingly detach her pump, flush the central line or use it for other medication, especially since no one understood the potentially dire implications of such a mistake. In his humble, polite and professional way he called a meeting with the entire floor of nurses and doctors and gave everyone a thorough and informative briefing. Even so, it felt risky. It was so easy for something to go wrong in a hospital where so little was known about this medication. I made a large sign for above Jenna's bed – "DO NOT STOP PUMP" – but also made the decision that one of us (or Ali, Shirl or Granny) must stay at her side until she went to sleep to ensure her safety. I also insisted that either Stu or I were there during the change of shift at 7 pm every night. In fact, this became our go-to hospital protocol every time Jen was in hospital. Besides, if something went wrong with the pump there was no one else who knew what to do.

Bright and early the next morning we were back in the ward. I was about to mix the medication for the first time. After yesterday we'd told Kristi she most definitely didn't have to learn to mix. As capable as she was, Stu and I had realised after watching the intensity of it that no one aged 16 should have to carry that sort of responsibility. All eyes were on me that morning and my hands were shaking. I had the chart in front of me and Nurse Debra was patiently and kindly talking me through the steps. Nurse Lizzie was assisting, double-checking everything I did. We quickly worked out that, in a country where there was absolutely no back-up, it was advisable, easier and safer to mix the medication in pairs so that one person was totally focused on checking, labelling and recording the mixing. This became especially essential months and months later when we had become really proficient at it, because that is when it is easier to make fatal mistakes. We needed these important checks and balances in place. I took a few deep breaths, and, with encouragement, I carried on. There were beads of sweat dripping down between my breasts under my hospital gown and my glasses kept steaming up. It took me just over one-and-a-half hours to mix my first batch of medication.

Jeez. This was hectic. Part of me really wanted to run away, or just hide under my duvet. But a bigger part of me was going to do whatever it took.

Next I had to programme the pump correctly, disconnect yesterday's pump, and then quickly connect today's one before switching it on. This was a really scary part as there were time limits. Plus it needed to be 100% sterile, sterile gloves always worn (there is a specific way to put them on, holding your hands high up in the air in front of you so you can see them at all times, ensuring you don't touch anything ... yes, just like doctors do in movies pre-surgery). Cleaning of the site and sterilising all equipment nearby it are also crucial.

Flolan has a 3.5-minute half-life. It is fast-acting and only stays in your system for 3.5 minutes. That meant we had a maximum of three minutes to do a successful change-over. I was trying not to show how nervous I was, but Jen knew. She put her hand on my arm and looked deep into my eyes. "You can do this, Mom," she said softly, with her gentle smile. I took a deep breath and focused. Of course I could. I had learned how to push through my fear, a skill that was useful but would also catch up with me later. I'd done it ... my first successful mix. The first of 365.

Within the first day Jen experienced side-effects from the Flolan. Prof. Badesch told us it was a good thing; it meant the Flolan was having an impact. Mild flushing, bone pain, tummy ache, headaches and first-bite jaw pain. As the dose increased, so the first-bite jaw pain intensified. Jenna's head would literally jerk back with the pain of the first bite of food or sip of a drink. It was awful to watch. It reminded me of rats being brainwashed with electrical pulses to programme them not to eat – something we could ill afford as Jen was so thin already. Prof. Badesch explained that the jaw pain spikes as the saliva rushes into glands but it dissipates quite quickly. All the side-effects were damn unpleasant, but they were far outweighed by the potential benefits. Many patients are well and functional on Flolan for as many as 10 years before transplant becomes necessary. Jen was as stoic as ever. She was not going to complain. This was her chance at a longer life.

Although the first three days in hospital were nerve-wracking, they also went smoothly. We got to know David and Debra and showed them a bit of Cape Town while family, Daffy, Kristi, Camilla, Celeste and a virtual army of friends came to visit Jenna every day. They chatted animatedly and supported Jen, somehow managing to get the balance just right between empathising and bringing stories of the outside world. Time was drawing near for her cousin Tayla to visit from Australia and everyone was excited to see her. Group Facetime calls helped keep Jen's mind off all things medical.

On the night of Wednesday, the 11th, we held the Cape Town PH Symposium at The Lung Institute. I worried that it may not be full as it was already halfway through December and PH had pretty much been an ignored condition here in SA, but the lecture theatre filled up with GPs, pulmonologists, nurses, PH patients and their families, as well as other interested medical practitioners and some of the bigwigs from Discovery. The Discovery team had done a good job ensuring it was well attended. It was quite exciting, actually. Stu leant over and took my hand. "Look what you've done, my love," he said.

Prof. Wilcox introduced the session and Prof. David Badesch thanked the Lowe family for everything we had done for PH. It was an unexpected but heartwarming acknowledgement. Prof. Badesch gave a fascinating, accessible and yet extensive lecture on early diagnosis, care and potential treatments for PH. Afterwards there were interviews with medical journalists and the humbling opportunity to meet other patients and patients' families, who also thanked us profusely for bringing this significant global expertise to South Africa. Everyone sent well-wishes to Jen. Until then I don't think I had truly looked up and taken stock of what was now happening to the landscape of pulmonary hypertension in South Africa but Jen and our campaign were making a material difference to other patients at the coalface. I choked back the tears.

By Thursday morning it was time to take Jen home to her own bed and test the brand-new drug den. We had only one last day with Prof. Badesch and Nurse Debra before they were flying off to the Johannesburg symposium and Lizzie and I were anxious to make sure everything worked just as smoothly at home. It didn't. We had the wrong lines. Hundreds and hundreds of them. Terror flooded my stomach as Nurse Debra stood in the middle of the room and said slowly, "Mmm, we may have a problem here." Shit! What were we going to do? There was a mad flurry of phone calls to GlaxoSmithKline in Cape Town. Because no other patient in Africa was on Flolan, they didn't have the lines we needed listed on their system. It was potentially disastrous. Prof. Badesch and Nurse Debra came to the rescue by having 10 lines couriered immediately, at great cost, from UC Denver Colorado Hospital, but they would arrive earliest on Monday. We had to push out one line change and re-use what we already had. This was not ideal by any means, but it was a plan. I spent the rest of the week ensuring that the local branch of GSK got the products listed, locked and loaded onto their system and then shipped over from the UK. From now on I would be in a heightened and adrenalised state on almost a daily basis. I didn't exactly feel secure saying goodbye to Prof. Badesch and Nurse Debra, but it was time to let them go. Another PH symposium and a full day clinic for difficult cases was planned in Johannesburg, to be hosted by Dr Paul Williams at Milpark Hospital.

Lizzie and I realised then that we needed to create some vital documents and get a water-tight system going: a mixing protocol document, an Excel spreadsheet for titrating the medication (I happily donated this job to Stu – numbers are not my forté), labels with date, time, dose and who mixed the meds to place onto each of the cassettes as we mixed so there was no room for error, emergency protocols and phone numbers and ... very important ... a massive stock-sheet. We needed a stock-sheet for all the elements and to ensure we had a minimum of three months' worth of stock of everything at all times, to allow time for shipping from the UK and Australia.

Nurse Debra had also suggested I store small quantities of medication over the road with Mary and in Prof. Wilcox's office in case of fire or theft. Raffaella from Discovery Health was on the phone to me daily to see how Jen was doing and how she could help. She had a brilliant idea and put me in touch with a colleague of hers, Ian Dunt, who was a medical manufacturer and had a sterile factory. He very kindly came to visit and agreed to make up specific sterile dressing trays for us that we could use for line changes and wound care. It made a big difference to the smooth running of everything. My pharmacist Brent at Nu Pharmacy in Cavendish Square and his team were also incredibly supportive. Brent allowed me to order in bulk and was happy to make deliveries to the house.

It had all been so hectic and overwhelming that we decided at the last minute to put Kristi on a bus to Plett to spend a week with our friends Johnny and Carrie and their two gorgeous daughters. Kristi was delighted. I could see that she needed to get away from all this adrenalised tension and total focus on Jenna. Carrie's family was the perfect place for her to "land". They nurtured her and looked after her with love. They baked together, walked together and gave Kristi the gentle family environment that we were unable to that week as we were so totally and utterly focused on medical logistics.

I spent the week while Kristi was away finding my feet with the new regime. By the time she returned, Lizzie and I had all our documentation and systems up and running. Nurse Debra had insisted that the whole family do a CPR course and also that I find a paramedic who was willing to teach Lizzie, Stuart and me how to insert an intravenous line. If, just *if*, something did happen with one of the pumps or Jenna's central line, then we would need to know how to take the line from the cassette of medication and insert it as an IV directly into her veins. She could not be off the medication ever; it would be life threatening. I planned the CPR course for when Kristi was home. She was coming back the following Friday to be back in Cape Town for Tayla's eagerly awaited arrival.

Meanwhile Jen had recovered the fastest from the adrenaline onslaught, or maybe she was just protected from it. Either way her absolute determination to get back up on her feet and out of the front door wearing her portable oxygen, on Chase and sporting her pump over her shoulder was as admirable as it was heartbreaking. She was so brave. It was when she and Daffy were busy planning a dinner out that I realised the full implication. What if something went wrong with the pump and I wasn't there? It was from that day that I started carrying my mobile phone with me all the time, even to go to the toilet, and it was then that we realised I couldn't be more than four or five minutes away from Jen at all times.

"Right," Jen said, "so Salushi it is then, Daffy."

Salushi or The Vineyard became our favourite restaurants; both were just a few minutes down the road from our home. They always found a spot for Jen.

The lines arrived from the UK, Kristi arrived safely back from a restorative and happy week in Plett and Tayla arrived from Australia.

It was beyond exciting to have Tayla with us. Born Tayla Jane Badings, Tayla is Jen and Kristi's cousin, the eldest daughter of Craig and Margo. She is a joy. Masses of dark hair frame her face and her huge green eyes twinkle constantly with mischievousness. Tayla is boisterous, loud, loving, kind, affectionate, fun, straightforward and uncomplicated. What you see is what you get. And she had a distinctive Aussie accent. Her arrival marked a new energy in our house. We needed to start taking Flolan in our stride and get used to our new normal. We needed to welcome people back into our home and start entertaining again. We needed to remember that this was a time of hope. It was our first Christmas without Natalie, so we wanted to make it as gentle a time as possible for Shirl and Kola. Jen's current condition crystallised the need to try and stay in the present moment in the most visceral of ways. Tayla's presence helped us to do that, and it also helped Jen to deal with Daffy's impending departure. He was leaving in January.

Between mixing meds, regular visits to Pathcare and ordering medical stock, I was also collecting hay for the bunnies and flea tablets for the dogs, grocery shopping, paying bills and generally keeping a normal household. On Sunday, the 22nd of December I left Tayla and Kristi with Jen and rushed off to Cavendish Square in a flurry to do Christmas present shopping (I'd neglected that) and stock up on groceries. We were hosting Christmas Eve dinner for the extended family and any "Christmas orphans" we knew who had no family in Cape Town ... best I get my act together! I rushed up and down the food aisles, tossing gammons and turkeys and heaven knows what else into my trolley. I also bought a huge blow-up Father Christmas. The girls thought it was hilarious and slightly creepy; they nicknamed him "Paedo Santa". Stu bought a tree and we all had so much fun decorating it, Jen directing proceedings from her day-bed and Tayla and Kristi dancing around with tinsel and large doses of enthusiasm to the sounds of Mariah Carey's Christmas carols. There were silver and gold baubles and strings of fairy lights.

The smell of gammon and the sound of laughter filled the house. "You are going to make your crispy roast potatoes and broccoli with cheese sauce, hey, Mom?" Jen had left the chaos of the lounge and snuck up behind me in the kitchen, hugging me gently from behind and whispering in my ear. She looked happy and she was clearly hungry. This was a good sign. We smiled at each other and hugged for a long time. Hope, we had hope. I spent all night wrapping prezzies while Tayla and Kristi moved furniture and laid a gorgeous Christmas table, complete with fairy lights and angels. We were dressed in our finest and ready for our guests, ice-cold bubbles in hand, by 6 pm on Christmas Eve.

There was so much pain and heartache at the loss of Natalie and yet there was intense joy in being with each other, in the present moment. We were discovering that pain and joy are different sides of the very same coin. The deeper the pain, the greater and more intense the joy when you find it.

CHAPTER 29

Shooting the lights out

Once or twice Jen forgot to strap her pump over her shoulder and walked away from it until it tugged painfully on her central line. But she only had to do that a few times before it started to become automatic. Her brain adjusted quickly, and so did she. A few days after Christmas she asked me to take her to Cavendish Square for some mommy-daughter shopping time.

It's extraordinary how the public at large respond to disability. It would enrage me to watch Jen having to cope with their fear as well as her own. The impact of Jen and Chase evoked different emotions in different people and it always seemed that, somehow, it was we who ended up managing these emotions for them. Jen hated it when strangers stared at her – and there were many who did, unashamedly – but she had developed a brilliant coping strategy. I watched her do it many times in Cavendish that day. She would disarm them with a huge smile and a bright "Hello". Some would smile back instantly and say "Hello" and walk on; others would flush with embarrassment at being caught out. Then there were people who were just downright inappropriate.

The classic was a woman in Woolworths. We were in the shoe

section trying on shoes … Jen did love an elegant high-heeled shoe … when Jen stood up from Chase to select a pair from the top shelf. The woman, who had been staring at us unabashed for many minutes, couldn't help herself. "Well, what are you doing on that thing if you don't need it?" she said loudly. I was flabbergasted. Somewhere in this person's pea brain, she believed that you should only use a mobility scooter if your legs didn't work at all or maybe if you didn't have any. My incredulity must have flashed across my face. "Smile and wave," Jen muttered softly to me under her breath. She was more practised at this than me. "Smile and wave, Mom, just like you taught me." We did, but that night the encounter kept going around and around in my head. Every day other people's ignorance and fear were being thrown at Jen. They found her condition confronting. I wanted to shake that woman, but I also knew it wasn't her fault. Western society, school, our parents don't equip us to deal with real life. We fear death. We fear illness and we fear, really fear, disability. It felt as if every mother out there was looking at me and thinking: "Thank God that's not my child."

Well, you know what? Thank God she *was* mine. It was an absolute privilege to be the mother of this incredible young human being. I lay in bed wondering where, in the myriad parenting books that I'd read, did they tell you that you cannot take away your children's pain. Where did you learn that? And why not? What was the point of loving so deeply, if you couldn't protect them? It felt so unfair and cruel. The layers of pain, challenge and complexity that my children had to bear. All I could do was bear it with them. I also thought about what it might feel like for my mother, for her as a parent to watch what I was going through, to watch my extreme pain. The reality is that we don't get to protect each other. Life will come at you and your kids in so many difficult and different ways no matter what you do. You don't get to control it. What you can do is teach them how to deal with it, how to live a life that matters *in spite of* pain and loss.

Jenna's journal
3rd January 2014
2 am; my room

Goodbye and good riddance 2013.

I have one month left with Daniel. Him leaving is going to break my heart. He'll be gone for 10 months. We discussed what we should do and although we haven't officially decided, I think we both know we are going to have to break up.

I want to smash stuff. I have zero opportunity to channel anger and frustration and no aspect of my life where I can be even slightly spontaneous or reckless. No exercise, no drinking, no wild partying … I can't do anything without careful logistical planning. It's a fucking nightmare.

Most of the time I accept it, and as each loss is a gradual increase on the previous losses, I tolerate it. But, at moments like this, late at night, I compare my life with those around me and think of what could have been and what's missing.

Everyone, including Tayla, has gone out after we hosted pre-drinks here and I am alone in bed at home. Stone cold sober and frustrated at myself for reading until 2 am and not sleeping.

I hate this tube. The worst thing right now is the restriction of bathing or showering. How hard it is to wash my hair.

There is also all the stuff about how easily I could die if anything goes wrong with this tube. But perhaps I will write about that another night. It's already 2:30 am and I need to sleep.

I have made peace with my heart and soul: please, if there is any good or God in this universe, may I now have my health back.

Jen was battling. Stuart and I talked about getting out of Cape Town. This was the first year we hadn't been to Plett in December because we hadn't known what kind of state we would all be in. Luckily Stu's aunt owns a home in Plett (not normally used by anyone except immediate family) and she very kindly offered it to us. The girls really wanted to go. They were yearning for the familiar faces and spaces of our beloved Plett and were desperate to share it with Tayla. Daffy wanted to spend every waking moment with his "Wen" (Daffy's nickname for Jen) before leaving for New Zealand, so he was dead keen on joining us. It would take a lot of meticulous organising, I knew that, but I was sure it was do-able. Patients in other parts of the world had been on Flolan for years; they certainly couldn't be confined to home all the time.

"Okay, Stu," I said, "if Lizzie can join us then let's do it."

I checked that we could use the pathology lab, Pathcare, at the Medi-Clinic in Plett for Jen's blood tests and of course Ian and Jillie were there and I had their local doctor on speed dial. By now we were able to self-dose the Warfarin based on the test results and if we needed to check anything urgently, Prof. Badesch always answered his phone on the second or third ring, no matter what time of the day or night it was in the US.

After hooking Jen up to her fresh meds on the morning of the 6th of January 2014 we set off for Plett, in two cars, packed to the hilt with medication and equipment. Lizzie wasn't going to be able to stay the entire time so she followed us in a third car. At least she would be with us for the first four days to help me get everything set up and sorted. We turned Auntie Aline's bedroom into a mixing den and sterilised the desk there. Then we sterilised a separate shelf in the fridge for Jen's medication. We identified a charging station to be dedicated to all the equipment. We were good to go.

I'm so glad we persisted in doing that trip. I think it was one of the happiest weeks of Jen's year. Tonnes of friends were still in Plett and the house was awash with youngsters visiting. It didn't matter that she couldn't swim (or bathe … her central line and site were not allowed to be immersed in water, ever) or hike or any of the other activities. There was hope in the air and Tayla's upbeat energy was infectious. We also had a close friend of Daffy's, James, come to join us for a few days.

The day after we arrived, Tayla and Kristi went to the beach to swim while Jen, Daffy and James sat anxiously on the couch together waiting for the National Senior Certificate final matric results from 2013 to be released. As the first "ping" sounded they all scrolled through the results website on their mobile phones. Daffy and James whooped with delight. They had both done really well, well enough to get into university, which was what mattered the most, and James had quite a few really good firsts as well. Daffy wanted one or two re-marks but, on the whole, they were pretty thrilled. Jen was sitting quietly.

"And you, Jen?" I asked when the noise died down.

"I did okay," she said timidly.

"Okay?" I asked slowly, my heart speeding up. Shit, was she disappointed? Was it possible that she didn't pass some of her subjects? Surely not? It would be the first time ever that she had failed anything. She did write in the most heinous circumstances, though. I tried to keep my voice even. "So tell us what you got, Jen?" I said. Pause.

"Um ..." Jen looked a tad embarrassed. "I got 91%, 92%, 93%, 94%, 95%, 96% and 97%," she said. And then her face broke into a big grin.

"That'll do!" said Stu, striding into the room with a massive beam on his face "Drinks on us at The Lookout Deck!"

The boys were both gobsmacked, jaws wide open "Whaaat!? Oh my God, Jen! You did 'okay'? What are you talking about? That's awesome, just unbelievable!"

I felt bad for the boys that their exciting results had paled into insignificance, but I was also so delighted for Jen.

As always, Stu led the charge to celebrate. "Time for a keg of beer, boys!" he said and everybody scrambled to their feet. We grabbed our stuff, messaged Kristi and Tayla, and made our way down to the deck for a "pint o' prawns" and a round of drinks.

The next day an invitation from Helen Zille, the Premier of the Western Cape, arrived in Jenna's inbox, inviting us to attend a ceremony at her official residence, Leeuwenhof. Jen was about to be recognised as one of the top 30 matriculants in the country. It was extraordinary really, in any circumstances, never mind Jen's.

Filled with hope for a much more stable year, a week later we drove home. For a moment in time life felt so good.

Part 4

CHAPTER 30

Painful new beginnings

Leeuwenhof is a grand old building, the backdrop to its sweeping lawns the magnificent Table Mountain. For the awards ceremony a huge white marquee had been set up on the lawn. It was a scorcher of a day, about 36°C, and even hotter in the marquee, where we sat on white plastic chairs among hundreds of students from Western Cape schools, all there to be honoured for their matric results, with their families.

The ceremony was not easy for us. Jen sat between Stu and me and as proceedings got under way and continued, and the heat worsened, Jen became more and more breathless. I was extremely worried. I was convinced she was about to have another collapse. I caught Stuart's eye and motioned to him to get some cold water. Helen Zille was in the middle of her speech, but my tiny hand movement must have caught her eye. She walked to the front of the stage and motioned to Stuart to come and take her own ice-cold, unused water bottle. We took it gratefully and the ceremony carried on. And on. It got hotter and hotter. Jen was getting worse, but she didn't want any negative attention. I wanted to take her home, but she refused. She was going to go up and collect that award no matter what. The Premier was keeping a quiet and concerned eye on the situation and just as I decided that we were now in trouble and I was going to get Jen home regardless of what she wanted, she motioned to the paramedic who was on standby. We got Jen out of the tent, under the shade of a tree and onto the paramedic's full-strength oxygen tank. Her portable machine was not effective enough in this kind of heat. The paramedic checked her blood pressure and vitals and put her into the vehicle. She managed to recover enough to go up on Chase and receive her award, but as soon as that was done we raced home. It wasn't fun.

Once Jenna was safely in bed in her air-conditioned bedroom, and stable and feeling better, I left her in Stu's capable hands and went down to Claremont with Kristi. The mundane side of life didn't go away. The first term of the new school year was starting the following day. Kristi needed school shoes and we hadn't yet done her stationery shopping ...

Kristi was not looking forward to Grade 10. It was going to be very different for her with Jen and her friends no longer on campus. She was nervous, recalling some of the negative memories from the previous year. There was also the fact that Jen had cast a very large shadow and her imprint was all over the school campus, which, I knew, would impact Kristi in multiple ways. Where was the space for her to just be her? Herschel is a truly excellent school, one of the best in the country, but also highly academic and relatively traditional. It suited Jen perfectly but wasn't necessarily the best fit for Kristi. She was, and still is, a good student, who got solid 70% and 80% for everything, but these awesome results could lose their gloss next to Jen's ridiculous academic achievements. So awful and grossly unfair. Her maths and Afrikaans results had suffered a bit with Natalie's death and Jen's illness and we agreed that extra maths and Afrikaans lessons outside of school would be helpful. Kristi agreed to try and find her feet again at Herschel but if she was really unhappy, we would look at moving her. That was the plan. She was going to try.

Within a few days of receiving her matric results Jen had received notification from UCT that she had official acceptance. We started gearing up to ensure that she was prepared and would be safe in her new environment. We invited Zelda and Chaeli from The Chaeli Campaign to come and have coffee with us. Chaeli, who had already been on campus for a year, shared all her hints and tips with Jen about navigating this large, rather daunting campus in a wheelchair. It made a huge difference to Jen. She was anxious about how she was going to cope, as were we all. Truthfully, I was terrified. What I really wanted was to keep Jen safe at home with me. But Stu and Jen would have none of it. That would be like rolling over and giving up. I knew they were right.

Stuart was working hard. Back in May he had started a business – WhyFive. Essentially it was a marketing consultancy, but one with a difference: it owned an innovative research and insights product called BrandMapp. BrandMapp is a large online national research study of the middle- and top-end consumers in South Africa. It helps marketers and business owners to profile their customers, and better understand their behaviour, product usage and decisions across thousands of brands and media types.

Stu was thrust back into working hard and I swiftly turned my attention to getting all the new MCC forms and paperwork filled in, checking on all our medication stocks, and updating medical data sheets. Plans were also hotting up for our Valentine's in the Valley fundraiser, which was scheduled for the 14th of February. Clearly there was lots to be done.

By now Jen had a really good, solid relationship with her therapist. I was so grateful that she did, because she was going to need it. She was about to say goodbye to both Daffy and Tayla.

Tayla and Kristi planned a pool party for Sunday, the 26th to celebrate Australia Day. It was also one of Daffy's last days in South Africa. During the day Camilla, Celeste and Kristi snuck off to set up a romantic table for Jen and Daffy under the umbrella, complete with candles, tea, cookies, fudge and a beer for Daffy. They also had a little chalk board sign made with a heart on it saying, "Daffy & Jenna". Oh my God – it was painful watching those two say goodbye.

A few days later Daffy's family, James, and our family took

Daffy to the airport to put him on the plane to New Zealand. He hugged each one of us tightly and said goodbye, giving Jen a long lingering kiss and whispering to James, "Look after my girl." Daffy's mom Karen and I wept openly as he walked through the doors. Jen was silent. My heart broke for her.

Stuart and I had recently reconnected with friends Gavin and Denise Levy. Gavin and Stu were good buddies from their water-skiing days when they were students; Stu and I had been at their wedding 27 years before. For no particular reason, we lost touch with them a few years after we were married, but they came back into our lives, in a significant and meaningful way, when Natalie was so ill.

Shortly after Natalie died, they invited all the Lowe family siblings and their families to spend a healing weekend with them up the west coast, where they owned a collection of beach houses as one of their businesses. Exquisitely beautiful, Denise has strawberry blonde hair, brown doe-like eyes and a light that shines from within. She is a highly talented and successful businesswoman and cook, and her warmth and generosity of spirit drew me to her during these, the most vulnerable years of my life. The two of us became very close friends. Gavin can probably best be described as a force of nature. Driven, focused, productive and highly successful, he is also loyal, committed and one of the most authentically generous and loving people I know. They have two wonderful children – a daughter, Kia, and her younger brother Josh.

Gavin has always given back to the community, and for many years he had been volunteering for the incredible Reach For A Dream Foundation. Reach For A Dream had been doing important work for 30 years, fulfilling the dreams of children with life-threatening illnesses, and Gavin was a member of their board. Jen had been on their radar since early 2013, but we were not ready to accept such a gift. Now it felt like time.

On the 30th of January 2014 the kind Heidi Rowley, who headed up the Western Cape division of the foundation, came to our home to see Jen. She spent many hours talking to us, drinking tea and trying to establish what Jen's one wish, one dream, would be if she had a magic wand. Something magical that would bring happiness, but which was also do-able.

Jen was so eager to travel and see more of the world, but of course long-haul flights were now out of the question. Then she had an idea, a very clever one … a local cruise liner! A luxurious floating palace perfectly equipped to deal with mobility devices and oxygen machines, complete with lifts, glorious pool decks, discos, casinos and restaurants. It was genius. Heidi was delighted and left promising as much as she could to try and make this happen, fast.

"Shit, Mom," Jen said, turning to me once Heidi had left. "I'm one of those children. I'm a 'reach for a dream' child."

Yes, Jen was one of those children who people fight to bring joy to because of the outrageous challenges they face. It was still so hard to believe.

Jenna's close friend Alex – her matric dance date – had been living in London with his family, but around this time he moved back to Cape Town. He was later to tell me that he couldn't stand being away from Jenna when she was in so much trouble. I think I'd always known he had feelings for Jen outside of friendship, but he never said so at the time. He visited her every day. As did James.

On the 1st of February I attended a "local parents" orientation lecture in Jameson Hall at UCT. It made me even more anxious about Jen coping on this massive, rather impersonal campus. Would she really be safe up here? What if something went wrong with the pump up on campus? Who was going to look out for her in among 40 000 students? A lot of her friends would be in the business studies and economics section whereas Jen had chosen to study philosophy and humanities, which had huge numbers of students. Would she be okay?

On my way home I had to pop past Groote Schuur Hospital to drop off my latest Medical Control Council paperwork and the pharmacy to collect medical supplies. I was so distracted that I drove straight past on the highway all the way into town before realising. I concentrated on my breathing to calm my adrenaline. "Eyes on the road, Gabs, eyes on the road," I whispered to myself, forcing myself to stay in the moment.

Since the inception of Flolan I'd noticed how adrenalised my body was. It was in a constant state of fight, fright or flight. The smallest of noises could make me jump right out of my skin. My neck and shoulders were constantly sore and hard as rock and I got diarrhoea easily. I was in a permanently heightened emotional state but trying not to show it. It was hard to access a sense of calm or serenity. Everything other than Jen's health paled into insignificance. I had a sense of time running out. Other than Kristi and Stu, even my most important relationships such as my parents and my closest friends, potential lifelines, had become secondary. Jen's survival was everything. It became my world.

Every morning was the same. I would wake up and instantly my heart was in my mouth. I would go through to the kitchen and gulp down a quick cup of coffee before making my way to the drug den to prepare for Nurse Lizzie, who would let herself in at 7 or 7:30 am so we could start our 1.5-hour morning ritual of measuring, mixing and recording. Then we would wake Jen to hook her up to her new meds. We would triple-check our stock and maths and then measure and record her vital signs. Once we were done Jenna would roll over and go back to sleep until at least 11 am. It was relentless.

I was also trying to wind down Upfront Marketing. I would really miss my business, and Jean, but I no longer had the time or space for it.

Jen was starting "O Week" (Orientation Week) in a few days and Tayla had extended her return ticket by a few weeks so that she could be with her for the first two days of it. I was so grateful. At the end of O Week we put Tayla on the plane back to Sydney. It felt like yet another blow for the girls, who were devastated to let her go, and the house felt very quiet without her.

The next week was Registration Week at UCT and lectures were due to start midway through February, on the 17th. My mind was churning with anxiety. How was Jenna even going to wake up on time, never mind anything else? One day at a time, I told myself, one day at a time.

The Valentine's picnic fundraiser that we'd been planning for three months took place in the magnificent valley of the Constantia Glen wine farm on Friday, the 14th of February with the indispensable help of "Jen's Angels" and friends who had formed a group called The Three Oaks. There was magic in the air that night. The immaculate lawns were scattered with red embroidered picnic blankets and the full moon rose behind the vineyard and Constantia mountains as Kristi's hauntingly beautiful voice floated across the valley. Solar glass jars lit the way for the roughly 400 guests to a groaning feast table and an abundance of delicious wines. Karen, Carlie and Melissa had worked for days decorating the pavilion, with Mary's help. And my old band, Seven, played some fabulous rock 'n roll standards as the night grew darker. It was an exceptional night, one that people still remember fondly. I spoke, Jen spoke, and the auction was so successful it covered another next six to eight months' worth of meds.

The next day Nurse Lizzie moved in with Jen and Kristi for one night because Stu and I, exhausted as we were, were driving six hours up to Plett to be at Jillie's 50th birthday celebration. It was hard core, but this was one party we just couldn't miss. We came back on Sunday morning, taking turns to drive. Jen was starting UCT and rehabilitative physiotherapy on the Monday. I felt like I could do with a week's sleep.

By the time Jen started on campus that Monday, Lizzie and I had put quite a few emergency protocols in place. Jenna had a sign on her pump in her bag that read DO NOT STOP PUMP. It was also populated with all our emergency numbers plus the paramedics'. She had a spare IV kit, which she carried with her, extra ice-packs at all times, additional batteries for Oxy-Jen, and always a fully charged mobile phone. I had a briefing with the entire Disability Department, as well as campus security and health services. Jenna had worked out her "best routes" with Tayla during O Week. We would have to wake up extra early to mix and hook up her meds, but she seemed pretty determined.

I don't think Jen was prepared for what she experienced on campus. She felt alone, very alone. Students would rush past her to lectures busy on their phones or in groups while she had to navigate alternative back routes on Chase, which often made her late for the start of a lecture. Many of the lecture halls slope downwards with many stairs, so her only option was to stay at the back of the lecture hall. This meant she wasn't able to find, or join, any of her friends and she was at a disadvantage for making new ones. She discovered that humanities lectures are attended by hundreds of students, which brings with it a mentality of anonymity. No one made an effort, perhaps because they assumed others had or would. No one took the lead to be inclusive. Maybe they just didn't know how or maybe they didn't want to single her out in case it was "politically incorrect". The mere fact that her eye-line was a different height from everyone else's, Jen said, meant she felt invisible and yet obvious at the same time. Wow. The things we take for granted.

Nevertheless Jenna enjoyed the content of her subjects and she found the tutorials easier because of the smaller groups of students and the fact that everyone sat at tables. But the bottom-line was that emotionally it was tough. Being surrounded by thousands of healthy young students, with tonnes of energy, and in the prime of their lives, highlighted just how much she wasn't able to do. There was nowhere to hide from that, and Jen began to feel more and more isolated. And she missed Daffy. Even though they spoke to each other just about every day, it wasn't the same as having him in Cape Town. She missed him. She was heartsore, Jen was so heartsore. Her friends, Cami, Celeste and Giulz visited often, as did James and Alex; but they had full and exciting lives in stark contrast with Jen's.

Kristi, too, was finding life hard and feeling alone. She had become so preoccupied with Jen over the past two years that she had neglected her own friends and now she found herself on the back foot with friendships at school. Also, with Jen no longer visible to them on a daily basis, it was easy for her mates to forget what Kristi was dealing with. It wasn't their role to make a safe space for her; they were simply getting on with their lives and being normal teenagers. I imagine Kristi had a role to play in all of the difficult dynamics as well. Her defences were up, and her mood was down. Plus, the academic pressure was mounting due to her falling behind in maths and Afrikaans. It was becoming a struggle to get her up and out of bed to school every day. Only horse-riding and her singing lessons with Kim would turn a dim light on inside.

Stu and I were stressed too. He was trying to find his way with a brand-new business and partnerships in the midst of huge emotional strain and financial pressure. There were now three people working full time in the office at our home and he had one major partnership with two people experienced in research. He had a lot to carry. Our grief, and Shirley's grief, weighed heavily on him too. He felt an enormous weight of responsibility keeping the ship on course. I was in my last month of earning from Upfront Marketing and although I hid my extreme levels of anxiety from everyone else, I couldn't hide them from Stu or my close girlfriends. Nursing Jen had become my life and it was taking its toll on me both physically and emotionally. Added to that was the fact that both my girls were battling depression and deep sadness. We were all missing Natalie desperately. For Stu and me, specifically, watching Shirley's pain was excruciating.

We increased our meditation/therapy sessions with Sue Cooper to every second week. Nothing could take away any of this brutal reality, but we needed healthy coping skills and a safe space in our home where we could really talk about what was going on for us individually. All the usual kids were out and about getting on with their first year of varsity, attending party after party and making friends. I asked Cami to let her girlfriends know that Jen needed them. Without Jen knowing, Cami sorted out a "roster" of visitors. Jen's friends started rallying and visiting more regularly.

At first, she told no one how tough it was for her up on campus, but slowly she let Cami in. Quite a few of her guy friends, including James, were visiting regularly. James, with his beautiful open face and huge green eyes, was a delight, and really good company. Intelligent and interested in the world around him, he was one of those rare young men who found it easy to have meaningful conversation and didn't shy away from the truth. He would seek me out whenever he visited to check in and find out what was really going on. How Jen really was. Jen was very private and avoided complaining at all costs. For her, pity was anathema. When friends visited, she would find the strength within herself to be upbeat and chatty, drinking in their company and their stories of the outside world without envy, self-pity, or a trace of victimhood. Only when they were gone would she weep into her pillow and admit to me how desperately she just wanted to be well. To be "normal".

The weeks of the first term were rolling by and we were doing the best we could. Kristi was reluctantly attending school and putting in some effort with her extra lessons. Her friendship with Kia, Gavin and Denise's daughter, had blossomed and they now spent every weekend together, which was a good distraction and a great help. Kia would move in with us on a Friday and leave on Sunday night. They partied a lot together, had friends over and also spent many hours chatting to Jen, sitting on the edge of her bed telling her stories of who liked whom and who was "hooking up" with whom. The weekend partying didn't worry me. The fact that Kristi spent all her time with Kia on the weekends probably made it harder to cement her friendships at school, but it felt so important for her to be happy and not spend all her time at home.

In the depth of the night Stuart and I talked constantly about whether the Flolan was actually making a difference or not. We were so desperate for it to be the miracle that she needed, it was hard to be objective. Jen's side-effects were pretty hectic, which could also confuse the picture, but for a while her breathing and extreme fatigue seemed to be improving. Nurse Lizzie and I were consistent in tracking her vitals and all her symptoms every day and keeping stringent records. Besides the continuous Flolan, Jenna swallowed handfuls of pills three times a day and forced herself to eat to try and "bulk up" (she weighed about 48 kg). Every now and then we would all have a spring in our step because Jenna would have a really good day. But when you looked at it on paper, there was no evidence of substantial improvement.

I worked hard to shake the impending sense of doom. I talked endlessly with Glynis about the dynamics in our household, trying to figure it out and make sense of it all. She always knew exactly what to say and what not to say. I felt totally unjudged when I spoke to her, no matter what I said or felt. Oftentimes I find that people listen to respond, but she listened to understand. Glynis understood that listening is an act of love, and I needed that so much. Nothing in my life felt simple any more. I was managing Jenna and Kristi's fears, our fear and all the accompanying layers of complexity on a minute-by-minute basis.

Every now and then Jen would attempt to go out with her friends for a short while and be a normal teenager, with her Flolan pump, Oxy-Jen and all. They would move around her in a circle and carry her when needed. Her friends were her warriors, her protectors, fiercely loyal. One night, after pre-drinks at ours, I dropped a group of them in Claremont as Jen was joining them at a nightclub for a short while. It wasn't long before I got a call to fetch them. When I did I could see Jen was very upset; she was shaking with anger and humiliation. She explained that after a bit of a wait, when they reached the front of the queue, the bouncer took one look at her wearing Oxy-Jen and announced loudly: "You can't come in here with that thing on your face." She was both embarrassed and outraged. She tried to reason with him and explain what it was but he wouldn't budge. In front of the small crowd that had now gathered, he told her flatly that she had to leave. Her friends were so angry, but powerless. The angrier they got the more this bouncer wouldn't budge. It was mortifying for Jen. I bundled them up and took them home, resisting the urge to go in there and take him out at the knees myself. I wrote the club an email the next day, but I never heard back from them.

Halfway through March, Kristi was getting ready to go on Step Out. Remember Step Out? The Grade 10 hike that had been so hideous for Jen. Now it was Kristi's turn. She was fit and healthy so rationally there was no reason to be nervous, but fear is not rational. Watching her pack and get ready to leave was triggering for me. I knew I wouldn't hear from her for six days and I was dreading it.

On the last day of Step Out I received a phone call.

"Mrs Lowe?" It was a teacher's voice and immediately my

heartbeat quickened. "Everything is all right, but Kristi has had a fall." My stomach lurched.

"What! Is she okay? What happened? Let me talk to her."

"She will be fine, but she fell off her bicycle on our last downhill off the mountain and has suffered a mild concussion. We're getting on the bus now to come home and I will sit with her the whole way home and keep her awake. But I think you should make an appointment with your doctor and take her for a check-up as soon as we get back. We arrive in Cape Town in about three hours."

By the time I'd collected Jen from varsity, taken her to therapy and physiotherapy and put her back in bed, the teacher called to say they were 10 minutes away. I raced down to the school grounds to fetch her. It was so good to see her. I hugged her gently, grabbed all her stuff and took her straight to our GP. Kristi purposefully downplayed everything so as not to worry me, but she didn't look great. She looked woozy. Our GP did a thorough examination and said I could take her home to rest, give her plenty of fluid to drink and observe her closely. Jen was so pleased to see her sister. We put ice on Kristi's large bump, gave her paracetamol for the headache and put her into bed. She was allowed to sleep, but not for longer than a few hours at a time so that I could check her pupils and her ability to talk normally. I set my alarm to check on her every two hours through the night and by the next morning I was relieved to see she seemed tired, but good. She went off to school normally. A few hours later the school called to say Kristi was having trouble with her eyesight and it was best for me to take her for an MRI. I took her straight to Constantiaberg. The imaging showed a small bleed on the brain. There was nothing to be done about it other than rest and avoid another knock. No physical contact sports and no horse-riding for the next two weeks.

Phew. Never a dull moment in the Lowe household.

CHAPTER 31

Reaching for a dream

A week later Heidi from Reach For A Dream arrived like an angel, bearing delicious chocolate cupcakes for Jen and a letter. It was done! We were going on a cruise liner in just three weeks' time! It was daunting but very exciting and we were determined to grab some fun, special moments with our girls. It would be a logistical nightmare, but that wasn't going to stop us. Jen's beaming face could have motivated an army. Preparation for the trip began in earnest.

"I think you should take at least three days' worth of extra Flolan and meds, Gabi, just in case," Nurse Lizzie advised as we packed for the trip, bustling about in the drug den, making sure I had everything I needed for the morning mixing. "What if you get stuck there or something? Three extra days would at least give me leeway if we need to courier anything."

It was April 2014 and cold and already wintry in Cape Town. This was madness. We both knew it, but we were doing it anyway.

"Okay, so ice-packs," Lizzie went on. "How are you going to freeze them and keep the medication cold?"

"I spoke to Heidi," I said. "There is a refrigerator on the same level as our cabin and they are happy to bring me fresh ice every morning."

"Yeah," Lizzie said, slowly, hesitantly, "but you know there can't be anything else kept in that fridge, right? No food or anything, okay? You are going to sterilise it, Gabi? Aren't you?"

"Yes, Lizzie," I said cheerfully, "I promise. Don't worry, it will be fine." Actually, I was pretty damn nervous. "It's going to be fine," I said again, trying more to convince myself than her.

We packed slowly and carefully, triple-checking our lists to ensure we had all the equipment, medications, portable oxygen, new batteries, cannulas, cartridges, lines, pumps, dressing packs, syringes, biohazard bin, etc. I'd called ahead to order a version of Thunder to be delivered by medical suppliers directly to the guest house we'd be staying in in KwaZulu-Natal. Oxy-Jen would also come, but by now a bigger one was better as Jen was most comfortable on at least five litres of oxygen a minute.

While Lizzie and I fussed over all things medical the girls packed their clothes for the cruise. I could hear their squeals – they were SO excited. This was an opportunity to really dress up and not hold back. They packed long dresses, short skirts, high heels, jewellery, bikinis and all their favourite girlie things. Jen, who barely got out of her PJs at this stage, was delighted to have an excuse to dress up.

We headed off to the airport on a rainy Friday morning in April to fly to Durban. I had found a friendly guest house online right on the water's edge where we would stay for four days before it was time to board the cruise liner. A very dear school friend of Stuart's, Russell, lived in Durban and ran a successful helicopter business. He was looking forward to reconnecting with us and to treating the girls to a special helicopter flip. The excitement was palpable as Granny and Grampa, plus a large shuttle bus for all our stuff, drove us to the airport.

Ridiculously, boarding the flight from Cape Town to Durban turned out to be the hardest part. SAA, our local national airline, made it outrageously difficult, even embarrassing, for Jenna. I had carefully ordered (online and over the phone) an oxygen cylinder for the flight. I'd also filled in the necessary additional forms required, complete with a medical letter from Prof. Wilcox giving Jen permission to fly. Plus, I'd attached copies of the information on Oxy-Jen, which clearly states that her particular mobile oxygen machine is totally safe, within flying regulations and permitted in the cabin. But they didn't want to let her on the plane. Kristi stood next to me protectively, urging me to stay calm and simultaneously glaring at anyone who was staring. Jen sat gracefully on Chase trying to hold onto her dignity and simultaneously wear a kind expression for the check-in counter lady, but it was hard. Stu was causing havoc, throwing in badly timed humour, leaving it to me to undo. The poor check-in counter lady, whose skin was already reddening, was further embarrassed by the officious man she'd called upon to help her and who was now standing at her shoulder announcing, loudly and gesticulating flamboyantly, "I don't think this is okay. We have NO record of you ordering the oxygen cylinder. Are you sure you did? You know it's so easy to forget things when you're packing."

Really? Wow. Don't antagonise the lioness, it's not a good idea. I put my shoulders back, leaned forward and murmured, "It's what my daughter uses to *breathe*. I didn't *forget*. And we *are* getting on that plane. There must be something you can do. Who else can we speak to?"

The officious man flounced off, most irritated with my persistence, but came back a few minutes later to tell me he had spoken to the captain. They would find an oxygen cylinder for the flight but "that thing –" (that would be Oxy-Jen he was referring to) "– that she's wearing on her face – that is not allowed to be used on the plane."

It was degrading and infuriating, but what hurt the most was watching Jenna have to split off and neatly pack away yet another hurt. Part of me wanted to throttle that ignorant flight attendant. I had even told him we were going on a "Reach For A Dream" trip. Everyone knew what that meant. Surely I didn't have to spell it out for him? The information made no difference. He just set his jaw at an even more officious angle. He was not letting our humanity get through to him.

We made it onto the plane, but all four of us consciously decided to leave the unpleasant incident behind and not let it ruin the holiday. Stuart's humour and Kristi's excitement saved the day and soon we were guffawing with laughter again.

Russell was waiting for us at the airport in Durban and made no fuss at all about the mountains of luggage, chatting happily as we packed it into every corner of his large car. He was such a caring teddy bear, my girls warmed to him instantly. There is something soothing about knowing that someone has been a friend of your dad's for most of his life. Russell bundled us into a helicopter to take us on a flip over the magnificent coast of Durban and to buzz the cruise liner, which was already docked in the harbour. We spent a few glorious days in Durban staying at a stunning guest house and spending quality time with Russell's family until it was time to board the MSC *Opera* cruise liner.

The ship was huge! An imposing beauty towering taller than a building. A long red carpet snaked its way to the check-in counters. But oh heavens – there were hundreds and hundreds of people waiting to board. I was immediately worried about Jen's energy levels, but I shouldn't have been. This check-in was a totally different experience from the one at Cape Town airport. We were directed off to a different queue. They were expecting Jen and made us all feel so special and welcome, with absolutely no pity involved, just efficiency and delight at having her on board. I was so grateful. Jen and Kristi were literally grinning. I hadn't seen this much happiness in a while.

Gold staircases, luxurious lifts large enough for Chase to do a full circle, huge and spacious entertainment areas, a multitude of specialty restaurants and bars to choose from, and of course stunning pool decks, a casino and a disco. The girls could hardly contain themselves. While I slowly unpacked all our medical equipment, set up my mixing station in our tiny cabin and introduced myself to our porter so that I could make the necessary refrigeration arrangements, Stu and the girls went whizzing off to explore and put our names down at their chosen restaurant for dinner. Their elation was infectious. Any trepidation about mixing on board a cruise liner seemed irrelevant in the face of their happiness. Once I was settled and everything was sorted, I joined them on the deck to watch our first sunset as the ship pulled out of Durban harbour on its way to the Portuguese islands.

Jenna may have been 19, but the vulnerability of her illness made her look younger. Kristi, on the other hand, was tall and often mistaken for the older sister. Jen didn't, and couldn't, drink or attend the disco. Kristi, on the other hand (16 going on 20), loved to have a sunset cocktail with us in the evening and a good boogie on the dance floor. We were so naughty: we swapped out the girls' ID cards to give Kristi more freedom. The five days on board were punctuated with so much laughter. We threw ourselves into the experience, playing bingo, singing karaoke, eating copious amounts of delicious food and spending every hour of every day and night together. We relished the warmth of the KwaZulu-Natal coastline. Stu and I found a way to mix the medication in our cabin early in the mornings, sterilising every surface, taking extra care and time to make up for the fact that Lizzie wasn't there to check us.

Kristi and Jen shared a cabin just two doors down from us, much to the horror of some 25-year-old who'd spotted Kristi on the dance floor at the disco and came knocking on her cabin door late at night. Oh my heavens, did we laugh! The girls had such fun dressing up every night, especially for the Captain's Dinner and flirting unashamedly with our poor young Czech waiter, who didn't know where to put himself. He folded pretty white paper roses for them each on the last night. Jen even "danced" with her dad one night, just for a few moments. It made me cry with sheer unadulterated happiness.

We flew home the day before my 50th birthday, a milestone I was feeling very conflicted about. Don't get me wrong, I love birthdays, but I was battling with the idea of celebrating my life in the face of Jenna's mortality, and of *not* celebrating it, because what else could we do but be in the moment to celebrate and show gratitude for what we did have – which was the most extraordinary family and community of friends? I shouldn't have worried about it at all because Ali, the fairy godmother, had taken care of everything and planned a full-blown 50th birthday party for me at her cottage in Sea Point, complete with a dance floor over the pool, great music, carefully thought out décor, a bar, snacks and a group of about 70 of my friends. The girls and Stu knew all about it and had helped draw up the guest list and plan the details. It was a very raw and special night. Kristi sang, and dedicated to me, John Legend's magnificent song "All of Me", which had me in tears; and Jen had written a heart-wrenching speech. It was a night of open-heartedness and special connections.

CHAPTER 32

The day I almost killed my child

We reluctantly returned to "normal" life. The extreme highs kept us going, but they also served to highlight just how relentless every day could be. For Jen the visits from close friends, both hers and ours, shone light into the cracks and made her days bearable.

James was visiting every other day. "Jeez, he's taking his job pretty seriously," Shirl said to me one day. I started watching their friendship with a different lens. I think we adults started noticing long before they did that the bond between James and Jen was strengthening and changing.

That week after we returned from the trip was a particularly heavy one for Jen on the media front. There was an early morning live television interview, three radio interviews and two sets of questions to complete for print journalists. University was not getting any easier and she had essays due. I wanted to lessen her load, but for Jen cutting back on her public awareness work was unthinkable. A few months earlier, shortly after her article had appeared in the Discovery magazine, the mother of a gorgeous little girl named Humayra had made contact with me. Shaakira had three children, one of whom had already passed away, possibly from undiagnosed pulmonary hypertension. Now she was afraid that five-year-old Humayra might have it too. It was Jen's story that had led this mother to our doctors and the medication Humayra needed, but also to Jenna herself, who had become a role model for the five-year-old. Shaakira told me that Humayra's life at school and within her community changed directly as a result of Jen. Now people understood her disease. She was no longer teased, and she was happy to wear her oxygen "because beautiful Jen did". Jenna's awareness campaign had made a measurable and substantial difference in Humayra's life, and she was one of many. We were regularly receiving calls like that and helping other families. For Jen, the fact that her story was making a difference to others' lives was what kept her going each and every day. It was the only way for her to make any sense of this awful and cruel journey.

I understood it. Jenna led many people, including me, to their life's purpose.

As the year dragged on Kristi was increasingly unhappy at school and Jen was struggling on campus more than ever. Much to our growing sadness, regardless of the Flolan, Jen was becoming more fatigued, more breathless. It was an impossible situation. We had tried to keep our hopes up that Jen would be less symptomatic as we titrated the amount of her meds up, but we were now at maximum dosage for her slight weight and there hadn't been a substantial improvement. Prof. Badesch and Prof. Wilcox agreed it was probably time to get Jen back up to Johannesburg to Dr Williams at Milpark Hospital for a final evaluation for transplant.

During this time there was this day, this one particular day ...

It was a cold and rainy Monday morning. As usual, my alarm was set to start mixing medication with Lizzie the minute I got home after dropping Kristi at school. We had a hot cup of coffee and a chat – I was updating Lizzie on how whacked Jen had been all weekend. Lizzie, who had become like a big sister to the girls and a friend to Stu and me, was an important member of the family by now. She arrived every morning (other than weekends) like a ray of sunshine with her compassionate, uplifting energy and sparkly blue eyes that were always filled with a zest for life. When Jen was particularly down, there was nothing like a little dose of Lizzie to improve her mood.

Not this day. This day Jen was really bad. She was lethargic, pale, blue lipped, tired and flat. When we went through to change her pump, she was not interested. It was a line-change day, which meant I had to put the light on and get her to sit up in bed and get involved. "I feel terrible, Mom," Jenna said. "Please, please let me sleep a few hours more. We can do it later." I should never have said yes. One of the rules with Flolan is *never* to change the time of day that you mix. Clearly this is because the medication runs out after 24 hours, right? But actually, that is not strictly true. In reality the medication, depending on the dose you are on as a patient, can sometimes only run out after 36 hours. I often wondered why, if this stuff was so incredibly expensive, we didn't push it to the last drop before changing over. Nurse Debra had explained that maintaining a routine was part of the protocol, part of staying safe, but technically there was some leeway with the time of day that you changed the pump. In our case, purely because Jen was so slight that her maximum dose was less than that of a larger person, there was quite a bit of leeway. When I saw how absolutely awful she was feeling and that there was still quite a bit of medication left in the cartridge, I capitulated. I agreed to change the pump later.

Bad move. Bad, bad, bad move. Because we had been mixing the meds every day at the same time for 110 days, because I had carried the new pump, medication and sterile tray through to her room, because I had taken her pulse and done my normal checks, and because I was so worn down with tiredness and flooded with cortisol, my brain thought I had done the change-over already and I forgot. I forgot. I forgot to change the pump, and Jen didn't remember either. She missed lectures that day and spent most of the day in bed. I kept checking on her and taking food, tea and shakes. By early afternoon she was able to sit up in bed and do some studying. She had a philosophy test on campus that evening. I went about the business of the day and helped her get up and dressed in time to go up to campus to write her test at 5 pm. Having dropped her off, I went back home to Kristi to take her to extra maths. I was sitting in the car outside, waiting for Kristi to finish her half-hour session, when my phone rang. It was Jen.

"MOM!" she said. "The pump alarm. It's going off! We forgot—"

As she said the words "pump alarm" my whole body flashed white-hot. I remembered in that instant that I'd forgotten to change the pump.

"Fuck! Fuck!" I shouted into the phone, slamming the car into gear. "Jesus. Jenna, I am on my way!" I sped up towards the university, hazard lights flashing, hand on the hooter. I did not stop. Not for a red light. Not for a stop street. Not for anything. I had to get to Jenna! I had to get to Jenna! What had I done? Oh my God, what had I done? I couldn't think straight. As I flew around the corner that leads into campus there she was, in the middle of the road. I screeched to a halt, jumped out, threw open the boot and tossed Chase in, by which time Jen had manoeuvred herself into the passenger seat. "Go, go, go!" she said. Staring pedestrians scattered as I slammed the car into gear and revved the engine.

"Mom, Mom," Jenna said, as I tore towards home. "Mom, slow down, you're going to kill us." The irony wasn't lost on either of us. "I re-programmed the pump to slow down the delivery of medication. I think I've bought us some time." Clever, very clever. I wouldn't have thought of that. But how much time? How could we know how many minutes Jen had bought? Eyes wide, neither of us spoke for the rest of the way. I drove like the traffic police, in the middle of the lanes, my hand on the hooter, my mind racing through what needed to happen the minute we got home, planning it down to the last millisecond.

I screeched to a halt in our driveway, jerked up the handbrake and leapt out of the car, leaving gates and doors wide open. I ran to the drug den and pulled on my mask and gloves with shaking hands. My breathing was coming fast. I grabbed the already mixed medication meant for this morning's change-over out of the fridge, found the pump and programmed it. I was so panicked I had to say the instructions out loud to myself as I went. By the time Jen had made her way out of the car and breathlessly down the passage to the drug den I had the new pump in hand. "No line-change today," I said. I hurriedly undid her old stat lock, sterilised a new one, attached the new pump and pushed start. No alarm. Silence. Blissful silence. We stood staring at each other, adrenalised and shaking. Jen was still standing on the top step of the drug den. She hadn't even made it down the stairs to the mixing desk. "I am SO sorry," I said. "I am so sorry, Jen." Then I burst into tears. Never again. Never again would we change the protocol. I had put Jenna's life at risk. It would take me a very long time to forgive myself.

When my mobile rang I nearly jumped out of my skin.

"Hey, Mom," said Kristi. "What happened? Where are you?" She was waiting in the dark on the pavement outside extra maths.

CHAPTER 33

Sterilising liquid and puke

"But she really needs to get out. Please, Gabi, please. We will be SO careful, I promise. I know exactly what to do."

Camilla stood in my kitchen with big pleading eyes. Like many of Jen's friends she was moving out of home and into student digs away from the watchful eye of her parents. It made a mockery of the fact that Jen couldn't be more than five minutes away from me. The total lack of independence, at an age when she needed it the most, was haunting Jen. She hungered for it. She fantasised about dancing in clubs, living with friends and getting drunk on tequila like any other first-year varsity student. But if she couldn't experience these things first-hand, then she wanted to be on the periphery. Camilla was having a flat-warming and she wanted Jenna to be there.

I was quiet. I was *not* keen. Camilla tried again.

"I know the protocol. Please, Gabi?"

Jenna was by now highly susceptible to infection, which meant we sterilised everything, not just the equipment in the drug den and other strategic places. There were random white bottles of hospital sterilising liquid all over the house.

"I'll think about it, Cami," I conceded. "I need to discuss it with Stu."

Those enormous green eyes. "I really think she needs it …"

Listless, tired and emotionally flat, Jen had been in bed for more than just a few days. I was not keen to let her go out. Not keen at all but also very torn. Maybe this would lift her spirits? Then I heard a determined little voice behind me. Jen had got up out of bed and walked down the passage to join us in the kitchen. "You don't have to talk *about* me, you can talk to me. I'm right here." She was facing me down. "Let me go, Mom," she said. "I can't be wrapped up in cotton wool all the time, it's not a life. I *want* to see Cami's apartment, I *want* to go." Her voice was unusually resolute and defiant, almost unlike her. Clearly, she really needed this.

"You can go, my darling, of course you can go. We will make a plan."

We had to keep reminding ourselves to let her *live* her life. After all she was here. Today.

It was Friday, the day had arrived. I helped Jen get dressed – she was way too breathless by now to do it on her own. Sexy dark denim jeans hugged her perfect bottom, folded up slightly to reveal her slim ankles. "Which top are you thinking?" I asked, standing at the cupboard door. "Oooh, the cherries, let's have the cherries," she said. I held up a short white top embellished with little red cherries; it showed off her flat stomach. She finished off the outfit with dangly red earrings and a dash of red lipstick and her red high heels. Red was Jen's colour.

Understanding Jen's love of fashion, Kristi had gone shopping for ribbons in different colours to tie on the pump pouch Jen slung over her shoulder every day to match her outfit. I looked through the box of ribbons in the cupboard and chose a dark red satin one to match her shoes. Smudgy, dark eye make-up and a generous spray of Clinique Happy meant Jen was ready.

"Bye, Nooglet!" she called.

"Wait, Jen-bean!" Kristi bolted out of her bedroom and stopped short. "You look beautiful," she told her sister. "Have fun! Have so much fun!"

Stuart had loaded Chase into the car when Cami phoned: "Bring an extra bottle of sterilising liquid!" she hollered happily down the phone. "We are ready!"

Meanwhile I was blabbering. "Okay, so Dad is taking you, I have packed the extra sterilising liquid, and I have my phone on loud, you drank your shake, right? Did you take your meds? Jen, did you take your meds? And what about the 9 pm ones, do you have them?"

"Mom, seriously, stop it. It's down the road, I'll be fine, I promise. I'm excited. Come, Dad, let's go. Dad!"

Cami and Alex were flatmates and had spent hours cleaning. The place was gleaming. A bar was carefully laid out with cocktails and gin, a large bowl of red punch, shot glasses and a special bottle of non-alcoholic bubbles for Jen. They had even marked out a special spot for her in the middle of the room where she could sit comfortably, but still be part of the group. Music was playing, and they were set up for card games and drinking games.

"Thank you! Thank you for bringing her!" Cami said when Jen and Stuart arrived. Jen wheelied in through the door on Chase at full speed. She was beaming, literally glowing, and full of life, silky hair streaming behind her. "Oh, Cami it's so lovely!" she said.

Stu took a few minutes wandering through the apartment, casting a protective eye over everything, making sure. At the door he handed a full bottle of sanitiser to Cami. "You've got my number," he said. "I'll fetch Jen the minute she is ready to come home."

"We know, Stu, we know," said Camilla.

"Love you, Dad. See you later," said Jenna.

We waited for the phone to ring. By 11 pm I was restless. "Should we just go get her?" I said. "No, Mom, no," said Kristi. "Let her have some fun." We waited and waited. Eventually we resorted to watching a series. Then I sent a WhatsApp.

"Jen, all good?" Jen responded immediately.

"Yes, all good."

Another series. I WhatsApped again. "All good, Jen-Jen?"

"Yes, Mommy, all good, I'm having fun."

We watched another series. As it was coming to an end, Stuart's phone pinged ... we both leapt on it. It was a message from Cami. It read: "Stu, please come and fetch Jen. And bring a change of clothing. Don't tell Gabi." A change of clothing! Why would she need a change of clothing? I ran next door to Jen's room, grabbed her favourite soft tracky pants and warm top out of her cupboard and shoved them at Stu. "Go get her, Stu," I said.

Stuart arrived in the carpark of Cami's apartment building to Alex and Mike pushing each other around at high speed in shopping trolleys. He hurriedly took the lift up to the apartment. When Cami opened the door, it was a totally different scene from the pristine space he'd inspected a few hours earlier. Music was thumping, the floor was drenched, and there were students everywhere. Jen was in the middle of the room, perched on the couch, in a weird ensemble of clothing. Her lips had a slightly blueish purple tinge. She looked tired, oh so tired, and she was very breathless, but her eyes were sparkling and alive. Stuart whisked her up and took her and Chase down to the car. As he drove her home, stories of the evening came tumbling from her lips. She had FUN, so much fun. All her friends were there, and she knew everyone. They had chatted and chatted and laughed non-stop. Then the drinking games had started, and more students arrived. There was this boy, a dark-haired boy she didn't know who couldn't take his eyes off her. Her friends were teasing him incessantly. He was apparently transfixed by Jen but clueless as to how to approach her, so he drank red punch, lots of it, to boost his courage. Jen had stood (yes, stood) at the bar area for a while before Cami insisted she sit on the couch to catch her breath. The music was loud and the party in full swing. Around 11:30 the boy finally approached to speak to this mysterious girl on oxygen, whose bottle of sterilising liquid was now floating, unnoticed, in a shallow pool of spilled alcohol on the floor. He sat down heavily next to Jen on the couch.

"Oh my God, you are so beautiful. You are so-o-o beautiful," he said, slurring. "How do you do this?"

"Do what?" Jen replied.

"You know ..." He looked sheepish.

"No, I don't," she said. "Do you mean the oxygen? Or the mobility scooter? Or …" There were many other things she could have listed, but she took mercy on the poor boy, who was squirming. He took a deep breath and moved closer. The girls were watching.

"I want you to go out with me," he said, slurring badly. "You are the bravest and most beautiful person I've ever met. Will you come out on a date with me?" And with that he vomited, depositing a large quantity of punch-coloured puke all over Jenna's sterilised lap.

As disgusting as the end of her evening was, Jenna was still pleased she'd gone to the party – and we had to admit she did have a very funny story to tell.

At the time I was admitting no such thing. I scrubbed Jen down and got her into bed.

CHAPTER 34

Emergency listed for transplant

By May of 2014 university was becoming increasingly difficult for Jen, and on Prof. Wilcox's instructions following the disappointing results of her latest six-minute walk test, Stu and I arranged to fly her to Johannesburg. Prof. David Badesch and Prof. Nazzareno Galie (from Italy) would both be in South Africa with the express purpose of helping Dr Williams and a local task force to create a White Paper on the guidelines for pulmonary hypertension in South Africa. This was a big step forward for the landscape of the disease. We arranged our trip to coincide with theirs, so that Jen could be examined by all three doctors simultaneously. We also arranged that Humayra and a few other patients could see them too. These doctors were so generous with their time and expertise.

On the 23rd of May 2014 we flew to Johannesburg. We sat in the waiting room with Shaakira and Humayra, who was so thrilled to meet Jen that she sat glued to her. The trip had been pretty harrowing. Since our last visit to Johannesburg, Jenna had deteriorated dramatically, in spite of all our efforts. Quite simply, for her, treatment had started too late. She had been listed for a double lung transplant since her trip to Johannesburg the year before but now, they all agreed, it was urgent. The day we had been hoping to push out for many years had arrived. Jen was "in extremis" and needed new lungs. Fast. We had known it was coming. I remember how the first time we'd ever heard the words "double lung transplant" it felt brutal. Now it was both brutal and hopeful.

New lungs meant a chance at life. A chance that Jen could live.

At the same time as Jen and I were flying back to Cape Town, Kristi was doing a sound check at the top of Table Mountain. On the morning of Sunday, the 25th she would sing for the second year at The Table of Peace and Unity, a few days before starting her mid-year Grade 10 exams. The contrast was ironic.

With a transplant now imminent, I turned my energy towards understanding the complexities. It made for difficult reading.

According to the National Heart, Lung and Blood Institute (NHLBI), the one-year survival rate of single-lung transplants is nearly 80 per cent. The five-year survival rate is more than 50 per cent. Survival rates vary by facility.

For these reasons, long-term survival after a lung transplant is not as promising as it is after other organ transplants, like kidney or liver. Still, more than 80 per cent of people survive at least one year after lung transplant. After three years, between 55 per cent and 70 per cent of those receiving lung transplants are alive.

Not exactly what we were hoping for. Plus we started to realise that in South Africa receiving organs is no slam dunk. In fact, it is highly unlikely. Once a patient is listed for emergency transplant, it doesn't mean they will get one. Having once dreaded the day that we would get to this point, we were now appalled to discover that South Africa, the "home of the heart transplant", has a precariously low organ donation rate. Up to 4 500 people are awaiting a lifesaving organ every day, and most will not receive one.

Lung transplants are trickier. In order to even be listed, a patient needs to have end-stage lung disease. They need to have exhausted all other available therapies without success and ideally have no other chronic medical conditions, no current infections or recent cancer. The recipient should be within an acceptable weight range (marked undernourishment or obesity are both associated with increased mortality) with an acceptable psychological profile and social support system in place. No alcohol, smoking, or drug abuse (some individuals who can cease these habits and comply with treatment may be given the chance) and potential recipients should be able to pay for expenses if they don't have appropriate medical insurance. A potential recipient must also be able to comply with the complex post-transplant regimen. A lung transplant is major and difficult surgery and, following transplant, the patient must be willing to adhere to a lifetime regimen of medications, as well as continuing and complex medical care.

Of course, Jen was able to meet these prerequisites to qualify, but it soon became apparent that lungs are the most difficult organs to come by. Not only do they need to be healthy, they also need to be a good size match for the recipient – large enough to oxygenate but small enough to fit within the recipient's chest cavity. Then a match in blood type is critical. The recipient's blood type must match the donor's, otherwise antigens present in the donated lungs can lead to a strong response by the immune system and subsequent rejection of the transplanted organs. Tissue type is also critical. The lung tissue must match as closely as possible in order to lessen the chance of rejection.

What a minefield.

Now that Jen was emergency listed, we needed to be contactable 24 hours a day and capable of rapid transport to Johannesburg (a two-hour commercial flight away) when the call came. Operation O2 had begun. We set about finding what we needed, from flights and helicopters to documents and updated tests. It became even more critical that Jen avoid infection. The quantities of disinfectant I was purchasing made us seem like a clinic. Kristi made signs for us to put up all over the house to remind visitors to wash and sanitise their hands regularly. No one could visit if they were sick or had been in contact with anyone they knew was sick.

Jen could not go back to university. Her doctors had agreed it was time for her to stay home and wait. While waiting, we took care of some important things. Vaccinations and dental appointments, paperwork for medical insurance approvals, updated and regular blood tests. We packed medical bags and put the necessary plans in place to be ready to up and leave at any time. I closed my office. Jean agreed to freelance and help me out with admin work from home, but Upfront Marketing was no longer servicing clients. Jenna's needs had become a full-time job.

I visited the Disability Department on campus and, with their guidance, we wrote to the necessary departments to request a Leave of Absence for Jen. Her wish was to carry on studying once she had recovered from transplant, to finish her undergraduate degree and then possibly apply to Oxford to do her Honours.

We made the house as comfortable as possible for Jen. My friend Nici and her husband Gregg built a cleverly crafted day-bed for Jen, which we set up in the lounge. It was fit for a princess, with plug points for charging her oxygen machine, a place to put her laptop, a food tray for meals in bed and padded sides she could sit up against. We gave it pride of place in the lounge so that she was still very much part of the action.

At the end of May Kristi started her mid-year Grade 10 exams. We had decided it was time to find an alternative for her in terms of schooling. She wasn't happy at school and just couldn't find her groove. An independent educational psychologist concurred that an alternative school environment would be a better option. With a heavy heart I visited the principal. The extraordinary commitment, kindness and support we'd experienced from him and the Herschel staff would never be forgotten. It was painful to leave, but more important for us as parents to keep an open mind about Kristi's needs. We decided she would complete her Grade 10 year at Abbotts College after her mid-year holidays. Abbotts is a co-ed school, with a non-traditional outlook but a focus on academics and individuality. It seemed like a good option for her.

Aniko phoned from Australia. She'd been talking to Jen and was devastated to hear she had been listed. She wanted to visit but could only make the trip in January. I was blatantly honest with her. "Book the trip, Aniko, but who knows where we will be, I told her. She understood. If Jen was in Johannesburg by then, she would come to Johannesburg. It was unsettling. The future was less and less certain. It was cold and wet, a dramatic Cape Town winter and Jen could not afford to get sick. We battened down the hatches ...

On Monday, the 18th of June 2014 Mary and Steve videoed Jen sitting in front of our fireplace. Gavin Levy had asked her to speak at a global YPO function on the upcoming Saturday night, but her health was so variable that he suggested she do a video in case she wasn't well enough to go. Thanks to Gavin's thoroughness, we have some wonderful footage of Jen speaking about her diagnosis and illness. She spoke off the cuff. No script, no multiple takes, no prompting. Jenna's ability to tell her story in a powerful and inspirational way, even at the worst of times, was truly astounding. She did make it to the function that Saturday night, wearing the gold dress she'd worn to her prefects' dance, and Gavin told me that she simply blew them away. Kristi led all the singers in darkness, and she and Robyn, the Dreamer, sang their rendition of "African Dream". Straws were handed out so that those brave enough could hold their nostrils closed and breathe through one while Jenna spoke. It was a frightening but effective way for people to identify with what she was going through.

That event was voted the best YPO event of the year.

However ill she was, Jenna continued to touch the hearts of many, even in her hours of darkness.

CHAPTER 35

Surprise visitors

On the 26th of June, Craig, Margo and Nic arrived from Australia – Tayla would follow a few days later – and there was a surprise visitor for Jenna: Daffy! The school he was stooging at in New Zealand had given him leave to come home and visit, and his parents, Karen and Bob, had gone out of their way to find the money to fund a trip. They knew there was a chance he might not see Jen again before transplant. Although Daffy and Jen had agreed when he left in January to just be friends, they had spoken, Skyped and messaged each other daily and talked about everything. Unsurprisingly, they slipped easily straight back into their romance. They loved each other deeply.

I busied myself with pressing medical stuff while Craig and his family spent time with their South African friends, many of whom they hadn't seen for years, and Jen and Daffy caught up.

The "gathering of the clans" was such a welcome relief. A special dinner at our home was arranged by Sue Cooper and a colleague of hers, Daniel Jardim, a talented vegetarian chef. The smell of delicious, healthy food wafted through the house while Sue led us all in a silent guided meditation – even the dogs joined in! Many members of my family hadn't experienced meditation before and they thoroughly enjoyed the calming reflective space. It was a magical night.

We had wonderful times together, some one-on-one time, some big gatherings and a celebration of Margo's 50th. But it was also tough and sad. It was hard for the people who loved Jen so much to see her so compromised. Margo hadn't seen her since her student exchange in Sydney and Daffy hadn't seen her for six months. She had got a lot worse since then. Daffy visited other friends and naturally spent time with his family, but he visited Jen every day. It was as if he had never left. They talked for hours, laughed, loved and cuddled … but lurking below the surface was always the knowledge that at any moment she could get called for a transplant. We were constantly on alert waiting for the phone to ring, for the call from Milpark to say we needed to get to Johannesburg fast.

Craig, Margo and Nic returned to Australia on the 10th of July, followed 10 days later by Daffy, who returned to New Zealand.

Jen had a sleepover at Daffy's house the night before he left.

"This second goodbye," Daffy would tell me, "was more difficult than the first. After the first goodbye I assumed I would take a gap year, Jen would have a year at uni, the new Flolan would help her and after the year we would resume. But, leaving the second time, I had no idea if I would see her again. That night before I left we had a small dance, her feet on my feet. I don't know what song was playing but my mum said my aunt saw us and began to cry before my mum shooed her away so that neither of us would notice her. The next morning you all came to take me to the airport and Jen and I were still snuggled up in my bed. It seemed like everyone was ready for me to get up and go, and I just wanted to lie in bed with Jen. I was actually late for my flight and almost missed it."

Only Tayla was left with us – and we were grateful for that.

CHAPTER 36

We nearly lose Jen

On Wednesday, the 23rd of July 2014, just three days after Daffy left, we nearly lost Jen.

Stuart had left for a business trip on the red-eye flight at 6 am that morning and Kristi was starting at Abbotts College that day. I dropped Kristi off and sat in the car watching her walk into her new school. It was the middle of the school year, and she knew no one, but her head was held high. She had her books under her arm and shoulders back. I got all choked up watching how brave she was and thinking about how much in her world had changed. Her long blonde hair was shiny and clean. She wore jeans and a white top, in stark contrast to a lot of the black I noticed the other kids wearing. I was proud of her determination to be herself, no matter what others thought, of her incredible ability to adapt and try something new.

With my heart full of love, I drove home hopeful that Abbotts was the right choice for her. I was meeting Lizzie at 8:30 in the drug den to mix Jenna's medication and do her pump change. It was also a line-change day and Lizzie and I talked lightly while we mixed and prepared a second tray. When we were ready, we wandered through to Jen's room with our masks and gloves on. Jen no longer came into the den for line-changes; we took everything to her now. We switched on the lights and opened the blind to let the natural light and air flood in. Jen sat up groggily. "Morning," she said sleepily. "How did Kristi go off, Mom?"

While we chatted, I covered her with a sterilised drape, cleaned around the central line, then disconnected her CADD pump, and connected the new one that was mixed and prepped for today. Then I programmed it while Lizzie and Jen checked me. I pushed start. "There you go," I said. "You can go back to sleep now." As Lizzie and I stood up to clean up the medical supplies scattered on the bed and started leaving the room, the pump alarm sounded. Beep beep beep beep beep. Everyone stiffened.

"Stop it and restart it, Gabi. Let's check we set it right." I stopped the pump deliberately and restarted it – calling my settings out loud so that Jen and Lizzie could check my numbers. Lizzie watched me closely. "Okay, push start," she said.

I did. Sweet silence.

But as we were both breathing sighs of relief, the alarm started again. Beep beep beep beep beep. Shit! My heart started beating faster.

"Maybe it's the cassette," I said. "I'll get tomorrow's one." I ran to the den and grabbed the medication cassette prepped for the next morning out of the fridge. While I did this, Lizzie disconnected the one we had just hooked up. I was starting to feel scattered and scared. I ran back into Jenna's room, where Lizzie was waiting, hand outstretched.

"Hand me the new one," she said. She took over and swiftly changed the cartridge. We needed to be quick. "I think we need to keep time," she said calmly from under her mask as she worked.

Jen was sitting bolt upright, attentive. "I've got it," she said, checking her watch. "You check Lizzie, Mom."

I did. I watched Lizzie like a hawk as she changed the cassette and re-set the pump. Again we reconnected it. This time she read out her numbers and settings. We took a deep breath and she pushed start. We waited. Silence.

And then … beep beep beep beep beep.

Now my heart was double pounding. Time was of the essence. What else could it be?

"Maybe it's the pump?" Jen suggested.

I ran back to the drug den to grab a back-up pump out of the box. It would take time to set it up. Tension was mounting. I stood in the centre of Jen's bedroom, my hands shaking, trying to block everything else out and concentrate only on re-setting the second pump. While I was doing this Lizzie ran through the possibilities.

"So we know it is not the line or the cassette because we already changed those. I can only think it must be the pump. This should work, Gabi." She removed the second cassette off the "defunct" pump and handed it to me. By now I had set the second pump and was connecting the cassette filled with medication.

"2.5 minutes," Jen said calmly.

I breathed deeply to still my hands, but my heart was racing.

"Here," I said, handing the second pump to Lizzie, who was perched, ready and waiting, beside Jen on the bed. She sanitised the stat lock quickly and connected it to Jenna's central Hickman line. She called out the numbers swiftly for us to check and then she pushed start.

We all stood staring at the pump. Waiting.

Beep beep beep beep beep.

"3.5 minutes," said Jen.

Jesus! I was panicking. What did we do now? I started pacing the room.

"Gabi!" Lizzie's voice broke through my fear. "Find our IV kit. We need to get this medication directly into Jenna's arm. Fast. Gabi?"

I couldn't believe this was happening. How could this be happening? I ran to the den again, passing a wide-eyed Queen, who had just arrived at work, in the passage. I flew straight past her and grabbed our container marked "Emergency – IV Kit". Now it was Lizzie's turn to shake. It is not easy to insert an intravenous line (IV) at the best of times, never mind under this kind of pressure in a home setting with none of the usual medical back-up. Thank goodness she had volunteered at a clinic a few months back in order to practise.

Lizzie was now kneeling on the floor next to Jenna's bed. Jen was sitting cross-legged facing her. At this stage we didn't know what had gone wrong, but we understood that we needed to get the Flolan into Jenna's system fast. It had already been quite a while, she was in real danger. The only thing to do now was get the medication into her veins another way, via her arm instead of her central line. She could not be off the medication any longer. It had already been too long.

I threw the IV start kit onto the bed – tourniquet, alcohol pads, gauze, tegaderm, tape and the right gauge IV needle. How it works is that an IV needle is inserted together with a small tube (a catheter) into the vein to deliver fluids directly into the bloodstream. Once inserted, the catheter stays, and the needle is removed and taped to protect the "IV" site. All this is usually done in a hospital environment, preferably when everyone is calm.

"4.5 minutes," said Jen.

"Gabi, call emergency services." Lizzie was staring up at me. I remember that her vivid blue eyes were wide and that they matched her face mask. "Go call emergency services," she said firmly.

I left Lizzie kneeling in front of Jen preparing to insert the IV needle. Jen looked straight at her, held her arm out steadily, and said, "You've got this, Lizzie."

I paced the dining room as I called emergency services. We needed an ambulance. Fast. And a paramedic who was experienced with IVs. Sheer terror took my breath away. My hands were shaking and so was my voice. I was flooded with adrenaline, but functional. "They are on their way, ma'am," the operator said.

Outside in Stu's office Brandon and his wife, Nikki, were having a meeting, oblivious to the unfolding drama. Stuart was in Johannesburg and Kristi had probably just finished her first lesson at her new school.

I tore back down the passage. "They're on their way," I said breathlessly.

When I walked into the bedroom, I was met with Jenna saying firmly, "Try again, Lizzie, you aren't hurting me." She was deathly calm. There was blood on the white linen and Lizzie was sweating under her mask. Her first few attempts at inserting the IV obviously hadn't gone smoothly, but she was persisting. I stood dead still, not wanting to distract her. This time it worked. The catheter was at the right angle, there was no back flow of blood. Lizzie started the pump. Silence … no alarm. We waited. No alarm. We watched the line. The medication started flowing.

"8.5 minutes," Jen said, looking up at us.

I fled to the toilet and vomited. Then I called Prof. Wilcox on his mobile to ask him to meet us at UCT Academic Hospital. I went back to Jen's bedroom. I could see she wasn't doing so well. Together Lizzie and I gently laid her on her pillow. Neither of us spoke.

When the doorbell rang Queen was waiting to let the paramedics in. The first time Brandon knew that anything was going on was when three paramedics rushed up the driveway and ran straight into the house. The gate was wide open, ambulance parked at an angle across the entrance. The dogs were agitated and getting underfoot.

Jen's blood pressure was crashing. She was pale and her lips were turning blueish. We had turned up her oxygen to maximum flow and Lizzie and I now had her lying on the floor with her legs up on the bed to help raise her blood pressure. The paramedics took in the scene quickly. The senior paramedic dropped to his knees at Jenna's head and spoke calmly and reassuringly to her. He asked her questions and ensured she stayed conscious. The second paramedic fired questions at Lizzie and me. The IV was perfect. They didn't touch it but wrapped it tightly in a gauze bandage to secure the line so that there was no risk of it coming loose. The first paramedic then instructed his team to bring in the trolley and once Jen seemed a little more stable, they lifted her onto it.

"I'll go in the ambulance with Jen," I told Lizzie. "You follow in your car."

As we wheeled her out the front door I saw Brandon standing at the top of the driveway. He looked horrified.

"What can I do?" he called after me.

"Find Stu!" I shouted over my shoulder before climbing into the ambulance.

Lizzie was right behind me running towards her car. She was

still covered in blood. Poor Brandon, he had no idea what had happened.

In the ambulance things weren't good. Jenna's blood pressure was crashing again when Stu phoned. "Gabs, Brandon called. What's going on?"

Prof. Wilcox was waiting for us at the hospital entrance. We got Jenna into ICU and onto monitors as fast as we could. We had worked out by now that Jenna's central line, the Hickman line, must be blocked. Prof. said she would need surgery to replace the line, but first she must stabilise. I called Stu again, who was busy rearranging things to fly home that night instead of in two days' time. I called Mary and asked her to fetch Kristi from school later. Then I turned my attention back to Jen. She was sleeping like an angel, and her vital signs were looking slightly better. As I sat at her bedside, silent tears leaked down my cheeks. An abandoned cup of tea sat on the hospital trolley. I put my forehead down on Jen's bed for a few minutes. Relief flooded my body. She was still with us. We were safe for now.

By early evening, when Prof. went home, it was clear that nothing was going to happen fast. There was a vascular conference in South Africa that week that just about all the vascular surgeons were attending. This meant that finding the right surgeon to do the job of replacing the line was difficult. One of the best had stayed behind to "hold the fort", but he was very booked up and busy, and we would have to wait. The procedure could only be booked for a few days' time. Prof. seemed to think that was fine. At least Jenna would have time to stabilise and get stronger.

But what about the Flolan? Surely the amount flowing into the veins in her arm was different from the amount pumping directly into her right heart chamber? I didn't want to take risks with the Flolan, so just to be sure I called Prof. Badesch in the US to apprise him of the situation and get his expert input. I'm glad I did. If the central line could only be replaced on Monday (it was Wednesday), then we would need to make another plan in the interim. And it would need to be done *today*. An IV needle into Jen's arm just wouldn't cut it. It was too risky to leave her like that

257

for any longer. It had already been eight hours.

We'd been advised that Dr Greg Symons, a young up and coming pulmonologist with a strong interest in PH, and a resident at Groote Schuur Hospital, would be looking after Jen's case while Prof. was away. So it was Dr Symons who was called and now had the tricky job of dealing with this mother (me) who was causing consternation in ICU, insisting that Jenna be seen and dealt with tonight. I wouldn't take "no" for an answer. Prof. Badesch had recommended that we insert a PICC line as the carrier for the Flolan until such time as surgery could take place. PICC stands for a peripherally inserted central catheter. It is an IV device that is threaded through the veins of the arm that end close to the heart. It is used for hospital in-patients and out-patients who require intravenous access for a prolonged period.

Commonplace in the States, there were none to be found in the hospital. I could see Dr Symons's enthusiasm waning. He thought maybe we should deal with it the following day when the theatre was open and things would be easier. A reasonable thought in normal circumstances, but I had spoken to Prof. Badesch. I knew we couldn't wait. So I ambushed him. I called Prof. Badesch and literally handed the phone to Dr Symons. "Here!" I said. "Chat to David. He will explain why it is important and urgent that we do this tonight." Dr Symons walked somewhere private to take the call.

When he returned he said, "Right, we are going to do this tonight."

We started placing calls to local hospitals to find a PICC line. Half an hour later we got lucky. A theatre nurse remembered seeing one at the back of a cupboard somewhere. She located it and said she would have it sent over to us with the hospital courier. Meanwhile Dr Symons had spoken to the anaesthetist on duty. When the anaesthetist arrived, he looked exhausted. He had clearly been on duty for quite some time. We suggested he go home to shower and eat while we waited for the PICC line.

Between calls I was talking to Mary and Kristi, keeping them updated and making sure Kristi was fine and looked after. Mary took her back to her house for dinner with the Berry family. I also sent Lizzie back home to mix more Flolan on her own. She would need to prep the pumps and do some sorting out in the den, which we had left in a state of disarray. Plus we needed stock of Flolan in the hospital fridge in ICU. We also needed additional for later that night because once the PICC line had been inserted, we would need to do a switch-over from the one pump to another.

By 8:30 pm Stuart had landed. He came straight to the hospital. It was such a relief to have him with me. The PICC line arrived shortly afterwards and our anaesthetist returned from dinner looking like a new person. Jen was far too compromised to be put under, and it wasn't necessary. Small amounts of local anaesthetic in her left arm allowed them to do the procedure in the ICU ward with the curtains closed. We could hear them reading the instructions on the pack, which felt weird. I had to be close by to do the CADD pump switch-over when they were ready. When it was done, before Dr Symons left, he told me that he wanted me to know that if Jen had been his child, he would have done exactly the same thing.

Once everyone was absolutely certain everything was functional and Jen had eventually gone to sleep, we went home. It was midnight.

Four days later Jen had a new central line inserted in theatre.

Jenna's journal
Friday, 1st August 2014
9:16 pm; my room

I just spent like a week in hospital, and I have a new line on the opposite side. I prefer the spot this one is in – it's further away and easier to hide with clothing. I'm just peeved at how many scars I am going to have on my chest.

I went in Wednesday through Tuesday. Had an emergency IV when my line blocked, then a PICC line, then a new central line. Lots of pricking and cutting and so forth.

I realised when I came out that I always emerge from hospital with some/a lot of anger. Cuz I go through so much and I'm always so calm and polite. It's exhausting how hyper-aware, vigilant and responsible I have to be about every little detail. There are some life-changing mistakes that nurses and doctors have almost made and that I have to be involved in to prevent.

I can't just lie back. No matter how sick I am, I feel like I have to watch out for myself. It's scary. Hospitals are supposed to be the ultimate safe place physically, but because of the uniqueness of my condition and my pump, hospitals are dangerous for me. It's exhausting.

I know exactly what Jenna meant. Going home at night and leaving Jen at the hospital was scary. Not that there wasn't intent from the staff to get things right and do the best by her; of course there was. But there was also a very real risk that someone could flush out the central line, forget to change ice-packs for the pump, confiscate her meds (so many of her meds weren't available in South Africa that she needed to have her own stash with her next to her bed) and many other potentially critical possibilities.

The six days in hospital went slowly, but we did our best to make Jen comfortable. As soon as she was out of ICU and allowed visitors Kristi went to visit every day, taking her sister news of the outside world and stories about her new school. Although I didn't get the feeling Abbotts College was a total match for her, she did seem happier. One night that week, in fact on the weekend, the nurses gathered around Jen's bed and Kristi sang for them all. We were forging relationships with the staff. This place was becoming way too familiar.

Mary continued to be the most incredible friend to me. When I arrived home late at night there would be a meal for the three of us, waiting on the front doorstep. She was a real gift, a crucial member of our support system – as were some of my other girlfriends. I still had lunch regularly with Vanessa, but we no longer met in town. Now she came to my side of the mountain so that I was never more than five minutes from the house. She was determined that once Jen got out of hospital, we were to arrange some exciting things for her at home. "Who does she want to meet?" she asked me. As editorial director at Associated Media, she had a fair whack of influence and knew a lot of people. When I told Jen about her offer, her face lit up. "Oh wow," she said. "Really? That's so kind. How long can the list be, Mom? There are so many people I want to meet!" She had many heroes and heroines. Vanessa's instincts were right. Jen was getting bored at home, waiting. Keeping her engaged and interested in the world by meeting interesting people was a great idea.

The minute Jenna was safely out of hospital, I met with Jen's Angels. It was time to plan another fundraiser. We had no idea how long it would take to get to transplant and it was nearing time to order another large batch of medication. I was no longer earning and even though Stu was working hard to build his business, it was going to take time. By now he had two experienced partners in BrandMapp – one based in Cape Town and one in Johannesburg – as well as a full-time sales manager. They were already doing pretty well, but there were overheads to cover and funds were becoming an issue for us. What would happen if the call came and we had to take off to Johannesburg? How would Stu earn? How would I? How long would we be there? How did we cover the costs of two homes? It was daunting. Stuart must have felt as if the world was resting on his shoulders.

I couldn't work, but I could fundraise.

This time the Angels and I went all out and together we came up with a fabulous plan – "Celebrity Sunday". The Baxter Theatre in Rondebosch offered us a night for free on Sunday, the 7th of September. We decided to put on an evening of sheer entertainment showcasing incredible acts drawn from theatre, music, dance and comedy. Our good friend and international singer Suanne Braun was coming out from London and she agreed to perform; and well-known author, journalist, and a close friend of ours, Marianne Thamm, agreed to be MC. We planned to include an auction, so we set about sourcing a variety of high-value items and offers. I met with Karen, Carlie and Melissa to continue our planning right down to the tiniest detail. It promised to be an exceptional night.

I contacted the Organ Donor Foundation, with whom we had already developed a relationship, to see if they would host a table that night for guests to sign up as donors if they were interested.

It's astonishing how much misinformation there is when it comes to organ donation. Most people don't even know the basics of what it entails or how to go about becoming a donor, nor – most critically – how much good it can do. And it costs nothing – you can do it for free.

Organ donation only takes place after an individual has been declared brain dead if they are still being supported by a respirator. The recipient will receive the donated organ shortly after retrieval. Medical tests will only be carried out at the time of death and they involve medical professionals evaluating medical history, carrying out blood and culture tests and conducting a physical examination to ensure that the organs are suitable for donation.

A single individual can save up to seven lives with their donated organs after their death: your heart, liver and pancreas can save up to three lives and your kidneys and lungs can help up to four more people. But there is also tissue donation, the difference between the two being that tissue retrieval can still take place several hours and even days after death. Tissue is stored in a special tissue bank, so it is available for use as and when needed. Corneas, skin, bone, tendons and heart valves are all tissue donations. You can help up to 50 people by donating your tissue.

Bone tissue transplants are the second most common transplant performed on patients, second only to blood transfusions. Many thousands of patients receive allograft tissue every year, most of which comes from non-living donors whose loved ones consented to donation.

It's also interesting to note that most religions support organ and tissue donation as it is consistent with life preservation. And, if you are happy to donate some of your organs, but not others, that can also be taken care of. I acknowledge that not everyone feels the same, but for me it really is a no-brainer. I find it oddly contradictory when people who say they won't donate are very happy to receive, either for themselves or a loved one, if they needed it. Where do they think those life-saving organs are going to come from?

It was important to Stuart and me that we use the Celebrity Sunday evening not just to raise funds, but awareness too. It also presented an opportunity for a different angle of interest for the media. In interviews Jen and I could start talking about the fact that she was emergency listed for transplant, what that meant, and also – because of the scarcity in SA of organ donors – for people to hear exactly why it was unlikely that she would get the lungs she now so desperately needed. We did numerous radio interviews, Jen from the safety of her bed, and myself usually in the station's studio.

In the midst of all this, 10 days before Celebrity Sunday, Kristi and Kia had a combined 17th Burlesque-themed birthday party at our house. Who does that? Apparently I do. Whatever our family was going through, I was determined that "normal life" would carry on. The night of the party Jen stayed in our bedroom at one end of the house so as to be far away from any risk of infection, and had her closest friends visiting, while we had a disco and smoke machines at the other end of the house. I think we must have been slightly mad. It was a great party, though. Apart from one unruly teen vomiting on my lounge curtains, all went well. There was a boy Kristi had met at Abbotts, called Reggie, whom she kissed for the first time that night. I know this because in typical Stuart fashion, my husband went straight over to where they were trying to have a private moment on the garden bench and sat down. "So," he said genially, "what are you two up to?" He does make me laugh. Poor Reggie. What must he have thought? But he got to know us soon enough and was able to giggle about it; and it wasn't long before he and Kristi were in a committed relationship and his friends were regular fixtures in our home.

Reggie had long hair, rode a motorbike and was an absolute sweetheart, with an angelic face, brown eyes and gorgeous smile. He watched in admiration 10 days later as Kristi sang for Jen at Celebrity Sunday. She and Kim Kallie Banner did an emotional duet, an extraordinary 15-minute medley that told Jen and Kristi's story through song, intertwining snippets of some of their favourite ballads. Accompanied only by piano, it was a mesmerising and memorable performance.

Kristi wore a long white sequinned dress – my wedding dress, in fact – and Kim wore shimmery black. The ultimate professional, Kim had supported and trained Kristi for weeks leading up to this day until they were note-perfect. Jen, made up, hair curled and wearing a red jacket, sat next to me in the audience, holding my hand tightly. We had a paramedic there just in case, and she was connected to his canister of high-flow oxygen. She wasn't well, but she didn't want to miss Kristi's performance. As Kristi sang the words "Stay with me, 'cause you're all I need", I heard a sob choke in Jenna's throat. One small sound in a silent theatre.

Jen was sick of waiting, of jumping every time she heard the doorbell or the phone ring. It was becoming unbearable. She was also getting worse and worse. She could barely leave the house. She still loved reading and did lots of it, but sometimes she was even too tired or flat for that. The one thing that perked her up was visits from friends, James in particular, or times when Kristi would cuddle up in bed with her and share stories about Reggie, seeking big sister advice. Those were precious moments.

Jenna's journal
Monday, 8th September 2014
3:15 pm, my room

Everyone went back to varsity today. I am at home. I realised that since Natalie's death I have lost faith in the fairness and justice of life. I have lost trust in the benevolence of the universe. I need to open up again – tap back into the energy around me. I have shut off spiritually. In the last few months I haven't been doing as much community work and "giving back" and I have barely written. I need to recharge my creative, spiritual and emotional energy.

CHAPTER 37

#GetMeTo21

"What are we going to do, Mom?"

I was sitting on Jen's bed and we were quietly drinking a cup of tea together. She never actually said the words, "I can't just lie here and wait to die", but we both knew that was what she meant.

"Something," I said. "We are going to do something."

Stuart and I had been talking to the Organ Donor Foundation in the background for a few months already. What could we do to change the state of organ donation in South Africa? How could we get involved? What could we do to alter Jenna's destiny and that of thousands of others who were awaiting transplants, but did not have the ear of the media? There had to be something we could do.

Now it became a preoccupation for Jen too. We started reading up on the statistics, on barriers to entry, on how it worked successfully in other parts of the world. Because Stuart is in the research business, he had access to some informative statistics. As we started to talk more regularly around the dinner table as to what we as a family could do to make a difference, Jen became more upbeat.

A year earlier, in September 2013, we had been contacted by the transplant unit at Milpark to pass on a message that an advertising agency in Cape Town, Mullen Lowe, had an idea for a campaign to raise awareness of organ donation. The campaign idea would only work, though, if it was driven by the right person – it needed someone waiting for a transplant who was erudite, comfortable in front of the camera and able to deal with the media. They had heard Jen on the radio and they were convinced she was the right ambassador. At the time Jen had not yet been listed for a transplant. In fact, we were in the process of negotiating Flolan, which we believed would give her many, many healthy years still to come. I remember discussing the campaign suggestion with her briefly and Jen saying she couldn't do it; it wouldn't feel authentic because she wasn't listed for transplant. I agreed with her and we left it at that.

Now it was different. She walked through to me one morning and said: "Mom, do you remember that agency who called a year ago—"

She hadn't finished the sentence before I answered, "Yes, my love, I remember them well." Pause.

"Well," she said, "it's time. If they still want to do the campaign, it's time."

Then she turned around and made her way slowly back down the passage to her bed. My heart was pounding. This was good. I emailed the agency and set up a meeting with Kirk for one evening that week.

Jenna was still a bit ambivalent. We didn't know Kirk and we didn't have a grasp yet on what a campaign like this would entail. Everything depended on how Jen felt about it all after the meeting. I shouldn't have worried. Kirk turned out to be an affable, clever, creative man and passionate about his work. He and Jen took to each other immediately. He was kind and sensitive, too, and there was a straightforward honesty between them from the beginning. Jen said she was happy to work with him. Kirk told me only recently that when I left the room to fetch some tea, Jen looked him straight in the eye and said, "You need to know I'm not convinced this will work. But I'm willing to try. I'm doing this for Mom. Mom, and all the other people who might die waiting."

It was an emotional meeting and I could see how much it impacted Kirk. We agreed to work together but, as was patently obvious, we would have to get moving.

The campaign would centre on a short video of Jen inviting the entire nation to her 21st birthday. All you had to do to come to her party was sign up to be an organ donor. It was a simple and powerful idea, one that took the focus off the dire situation of organ donation statistics in South Africa and flipped it into a conversation about life and the celebration of life. Jen understood better than most that 21st birthdays aren't like any others. Turning 21 symbolises adulthood, independence and the potential of making one's own way in the world. It is the ultimate celebration that teenagers and adults alike can relate to. Jen was turning 20 in six weeks' time. The timing for the idea was perfect.

As simple as it seemed, it had been carefully thought out. Years of working with the Organ Donor Foundation had shown Kirk and his team that the general public are far more moved by the plight of one person they identify with than scary, generalised statistics. Jen would put a face to the harsh reality that she and so many other South Africans were facing. She would become a face for organ donation.

There was much to be done. Kirk and his team set about finding the right teams of people to come on board. This was pro bono, cause-based work and it required dedication, commitment and sensitivity. A specialist digital agency called GSDH started building the #GetMeTo21 app. It was imperative that at the end of Jen's video you could click through to sign up to be an organ donor. It was a call to action, after all. Then there was Match Creative, who ran all the public relations and media liaison, and Egg Films, who did the video production. Everyone gave of their time and expertise willingly and with love. They were united in the cause. It was important that Dani, the director at Egg Films found the right crew. They would shoot in Jen's bedroom, up close and personal.

I could see that the idea of the campaign and what it might achieve was bringing a renewed sense of purpose to Jen's long painful days of waiting.

The day of the shoot was looming. We needed to be sure no member of the crew was sick. They followed strict protocols, sterilising their equipment, washing their hands and respecting the space. Dani was the producer and she was the ideal choice. Warm, funny and easy-going but naturally caring, she handled the process with care and empathy. Jenna trusted her.

Kirk had shown Jen the agency's carefully crafted script. It was a discussion that didn't last long. "If I am to be the poster girl for dying," Jen said, "then it will be my words, words that are more representative of me." I left it to them to work it out. I trusted her implicitly.

The camera, lights and sound were set up and ready to go, with Steve and Mary squashed into the back corner of Jen's bedroom so that they could capture what the team was capturing on video. They did the shoot in just a couple of hours. Jen looked straight into the camera. She was breathless, but animated. The slight hissing sound in the background couldn't be avoided; it was the sound of Thunder. You can watch it on www.getmeto21.com

"Hi, I'm Jenna. I'm 19 and I'm planning my 21st birthday party now, and I'm inviting you. Now that might seem a bit odd, because I probably don't know you, but I would like you to come anyway.

"And I don't care what shape, size, colour or age you are, I want you to be there with me, and I want you to bring your friends. Because the more people there are, and the more people who sign up now, the more likely it is that I'll be able to join you.

"All you really have to do to come to my party is sign up to be an organ donor, because in order to make it to 21, I'm going to need new lungs ..."

The 55-second video had a massive impact on South Africans.

It launched on Tuesday, the 7th of October 2014 on YouTube, Facebook and Twitter, and within the first 24 hours, her video invitation had generated 2 105 788 Twitter impressions.

Jenna's message went viral overnight!

Within days it was picked up by traditional media. Our phones were ringing off the hook with radio producers, journalists, research students and patients all wanting to speak to Jen. It was insane. The conversation about organ donation was on everybody's lips and in everybody's home. Our wildest dreams could not have imagined this response.

At the bottom of the web page was a number-counter that ticked over every time another person signed up via the #GetMeTo21 digital app. Of course there are other ways to register as a donor, but even so, many used Jen's app and watching that counter clock go up and up by thousands was exhilarating. Everyone who became a donor had a sense of agency, a sense of belonging to a significant cause. They could be superheroes. It gave Jenna great joy watching that counter. I remember how, for the first few days, every time another donor signed up she would shout breathlessly from her bedroom: "Another seven lives saved!"

On Tuesday, the 28th of October 2014 Jenna turned 20 years old.

On the day of her birthday she was visited by Primedia, who had chosen her as their Lead SA Youth Hero of the Month for the Western Cape. Jen didn't know but Stu and I had been warned, and we'd arranged for a small group of her friends to visit that afternoon. They were all sitting with Jen on the day-bed when the Lead SA team arrived. Although slightly embarrassed about receiving the award, at the same time Jen was totally delighted and dinner that night was a celebration!

Jenna and Kristi's friends were incredibly supportive. They advocated for the cause wherever and however they could. There were flash-mobs at Newlands rugby stadium, as well as on various university campuses; videos were made and posted by close friends; everyone was urging everyone they could think of to sign up and spread the word.

Other South African brands and businesses joined the fever. On the 23rd of October the Spur Foundation pledged their support, and on the 7th of November they launched a supportive auxiliary "Save 7" campaign, working hand in hand with myself, Mullen Lowe and the Organ Donor Foundation. Soccer Laduma also joined the fight, committing to a consistent educational campaign through their publication, which had a readership of millions. They encouraged the involvement of one of the Western Cape's well-known soccer teams, Ajax Cape Town, to visit Jenna at our home to show a display of support for their advocacy campaign.

A large group of about 50 of our friends showed up for the annual Organ Donor Foundation 5 km walk in Mouille Point and we walked with a huge #GetMeTo21 banner. And in November the Western Province rugby team posed with the same banner to show their support. On the 5th of December Premier Helen Zille paid a visit to our home to have tea with Jenna as a show of support for her courage and her campaign.

Jenna's digitally led campaign ran for 67 days in total. During that period not one single cent was spent on media. The massive coverage was genuine cause-led publicity. The campaign went on, much later, to win many prestigious awards in the advertising industry, among them: Loeries 2015: Gold for the "Get Me To 21" campaign in the PR category and Bronze for the "Get Me To 21" campaign in the Social Media category; ACA Apex Awards for Effectiveness: Gold (in the Change category) for the "Get Me To 21" campaign; Grand Prix for the "Get Me To 21" campaign; the "Special Award" for the most successful submission for a charity or non-profit organisation for the "Get Me To 21" campaign; and IAB Bookmark awards: Silver Bookmark for the "Get Me To 21" integrated social media campaign.

It was really exciting, but between the numerous shoots taking place at our home and the radio and television interviews taking place from Jenna's bed, life and its challenges carried on as normal. Regular visits from the Pathcare nurse to draw blood, regular visits to Prof. (he'd started coming to us if Jen was too ill), an hour of mixing medication and changing pumps every day, six-hourly ice-packs, school lifts for Kristi, and listening for the little bell next to Jenna's bed in case she needed me.

But mostly we were listening intently every minute of every day for the phone to ring and someone to say, "We've got lungs."

The waiting was exhausting. In the mornings, a few times a week, I would walk around the neighbourhood with Mary and

Sue. Sometimes I couldn't even get around the first corner before crying. At home I was the rock of Gibraltar, but with my friends I could show my extreme anxiety and vulnerability.

Jenna's friend Alex continued to visit regularly, just about every day, often in his cycling kit. When he arrived, bike under his arm, in his bright yellow outfit Jen would look at him quizzically and tell him in no uncertain terms that he looked like a giant banana. When he wore the white cycling kit she would tease even more. "Yuck, Alex, really? Men in white lycra are not a good look!" They had such fun times together. He would perch on the end of her bed and they would play word games, argue about Disney movies (Jen was a massive fan, Alex not so much) and chat and giggle.

Jenna was really good company – funny, quick-witted, entertaining and hungry for news of the outside world. Chatting to her was the easiest thing in the world.

Knowing this, and loving Jen, Vanessa kept her promise to arrange for some exciting, inspirational people to visit. At the top of Jen's wish-list was Archbishop Emeritus Desmond Tutu, but unfortunately we didn't get that one right. She did, however, also ask to meet radio talk show host John Maytham. John had interviewed just about everyone who was anyone over the past 20 years. He is one of the most informed and intelligent people I have had the privilege of listening to on radio. I found the idea of having him in my home a little scary, to be honest, but Jen couldn't wait to meet him. It turned out to be a wonderful visit. John sat on a chair in Jen's room, and Stu and I sat on the bed with her. I think he arrived with the intention of chatting for a bit and then leaving as soon as possible. He can be quite a cynic, so he couldn't quite understand why this young girl would want to meet him. They got on so well that John ended up staying for a good two hours. What a fantastic man, and how good it was to see Jen light up again with intelligent debate and conversation.

She was also visited by South African author, scriptwriter and columnist Lauren Beukes. Jenna was toying with the idea of writing a book and was intrigued to talk to authors and get a sense of their processes. She had a million questions to ask. Lauren arrived with an armful of her books, each one signed for Jen, and they sat happily discussing reading and writing ad nauseam, one book nerd to another.

It was so uplifting to experience these happy times and see Jen so enthused and engaged. In darker moments, if I allowed myself to think about what she was missing out on, the adventure and possibilities awaiting her outside of these four walls, if I allowed myself to dwell on the losses she was facing, it would leave me feeling desolate. I wanted to rage at the world and its injustices, to curl up in a ball and give up. But I did not allow myself that. It was not an option.

Even though we had many exciting new visitors to our home, none brought quite as broad a smile to Jen's face as James. She simply lit up when he arrived – and so did he. It was a problem, one that Stuart and I had seen coming for quite some time, long before anyone else did. Including Jenna and James. The complexities of it were outrageous. James and Daffy were good friends, and had been for most of their lives. They were also both part of a tight-knit friendship group who'd been together since Grade 1. If Jen and James fell for each other, it could affect not only their very close friendship but it would cause discomfort in the whole group. Then, most importantly, there was Jen and Daffy's special relationship, years and years of friendship and romantic love. Jen would always love Daffy and he would always love her. From the outside looking in, it seemed so simple – this couldn't and shouldn't happen. It was too complicated and potentially too many people could get hurt. Not least of all James. Jen was not well. This was no picnic. Falling in love with Jen was risky in the extreme. But, again, the truth is that nothing is simple. Conflicting emotions, difficult complexities and brutal reality layer our lives every minute of the day. What matters most is our intention, our intention for love, courage, kindness and generosity of spirit.

Jenna and James had no intention of hurting anyone. They had no intention of falling in love either. But they did. What they shared during this extremely difficult time in Jenna's life was something that two young people should never have to cope with. It was intense. A situation that resulted in their feelings for each other becoming deep, very quickly. Looking back now, I can see that it was inevitable. There is nothing quite like the imminent threat of death to make the present moment have a ferocity that is difficult to explain. Everything else falls away. Life and love hold a new perspective.

It was the beginning of November, just a few days after Jenna's 20th birthday. James arrived at our house uncharacteristically early in the morning. He knew Jenna wouldn't be awake yet. He looked nervous and said he needed to talk to me. "Sure," I said, taking a deep breath. We made tea and went outside to sit on a bench in the garden. He looked strained. "What is it, James?" I asked. I was worried. Over the past 10 months I'd grown to love this boy who had visited my home every week. I had come to know him well. He was fun-loving and animated but he also took life seriously and had substance, integrity and a curious mind. James had been an unbelievable friend and support to both Jenna and Kristi over the months and years, and we had all become close. Unlike some of the youngsters who visited, he never avoided "time with the parents"; in fact, he would seek us out and spend hours talking to us around the kitchen counter, often having deeply honest conversations about how Jen really was. There was nothing he didn't know about the truth of her condition.

Today James looked distressed. "What is it?" I asked again. "James, you know you can talk to me about anything, right?"

And then it all came out. He explained that he had fallen "head over heels in love" with Jen and had absolutely no idea what to do. He talked and talked. It was clear just how excruciating this was for both of them. It was a situation that they had only acknowledged to each other fully for the first time the day before. It was a real dilemma. Our beloved Daffy, the myriad combined and intertwined friendships, James's family … this would impact everyone. I didn't know what to say. I was just as confused as he was. We talked for a very long time, exploring every angle. If James intended to go through with this, he had better be damn sure. He needed to know what he was getting into and what he could lose. Not only his friendship with Daffy and others, but also Jen. He needed to know he could lose Jen. He was so conflicted in so many ways and clearly in pain. We talked around and around in circles. Then there was a long silence.

Eventually I said: "James. You know this is going to get messy, right?"

"Yes, of course," he said, looking down at his feet.

"Then I have only one question left to ask you." Pause. "Are you able to walk away, James? If you are, then now is the time."

He thought about it for a long while, then looked up at me, his huge green eyes full of tears. "No," he said. "There is no way I can walk away from Jen now." Of that he was sure. He was resolute.

"Then you have your answer," I said. "You have your answer no matter the consequences."

Jenna phoned Daffy that night. It was one of the hardest things she had ever done. She wept before, during and after for many days, but she wanted to be with James. And Daffy was not there. He was on the other side of the world. It was tough and there was a lot of anger. I went to see Karen, Daffy's mom, and we cried together too. But as adults we also both understood. Karen loved Jen just about as much as she loved her own son and she understood that what Jen was facing was unthinkable. None of the normal "rules" applied. Part of us was grateful that Jen had James, at her side.

Daffy loved Jen so much that he phoned a few days later to tell her there was no way he could face losing her and his friendship with James at the same time. He was angry and hurt and sad, but he also understood. Then he spoke to James and told him he forgave him; no one could understand better than he how easy it was to fall head over heels in love with Jen. "But," Daffy said, "you had better not hurt her or let her down. You had better love each other fully and until the end or I will never forgive either of you."

Those boys astonished me. In fact they were not boys at all. They were incredible young men who, in the most difficult of circumstances, were loyal, committed and loving to the bitter end.

James, Daffy and Jenna all understood something that takes

most of us a lifetime to learn. They understood that loving and letting go are the same thing. They understood that real love is expansive, allowing and selfless. Holding on too tightly would have caused more pain and more anger. Daffy and Jen still spoke regularly; they remained very close. I don't know how he did it, but because of Daffy's understanding and generosity of spirit, Jenna and James's relationship took on a new dimension.

There was a new energy in the house and it was good to see and feel joy. We may not realise it but repressing feelings, good or bad, takes energy. Jen's spirit was enlivened and we all fed off that.

Apart from the odd exception to the rule, outings for Jen were pretty much now a thing of the past. Friends and family came to us and were met at the front door with a large sign that read "STOP. If you are even slightly sick, or have been in touch with someone who is, please don't visit. You will put Jenna at risk." Our little family had expanded. We often had six or more around the dinner table at night. It was the one thing Jen still managed to do; she still ate dinner at the dining room table with the family just about every night. Thunder would be rolled down the passage and plugged in at the front door. From there her seven-metre-long tube could reach just about anywhere in the house. I looked forward to dinner times when there was often laughter and happy debate around the table.

But always, just below the surface, there was a sense of waiting, of expectation and the knowledge that Jen was running out of time. Late one night Jen said to me: "I think one of the hardest parts of waiting for a transplant is that I don't know if I am preparing to live or preparing to die."

There were many times we were able to live in the moment and push aside our darkest fears. And then there were other, unforgettable moments, when the brutal reality was unavoidable. This is a journal entry Kristi wrote, four years later, in September 2018:

"Looking back it surprises me how we can become accustomed to even the most arduous of circumstances. Constant stress and fear just became a part of our day-to-day lives. Being as young as I was at the time, it was hard for me to constantly identify, confront or even understand the complex emotions I was experiencing when Jen was so ill, they were part of my normal daily routine. It is only now that I have truly begun to understand what my mind and body have endured over the years and, in all honesty, I still haven't fully come to terms with the impact Jenna's (and my own) trauma has had on me mentally, physically and emotionally. There are times when I can't remember whole periods, as if I erased the memories from my mind. And then there are some incredibly vivid memories, memories which, when I hold in my mind, take me back to that exact moment in time – I can smell, taste, feel everything all over again …

"I remember hugging Jenna, just a couple months before her transplant. She was so sick that she could barely walk to the bathroom without breaking to catch her breath. She had just got out of bed and I embraced her, both as a source of affection and comfort, and as a physical aid for her to catch her breath. She leant into me, and it struck me – not for the first time, but probably the most memorable – just how different she felt. Her head rested in my neck, the hissing of her oxygen loud in my ears. As I wrapped my arms around her, I could feel every vertebra in her back. Her tiny arms held my waist, and I could feel her ribcage expand and contract as she fought to pull more air into her lungs. But the scariest part was her heart. It fluttered against me, fast and urgent. It felt as if there was a hummingbird in her chest desperately trying to burst free. In that moment I could literally feel how hard her little body was working to keep her alive. A part of me was terrified, I wanted to let go, to have my Jenna back, with her strong arms and athletic build that could squeeze me back and tell me that everything would be okay, that she would always be there for me. But an even bigger part wanted to hold her even tighter, to sweep her up and take away her pain. To never let her go."

CHAPTER 38

Down the rabbit hole

We didn't need more, but just a few weeks later, on an ordinary week night, there was another drama. We had just finished dinner. Jen walked down the passage slowly, her long oxygen tube trailing behind her, and flopped down onto Kristi's bed. Reggie was visiting and the three of them lay together, chatting, sharing memes and scrolling through Facebook. I was in the lounge, contemplating watching some TV, when suddenly I heard Kristi shout, loudly and urgently.

"MOM! Mom! Come quick, we need to change Jen's pump!"

Change her pump? But we did that this morning ... we only change pumps in the morning. Something must have gone wrong. I all but levitated and ran down the passage. Kristi and Jen were already a few paces towards the drug den. The line from Jen's pump that carried her medication to the port in her chest was severed.

"What the fuck happened?" I shouted, my heart racing.

"Mellow, it was Mellow," Kristi said.

Mellow, one of our "adorable" white angora bunnies, had quietly hopped into the room unnoticed. Jen had placed her pump on the floor next to the bed and Mellow had eaten *straight through* her line.

"When?" I said, staring at her in shock. "When, Jen? Kristi? *When* did it happen? How many minutes?"

"We don't know, Mom."

There was no way of knowing how many minutes had passed since Mellow had done the damage. With the threat of Flolan's short 3.5-minute half-life, we could be in serious trouble. My mind was racing.

"Mom!" Kristi's voice broke through my fog.

I was standing in front of the fridge in the drug den, door wide open, staring at it, paralysed. I snapped back into action, grabbing the already mixed cartridge of medication from the fridge (so this was why we always mixed two!) and barked at Kristi to find a dressing pack on the shelf.

While she did so I shook up the cartridge, checked it and got out a spare pump to start programming it. My mind was all over the place. How many nanograms were we on? What setting did I need? What speed? How did I do this? White-hot panic can totally scatter your thoughts. "Focus," I told myself. "Focus." My hands were shaking violently as I put on my mask and surgical gloves. "Give me instructions, Mom, what must I do?" It was Kristi. I needed her assistance. Once the sterile gloves are on you can't touch anything. Over 100 hours of practice kicked into action. I started issuing instructions.

"Wipe down the surface with an alcohol swab, quickly. Okay, now do it again. Put on those gloves. No, those ones. Now, unwrap the sterile dressing tray, quick! Okay good. Pass me another alcohol swab, yes, another one, tear it, tear it and pass it to me." Everything else receded into nothingness. There was just Kristi and me, totally focused, working as a team. "Right, pour that Biotane into the tray and pass me the gauze. I need a new stat lock and line." We were working as quickly as we could. Jen, meanwhile, had sterilised her hands, unscrewed the stat lock from the chewed-through line and placed the discarded pump on the bench. I primed a new line. It felt like everything was taking so long! Finally, everything was ready. I sterilised her port and then twisted the new stat lock and line into place … there … connected! I switched on the pump. Silence. No alarm. It was good.

278

Oh my God. I stared at Jen. She was pale but seemed all right. Kristi and I were shell-shocked. My hands were still shaking. At that moment Jen's phone rang in her back pocket. It was Radio 702. We had forgotten she had a live interview on national radio scheduled for 8:30 pm. "Pass me the phone," I said. "I'll cancel it for you." She looked at me as if I was crazy and walked slowly up the two steps that led out of the drug den. She leaned against the passage wall and said, "Hello!" Her voice was calm, bordering on cheerful. "Yes, it's Jen. Thank you for having me on the show. How are you?" Not a word of what had just happened. Kristi looked at me and shrugged. Reggie was standing in the doorway, white and wide-eyed with shock. Medical equipment lay strewn all over the den.

As for me, I was in a heap. Bunny stew seemed like a good option.

CHAPTER 39

Presenting to Parliament

For a while now the Flolan had been titrated to its maximum levels, as had the rest of Jenna's medications. Plus we had her on maximum levels of oxygen, all the right supplements, alternative remedies, meditation, rest, love and anything else you could think of. There was nothing left to do but wait for transplant, and it couldn't happen soon enough.

One of the incredible things that resulted from the general uptake of the #GetMeTo21 campaign was that Stuart and I were contacted by a member of Rotary. He knew the secretary for the Portfolio Committee on Health and he asked us if we would like an opportunity to speak in Parliament and address the committee regarding PH and the legislation surrounding organ donation in South Africa. It was a fairly nerve-wracking prospect but we jumped at the chance. This could potentially make a difference at government level, which was what was needed. Countries around the world who have an "opt out" system fare much better in terms of the quantity and quality of transplant surgeries, which in turn impacts excellence in all areas of medicine.

Stu and I prepared a detailed presentation, using Jenna's story as the narrative for a much bigger conversation which highlighted the facts and statistics surrounding organ donation and transplant in South Africa. We checked our details with the ODF, Stuart's research and a local transplant co-ordinator to ensure factual correctness, but the presentation was our take on it. Steve and Mary offered to video a message from Jen for the committee. She would have given anything to have been there in person to address them. Jen believed that transplant is the ultimate "rainbow nation" life-saving gift. Why? Organs are not only colour blind, but they don't care what age or gender you are. As she used to say: "You certainly don't need your organs in heaven, but Lord knows we need them here on earth." The activist in Jen was fiercely determined to address local government, and the United Nations if she could, when she was well enough on the other side of transplant. She wanted to influence the laws around the globe so that everyone has access to lifesaving medication and organs.

On Wednesday, the 12th of November Stu and I got dressed in formal gear, laptops under our arms, and made our way to Parliament. What an experience. There were rows and rows of desk-type tables with small microphones on them that looked like thin desk lamps. We had to push a button every time we spoke so that the whole room could hear. Stu and I were seated facing everyone else in the room. In some ways I felt like I was on trial in front of a panel. There was so much at stake here. Then there was the protocol, all totally new to us other than Parliamentary debates we had watched on television. It is actually really like that. Every time we addressed an Honourable Member, or answered a question we had to do so through "Madam Speaker". Yikes. We both got it wrong at first and Stu held my hand under the counter to give me encouragement, but after a while we found our feet. Our presentation, which was about half an hour long, went really well and our audience seemed captivated. Afterwards we fielded questions.

By the time we got home I was sweaty and exhausted, but it was so good to be welcomed by a very proud Jenna who wanted to know every single detail about her parents' Parliamentary début.

The next day, Thursday, the 13th of November, was the first anniversary of Natalie's death. Was it possible that an entire year had gone past already? Grief and time have a weird way of entwining themselves, merging into a timeless dimension. It felt as though it had been both 10 years and 10 days. We gathered to commemorate her death and celebrate her life, to be together. It felt surreal.

Operation O2 was prepped and ready to be actioned but the waiting went on.

At the end of November Jen was visited by another writer, this time also a political commentator, Melanie Verwoerd. To mark the "coming of age" of the South African nation, Melanie was in the process of collecting 21 life stories of people born in 1994 for a book she was co-authoring with Sonwabiso Ngcowa. Publication was scheduled for the following year, the year of Jenna's much-anticipated 21st birthday. Melanie came to interview Jen and they got along so well that Jen asked me to invite her to join us for a braai a few weeks later. Jenna's story is the first chapter of Melanie's book, which is called *21 at 21*.

By now Kristi and Reggie were pretty much inseparable. He was in the middle of writing his final year exams and Kristi was writing her finals for Grade 10. Already one year older than most in her class, at 17, she had her learner's licence and could now drive as long as a licensed adult was with her in the car. Aside from studying and Kristi, Reggie's mind was on leaving school and Matric Rage with his mates. He was torn between the excitement and anticipation and not wanting to go without Kristi. Naturally Kristi was also keen. She badly wanted to go.

Stuart and I weren't sure how to deal with the dilemma and we discussed it for hours. It had been a rough couple of years for Kristi and it was true that she had dealt with and seen things that most adults haven't had to face. We trusted her, but more than that we wanted her to have the experience of some carefree teenage time. Stu and I decided that the only way it could work was if Reggie went on his own for the first week and then I drove Kristi up to join him for the last six days. I would stay in Plett, not far from them, and that way I could ensure she was okay and we would be together in case the call came for Jenna's transplant. It was a big decision. A very big decision. What if the call came in the six days that I was away? I was very nervous about the idea. But then again, what were the chances? What were the chances that in all these months of waiting the call would come in those six days? What were the chances that we would even get a call? Very slim. Very, very slim indeed. Still, I was nervous.

Lizzie was on standby and would be there every day to help Jen, and besides, Stu said, "You really need the break, my love. You look exhausted."

And so the decision was made. Kristi was beyond excited, and so was Jen. She was delighted Kristi would have this time.

"I want to hear all about it, Nooglet," she told her sister. "All about it." And then, looking at me sternly, "And you, Mom," she said, "you need some rest."

Stu and Jen were right. I did. I did need some rest. And Kristi needed to be a normal teen and have some fun.

In the days leading up to the Plett trip Stu and I called a meeting in his office at the top of our driveway with Mary, Sue, Brandon and Lizzie to go through the Operation O2 documentation in minute detail. Everyone had to know exactly what was going on, and to have their own copy just in case. Lizzie and I checked all the already packed suitcases of medication yet again and we also made sure all the contact numbers on the phone tree were current and functional. From a logistical point of view we were "good to go".

On Wednesday, the 3rd of December, as Kristi's school year finished, Kristi, Kia and I piled into the car together and drove to Plett. For me it felt completely counter-intuitive driving away from Cape Town. I had to keep reminding myself that this had been a carefully considered decision.

Everything went well. Reggie and Kristi were happy to be together and met up with numerous friends from all over Cape Town and Plett. In fact they had the best time. Kristi was safe and she stayed in contact with me regularly. Meanwhile I made sure that I rested, slept, walked, wept and spent valuable time catching up with Ian and Jillie. I spoke to Jenna, and Lizzie and Stuart so many times a day they got irritated with me. Everything was fine at home. "Stop worrying, my love," said Stu. "We will see you on the weekend."

We were leaving Plett to head back to Cape Town in two days' time.

And then ... on Wednesday, the 10th of December 2014, at 9:10 am, the ringing of my cellphone shocked me awake.

Part 5

Lead SA Hero of the Month for her organ donor campaigning

Top: Gabi and extended Lowe family – Shirley, Alison and Stuart
Bottom left: Gabi and Mary Berry – ultimate friend and neighbour
Bottom right: The Hunters, Ian and Jillie

Top: Gabi with her Angels – Carlie, Karen and Melissa
Bottom: Stuart with the 'boys', James and Reggie, at the Rivonia house

Top: Jen and James in the jet en route to Joburg for the transplant
Bottom: Nurse Lizzie and Stu watch as Jen is airlifted by helicopter
from Lanseria to Milpark

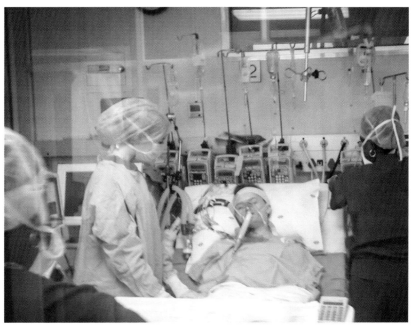

Top left: Kristi and Gabi saying goodbye as Jen goes into theatre
Top right: Waiting outside ICU
Bottom: Kristi sings to her sister post-transplant

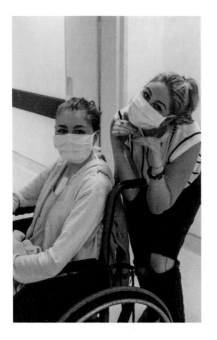
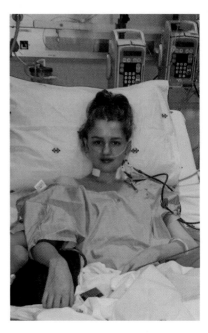
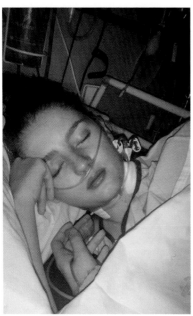

Top left: Aniko and Jen doing 'wheelies' down the passage at Milpark
Top right: Doing so well post-transplant, early January 2015
Bottom left: Our sleeping angel between dialysis
Bottom right: Valentine's Day 2015 – James puts on a show for Jen in Milpark Hospital

Top: Jen's friends speak at the memorial service – Daffy, Aniko, Tayla, James, Camilla, Julia, Giulietta, Michael and Celeste
Bottom: A beautiful montage put together in memory of Jen

When we were ready, we took a family road trip to sprinkle 'Jen-Dust' around the country at her favourite and most special spots

CHAPTER 40

Transplant: Wednesday, 10th December 2014

Jenna looks back at me as her hospital bed is pulled through the theatre doors. She smiles at us, so full of hope, fear and courage. She is the bravest person I know.

We stand outside the theatre doors staring at each other, Stuart, Kristi, James, Lizzie and myself, the noise of the double doors thudding softly slower and slower until they come to a stop. It is just after 6 pm and already it's getting dark. I am rooted to the ground. Alternating waves of hope and nausea threaten to overwhelm me. The air on my skin feels cold. Stu puts his arm around me, and we move gently down the passage to the waiting room. It is small, square, with brown carpets and bare walls. It feels more like a prison than a family waiting room. I can't sit. I stare up at the only redeeming feature, a skylight in the centre of the room, watching as heavy raindrops fall from high up in the sky down, down, down onto the plastic.

Dr Williams (Paul) arrives and explains calmly that it is time for us to leave the hospital. "Surgery will take many, many hours," he says. "You need to go to your hotel and rest. I will stay in touch, as and when I hear from the theatre." His tone is gentle but firm. "We will let you know as the surgery is coming to an end so that you can get back here in time for when she comes out."

Dr Williams is Jen's critical care expert, her lead doctor, our person, but he isn't the surgeon. There is a full team inside the theatre doing the transplant. Once surgery is over, they will hand over to him.

It feels impossible to leave the hospital, but staying in this airless room is not an option. We make our way to The Parkwood, which is just 15 minutes away, where our friends Dean and Sarah are kindly waiting to welcome us. Usually fully booked, it's a blessing that Johannesburg empties like bathwater in December.

We collapse onto the big couches under shelter on their deep veranda and nurse a bottle of wine. I notice James is still in his gym shorts and T-shirt from this morning's evacuation. Everyone starts to share stories, their unique experiences of the day. I'm hungry for every detail. It feels surreal. Stu, Kristi and I sit huddled together on one couch. Everyone is tired, but wired. I won't remember much of those eight hours of waiting except that it takes forever. The storm is building, and the skies are dramatic. Forked lightning lights up the night sky and thunderbolts crack open the heavens. Rain pours down in sheets. Waves of fear threaten to overwhelm me as the hours tick by: 10 pm comes and goes, 11 pm ... midnight ... Eventually I put Kristi into bed. She is exhausted and still in shock. Her coping mechanism is to sleep and shut out the world. James can't sleep. He sits up waiting with Stu, myself and Shirley.

Thursday, 11th December 2014

At 1:10 am Dr Williams' message comes through. "Come to the hospital. Jen will be coming out of theatre soon."

Deafening thunderbolts shake the heavens and hailstones fall from the sky. The skyline lights up again and again as jagged forks of lightning slash and vanish. There are no other cars on the road. The scene outside our little vehicle reflects the turmoil going on inside. We make it back to the hospital and hurry down the deserted passage to the waiting room. The skylight is our only window to the storm still raging outside. Twice I levitate right off my chair because the thundercracks are so loud. They are directly above us.

A little after 2 am we are called to ICU. There is a bell at the entrance to the double doors and a hand-washing station on the right as you enter, complete with masks and gloves. The rectangular room has no windows. Square fluorescent ceiling panels flood the space with unnatural light. What look like glass boxes flank the room along each side. These are the isolation wards. The main part of the room is for intensive care patients not in need of isolation, their beds screened only by a curtain, if at all. There are no "healthy-looking" patients in ICU. It is not a gentle place, but in the dead of night, except for the non-stop beeping of machines, it is at least quiet.

We sit awkwardly in the middle of the room between the rows of isolation cubicles.

Then there is a sudden flurry of activity. The double doors from theatre burst open. Three nurses and two surgeons pull a bed through from theatre and into ICU. It's Jenna. All the nurses spring into action. Everyone is on high alert, focused, paying attention. We stay out of the way as they wheel Jen past us and into her isolation ward, which has been prepped and is ready and waiting for her. I stare at her as they wheel her past. It is a shock. She is hooked up to so many tubes and machines. We watch in silence through the glass doors as they hook her up to more monitors and additional machines. It is a frightening sight, but somehow she has made it through the eight-hour surgery.

There were two surgeons in the operating theatre and the lead surgeon makes no bones about the procedure. "It was a very long and very difficult surgery," he tells us. His words and his no-nonsense tone of voice indicate that Jenna is far from out of the woods. "Nothing is predictable," he says to Stuart and me, "but she is a fighter, that is for sure."

I stare at my girl. Is this really my child? It seems unreal.

A green theatre gown covers Jenna's chest, but I know that

underneath it there is a "clamshell" incision that extends from one armpit around to the sternum and then back towards the other armpit. It will be stapled from end to end. Jen is far from conscious, and her skin is deathly pale and waxy. Her head is wrapped in a large bandage (why?) and there are pipes everywhere.

Everything I have read up to this point has been in an effort to prepare myself for this moment. Those efforts have been futile, I realise. Nothing could have prepared me. Nothing. I push my terror aside. I need to stay calm and strong for Jenna.

At 4 am we drive back to The Parkwood. We are shattered. We brush our teeth in silence. There are no words. Stuart is asleep before his head hits the pillow. But I can't sleep. Not one single wink. Images of Jen being wheeled out of theatre flash across my mind again and again. I just want to get back to ICU.

Stu and I are back at the hospital before 7 am. Shirley stays at the guest house with the kids, who need to sleep. We stand looking at Jenna through the glass. Two full-time ICU nurses are inside the isolation ward with Jen at all times. They are constantly busy – monitoring, writing things down, taking vital signs, adjusting and administering medications. It is mind-blowing.

Jen is attached to an ECMO (extracorporeal membrane oxygenation) machine which pumps and oxygenates her blood outside her body, allowing her heart and lungs to rest. Two thick tubes carry the blood out from her body, through the ECMO machine and back again constantly. "The machine is currently doing the work of her heart and lungs," Dr Williams explains when we see him, "and the large bandage on her head is simply there to hold the ECMO tubes in place."

She is also intubated, meaning she has a pipe down her airway which is connected to a ventilator to help her breathe. A ventilator delivers breath to the lungs when a patient can't.

There are the standard hospital monitors – the graph of the heartbeat, to keep track of her heart rate, oxygen saturation levels and blood pressure. We will quickly become adept at reading these at a glance to get a top-level overview of how Jen is doing. Then there are the drains – thick tubes filled with dark yellow fluid –

coming out from either side of her chest to help remove excess fluid build-up. Plus there is an additional port with intravenous lines coming out from her neck on the opposite side to the ECMO tubes. These provide direct access to her veins for medication. And behind Jen's bed a bank of further machines, specialised medication pumps, and several drip stands. Doctors come and go. It is tense.

Kristi and James are allowed into ICU for a short while to gaze through the glass doors, but not into her glass cubicle. We take turns so there aren't too many of us crowding the place.

At 2 pm Stu insists on taking me home to rest. Ali has arrived in Johannesburg. It is so good to have her here. I manage to eat a banana and sleep for two hours before going back to the hospital. When I get back to Milpark at 4 pm Jen is battling. She is unstable. They are trying to keep her completely sedated but she is fighting for consciousness. Paul (Dr Williams) will allow me one minute in the cubicle. I wash up and put on a mask and gloves and a sterilised gown over my clothing. He is inside the cubicle, watching carefully. If my presence calms Jen, it will be very helpful for everyone, but if she gets excited or agitated then I will be whisked away. I take a few deep breaths and enter. I am careful not to bump anything or touch any of the tubes. It feels so foreign in here. I find a space to stand between the machines, next to Jen's bed. Gently I take one delicate hand in mine. Her eyes are closed but agitated and darting from side to side. The minute I start talking they stop. "Jen. Jen, my darling, you are doing so well. I am so proud of you, my baby. The doctors are very happy. Everything went well and is as it should be. We are all here all of the time. You are not alone. I love you, Jen."

Her heart slows a bit.

Paul nods to me. I have done well but I am not allowed to stay longer. It is too soon after the surgery.

When I get out, I cry. It felt so good to be inside with Jen, to touch our special "Jen-Bean".

James is taking strain. Stu has been speaking to his dad; we need to get James home to his family. That night we eat a simple meal, we phone Granny and Grampa in Cape Town, and Craig and

Margo in Australia. It is good to have Ali's energy here. She insists I take a sleeping tablet so that I can have a good night's sleep. She takes my phone away and gives it to Shirl. I make Shirley promise they will wake me and take me to the hospital if ICU calls. I get seven straight hours of sleep and feel vaguely human again.

Friday, 12th December

Today Jen is unstable. She has had two blood transfusions and is going onto dialysis at 2 pm because her kidneys have stopped functioning. Stu and I take turns being at the hospital all day. I'm glad James has flown home; this would be too hard to see. Kristi comes back and forth, either with me, or Stu, or Shirl, but she is very quiet. It is not easy for her to see her sister in this environment.

Saturday, 13th December

Three days post-transplant, Jen is fighting for her life. For three hours this morning it has been touch and go. She has been put onto inhaled nitric oxide and adrenaline through the ventilator.

Both are used to treat respiratory failure. She does not give up. By mid-afternoon she stabilises again and the nurses send me away. I go to help everyone move from The Parkwood to Christine and Mark's apartment. They have been ridiculously kind and are lending us their apartment. I can't believe it. Christine is going to Plett for a month and has given us the keys to her home and her car. It's only 15 minutes from the hospital and so is a real lifesaver. How do you thank people for this sort of kindness? What would we do without it?

Messages of support are flooding in for Jen. Sandy Harper, a dear friend who moved to Johannesburg a few years back, arrives with some ready-made meals for us. They are much needed and I'm so grateful for her thoughtfulness. And Shirl is being a support in ways I don't even know I need. Tayla and Daffy are messaging James frequently and he has the idea to set up a WhatsApp group for all Jen's friends so that he can keep them informed. He calls us two to three times a day to hear how she's doing. Stu and I have asked Kristi if she would like Reggie to come up to support her and she says yes. He will fly up to join us on Tuesday. Alex has moved into our house in Cape Town to house- and dog-sit; he says all is going well, although the dogs keep looking for us and Sahara follows him around everywhere, whining.

Today has been a big day. In the shower this evening I have what I think might be some sort of an anxiety attack. I can't breathe. I've never had this before. But it doesn't last long. I talk myself down.

Sunday, 14th December

Stu and I wake early and go straight to the hospital, leaving Shirley and Kristi to sleep in. Jen is a little better and more stable today. Still critical, but stable. I think we may be creeping in the right direction. She is still on ventilation, on ECMO and on dialysis, but on a slightly more even keel. Stu and I are starting to get to know the staff at the coffee shop. Shirley brings Kristi through in the afternoon. Jen is quite wakeful and while the four of us stand watching, Paul goes in to talk to her.

She opens her eyes briefly and tries to smile at him – with all those tubes! And he gets her to squeeze his hand. He lets me go in to see her, but she is fast asleep again. On the phone I tell James the good news about Jen opening her eyes and smiling. He is really battling with being away, he wants to come back. He is visiting Cami in Cape Town today so that they can be together.

I go back to the hospital again after supper. Things have changed and they're not good. Jen is in tachycardia, her heart rate is fast and irregular. The ICU staff call Paul to come to the hospital. Jen is very distressed. It is awful. Paul and I decide I should see if I can calm her down. It is the third time I have been allowed in to be with her. I wash up and put on my mask, gloves, cap and gown. I can't wait to get to her side. In the isolation room I keep my voice stable, calm.

"Jen, it's Mom. I am here with Dr Williams. You are doing so well, my love, you are doing so well. Right now you have only one job, my baby, only one job, and that is to stay calm. We need you to stay calm. Can you try, my love? Everything is fine, but you need to rest. Okay, my love?"

Her eyes are closed but she nods and squeezes my hand.

"I love you, Jen. I love you so much. You are doing so well."

This is so hard.

Monday, 15th December

Five days post-transplant. Some meds have been altered, Jen's heart rate is down and her blood pressure is more stable. She goes briefly into theatre today for a bronchoscopy to remove some mucus from the new lungs because she can't cough naturally yet to clear them. While she is there they will have a look inside. Paul says her lungs are looking pink, much better than before. This is good news.

So many people are sending beautiful messages from all over the country and lighting candles for you, Jen, I tell her in my heart. The world is on your side, my love, thinking of you and praying for you.

Just keep fighting.

Tuesday, 16th December

It is so good to have Reggie here for Kristi. He is being so kind and gentle with her and is totally involved. It's a relief to know she has him here as a support, as I am mostly at the hospital.

We are all standing at the glass doors when Paul goes in to see Jen today. He tells her we are all outside, and for the first time since surgery she lifts her eyes towards the door to look at us through the glass. She lifts her hand a tiny bit and tries to wave. I think I might burst with happiness. We blow Jen kisses before she drifts back into sleep.

This time Stu and I are both allowed to spend time inside the isolation ward with Jen. She is still intubated so she can't talk and instead is making small hand signals, which we are trying to work out. It's such a sense of relief when we do, and so frustrating when we can't.

Wednesday, 17th December

Six days post-transplant. A really good day. Stu and I get to the hospital early. Jen's heart rate is good and her blood pressure is down. There is talk of extubating her – removing the ventilation tube – of getting her off the ventilator. I call Shirl to let her know and she comes through to the hospital with Kristi and Reggie. Paul explains to us that because Jen has been intubated for so many days there is a chance her vocal cords will be damaged. She is still very drugged up but vaguely conscious and so now is a good time. It won't be done under sedation, she must be conscious. I explain to him that the best chance we have of the extubation going smoothly is if he explains to Jen exactly what he is going to do before and while he does it. I know my Jen. The more information she has, the calmer she will be.

When you extubate a patient it can feel weird and scary, and uncomfortable. But more than anything this is a massive moment as Jen will be off the ventilator for the first time. And for the first time she will breathe on her own with her new lungs.

We watch as Paul explains carefully and precisely to Jen what he is going to do. I know every subtle nuance of her body language, and I can visibly see her relaxing her body and taking her mind to a place of calm.

Paul removes the tube. No one moves.

"Jen ... Jen," he says, "I need to hear your voice. Jen? Can you hear me? Talk to me, Jen."

Silence. And then we hear her voice for the first time since surgery. It is hoarse.

"Thank you, thank you, thank you, thank you, thank you." She can't stop saying it. "Thank you, thank you, thank you." Tears stream down her cheeks.

Dr Williams looks up at us. Tears are running down his cheeks too. We are all in tears. We watch from outside the glass doors and weep with relief and joy.

Stuart and I are allowed to go in to be with Jen, at her side, almost immediately after her extubation. I can see she is a bit anxious about breathing on her own. Paul has warned us it will be a big step for her, and the nurses give her a small oxygen mask to help with the transition. We talk her gently through it and put her mind at rest. These lungs work, I remind her. These are healthy lungs. Somehow in my fantasies this moment of her first breath with her new lungs was very different from this. I imagined her taking huge, unhindered gulps of air, but of course it's not like that. She is sore and weak and has to learn how to use these lungs, slowly.

At 2 pm we are sent home so that Jen can rest. I take the opportunity to call my family, James and all my girlfriends with the news that Jen is off the ventilator. It is the first time since surgery that I speak to anyone other than my direct family. I phone Glynis, Vanessa, Mary, Lani, Karen, Jillie, Tess, Nici and more ... I phone my inner circle while I have the impetus of good news to carry me through hearing their voices outside of the horror that is ICU.

Now I have a monster headache. It has been brewing all day. It's really sore. At 6 pm I go back to the hospital. Jen is so tired from breathing on her own. I stay for a while, but the nurses think it's better if I leave her to sleep. I'm going to do the same. Paul says I really need to get some rest now. He says that soon there is a chance that Jen will experience some psychosis as a result of the hectic combinations of medication she is on. All patients experience it differently, so there is no way of knowing what it will look like for Jen, but few patients escape it. When it happens, I want to be ready. I take some strong headache tablets; even my face aches. Stu is looking after me and puts me to bed. I love him. How would we get through this without each other?

Thursday, 18th December

It is one week since transplant today. I call ICU at 6:30 am, as I have done every day so far, to check in. By now we know that if we want a detailed report on how Jen's night has been it is best to speak to the night nurse before shift change at 7 am.

Jenna has had a good night, the night nurse tells me, no drama, and is fast asleep. She has even had a few tiny mouthfuls of yoghurt.

She has to start eating. As all is calm, I take the opportunity to do some washing. Both Kristi and I still only have our Plett clothing with us. I pay some bills, check emails and do general admin. It feels surreal to do even the smallest of ordinary tasks.

We get to the hospital later than usual today and at 9:30 am we meet the hospital GM and Raffaella from Discovery for coffee in the coffee shop. We hear the "chopper drama" for the first time. Apparently, there was a delay with the lungs when Jen was in surgery. The storm last week had played havoc with arrangements and so an army chopper had to be sent in – all the international air traffic at OR Tambo International Airport had to be stopped – to collect the lungs to transport them to Milpark. Only army choppers are cleared to fly at night and time was of the essence. It was the only way.

I spend the morning with Jen and swap out with Stu for a brief rest mid-afternoon before heading back at 5 pm.

When I get back to ICU it is hectic. Psychosis has set in.

Paul calls me in to be with Jen.

She is very much awake. Her eyes are wide open, and she is staring up at the ceiling, barely blinking. She is completely non-conversant, as if she is in an altered universe. And she looks terrified. Every few seconds she sucks air in through her lips in short sharp breaths. Try as I may, I cannot get her to look at me or respond in any way. I notice she is trying not to swallow. She hasn't eaten a morsel since this morning, won't sip water or respond to anyone.

I talk to her gently and sing some of the lullabies I used to sing to her as a baby. Nothing seems to make a difference. She stares and gulps, and stares and gulps. In desperation I start telling Jen her life story. From how she was in my tummy, to how she was as a newborn, a baby, an infant, a toddler. I tell her in minute and intricate detail. I remember every small detail. Every smell, every sound, every touch, place, experience, person or pet who has mattered to her. I stay beside her until midnight. Sweat is dripping down my back inside the gown and my hands are itching from the gloves. The air inside my mask is damp and warm. I concentrate on keeping my voice calm and even. I am thirsty and I need to wee, but I don't move. The only way we know that she can hear me is that her heart rate is more constant. But for the rest, she stays exactly the same. Non-conversant, short, sharp, erratic breathing and staring up at the ceiling wide-eyed like a frightened deer. She is in some kind of awful hell. Every now and then her eyes close and she appears to fall asleep for a few seconds, only to wake in terror. Her eyes snap open and she gasps again.

Paul recommended some sleep meds, but they haven't touched sides. More are given. Jen falls asleep at midnight and I am sent home. Shirley puts me in a hot bath. My heart is broken. I can't eat. My stomach is a bundle of tight knots. I have lost 3 kg in a week. When will this get easier for Jen?

Friday, 19th December

I wake ridiculously early and cook clear chicken soup. Jen's favourite. I have to tempt her to eat. Even just a few mouthfuls. She slept for six hours but now that she is awake again she is still using every inch of her energy to focus on breathing, swallowing and staying calm. She has such grit. I can see she is trying to help the nurses and to cough. This morning's chest X-ray showed mucus build-up in her lungs again. They send me out of ICU at 11:30 am so that Jen can have a wipe-down and a rub.

I go and sit in the coffee shop, where I look at my phone. I'm so filled with gratitude at the incredible messages and outpouring of love. Everyone is rooting for Jen. Ali and Les are going to fly up for Christmas with Matt and Kola. Yay. Christmas. Heavens. I haven't even thought about that. What would we do without Mark and Christine's home? Where would we be? We are so blessed to have such love and support. And we have a second car. A friend of Charles's just arrived to give the keys to Stu. We don't even know them. People's kindness and generosity are humbling.

I walk back down the long passage to ICU. I square my shoulders, take a deep breath. Jen is much the same. Staring up at the ceiling, battling to breathe, to swallow and to sleep. She can't eat in this state and I am worried about how thin she is getting. Paul and I discuss it. She will go onto a nasogastric tube tomorrow. I don my gown, mask, cap and gloves and pick up where I left off yesterday. I continue telling Jenna her life story in minute detail. It is all I can think to do. In between I sing to her, softly. Every now and then she catnaps before waking up and gasping again. I can't stand to see her so scared, but nothing I say seems to change it. She must be so tired. She seems to be in a never-ending loop.

By night time Paul decides to sedate her again.

Saturday, 20th December

Today isn't a good day.

There is a lot of fluid on Jenna's lungs and she is really battling to breathe. She goes back into theatre for another bronchoscopy and to be intubated again. She is also put back on the ventilator. Initially it feels like a step backwards, but it is such a relief to see her get some respite. And the nasogastric feeding tube means that at least she is getting some nutrition.

James phones regularly. He is hating being away and wants to come up, but it's not the right time. This is too tough.

By the afternoon Jen is looking better. Her heart rate is down. Her oxygen sats have improved since the bronchoscopy and she's had some sleep. Paul extubates her again. She is compliant. Clinically she is doing much better but once she is able to talk she tells us that she is fed up, *gatvol*. She throws us out. First Stu and then me. The nurses say she has been quietly "on strike" all day. This is good. Maybe Jen is getting her spirit back.

We send Kristi in, who spends the longest time at her bedside. She sings to Jen, song after song after song. Stu and I watch through the glass doors. It is so poignant to see Kristi stand at her sister's bedside with such love and courage and sing and sing. Tears pour down our faces. The two ICU nurses are crying too, I can see the tears on their cheeks underneath their masks. Kristi's singing is deeply moving ... and it is the only comfort that Jen will accept today.

Sunday, 21st December

It is 10 days post-transplant. Jen is, understandably, unusually grumpy and scared. She tells me she has been forced by the physiotherapist to get out of bed and sit up in the La-Z-Boy chair that has now been squashed into her glass cubicle. It's very tiring and she's pissed off but vaguely co-operative. And she is sitting up! Jen won't show her anger to the nurses, just to Stu and me. But she asks me for tea. That is a good sign. I have brought her iPod and loaded it with her favourite Disney songs. When Paul does his evening visit, Jen tells him just how irritated she is with the millions of tubes. He seems pleased she is irritated. I can understand. Irritation is a damn sight better than the child who lay staring at the ceiling less that 24 hours ago.

Monday, 22nd December

Today is a huge day. Today Jen goes into theatre to have the old Hickman line taken out, her neck lines taken out and two dialysis lines put in on the opposite side of her neck. She comes off the ECMO machine, off the nasogastric feeding tube and off the catheter.

When Jen comes round, she is incredibly chatty. The combination of the relative "freedom" of fewer tubes and left-over anaesthetic make her pain free, comfortable and very animated. She talks in fast but soft bursts, non-stop, and she wants both Stuart and me at her bedside. We are mesmerised as she tells us in detail about the book that she wants to write and publish before her 21st birthday. She says she also wants to learn to cook, and to speak conversational isiZulu. Once she is out of hospital she wants to exercise every day – she can't wait to be able to exercise, it's been so many years – and to eat good food. I can see she is starting to get excited about getting better and having a new lease on life. I feed her small mouthfuls of my chicken soup as she describes a "secret Santa" plan she has for the ICU nurses. It is nearly Christmas, isn't it? There are gaudy paper decorations all over ICU. She can see them through the window. Yes, we confirm, it is the 22nd and Christmas is three days away. We set off to shop for the nurses' goodie-bags as instructed. Jen has requested that Nooglet go and sit with her while we're gone so they can chat. Kristi is delighted.

While Stu and I are shopping at Pick n Pay in Cresta shopping centre we find a pile of magazines on the shelf with Jen in them. I drop the December issue of *Woman & Home*, *Huisgenoot* and *YOU*, plus the January issues of *Cosmopolitan*, *Your Family* and *Good Housekeeping* into our trolley. Jen is everywhere in the media right now and we didn't even know! We have been operating in a parallel universe since we got to Johannesburg. After the intensity of ICU it feels strange to be walking around the shops like normal people. We race home to dump the shopping bags and tell Shirley all the stories. Then we go back to the hospital to relieve Kristi.

Jen wants to know when James is coming up. She is ready to see him.

Tuesday, 23rd December

Jen comes crashing down after the excitement of yesterday. She still has drains on either side of her lungs so lying on her side is sore and she has terrible discomfort everywhere. Breathing is becoming hard again, and she is battling to cough up mucus on her own. Dialysis also makes her very tired. They have her on a different machine today, a sled. Apparently it takes a shorter time but is pretty harsh on her little body. Paul is not happy with today's chest X-ray. She has fluid on her lungs again. What a roller-coaster we are on.

Wednesday, 24th December

It's two weeks today since transplant. Stu and I are at the hospital early as usual. We have dispatched all 30 gift bags to the nursing staff, which have been packed in 24 hours by Shirley, Kristi and Reggie, and are taking turns alternating between the coffee shop and ICU. By now we know everyone by name. The coffee shop staff and owners, the nurses, the parking attendants. Jen is back on full-time dialysis again and it's making her really sleepy and queasy. Her numbers appear stable, but she is quiet and just wants to sleep. The nurses suggest we leave her to sleep and so we do.

We pop to the shops quickly to buy a few gifts for Christmas – which, we realise, is tomorrow. Kola arrives today; he is flying up with Ali, Les and Matt. Kola will be staying with us, and Shirl can't wait to see him. She is so excited. Tonight the whole family will gather for dinner at the Hyde Park Hotel – Ali has arranged it all. Hyde Park is relatively close to the hospital so we can move between the two if we need to. Johannesburg is empty. There is no traffic. No queues at the shops. This place is like a ghost city at Christmas time.

We go back to the ICU late afternoon. Jen just wants to sleep.

Ali has decorated the table in the hotel restaurant with Christmas crackers and chocolate baubles. Everyone has dressed up. The food is delicious and there is good wine and everyone is making an effort to be cheerful. Shirley has suggested we write messages on a red poster for Jen and take it to her tomorrow.

It is Christmas Eve. Without Jen.

But next year will be different.

I excuse myself to phone ICU.

CHAPTER 41

Christmas and New Year in ICU

I wake up on Christmas Day with my heart pounding. I just want to get to the hospital. Stu feels the same. We sneak out of the house, leaving everyone to sleep.

Jenna is not doing well. She is nauseous, dizzy and very drowsy. She has chest pain and an erratic heartbeat. Paul wants to get her dialysed soon. Stu and I spend four hours with her, taking turns to nurse her, with ice for her lips, moving pillows around to make her more comfortable and warming up her "happy hugger" to help ease the chest pain. We put the red poster we all made for her last night up on the wall. At 11:30 am we go home to change and open prezzies with Kristi, Reggie, Shirl and Kola.

Dean and Sarah are hosting us all for Christmas lunch at the guest house in Parkwood. Sarah has set the most beautiful table and has been cooking for days. Stu and I are both very present and very distracted at the same time. We are grateful for their caring and kindness but it's hard to sit still. We spend the day moving between the hospital and Christmas lunch. Back and forth – at 2 pm, 4 pm and 5:30 pm. Jen is tired, and her blood pressure is low, very low. From 5:30–7:30 pm we sit on Dean and Sarah's veranda, just as we'd done the night we arrived, and watch another impressive Johannesburg thunderstorm. It's not quite as dramatic as the night of Jen's surgery, but it's big. Massive hailstones fall from the sky by the bucketload and the heavens flash and echo with thunder and lightning.

At 7:30 pm Stu, myself and Kristi go back to the hospital. We spend three hours nursing Jenna. She is overheating and desperate for ice on her lips and her forehead. She is terribly nauseous and dizzy and she has a very erratic heartbeat. This is really shit. She is back on slow, constant dialysis now. It is late when we are sent home to bed. James is coming up tomorrow.

For a few days now, Stu and I have been discussing the fact that Kristi needs a break from all of this. It is relentless. It is brutal seeing Jen like this day in and day out. Kola needs to go to Port Elizabeth to go surfing with his dad but, ideally, he shouldn't fly alone. Stu has been talking to Gavin Levy. Gavin and his family are on holiday in St Francis. Kia and Kristi are missing each other, and it seems like a good idea to send Kristi to join them for a while. Reggie has to go back to Cape Town to see his family and we could fly Kristi to PE to accompany Kola on the flight. She can then join the Levys for a bit and drive back to Cape Town with them in early January. We think it will be good for Kristi to be home, to see the dogs and the bunnies, and sleep in her own room. Alex is still house-sitting for us so she won't be alone. It may be good for her to have some "normal" grounding time away from the hospital and ICU.

We want Kristi here with us, but it is so hard, so tough, so brutal. We think she should have a break from it.

On Boxing Day Jen is feeling a little better. She is coughing slightly. Her chest X-ray is better, and her blood pressure has normalised. But there are dark rings under her eyes and she is so very thin. The nutritionist is urging her to eat and has put her onto all sorts of shakes and supplements.

Stu and Shirley have been spending hours researching places for us to rent. Christine comes home in a few weeks, so we need to find a rental. For how long we don't know, but Paul says we need to be close to the hospital for at least three to six months.

James arrives. He and Jen are both nervous about seeing each other but that only lasts a very short time. He turns out to be a really good nurse and the next day the two of us take turns to nurse Jen while Stu takes Kola, Kristi and Reggie to the airport. Before the kids leave they come to the hospital to say goodbye to Jen. It is very hard to say goodbye to Kristi. I hope Stu and I have made the right decision.

Today Jen cannot get comfortable. She is hot and cold, and her tummy is sore. She needs to start mobilising more, but it's so hard when she's on dialysis for hours and hours. Once she is hooked up to the dialysis machine (through the lines in her neck) she can't move. It also makes her really tired. I wish her kidneys would start working. Jen is committed to eating as much as she can, and we are following strict instructions from the nutritionist. I have made a chart and we carefully tick off all her supplements and protein shakes as she gets them down. The problem is that eating makes her tummy really, really sore. But she is determined and persists.

We begin taking turns being in ICU with Jen now – sometimes me, sometimes James and sometimes Stu. While James is with her Stu, Shirl and I drive around Johannesburg looking at potential rentals. Maybe I'm just in a bad mood but so far they are all awful and depressing. I'm tired and hungry. I don't want to stay in any of these places. What we are going to need is a place of healing, a sanctuary for us to go home to after ICU every day and for Jen to come home to when she leaves the hospital, hopefully in a few weeks' time.

I speak to Kristi every day. She is finding it really hard to be away and is anxious and missing us. The world around her is joyous and on holiday, a stark contrast to how she is feeling, still haunted by hectic images of ICU and worried about her sister. She can't relate to all the festivity, she says. It's like a parody. I can't help berating myself; I should have known it would be like this for her. I feel the same, even if I just go to the shop to buy groceries.

The morning session appears to have become mine and on Tuesday, the 30th of December I'm up early to make smoothies, fry bacon and freeze homemade juices to take to Jen. When I get to the hospital the physio has already arrived. She wants to make Jen use the walker for the first time today and suggests I go to the coffee shop while they try. Jen looks wiped out when I get back, but this has to be a significant milestone. She has taken her first few steps. We phone Stu and Kristi to tell them and they are thrilled.

But the rest of the day isn't good and Jen remains tired.

Week 4 post-transplant (Wednesday, 31st December 2014)

I get to the hospital early, before 7 am, and James comes by to say goodbye to us in the ward on his way to catch his flight back to Cape Town. Jen is really down. She is feeling drained and scared. Her oxygen is being turned down all the time because the team want her off the mask, but she can't bring herself to trust the lungs yet and has become psychologically dependent on the oxygen. This isn't surprising, seeing that she's not breathed without it for two years. She is very tired all day and her blood pressure is unstable again.

For the first time Jen begs me to ask the nurses for sedation. She is battling. She is sad. She is angry and frustrated and tired. She wants to block out the world. So do I, but I don't tell her that the nurses say there can be no more drugs; I must make another plan. It takes a long time to get Jenna comfortable. I stack pillows between her bony knees and ankles, adjust the bed, and make sure her lines aren't pulling. Then I settle in to gently massage her feet and talk to her quietly. I take her back to her childhood. To times of playing at Granny and Grampa, of visiting Knysna, to the smell of the wooden decks and of the forest after the rain. To the feel of sand under her feet and how it will feel when she can sink into a bath of warm water for the first time. I paint beautiful pictures with words as I rhythmically massage her feet. Her feet are practically the only place on her body without scars and tubes. Eventually Jen falls into a deep and long sleep. I sneak out quietly at 5:30 pm.

It is New Year's Eve.

Stu, myself and Shirl go to Dean and Sarah's for prawns and at

9:30 pm Stu goes back to ICU to check in on Jenna. Afterwards he comes back to join us to see in the new year. Please, Lord, may it be just that. A new year and a new start. For all of us, but especially for Jenna. Stu and I cling to each other tightly and at midnight we shed a few tears. We phone Kristi. She is also tearful. She wants to come back to be with us. This is unbearably hard.

CHAPTER 42

Rivonia

One good thing that happens is that Stuart and Shirley find our Johannesburg "home to be". It is incredibly quaint, leafy and green and owned by a wonderful family who are renting it out for the first time. They are happy to let us have it for three months with an option to renew monthly. They understand and empathise with our situation. What a relief. It's in Rivonia, half an hour from the hospital.

Jen is determined to get better but she needs to find ways to stay positive in the face of all this. I make charts for her walls. The first chart is called "Pharewell PH! Good Riddance To ..." and on it we list all of the things she has said goodbye to: breathlessness, excessive fatigue, nosebleeds, flushing, Flolan, pumps, first-bite jaw pain, cassettes, line-changes, ice-packs, dressings, the drug den, Thunder, Oxy-Jen, oxygen cylinders, Chase, blood thinners, Bosentan, Revatio, drug box, IV kit, biohazard bin, sharps bin, not being able to exercise, ringing a bell for help, not being able to walk ... etc. Then I make a second chart: "Things to look forward to in the weeks ahead", as decided by Jen. Walking; sitting up in bed; talking and laughing; bathing; washing my hair; receiving visitors; going to the toilet; seeing daylight; going outside; ditching dialysis; phone conversations; walking to the nurses' station; leaving the hospital; seeing our Rivonia home.

I put both charts up on the wall where she can see them.

Jenna swings between total determination and being flattened by terrible nausea and abdominal cramps. Her arterial line starts bleeding and needs to be changed, as do her neck lines. Her neck needs a break, so new lines are inserted into her groin, but they keep bleeding. It's tricky to keep finding new sites. Lines have a "shelf life" because of the risk of infection.

Granny arrives from Cape Town on the 5th of January. It is so good to see her, but I am worried about how it will be for her to see Jen. Jen is still being dialysed regularly, although she can now sit up in the chair every day and is forcing herself to do the small exercises her physio has given her to do in her bed. She is so brave. She deals with everything with such courage. What is the most debilitating for her is the nausea that comes over her every time she eats. "Give me pain over nausea any day," she says. Jen is still skin and bone, but now her face is starting to swell from all the meds. The rest of her is not affected, just her face.

Granny and Shirl take shifts nursing Jenna, relieving Stu and me. Every time I leave the hospital, I look at the skyline, the horizon. Jen has not seen outside that tiny glass cubicle for a month now. No view. No natural light. No faces that aren't covered in masks or bodies that aren't wearing sterile coats. We have started to knock on the glass doors from outside so she can see our smiling faces before we mask up. I take pictures for her from the car so that she can see what the weather is like outside. That there is a world outside.

Week 5 post-transplant (Wednesday, 7th January 2015)

Daffy and his mom Karen are coming. Daffy's year of stooging in New Zealand is over and he is flying through Johannesburg en route back to Cape Town. Karen will fly up to meet him here so they can both visit Jen. Stu will fetch them from the airport and take them to the apartment for a "debrief" first; they need to know what they are facing. Daffy can't wait to see Jen. Stuart brings him through to ICU at 8:45 pm for a short visit. I'm still here because

Jen has severe back and tummy pain. I'm so happy to see Daffy and we hug for a long time. Then I show him how to scrub up and get ready to go in and see Jen. They have both been anxious about seeing each other but are comfortable within seconds. Everything else falls away in the face of this kind of fight. I think it is a shock for Daffy to see Jen, but he doesn't show it.

He and Stu go home. I leave at midnight and swap out with Stu. Dialysis only finishes at 1 am and he rubs Jenna's back and feet and stays with her until, at around 3 am, she falls asleep.

Kristi is back in Cape Town now, at home with our beloved dogs. She is having some downtime, recovery time. She and I talk regularly, every day, on the phone. She doesn't like telephone conversations so it's difficult. I understand, I'm not naturally great on the phone either, I have had to learn over the years. She is missing us terribly. We have made a plan for her to come up to Joburg next week, and Kia might come with her. We keep Kristi up to date daily with Jen's progress, but it's not all good news and I find myself choosing my words very carefully.

Daffy and Karen stay with us for a few days and Daffy visits Jen every day. They have loved seeing each other but Jen is feeling a little more nauseous each day, which is not great. On the 8th of January, before he and his mom fly to Cape Town, he spends some time alone with Jen at the hospital early in the morning. He has downloaded some music for her on her iPod. He tells me that he and James spend many hours talking, with James keeping him updated on how Jen is. They even planned his visit to Johannesburg together so that they could see her separately. To this day they are still good friends. I don't think that will ever change.

The day Daffy leaves is not a good day. Jen is nauseous, shaky and has blurred vision. Paul is away on leave, but his team is on watch. On Friday the 9th Jen goes back into theatre to have the lines in her groin removed and new ones inserted in her clavicle. They will do a post-transplant biopsy on her lungs at the same time. They will also do a stomach X-ray and sonar and maybe find what is going on with her tummy. Jen now has severe tremors and shakes.

During the time she has been here Granny has either been relieving me at the hospital or at home cooking, to ensure we are all looked after. She leaves to go back to Cape Town on Sunday, but comes by the hospital first to say goodbye to Jenna.

Sunday is another bad day for Jen, with lots of vomiting. She is unable to eat and is fading away. The team decides it is time for her to go back onto a nasogastric tube to take the pressure off her.

A few weeks ago, Shirley introduced me to colouring in, a tool she discovered in Boston during her long months at Natalie's bedside. It has become a form of "therapy" for me. I can do it anywhere, including sitting at Jen's bedside when she sleeps. It is a form of meditation and decoration all in one. Clever. Sometimes Jen chooses the colours. She is too weak to draw or do anything herself, but she gets involved. Once my "artworks" are complete she chooses where to put them up on the wall to decorate her otherwise characterless isolation ward.

Monday the 12th brings some good news. The results of the biopsy of Jenna's new lungs show absolutely no signs of rejection and a Doppler of her neck is clear. The facial swelling must be drug-related. She will be dialysed again tomorrow to remove the build-up of fluid because her kidneys can't.

Jenna has a comprehensive team – Paul (who is still away on leave), two surgeons, the physiotherapists, nutritionists, dialysis doctor and team, cardiologist, radiology team and a neurologist. Plus all the nurses, the transplant co-ordinator and the transplant psychologist. But we are her emotional support system, without which I don't know how she would cope.

We have been made acutely aware that ICU has official visiting hours – one hour in the morning, one hour in the afternoon and one hour in the evening only – and we are not observing any of them. It feels unfair that in addition to the trauma of seeing Jen battle like this every day there are also hospital "politics" to deal with, that I have to start managing these dynamics as well. My constant presence in ICU is apparently causing some trouble. Many of the nurses are really pleased to have me there – it is obvious how it helps Jen, lifts her mood and keeps her engaged in the fight – but others are not. They would rather not be "watched". I understand that my vigilance is an extra pressure, but I always try to be careful, to remain calm, considerate and out of the way when necessary. One of the sisters believes it is not sustainable, that I will collapse and won't be able to stay the distance. She doesn't know me. I will stay the distance no matter what it takes, and I won't leave my child's side. I promised Jenna that.

They do have a point, however, about it being unsustainable. I have been talking to Glynis. She has offered to take a week off work and come up to Johannesburg to help me. I am beyond pleased. Granny has gone back home, and Shirl is heading home soon too. She has been phenomenal, but now that the school holidays are over she must go back to her life and her son.

Stuart has started working during the day so I do day duty while he takes the evenings. I don't know how he does it. This is totally all-consuming in every way. But he says work helps him to take his mind off things. We've worked out that it takes a minimum of two (ideally three) hands-on people Jenna trusts for someone to be with her round the clock and not fall apart from exhaustion.

On Monday, the 12th of January Stu collects Kristi and Kia from the airport. They will be here for a few days before going back home so that Kristi can start her Grade 11 year at Abbotts College. We have talked at length about moving her to Johannesburg, but we have no idea how long we will be here. She doesn't want to leave her home, Reggie, her horse – Riaan is now stabled in Tokai – and our dogs. Kristi has always been a homebody, she feels secure there. Besides, it might only be one term that we are not at home. Our thinking is that Stu can move back to Cape Town at the end of the first school term and he and Kristi can live at home during the week and come up to Johannesburg together on weekends. I will stay here. Jen should be out of hospital by then and recovering in Rivonia. It's hard to know what is best, but for now we will take it one week at a time. Alex will help with lifting Kristi to and from school in the meantime, but the good news is that Aniko – our Ko-Ko – is arriving in Cape Town on the 20th. Kristi is torn, but she would prefer to stay in Cape Town. She doesn't know anyone in Joburg and it would also mean starting at yet another new school. Besides, I spend most of my time in ICU so she would be very much alone. That can't work. It is an impossible situation. For now, Cape Town is the better option. The Berrys are across the road, Sue is two houses away and all our family are there. We decide that Kristi will stay in Cape Town for now.

Week 6 post-transplant (Wednesday, 14th January 2015)

It is mid-January and with everyone going back to work and to school, Johannesburg has filled up. The traffic, as I have discovered, is appalling. It now takes me twice as long to get to the hospital. Parking at Milpark is also a nightmare. They are renovating the hospital and the builders are back in force. I had no idea how aggressive Johannesburg drivers are. Taxis hoot non-stop, and they just about drive you off the road; they don't obey stop signs or red lights either, it seems. It's nerve-wracking. My body is always on high alert. It seems to have a mind all of its own. I jump at the slightest thing. Headaches and excessive tension in my neck mean that I am in some pain, and the butterflies that are always in my tummy give me intermittent diarrhoea. I spend hours not eating or drinking once I'm in ICU with Jen as it is demanding and difficult to leave. Hard for me to leave, and hard for her not to have me there. She doesn't want to let me out of her sight. The mask, gloves and coat mean I sweat and dehydrate easily, and I can't drink unless I leave the room, which means I must disrobe and start all over again when I come back in. It's physically, mentally and emotionally brutal, but in truth my own bodily functions have become minor details.

Dr Williams – Paul – is back from leave and it is so good to see him. I am relieved to have him here and Jen is delighted. We feel safer now that he has returned. Maybe he can shed some light on Jen's nausea and vomiting. We have a long talk. He says he is keen to move Jen out of ICU and into the Isolation Ward in Section 7 downstairs. He thinks it's a good idea to get out of here, away from the trauma of ICU where she can be alone and see some daylight.

313

It will also be easier for us to be with her at any time of the day or night. It sounds like a very good idea to me. This is progress. Even though Jen is feeling awful, a move is exciting news. Paul increases the amount of feed going through her tube and ensures all her meds are now given intravenously rather than orally. It should help with the nausea and relieve the pressure to eat.

Kristi and Kia have arrived! It is just wonderful to see my Nooglet. I take the two girls shopping for an hour and we have a meal together. It feels so good to be out in the world and act normally for an hour or two. After that it is straight back to hospital. Jen is not well. BP unstable. Tachycardia again. Bloods show some infection. We can't move as promised. She is bitterly disappointed but also frightened. Stuart and the psychologist sit with her for hours trying to keep her calm because her heart rate is dangerously high. It takes many hours for it to come down.

On Thursday Jen calls me at 6 am. She is vomiting again, non-stop, even though she is not eating. The anti-nausea meds don't seem to be doing anything. I race to the hospital to beat the traffic, where I spend all day holding silver kidney-shaped bowls for her to vomit into. I wash out one bowl and sterilise it while I hold another at her chin, then swap. I do this all day. Every now and then Jen can nibble ice, but then she vomits again. Eventually in the afternoon she falls asleep, exhausted. I go back to the apartment where Stu and the girls are packing up. Tomorrow we must move out and move into the Rivonia house. Thank God Kristi and Kia are here to help, but at the same time I am sad they aren't able to spend more time with Jen. Jen simply can't face anyone. They stay home, waiting, just in case.

By evening Jen has stabilised enough for us to move her. It's an intricate job with all the tubes and medications but at 7 pm we move Jen to Ward 14 in Section 7. She is now in an isolation ward downstairs from ICU. It is big and spacious. It has a door and a window that looks onto a small unkempt courtyard. Right now it is dark and Jen is still nauseous so she can't appreciate it, but Stu and I are pleased. We decorate the walls with my colouring in and our charts and family photos. We go up and down the passage finding extra chairs and tables. I love this about Stu. He is happy to break the rules. He walks into every empty ward collecting furniture to make it as beautiful and comfortable as we can for our "Jen-Bean".

On Friday, the 16th of January Jen wakes up to daylight for the first time in 35 days.

I do not leave her side. She is vomiting up a white, foamy, phlegm-like substance every 20 minutes and she is exhausted and miserable. Everyone is flummoxed. No one knows what is going on. I wonder if it's the combination of meds she's on.

Kia has gone back home and Kristi visits in the evening, but Jen is in a bad way. Eventually she manages to keep down a sleeping tablet and at 10:30 pm she passes out.

Kristi and Stu have moved us into the new house. We will sleep in Rivonia tonight. I drive home in a daze on the highway. Cars whizz past me. It takes 35 minutes. Rivonia is further from the hospital than I thought.

Kristi starts school in Cape Town on Tuesday and Aniko arrives the same day. Kristi is so excited to see her. The timing has worked out perfectly. Aniko will stay in the house with Kristi. But first Stuart will fly home with her this weekend to settle her in … it will be his first time home since the 10th of December. Neither of them wants to leave while Jen is so bad, but they must. I can't cope here on my own, however – it is too intense right now and Jen needs constant minute-by-minute nursing – so James is coming up tomorrow and Glynis will fly up on Sunday. That will be our team of three for the next week.

Our Rivonia rental home is beautiful. Stuart and Shirley were right. It is a sanctuary. Tranquil, quiet and with beautiful gardens that Gail, the owner, has spent decades tending. When I get home I cuddle in bed with Kristi. I can't believe she is going back to Cape Town already. I want my baby with me. But I think this is the right decision. We will make her room here beautiful and she will come up as often as she wants to. I think it's the right choice, but even so it is breaking my heart.

CHAPTER 43

Nausea, nursing and seizures

Jen is very pleased to see James, but she still feels like crap. He sits with her all afternoon so that Stu and I can go to Makro with Kristi and buy things for the house – cutlery, crockery, towels, wine glasses. I'm back at the hospital by 5:30 pm and send James home in an Uber. We are having Mark and Christine over for supper tonight to thank them (can we ever?) for so generously loaning us their apartment and car for a whole month. I wonder if I remember how to cook …

Sunday is awful. Stu and Kristi fly home to Cape Town. Jen vomits all day. Mid-afternoon in desperation I text Paul. This is unbearable. Jen is gagging non-stop even though there is nothing in her tummy. Even in her sleep. Paul removes her feeding tube in case it's the tube that's causing the nausea; maybe it's infected. I've been with Jen all day. James will take over this evening for a few hours – I hope he will cope – and Glynis is arriving. I am so relieved she will be here.

On Monday Jen is worse. Yesterday Paul ordered special anti-nausea meds that are normally reserved for chemo patients but they take all day to arrive. He has also ordered a CT scan of Jen's stomach and chest but this hasn't happened yet. Glynis and I stay at the hospital the whole day. Glynis is really good with Jenna. She is nervous at first to get it right, but she is patient, kind and attentive. It is a relief to have the company and Jen trusts Glynis and feels comfortable with her.

By 9:40 pm the CT scan has still not been done. We have been waiting all day and now I am furious. Tonight's night nurse is not on form. She "forgot" to give the contrast medication, so after waiting the whole day Jen now can't do the CT scan tonight. Jen is exhausted. She is still vomiting white stuff, it hasn't let up, and she looks really ill. I can't leave because the nurse appears to be semi on strike. At 11 pm I bump into Paul in the passage. He works ridiculous hours, I don't know how these doctors cope. He decides to move Jen back into ICU. Tomorrow he will get her into theatre to do a gastroscopy to see what is going on inside her stomach.

Glynis goes to the hospital at 6:30 am so that I can sleep for a few hours. At 9:30 am Jen has her CT scan and is taken back to ICU and put in her same glass cubicle. While I am on the phone to Glynis telling her I'm on my way, Jenna has a seizure. There are two doctors and nurses with her and they manage to stop the seizure within a few minutes with an Ativan injection. By the time I get there Jen is sedated. A seizure? Why? Glynis and I wait outside the glass cubicle watching her sleep. Paul says the gastroscopy will go ahead later today – he needs to know what is going on. I phone Stu, who says he will get on a plane and be here in time for theatre at 4:30 pm. In the meantime Jenna is having an EEG to check her brain activity. There are probes and wires all over her head. It looks scary, like something out of a sci-fi movie. But the practitioner says it all looks good. Stu arrives at 4:30 pm but Jen only goes into theatre at 8:30 pm as there is an emergency before her. We are anxious. Post-transplant patients should avoid theatre because of their very high risk of infection. This is far from ideal.

Week 7 post-transplant (Wednesday, 21st January 2015)

When Jen went into theatre yesterday, besides the gastroscopy she also had a bronchoscopy and a lung biopsy. And they moved her dialysis lines again. With the gastroscopy they may just have found the problem. The gastric surgeon found and removed what is known as a bezoar from her stomach. This is a solid mass of indigestible material that accumulates in the digestive tract, which, if partially or completely obstructing the stomach, small intestine, or large intestine, can cause cramps, bloating, loss of appetite, nausea and vomiting.

This is good news – I think. "But," I ask the gastro doc, "why? Why would that happen? Why is she not digesting?" This is the first time I hear the word "gastroparesis". A Google search tells me: "Gastroparesis is a condition in which your stomach cannot empty itself of food in a normal fashion ... A damaged vagus nerve prevents the muscles in the stomach and intestine from functioning, preventing food from moving through the digestive system properly."[5] The vagus nerve can apparently easily be damaged during surgery. Could this have happened to Jenna?

Paul tells me the masses of medication Jen's body has been subjected to are more likely to be the cause and the nausea should ease now.

Jenna wakes up starving. It's the first day in weeks that she has no nausea or vomiting. She is so, so hungry – but she can't eat yet. It feels cruel, but the gastro doc insists she must wait. She is allowed juice, 70 ml, measured precisely, after which the NT tube in her stomach is clamped so that the doc can check to see how much liquid goes into the tube. Jen is grateful not to be vomiting but she is hungry and irritable. Understandably. Paul, myself and Jen agree that tomorrow she will be intubated and have sedation meds so that she doesn't have to feel the debilitating hunger. She has not eaten in weeks. While Jen is sedated, Stu and I will have our first day off in 42 days.

Stu stayed up very late the night before typing a long letter to hospital management about the communication gaps between doctors and carers. In the past few weeks we have observed that

---

1   https://www.webmd.com/digestive-disorders/digestive-disorders-gastroparesis

often instructions haven't been carried out, drugs haven't been ordered timeously, and often proper handovers between day and night shifts have fallen short. It seems to us that there is a gap in care and we are concerned. We have also had to move Jenna in ICU from one glass cubicle to another because of flooding. In one of these wards her glass doors didn't shut – the whole point of isolation is infection control. Also, when it comes to the nursing care, there is a noticeable difference in quality. While some of the nursing staff are world class, others are indifferent, uncaring, slow to respond (bordering on neglectful), careless and sometimes rude to Jen, treating her like a three-year-old who has no right to ask questions about her own health. I am not sure it's a good idea to put this all into a letter, but Stu doesn't agree. I want to protect Jen and am worried about possible backlash. Stu feels strongly that these issues need to be addressed. He pushes "send" on the mail.

Week 7 post-transplant (Wednesday, 21st January 2015)

On Thursday morning Stuart and I lie in bed, the curtains and doors open onto a garden full of birds. The sound of trickling water from a water feature outside on the grass is soothing. Glynis and James are in the kitchen making breakfast. We are going to rest today and spend time together. It feels blissful.

I'm imagining Jen fast asleep in her bed, intubated and sedated, when the phone rings. I can't believe what I am seeing. It's Jen's number. She has been "accidentally" extubated. The tube has been bumped and pulled out. We rush to the hospital. Jen is hungry, weak and her throat is sore. But she is also powerful in her rage. It is almost good to see her angry. That means there is fight in her. While I calm her down Stuart is called to a meeting with the hospital's management. They have received his email.

The meeting does not go well. Management threatens to stop us seeing Jenna, reminding us that they can restrict us to visiting hours, or even throw us out. This is exactly what I was scared of but it's not going to happen. Jen won't survive it, and neither will we. The hospital has many patients, but we have only one sick child and there is no way we are going to leave her side. I may not be a qualified nurse, but I am her mother, and no one can read my daughter's needs like I can. I am also the only person who has seen it all. The only one who has been here every single day through just about every procedure, change and nuance. Nurses come and go, change shifts, move wards, change patients. But I don't. I have one patient – Jenna. Also, the nurses are contract staff, not permanent. The philosophy is to rotate them to avoid nurses getting emotionally involved in Jenna's case. This makes no sense to me. Transplant patients are often in ICU for a very long time. By their very nature these are complex cases. Surely it would make sense for a transplant patient to have one dedicated team of highly qualified transplant nurses? The same people day in and day out who get to know every aspect of a patient's care? In fact, I don't just think it makes sense, I think it is essential.

Statistics show that transplant patients fare much better when they have unlimited access to family. Of course they do. It is an arduous journey they have undertaken.

Distressing though all this is, I have to put it aside so that I can be there for Jen. She wants to know why Stu is in a meeting. I don't want her to know about all the politics, she doesn't need the extra burden, but she can sense something is going on. She is extremely anxious that they will limit her access to her mom and her dad. It turns into a very long day.

Stu and Glynis take over from me early evening. A bit later they will meet me at Raffaella's, who has invited us for supper, and James will "Jen-sit". He is hoping to distract her with a series. Until now she hasn't been well enough to watch anything.

On Friday morning Stuart has to attend a meeting in Cape Town so he takes the red-eye flight and I get to Milpark at around 8:30 am. Jenna has just had another seizure. I can't believe it. The nurse tells me everything is under control. We settle her. She is starving hungry – she now weighs just 40 kg – and after her seizure a little "out of it". I am allowed to give her some baby food and she loves it.

At 11:20 am Jen has another seizure. I am sitting at the end of her bed when her eyes start tracking weirdly to the right. "Jen?" I say. "Jen! Are you okay?" Suddenly her whole body starts shaking violently. I scream for the nurse, who has just stepped out of the room. I put my hand on Jen's back and start talking to her loudly. "I am right here, Jen. I am right here." Three nurses fly into the room and take over. My hands are shaking almost as violently as Jenna is. I step outside to let them do their work. When the seizure is over Jen is disorientated, confused and terribly distressed. It's awful to watch. Dr Williams arrives. He medicates Jen, bit by bit, more and more, to sedate her. The neurologist comes to check on her. There is no damage. Paul changes her meds. It could be the meds that are causing the seizures ...

Earlier I phoned James and told him not to come to the hospital today. I sit with Jenna, who is absolutely exhausted. At 10:30 pm I leave. I am exhausted too. It is beyond painful to see my child like this.

Saturday is a better day. Glynis, myself and James wake up to messages from Jen saying, "Please bring rice and mince!" She must be feeling better! We jump into action. Glynis rushes to the Engen Woolies on the corner to get what I need, and I start cooking. We are there with Jenna's food by 9:30 am. She has been on dialysis since 5 am and looks much better. She eats well and is looking forward to seeing James, who will come in the afternoon. Her little face is like a moon, all swollen from the steroids and anti-rejection meds, and her body is unbearably thin, but her spirit is strong.

She has a good visit with James, he is so amazing with her. Stuart is due in at 5:30 pm and he will take over so that I can take Glynis and James out for dinner, to thank them. I don't know what I would have done without them this week, I really don't. The respite has been invaluable. We are careful to try and protect James from the worst times, but he insists he really wants to be here. Even so, this is very tough for him. Glynis is a rock. She helps us emotionally process some of what we are holding and experiencing. She is a professional, but more than anything she is a deeply loving, dependable, empathetic and emotionally robust friend. Every night Stu has been away Glynis has "debriefed" me and James – and we have needed it.

CHAPTER 44

Moments of relief

Week 8 post-transplant (Wednesday, 26th January 2015)

Jen has been moved out of ICU and back into Section 7. She is sitting up and drinking tea. I think my heart might pop with happiness. She still has mild nausea after eating but is much better. She is consuming small amounts every two to two-and-a-half hours to try and build her strength and put on weight. We are trying to turn her room into a homelier space and have bought a mini-fridge and microwave for food and for warming up her happy huggers to help with her back and tummy pain. She has three of these small bean bags (she loves that I call them that), which we wash and rotate.

The big news is that she is being dialysed only every second day because she is starting to urinate on her own. This alone is a massive step forward. Another step forward is a literal one: today Jenna stood. She stood! Her muscles have totally wasted away and so, in addition to physio, she has started biokinetics.

Shirley has arrived to spend five days with us – we are so happy to see her. And Kristi is coming up too – I have arranged permission for her to skip two days of school and I can't wait to see her. I am so excited! Glynis and I spent hours the other night moving furniture around in Kristi's room in the Rivonia house and redecorating to make it beautiful.

All in all it is a good week. A very good week.

Kristi arrives on Thursday night. She is thrilled to see Jen so much better and they have a fabulous time together. More good news is that Camilla is flying up, which makes Jen very happy. Shirley goes back to Cape Town with a smile on her face and Cami arrives with a smile on hers. Jen loves having Cami and Kristi here. It brings me so much joy to see her enjoy their visits, even on days when she is not feeling up to talking much.

Jenna still has mild nausea and abdominal cramps when she eats, but it is much better. She is eating every two hours, fighting to put on weight and get stronger. On Monday, when we weigh her, the scale shows that she has managed to put on 5 kg in a week. She weighs 45 kg now. She is so, so proud of herself. Plus, she walked six steps today with the walker. Six steps!

An old childhood friend of mine, Jane, who has lived just outside London for nearly 30 years, is visiting South Africa. We have remained in contact and she is making a special trip to Johannesburg to see me. To see Jenna. She arrives with a large envelope stuffed full of beautiful letters from all the children at her son's junior school. She tells me that the children have been following Jenna's story for months and their art teacher has helped them make get-well cards and drawings for her. Jane has also done some fundraising. I wonder if she knows just how much her hard-earned pounds mean to us. They cover the costs of one more month in Johannesburg. I am so grateful and it is really good to see her.

On Tuesday, at Paul's suggestion, the nurse and I take Jen out into the courtyard outside her room. Jen is in a wheelchair – and we have ordered an oxygen cylinder just in case – but this is the first time she has felt fresh air and sunlight on her skin in eight weeks. I take a picture of her on my phone and I look at it often. She is sitting in the wheelchair, with her moon face and her skinny legs sticking out of her green gown, sunlight on her face, eating an orange ice-lolly. She looks so happy! You can't see it in the photo, but she is breathing fresh air into her new lungs.

Week 9 post-transplant (Wednesday, 4th February 2015)

This week it is only Stu and I who are in Joburg with Jen. Stu is working full days now while I am at the hospital. We swap out in the evenings and spend time together there with Jen before I go home. We always make sure someone is there for shift change-over because often there is a gap in the nursing, or doctors' messages fail to get passed on. For eight weeks now, Stu and I have barely had any time alone together. Stolen moments in the passageway, at home in the morning before I leave or at change-over. We talk often though on the phone, at least six times a day. Teamwork. We might be exhausted and traumatised, but we are a real team. I adore this man of mine. We play such different roles in Jen's care. When Stu arrives, he brings energy from the outside world, stories of his day and funny anecdotes. I am envious of the fact that he is always able to bring humour. Even at the worst of times he can make us laugh. And clumsiness. He also brings clumsiness. Oh heavens, when Stu is here you can be sure he will touch a monitor that shouldn't be touched, sit on the bed too hard or hook a tube on the food trolley. Jen chastises and scolds him. We both do. But lovingly. He massages Jen's feet – Stu is the best massager in the world – and brings lemon iced tea and orange ice-lollies. He lifts our spirits no matter what.

It is another good week. Nikita and Tessa visit from Cape Town for three days. Jen still has a moon face and mild nausea, but she is able to eat, able to chat, able to stand and to walk a few steps with her walker. But her breathing is laboured. Paul orders a CT scan. The nurse and I prepare her with an oxygen cylinder, masks and drip-stands to transport her meds, and wheel her bed down the passage to Radiology. For Jen it is like an outing. She gets to see life outside her isolation ward. People in the passage. Those few moments out of isolation are like an adventure.

The scan shows there is fluid in the space between her lungs and the chest wall and it must be aspirated, which means the fluid must be drawn out. The procedure, called a pleural tap, requires a small needle or tube to be inserted into the space between the lung and chest wall to remove fluid that has accumulated around the lung. It is done in the ward.

The young doctor who will do the procedure and his assistant arrive with their steel trolley and instruments. They explain to Jen exactly what they are going to do. She needs to be upright and totally still, but this is hard as she is not yet strong enough to sit unaided for long periods of time. We devise a system. I stand in front of her with a pillow on my chest and she leans her head into it. This helps her to sit up for long enough (about 20 minutes) for the doctor to inject, make the incision and draw off about a litre of fluid. She has pressure, discomfort and weird chest pain but, as always, Jen is brave and doesn't move. I talk to her gently throughout. Underneath my sterile gown the sweat pours in rivulets between my breasts.

Afterwards Jen's breathing is easier and she is feeling better. She is able to sleep. While she is sleeping I go with Tess to her brother Gavin and his wife Lou for lunch. Then it is back to the hospital until Stuart comes to relieve me. He will do the night shift and I will drive back to Rivonia and try to get some rest.

On Saturday morning, the 7th, I shop for groceries and go to the hospital in the afternoon. Tonight Nikita is going to "Jen-sit" and Tessa is going to help me prepare dinner. We are having people over. Imagine that! I'm so excited. I am going to light candles and make yummy food. I have invited Mike and Sandy Harper (who constantly offer us their home as a sanctuary if and when we need a few hours away from the hospital), Raffaella and her husband, Gavin and Lou, and of course Stu, myself and Tess.

The evening is lovely, a really happy time. Jen will love this Rivonia home when she comes out.

Tess and Nikita leave early on Sunday morning. In the afternoon Sarah Holloway, a very dear friend of the family, comes to the hospital to visit. Sarah is efficient, fearless and kind – and she is very creative. She has offered to do some nail art for Jen. We spend most of the afternoon with Jen on dialysis while Sarah does intricate art on her nails. Her energy is uplifting and it is good to have the relief and distraction for a short while.

On Monday Jen manages to walk from her bed to the door of the ward and back with her walker. To celebrate we organise her first bath. It is a logistical mission as she is still hooked up to meds and tubes, she can't wet any of her ports and she is not nearly strong enough to sit up in the bath for long. But she can use the walker to reach the door, which means she can also reach the bathroom. She begs us for a bath. She is chatty and lovely and funny. So much more like her old self.

Two nurses and I set to work. We need sterilised towels, Steriscrub, fresh sterilised linen and a fresh hospital gown for Jen to get into afterwards. The meds need to be checked; those that can be disconnected are and those that can't need to be put onto a dripstand. We are ready. I run the bath and add a few drops of Steriscrub to make bubbles. Slowly we walk Jen with the walker, and all the drip-stands, step by step to the bathroom. She leans against the wall, holding onto the walker and me, to catch her breath. We undress her, making sure to feed tubes through the arms of the gown.

I see Jenna's body, naked, standing up for the first time. I barely recognise it. I watch her eyes staring at herself in the mirror. It is as if she is seeing a stranger. She is covered in scars and she is so thin and wasted that her legs sway back weirdly. Her knees and elbows look enormous. I hug her.

"Now," I say, "how do we get you into this bath?"

We sit her bony bottom down at the top of the tub, then lift her up like a baby and lower her in. Hours of nursing and lifting Chase for two years have made my arms strong but I am shaking. As I lower her carefully into the water she draws in a slow deep breath. I am holding under her arms firmly so that she doesn't slide under the water. One nurse is on stand-by with me in the bathroom, watching carefully, while the other nurse changes bedlinen and sorts out the room. We are a good team.

Jen looks up at me and her face breaks into a broad, beautiful smile. "Thank you, Mommy, thank you," she says. "It's delicious." Her first time submerged in water in over a year.

Gently, we wash her hair. James is coming up tomorrow.

With Jen doing so much better Stu suggests it's time for me to go home to Cape Town for a few days and I really want to see Kristi. I have not been home since she and I left for Plett Rage – two-and-a-half months ago! Shirley has agreed to come up to Joburg while I'm away to be with Stu and James. I am nervous about leaving, but it is decided. The flight is booked for the 11th.

Week 10 post-transplant (Wednesday, 11th February 2015)

Cape Town feels surreal. It is as if I am in a dreamlike state, outside my body. There is a world out here free from the horrors of hospital. I notice things in a way I've never noticed them before, every detail. Light, trees, smells, sounds; people's body language.

When I arrive home the dogs go crazy. I unpack and walk around my house, staring at familiar things with new eyes. I feel like a stranger in my own home. Later I fetch Kristi from school … what a treat! Something I've done for years has become an absolute privilege.

Aniko is there – she is in Jenna's room – and it is so lovely to see her. She, Alex, Kristi and I go to Granny and Grampa for dinner. We laugh and talk and share stories.

It feels odd to sleep in my own bed.

I spend Friday, Saturday and Sunday catching up with my friends and family. We walk, go for brunch, go for lunch, have coffee, talk, cry and drink wine. I do admin, sort out the house and swap out clothes. I pack a new wardrobe to take back with me to Johannesburg. I take the dogs to the vet for their check-ups and vaccinations. I pay accounts and do a few months' worth of filing.

On Sunday night Kristi and I have a long talk. Over and above the trips to Joburg, Kristi has missed a number of days at school. She says she has been sick a lot – colds, sore throats, headaches; Aniko's confirmed this – but hasn't wanted to bother us because our plates are so full already with Jen. When she wasn't feeling well she just stayed home. I know how stress affects your immune system and Kristi is dealing with so much. I'm worried about her. They are all doing their best but between Aniko, Alex, Kristi and Reggie – who is at the house a lot – home really is more like student digs than the structured environment a 17-year-old needs. If I was living alone at home with no adults at Kristi's age, I would also miss a lot of school! Some of this is therefore probably normal teenage behaviour, but clearly Kristi is battling and doesn't want to say so. We agree to put more checks and balances in place and together we plan a schedule of all her trips up to Johannesburg in the next six weeks.

On Monday I arrange a check-up for Kristi with our GP and while she is at school I visit my therapist. Later Kristi and I have a meeting with her teachers at Abbotts. Her first trip to Joburg will be in 10 days' time for five days. I explain to her teachers that although she will be missing more school, I think it's more important that Kristi is with us so that we can keep a closer eye on her.

I talk to Stuart every day, several times a day, to hear how Jen is doing. She has low-level nausea, and every now and then she does a big vomit, he says, but she is now standing for up to 15 minutes at a time during biokinetics. It is astounding. And the more upbeat parts of her personality are back. She is funny, engaging and interested in the world around her. She jokes with the nurses and spends hours chatting to them, finding out all about their lives. I have missed this side of my "Bean". We all have. I talk to Jen every day too.

Saturday was Valentine's Day and James had been carefully planning a "date night" with Jen in the hospital. Stu and Shirl were in on the arrangements. They organised for Sarah to go to the ward in the afternoon to wash Jen's hair, do her nails and put on a bit of make-up. I had spoken to Jen on the phone and I could hear how bittersweet it felt for her. She was so aware of how it must be for James because physically she had changed so much – "My body is like a skeleton, Mom." Her hair had thinned dramatically, her cheeks were swollen and she had so many scars and bandages. To add insult to injury she also now had slight Bell's palsy on one side of her face, although Paul had told her it would dissipate soon. She worried that rather than enhancing her, make-up would only highlight all the "defects". On the other hand, she wanted to make an effort for James ...

I let her talk and I listened. What she described to me is not what any of us sees. We see a young woman so full of courage, integrity and grace that her beauty radiates from within like a magnet.

James had special permission from the nurses to "make an entrance" without his sterile coat and mask. At 7 pm he walked through the door. He was all dressed up, in black suit and tie, carrying a bunch of red roses (fake ones, because you can't have fresh flowers in an isolation ward) and a huge bunch of red and white helium balloons.

"Oh my God," Jenna said. "You look so HOT!"

I think that made James's year.

Not only had he brought roses and balloons, he had another surprise: Jenna's beautiful high-heeled red shoes which he'd brought up from Cape Town. When he produced them with a flourish Jen clapped her hands in delight. "Yay!" she said. "My 'slut' shoes!" James carefully placed the shoes on her feet under the sheets and they beamed at each other. Stu took this as his cue to leave them – to have some private time together, to talk and laugh, message friends and enjoy the special meal James had arranged. It might not have been a conventional Valentine's but it was a happy one.

On Monday Paul starts weaning Jenna off the O2; she doesn't need the cannula any more. Her new lungs must do the work on their own. On Tuesday Stu and Shirley put Jen into the wheelchair, with a mask, and wheel her down the long passage that we have walked so many times, out of the hospital's main entrance and into the fresh air. They wheel her round the carpark. It is the first time she has left the building in 69 days.

On Wednesday I am flying back to Joburg. I cannot wait to see Jen.

Week 11 post-transplant (Wednesday, 18th February 2015)

When I walk into Jenna's ward in Section 7, she is not in her bed. She is sitting outside in her courtyard at a table with Stuart and the nurse chatting and having tea. I cry tears of joy.

"Wait," Jen says, "that's not all. Watch this, Mommy."

I watch her walk, slowly, from the door of her room all the way to the bathroom – without a walker. On her own. Her gait is a little strange, but she is doing it. She is walking unaided. Now I am weeping. We hug tightly through my coat. I wish with all my heart that I could kiss her without my mask on. Oh my God, she has done it. Jenna has turned the corner.

Later that day we hear from Kirk at Mullen Lowe that #GetMeTo21 has won the Silver Bookmark for the Integrated Social Media category at the IIAB Awards. It is a huge accolade and Jen is thrilled. People are still signing up as organ donors because of her campaign. In fact, I have media phoning me off the hook. There is a frenzy of people wanting to interview Jenna again once she is out. Everyone has a sense that she is getting better and will be back in the world again soon. She, too, is starting to talk about how to continue to encourage donor sign-ups and wants to discuss plans for her 21st in October. Thousands and thousands have already joined up and Jen wants thousands more. It will be a massive celebration of life, just as we promised.

On Thursday Jen walks all the way down the section 7 passage with her physio.

She also has a brief visit from a young man named Blake, who had been so taken with Jen's courage many months back that he'd insisted on meeting her in Cape Town. He has been spreading the word of organ donation ever since and supporting the cause in whatever way he could. He has even run races for her. Now he wants to know what he can do to help us in Johannesburg. We have given back the vehicle we were borrowing and have brought our car up to Johannesburg by train, but we really need a second car. Johannesburg is a huge city and difficult to get around without transport. Currently we rent, borrow where we can or Uber, but it is draining our resources. Astoundingly, Blake manages to arrange a free rental for us from Europcar, on a compassionate basis, for as long as we need it. It will make a massive difference getting to and from the hospital. We are so grateful.

Friday, the 20th of February is a big day. Not only is Jen's friend

Giulietta coming up to visit, but it is Jen's first day with absolutely no oxygen, no dialysis and no monitors. She is so much more mobile as a result. It is odd not to hear the constant beeping of the monitors. It's a strangely insecure feeling. But Giulz is a ray of sunshine – she fills the room for the three days of her visit with banter and chatter. She and Jen make a list of 50 things Jen wants to do when she gets out of the hospital. We laugh so hard when Guilz and I tell Jen the story of our Uber driver and how he got out of the car, mid-ride, to take a wee on the pavement. It feels so good to laugh. Guilz has such a positive energy about her. There is hope and anticipation in the air.

After Guilz goes back to Cape Town it's just Stu and me again but we are coping fine because Jen is doing so much better. Mostly I do the day shifts while Stu works, and Stu does evenings. Jen is walking further every day and managing her nausea carefully. She has learned that if she keeps her meals very small and regular, and times them just right, taking the anti-nausea medication 15 minutes before she eats, then she can manage it. If she doesn't, then "It all goes wrong." She is determined to go home soon. Bit by bit she makes us pack up a few of her belongings and take them to the Rivonia house.

Kirk visits while on a business trip to Joburg and the four of us sit and discuss the 21st party and all the people, sponsors and companies who want to get involved. He reminds Jen that thousands of people who are following her journey would love to hear from her when she is up for it.

Week 12 post-transplant (Wednesday, 25th February 2015)

Jen blogs for the first time since the transplant. Seeing her write again is so poignant. I sit in the chair watching her. A few weeks ago she couldn't do this, and for many months before that she was too breathless to pick up her laptop. Now she swings the laptop onto her lap easily. She sits up in bed and starts typing:

Blogpost from Jenna
25th February 2015; 11:05 am
Section 7; Milpark Hospital
www.jennalowe.org

Hello everyone

I'm finally getting there ... eating, breathing, even slowly walking. Very soon I'll be able to leave this ward. I'll be nursed by my parents at our temporary home, close to hospital, but come in often for treatment.

I have been off oxygen for five whole days. It's been two years since I last breathed without that tube trailing me. To be free of the plastic across my face and the hissing in my ears, to not be tethered to a machine ... it's the most incredible feeling. I send endless love to the many patients on O2, especially with the recent load-shedding.

I walked up seven stairs today, one for each life a donor could save.

I keep thinking it's not possible to be more grateful for my lungs but with each milestone my gratitude to my angel donor grows.

I'll write again soon, but for now all my love

Jen

But that night, alone in her isolation ward, Jen does a much more private video log into her laptop. Stuart and I have left for Rivonia when she switches on her webcam for the first time. Looking straight into the camera, she starts recording. She talks quietly and calmly in a gentle voice, with no breathlessness, showing barely any emotion. We only found these webcams much later and it has taken me many years to watch them. I have just done so right now for the first time, while writing this book, just minutes before sharing her words with you.

10:24 pm – General check-in …

This is kind of like a stream of consciousness thing, I guess ….
It's the 25th of Feb and I'm mainly just doing this to record how
fat my face is and to check on my Bell's palsy which makes one
eyebrow frickin raise higher than the other! I may be out next
Tuesday – I just came back from Netcafé with Dad which was
lovely! My kidneys are still mainly fucked but are getting better –
last time I was dialysed was two days ago and I still feel good – so
there is improvement there! Unfortunately, the nausea is hideous
– and the doctors don't know what it's from – Dr Williams said
tonight … "You just have to live with it and it's not really affecting
your health." It's really bad though and I do vomit – but it's not
affecting my life and if they do any procedures it could really
unbalance things – and there are much more serious issues to deal
with like renal failure. So they can't do anything about it now.
So I'm having to deal with some really shit nausea … mainly in
the mornings … and I just feel green and I just can't move …
and I just have to lie here – so I'm kinda trying to vary things …
and eat before my meds or not eat before my meds – so we will
just see how that goes – that's a basic check-in of my state. I am
walking up to 200 metres at a time – totally fine. This evening
I walked 100 metres unsupported – I wasn't out of breath – I was
having a full-on conversation with Dad. It was at a fair pace and
I didn't look like a weird spastic person. My body is starting to
return to a normal shape … I am most resentful about my cheeks
and my stupid hair is still coming out by the handful. So I have a
scattered little rash on my face, fat cheeks and a receding hairline
… and eyebrows that don't work … so I'm not very attractive at
the moment! But the rest of my body is slowly going from little
pot-belly and a hunch and sway-back knees to being able to stand
upright. My belly still protrudes more than it should but that's
because my muscles are still learning to hold themselves in. My
knees are still wider than my thighs and my calves but I'm actually
starting to get calves – like they are tiny – but they exist – and
I'm starting to look more like a human being. So that is a general

check-in of my state … The worst is probably the cortisone side-effects which include the things I've already listed but also my skin is really dry and flaking and my teeth – I think they are more porous because they kinda stain easily … and all this raaandom shit. Anyway – we'll get there!

10:32 pm – Emotional check-in …

So I can easily delete this – so I think I can use it as an honest thing – because the previous video was like a check-in of my general physical state post-transplant. It is almost 12 weeks now – and this could be an emotional check-in which is quite a broad thing to say and a weird … um … bit of pressure to put on myself right now because I don't think I could sum up my emotional state – I would have to go topic by topic – but I mean I am generally fine. I'm terrified of this nausea – and the moment it turns to evening it makes me anxious. It makes me anxious to go to sleep because I am scared to wake up – so … I guess … if not for the nausea I really don't think I would be as terrified of the passing of time – but I am quite scared of … tomorrow – scared of how I will feel – um – I do a lot of managing it throughout the day – and whenever I'm not feeling it … I kinda forget … how bad it is and when I am feeling it I think I must … I can't forget again … to tell someone how bad this is … but I do … and everyone's kinda like … "Well, that sucks but we can't fix it" … so … that's really horrible – it's really scary – but Dr Williams today prescribed a new drug which is supposed to give symptomatic nausea relief – so hopefully we can use that tomorrow – because today it was horrible! I don't even mind throwing up as much as I mind the feeling that comes before and after it. That "really just can't move" feeling – it's just not knowing when it's going to go away – you know you lie there and this could last all day – or this could leave right now. And it always comes in waves … so … and it's weird because I always get hungry and nauseous at the same time – so the way I manage my nausea is to eat regularly – but then I have to be careful with what and how I eat – I have to take my nausea muti at the correct time – which is 15 minutes before a main meal. So it kinda feels like my day revolves around food. Which it sort of does at the moment – which is fine – but when I'm nauseous … it just becomes a lot harder! So anyway – I have a whole plan for tomorrow morning which involves waking up at 6 am and taking the one tablet – then waking up at 7:45 and taking another – and then eating and taking the rest. So … I hope that will help … It's sometimes hard to believe that such small changes such as having a piece of toast can affect the next four hours – of whether I lie groaning or whether I am fine. But we'll see … I don't have biokinetics tomorrow – which is another thing because I realised that I'm scared of the days I have biokinetics … during the sessions I'm fine … but I'm scared of the sessions beforehand … um, which is stupid – the moment I think about it in detail then I'm okay. It's the same with the evenings – and like … the moment that I start questioning what I'm afraid of and breaking things down into individual parts like … Am I afraid of being with the nurses? … No. Am I afraid of going to sleep? … No.

Then I'm okay – it's just the general impression I get … this terrified feeling … But … It is scary being in hospital – this room is … beautiful compared to other patients' because my family has made it beautiful – but it's still … it's not where you want to be for this long and actually I think it's going to be safer and more sanitary at home. It sounds like home – Rivonia home – which I haven't seen – is really peaceful and healing – I just need to get out of here and go there. I need to be able to lie when I'm nauseous in bed and have the distraction of my laptop or read or something – I just need something other than being in this room. And I'm just feeling … I can't describe it … it's the absolute worst – and I find pain is easier to manage. I hate saying that because it feels like a jinx … like I'm asking for pain … but I find that pain is … it's just mentally easier to deal with than nausea. Anyway … I think looking at myself while I speak – it's quite important; because I've just seen my face move slightly – and, well at least I just caught a glimpse of Jenna. Because this face and … whatnot … makes it kinda hard to recognise myself. My whole body has changed – things have moved around.

10:35 pm – Head-to-toe catalogue of changes

My feet are currently very swollen, my calves are non-existent, my knees are so-o-o dry and painful ... anyway ... my thighs are almost non-existent, my ass is non-existent, the skin on my legs is super dry, my stomach protrudes, my back ... kinda pulls tighter and straighter – which is a good thing, I guess. My chest obviously is scarred and contains different lungs ... and fits differently ... I think that I feel my torso sits a bit broader. My underarms feel different – certainly when I stand my shoulders pull back a bit more – and the top part of me seems to take up more space. My lungs are apparently good. The skin on my back is dry as all hell. My shoulders no longer have the same points of tension when I roll them. Pressure, trigger points, noises that my body used to make are all different. My freckles are the same ... thank God! My arms are similar – although the muscles are obviously slowly coming back. My hands and wrists are the same. My neck is scarred but similar. My ears are the same. My cheeks are massive and bad. My teeth are more porous and getting marked more easily. My jaws are the same. My lips are pushed together by my cheeks so are a different shape. My nose is the same but dryer – the skin on my face is all dry. The skin on my face has a little rash on it. My eyebrows are uneven, and the top half of my face is semi-paralysed on one side but my eyes are the same. My eyebrows might be a tiny bit bigger. The hair on my body is approximately the same. Apart from the hair on my head. The hair on my head is coming out by the handful. My hairline is receding.

That's ... some ... of the changes that are going on ... And it's really confusing ... because I'll just kinda assume something about myself and look down and go, like, WHEN did that happen? – that's really different! Anyway ... hopefully, a lot of this will go ... back to normal.

Kristi and Aniko are coming up in two days' time. Jen cannot wait to see them but she is also apprehensive. She hasn't seen Ko-Ko since Australia and doesn't want her to get a fright. But, apart from the nausea, her recovery is going so well now. Paul is pretty sure she will come home any day! We are really excited and hope to plan it to coincide with Kristi and Aniko's trip to Johannesburg this weekend or next week.

There is cautious but real excitement in the air!

On Friday morning Jenna calls me early. She is feeling very nauseous. I get to the hospital as quickly as I can. I am sitting with her talking quietly when I notice her eyes start to flicker. My adrenaline spikes immediately.

"Jen?" She looks at me.

"Yes, Mom?" Relief.

Two seconds later her eyes start pulling weirdly to the right again. I know what's coming. My heart starts racing.

"Jen? Jen?"

Her body starts shaking violently and her eyes are rolling around. It's another seizure and there isn't a nurse in sight. I'm on high alert. I roll her onto her side and pull up the cot side of the bed. I step out into the passage and scream loudly – "Help! Help! Somebody! We need help!" – then rush back into the room. I can't believe this is happening again. Jen is shaking violently. I talk calmly to her but I am scared as hell. Where are the nurses? "Help!" I scream again over my shoulder. Two nurses and the shift leader fly into the room with a crash-cart. It's been less than a minute, but it feels like forever. They inject Jen quickly with Ativan and manage to stop the seizure. I pace up and down the room, shaking. I phone Paul and I call Stu and tell him to come. This is unexpected. A shock. She has been doing so well.

Jenna is not herself. She is confused and looks exhausted. On Paul's instructions the nurses hook her up to the monitors again and do an EEG. I sit and watch as they hook her up to all the probes.

Stuart and I try not to feel despondent. On Saturday, although she is very tired, Jen recovers quickly. She refuses to be thrown off track. By the time Kristi and Aniko arrive to visit, she is much stronger and looking good and the three of them chat and laugh all afternoon. Ko-Ko and Kristi wheel her around the hospital for an outing, doing "wheelies" and skids up and down the passages.

It is good to see her laughing and having fun. We even have lunch at the hospital café, all four of us, including Jen, who spoons the food up under her mask. I can see her eyes smiling.

That night Kristi and Aniko spend the evening with Jen while Stu and I go down the road for dinner with old university friends, Japi and Lupi, who live close by. It is a fabulous evening. Their family and friends are so welcoming and supportive, we feel loved and held and happy. We eat delicious food and laugh and drink wine. Later we Uber back to the hospital to fetch the girls and bump into Paul in the passage. He is beaming and delighted to see Jen so happy and well. She will likely come home next week sometime! On Sunday we pack up more of Jen's belongings. After 82 days in hospital we have accumulated quite a bit of stuff.

We have already started the process of scrubbing and sterilising the Rivonia house from top to toe in preparation for Jenna. By Sunday evening her room is ready. I have bought and sterilised new crisp white linen for her and fake flowers to make her room beautiful. I have unpacked all her things carefully into the cupboards and been to the pharmacy to stock up on supplies: a blood pressure machine, thermometers, dressings, sterilising liquid and all the things I will need to nurse Jen and monitor her at home. I have framed some pics of the family for the walls. She is going to love the Rivonia house, I know she is. When she lies on her bed she will gaze upon white rose bushes, greenery and the most magnificent birdlife. I watch the birds every day when I get home from the hospital.

I do one last check and then close the door. No one is allowed in her bedroom now that it is immaculate and ready. We close the door to keep it "just so".

On Monday Jen is doing brilliantly. She is full of energy. She is so determined to come home that this morning, with her physio and me, she walks out of Section 7, down the passage and up the stairs. Yes, up the stairs. And then down another small length of passage and into ICU. She wants to visit her ICU nurses and find Dr Williams to tell him she wants to go home. The whole place bursts into spontanous applause when they see her, and what's more – Dr Williams gives his permission. She can go home later this week.

I can't believe it. I can't believe it. This hell is over. We can take Jen home. I weep with happiness. I phone James, who immediately books a flight to come up at the weekend. We phone everyone we love to share the good news.

Stuart, Aniko, Kristi and I go out for dinner to celebrate but also because the girls are flying back to Cape Town tomorrow. Kristi must go back to school. There's a Thai restaurant close to home that Stu and I have been wanting to try so that's where we go. We chat and eat yummy food and voice-note Jen and send her pics of our meals. We promise we'll bring her there as soon as she is allowed to eat in restaurants again.

At about 10 pm, as we are about to leave the restaurant, Jen calls. She is not feeling good. She has terrible nausea. I rush back to the hospital.

CHAPTER 45

You've got to be kidding me

Tuesday is a really bad day. A really, really bad day. Jen can barely move. She has hideous nausea, a terrible headache, red eyes and a very sore tummy. I am at her side from very early in the morning and I stay with her all day.

After yesterday, Jen is terribly disappointed, inconsolable in fact. When Paul comes to see her he asks a lot of questions, trying to find out what is going on. When he suggests that maybe she is just really nervous about going home … it wouldn't be uncommon … after all this time in the hospital … Jen gives him a scathing look. It's the first time in all these months that I have seen her bordering on even vaguely rude.

"Okay, Jen," Paul says, "I believe you. Let's find out what's going on." He orders a CT scan for the afternoon.

At 1 pm Stuart takes Kristi and Aniko to the airport. I sit with Jen, waiting for her to be taken for the CT scan. She looks awful. She is curled up in pain. At 4:45 pm she has another seizure. At 8 pm she has a second one, a bigger one. These seizures are completely terrifying. To see that tiny body shaking so violently … Even in her confused and dazed post-seizure state she clutches her stomach. She looks dreadful.

By 10 pm she is moved back to ICU and sedated. We are devastated. Utterly devastated.

Week 13 post-transplant (Wednesday, 4th March 2015)

On Wednesday morning I get to the hospital early. Jen is irritable about being back in ICU. She doesn't want the tubes or the monitors. She wants to go home. She politely tells anyone who will listen that she is fine. I remind her that she had two seizures yesterday. She doesn't remember them. She is not completely compos mentis but trying very hard to convince us all she is. She has tummy pain but looks much better than yesterday. She asks for tea. I pull the tea-tray close to her bed and start pouring. "I will do it," she says defiantly. "No problem," I say and push the tea table closer. She picks up the pot with a slightly shaky hand and starts pouring, talking to me at the same time. She pours the amber-coloured liquid into the milk jug instead of the tea cup and it overflows all over the tray. I take the pot gently from her. We giggle about it, but it's worrying. She didn't even realise she was doing it.

We are in a different room, a different "suite" as Jen calls it, in ICU this time. The back far left corner. It makes for a pleasant change. In addition to yesterday's CT scan Paul has ordered a lumbar puncture. They need to check her spinal fluid post the seizures. The neurologist arrives with his trolley and explains the procedure carefully to Jen. It is important that she lies completely still, even if there is pain. She is vaguely dismissive. Pain doesn't scare her. She lies on her side holding my hands and looking me straight in the eyes while he works. I tell her stories. At one stage her eyes glaze over slightly, but she doesn't flinch. My heart squeezes. I keep talking gently, describing her favourite place in Newlands forest back home. After the procedure her back is sore but she manages to sleep.

While I am sitting in the chair beside Jen's bed my phone vibrates with a message coming through. I click on the pic. I must be seeing things. I enlarge the pic and look again. It is Riaan, Kristi's Friesian stallion, with his head through my lounge door at our home in Cape Town. He is in our garden in the middle of the residential Southern Suburbs; in fact he is half inside my house! I am flabbergasted. Kristi has lost the plot. I storm out of ICU to phone her.

My anger soon turns to dismay. Yesterday, while Stu and I were coping with the shock of Jen's seizures, Kristi was fighting her own fight.

The Cape is battling massive fires at the moment – we have been horrified by some of the pictures we've seen on social media – and fires are raging in different areas around Cape Town. As Kristi and Ko-Ko's plane came in to land yesterday they could see from the air the extent of the fires. The mountains were ablaze in several spots. It looked as though the whole of the Tokai and Constantia area, where Riaan is stabled, was under threat. The minute they landed Kristi made Aniko drive her straight to the stables. She had to get him out of there. She phoned Tarryn, the young woman who helps us manage and feed Riaan in our absence. She was already on her way. The horses had to be evacuated. She would lend Kristi her horse-box. They managed to coax Riaan into the horse-box but there was nowhere else to take him other than home to our house … and that, it seems, is why we now have a black stallion in our back garden.

Life feels upside down. I don't have the heart to be angry with Kristi. Actually, I am proud of her, but at the same time I'm worried. She is dealing with way too much on her own. I phone Mary and ask her to go over and check on the girls. She sends me more horse pictures captioned "Just another normal day in the mad Lowe household".

Jen wants nothing to do with ICU, this is not in her plan, and she begs Paul to move her back into Section 7, which he does the next day. She is weak and still has tummy pain but is doing better than yesterday. On Friday she wakes up with bad nausea and even more severe tummy pain than before. She's had a very bad night apparently and when I get to the hospital I can see she is in agony.

Writhing. Paul orders a sonar. They come to her room to do it. The practitioners are gobsmacked. Jen has appendicitis.

Appendicitis! You've got to be kidding me! We cannot believe it. Neither can Paul. He books a CT scan just to be sure. The nurse and I wheel Jen down the passage to Radiology. She is in a bad way, curled up on her side, clutching her tummy. James flies up at lunchtime (he always seems to get the worst of it …) and he comes straight to the hospital.

The CT scan results confirm appendicitis. Paul phones the surgeon who did Jen's gastroscopy and he comes to see Jen to discuss what needs to happen. In short Jen must have an appendectomy. The prospect scares us rigid because transplant patients should avoid surgery. Jenna will be at great risk. In her condition and so soon after transplant, surgery is extremely dangerous. But there is no choice. It has to be done. Jen is too sick to even respond. She just wants the pain to go away. The surgeon is nervous too. He tells us he doesn't want to be responsible for her death. Encouraging.

At 7 pm she is wheeled into theatre. Stuart and I are white with anxiety. We wait in the courtyard outside Jen's Section 7 room and sip wine straight from the bottle. We wait. An hour and a half later the doctor comes to find us. Jen is out and in ICU. We can visit. "She is a fighter, that one," he says. We know. No one is more of a fighter than Jenna. The depth of her courage is extraordinary.

The next morning Jen's heart rate is high, but she is quite chipper and has no pain due to post-op pain meds. She is back on oxygen and being closely monitored.

She calls me early on Sunday morning, craving crispy chicken wings and roast potatoes. I jump out of bed and switch on the oven, more than happy to oblige. She is nibbling on them delicately when the surgeon arrives mid-morning to check on her. He is impressed that she's eating, but advises that she keeps the amounts very small for now. And she must be sure to mobilise. Never mind that she has just had an appendectomy, Jen gets out of bed and stands for a while, but by evening she starts to go downhill. She is battling to breathe, and her nausea is back with a vengeance.

I wake up on Monday with a sore throat and a bad cough,

and I have a high temperature. My first thought is that I can't see Jen. I go and see a doctor right away and am put on a course of strong antibiotics, but I am not allowed anywhere near my daughter. Stuart goes to be with Jen and the plan is that James will relieve him in the afternoon before he heads for the airport; he is returning to Cape Town tonight. I am so upset. I sleep and check my phone, sleep and check my phone, sleep and check my phone. I need to get well, and fast.

Stuart says Jenna is still struggling to breathe and her stomach is distended. A chest X-ray shows fluid on the lungs, and Paul has ordered another pleural tap and dialysis to remove it. Plus, she is vomiting badly, which is painful so soon after surgery. A nasogastric tube is inserted. Paul doesn't want Jen to start losing weight again. Stu tells James not to come after all and he stays with Jen all day. Paul orders another CT scan and a sonar.

Tuesday morning Jen is weak and nauseous. She has had diarrhoea all night and no sleep. The CT scan shows nothing sinister, but she is full of fluid, so they dialyse again. I am on my antibiotics and starting to feel better and Paul says I can go in tomorrow. Thank heavens! Not only because I can't bear to be away from Jenna's side but because Stu has to go to Cape Town tomorrow; he has an important business meeting. And we are worried about Kristi, who is sick again and starts test-week next week. Stu needs to check on her.

Week 14 post-transplant (Wednesday, 11th March 2015)

Stuart visits Jen in the morning before he catches his flight. He reports that she is looking slightly better – her tummy is less distended – but she is very nauseous. I get to the hospital as Stu is leaving. Three days has felt like a lifetime and Jen and I are very happy to see each other, but she doesn't look good. Today's chest X-ray still shows fluid so she is dialysed again.

On Thursday I am at the hospital very early. Jenna looks awful. She is weak, pale, swollen. And she is vomiting non-stop. The night nurse tells me she vomited and had diarrhoea the whole of last night. I insist we call Paul and he comes right away. He is not happy and phones the gastro surgeon. Tonight they will take Jen into theatre again and do another gastroscopy. They need to find out what is going on.

The gastroscopy reveals more gunk (another bezoar?) in Jen's stomach and the surgeon removes it. Why is this happening? Jen goes back into ICU for the night so that they can monitor her.

Around 9:30 pm I drive home. It's been a really bad day.

CHAPTER 46

Mama, come quick!

Friday, the 13th of March and the sound of my cellphone ringing pierces my sleep. A stripe of light cracks through an opening in the curtain and my eyes sting when I open them.

I grab the phone. It is Jen's number but there is a deep unfamiliar adult female voice on the other end. "Mama! Mama! Come quick! Jenna can't breathe. You must come now. Come. Now. Mama!" The phone goes dead. My heart is racing. I have not been phoned directly by a nurse in ICU, not in the 100 days that Jen has been at Milpark. It must be an emergency.

I launch myself out of bed, throwing on the tracksuit pants that lie discarded at the bottom of my bed. I can't find a top or even remember where I keep my clothes. I can't think straight. All I know is that I need to get there. I run, grabbing my keys on the way. The front door lock sticks, I pull it hard and it flies open, banging the wall and then my hip bone. I barely notice and slam it behind me.

I'm in the car and speeding up the hill. Did I close the gate? I don't know. Don't care. I drive faster. The car clock says 7:20 am. I get to the main road. Shit. Traffic, so much traffic. It's backed up, everyone is on their way to work and to school. I forgot to go to the toilet. I need to pee.

There is nothing to be done, it is literally bumper to bumper.

I phone Paul, my hands shaky. No answer. I slam on brakes. I nearly hit the car in front of me. The guy in the lane beside me hoots and gesticulates angrily. "Get off the phone, asshole!" he shouts at me. He's right. I shouldn't be on my phone. I ignore him and dial again. No answer from Paul. I try ICU but the phone there just rings. Then I phone Angela, the transplant co-ordinator. Someone closer to the hospital than I am has to get to ICU and get hold of Paul.

Angela picks up right away. "Gabi?"

"Angela, something's wrong with Jen, something is terribly wrong." I am speaking fast, tripping over the words. "The hospital called, the nurse said she can't breathe, and I can't get hold of anyone—"

"Gabi, where are you?"

"I'm stuck in peak hour traffic on the M3, on the highway."

"How close are you?"

"Far, I'm far, and the traffic is not moving. It's bumper to bumper." My stomach lurches again as I realise it's going to take me at least an hour to get there. I want to vomit. "Oh Jesus," I groan. "Angela? Can you get there? Please. Someone needs to get there." I want to cry, and my bladder is burning. I really need to pee. My stomach starts to churn and gurgle as well, the fear dripping into it like acid, making it really loose. It's my fear response, always – instant runny tummy.

"Gabi." Angela's voice brings me back. "Stay focused, drive carefully. I will phone the hospital. I will find Paul. I will make a plan. Leave it with me. You just get here safely."

I am stuck behind kilometres and kilometres of cars, with no way out and nothing I can do. It is excruciating. My body is coursing with adrenaline and I really, really need the loo. I am literally writhing in my car seat with the agony of it, trying to breathe and calm down but I'm desperate. Desperate with worry. Desperate with fear. Desperate to get to Jen. Desperate for the toilet. I don't know if I'm going to make it, but I cannot pull over. I will not give in to my body's needs until I get to the hospital. I have to get to the hospital.

It is one of the longest hours of my life. When I get to Milpark I run straight to the loo. I wash my hands and sprint down the long passage and into ICU. I run inside … I must look a fright because the shift manager puts an arm out and stops me in my tracks. "Stop, Gabi," she says. "She is okay. Jenna is okay. Take a deep breath." She puts two hands on my shoulders. "Calm yourself." I bend down over my knees and catch my breath, like a runner who has just finished a race. I get my breath back, stand up straight and look at her. "Thank you," I say. "I'm fine now."

I put on my mask, gloves, cap and coat and look at Jen through the glass doors. She is sitting up in bed. Her face is really swollen and she is on a ventilator, but not the ventilator I have seen before. She is also being dialysed. One of the transplant surgeons on Jen's team is standing next to her. There are three nurses in the room. I have not seen Jenna's eyes so full of fear, not since the psychosis.

Before I go in the doctor comes out to speak to me. She confirms that Jen had a terrible, terrible night. Not only did she vomit all night but she was having a lot of trouble breathing. It was lucky she'd just happened to be walking past this morning to check on another patient when the nurse brought her attention to how much trouble Jen was in. Lucky? I feel rage rising inside me. Why didn't ICU call Paul in the middle of the night? Why didn't they call me? How could they let my child go through that? Why would they let it get that bad? The night nurse who called me earlier on Jenna's cellphone is no longer here. There has been a change of shift.

I push my rage aside. I can't let Jen see it. She needs to trust her carers and she won't if she thinks I don't.

I ask about the ventilator. The doctor explains that it's called a Bipap. It is a non-invasive ventilator that gives airway support by way of a face mask instead of an endotracheal tube. It pushes air into your lungs and will ensure Jen gets the oxygen she needs. The dialysis will help reduce her pulmonary oedema.

I go in to see Jen. She is so relieved to have me there. I stroke her hair, kiss her forehead through my mask and talk soothingly to her. Her heart rate is alarmingly high.

I can't stand to see Jen like this. She can't eat or drink. Her stomach is very distended and even on the ventilator mask she is breathing with difficulty. She has a temperature, and the vomiting is continuous. Every time she needs to vomit, she indicates with her hand. I whip off the ventilator mask and hold the silver kidney-shaped bowl under her chin. When she is done, I replace the mask to help her breathe. Then we do it again. And again.

Paul comes back and forth a few times during the day. Late afternoon Shirley arrives from Cape Town. I show her our system of Bipap and vomit bowl and she relieves me for a while so I can have something to eat and drink. Considering what Natalie went through in Boston, it must be so hectic for Shirl to see Jen like this. I shouldn't be letting her see this, let alone help me. I feel terrible, but I need the support.

We have a hectic weekend. By Sunday Jen can sip some black tea and water, or clear juice, without throwing up. She is very weak but improving. If this keeps going in the right direction, Paul and I would like to get her out of ICU and back into Section 7 as fast as possible. This setback is damaging her morale. On Monday we move Jen back to Section 7, to her isolation ward. Her heart rate is still erratic and quite high, her meds are now all being given intravenously, and she is off the Bipap and back on a cannula. But she has a day free of nausea and vomiting. It is a massive relief. She is being fed via TPN. In addition to everything else, she has also developed shingles. Shingles can be very painful but it seems Jen barely notices. It is the least of her worries.

In the afternoon we get a visit from Jen's godfather and our dear friend Ian. It is so, so wonderful to see him. He dons a coat and mask and sits in the ward with us. If he is shocked by how Jen is, he does not show it. He is calm and caring and kind. Jen is happy to see him. We all are. He comes home with us for supper in Rivonia. Shirl does the evening shift so Stuart and I can spend time with Ian. After chatting most of the evening Ian asks what our friends in Cape Town can do to help. He won't take "no" for an answer. They are all waiting to hear from him. We do know what we need, but it is so hard to ask. After much convincing, we put our pride in our pocket and tell him: Voyager Miles or cash to help with flights to bring our family members and James up to visit regularly. That is what is needed the most. Ian doesn't hesitate. "Consider it done," he says. We know he will go back and request help on our behalf. There is a group of six couples (we call ourselves the "Wazzup's") who go away together once a year. Stu and I have had to miss these holidays a few times because of Jen's illness but there is a unique bond among us. I suspect it is these friends, along with a few others, that Ian will approach for assistance. I see reflected on his face the depth and breadth of the strain on us. We are 105 days into an epic battle that we could never have imagined would be this hard. We need all the support we can get. There is no room for pride.

Why, Ian probes, have we not reached out to more of our Johannesburg contacts? We know a lot of people here, after all, and they are on standby waiting to support. It's a valid question. To be honest, we haven't been able to lift our heads to see more than a few steps in front of us. Things have been so horrifically hard that we don't want anyone else to witness this or have to bear it. And we keep expecting it to improve. Of course, we've had some incredible support but truth be told, we have not really let anybody in properly. We have been in lock-down. Ian can see how run-down and emotionally battered we are. He is deeply concerned.

Week 15 post-transplant (Wednesday, 18th March 2015)

Jen has lost weight again. She is managing to stand but there is no walking, she is too weak. She is being fed intravenously and her shingles is getting worse. It is now noticeably sore, and she has had a mild temperature for days.

With the encouragement of her nutritionist I am trying to get Jen to sip clear soups and juices. I make these myself at home in a sterile kitchen environment (everything gets washed in baby bottle steriliser) to supplement her intravenous feed. My friend Libby has sent her special juice-extractor machine up from Cape Town for me to use.

Jen is listless and her temperature is slowly rising more each day.

When I think of how well she was just a few weeks back before the appendicitis, it makes my stomach lurch. She was doing so well ... walking upstairs, no oxygen, no monitors, so hopeful and about to come home to Rivonia to really start her recovery and reintroduction to the world. Now she is tired and flat, weak, unable to eat again, back on dialysis, with a distended stomach and constant diarrhoea. I am watching her fade away in front of my eyes all over again. She is vomiting at least once or twice a day.

On Friday Paul comes to see me. He believes Jen has a CMV infection so he's going to start her on a strong antiviral called Cymevene. Research tells me: "Cytomegalovirus (CMV) is a common virus that can infect almost anyone. Once infected, your body retains the virus for life. Most people don't know they have CMV because it rarely causes problems in healthy people. But if you have a weakened immune system, CMV is cause for concern. For people with compromised immunity, especially due to organ transplantation, CMV infection can be fatal. If your immune system is weakened, you might experience more serious signs and symptoms affecting your eyes, lungs, liver, oesophagus, stomach, intestines and brain."[6]

For most of the weekend I sit at Jen's side. I cannot believe she has more to deal with. How can this be possible? I don't explain the severity of the CMV virus in transplant patients to her, she doesn't need to know that part. By Sunday night she has full-blown rigors and fever and her heart rate is right up again.

Paul comes in early on Monday. Lab results also show a yeast infection, which will be from her lines. They must be removed, and new ones inserted. Today. He books a theatre for this afternoon.

Jen is so sick. But today's nurse is dragging her feet, literally. Everything appears to be an effort for her. She acts as though she really doesn't want to be here, and Jen can feel it. I try to bear the brunt and make up for the careless nursing. She takes extra-long tea breaks, disappears for long periods during the day, resents any requests and does everything at a snail's pace. I don't leave Jenna's

---

6   https://www.mayoclinic.org/diseases-conditions/cmv/symptoms-causes/syc-20355358

side. Eventually I phone Stu for back-up. Jen is really battling and I'm so tired. He comes through and we help the nurse get her ready to move to theatre. With all her lines and meds, it is a complex process.

Jen goes into theatre at 4 pm. By the time she comes out and back down to her isolation ward in Section 7, it is 5:45 pm. The new lines in her neck are very high up and there is a lot of blood on the sheets. She is restless and upset, and she is getting absolutely no sympathy from the nurse, who is irritated that Jen has come out of theatre so late. Clearly, she would rather be preparing to go home. I am angry but stay calm and focus my attention on helping Jen settle. She has bad diarrhoea, is sore, and unusually anxious. I watch the nurse hurry through giving Jen all her meds and I have a bad feeling. At 6:45 pm she races out the door to catch her taxi home, not even bothering to stay for the 7 pm handover. Jen is still lying in bloodied sheets. I am horrified. I feel helpless.

The night nurse is on it. She quickly changes the linen and helps me settle Jen. When Paul comes to do his rounds and check on her, I take him aside outside in the passage and explain how bad things have been today. I am worried that the nurse has made a mistake with the meds because she was so rushed and careless. I am especially worried about the antiviral, which is very potent. I have a bad feeling. Paul takes me seriously and checks very carefully everything the nurse has written down on Jenna's chart. And there it is, in black and white: instead of 0.5 mg of the antiviral medication, the nurse has given Jen the entire vial – 500 mg. I feel panic rising. "It's not possible," Paul says, incredulous. We have to make sure. He reads it again and again, as if looking at it will change the outcome. Then the night nurse rummages through the waste bin to find the vial. It is empty. Paul still can't believe it. I can't either and yet I can. I can because I watched the nurse rushing. I could see she was distracted. She took no care, she took no care at all.

Leaving the night nurse with Jen, Paul and I go back out into the passage to talk. We pace up and down. I am so worried. So is he. But first he has to be sure. He instructs the hospital to track down the day nurse to ask her. We have to find out. We have to be sure. When he leaves I sit at Jen's bedside, distraught. She is so weak and compromised already. Now she is even more at risk. I don't know what to do with myself. Anger rises up inside like waves threatening to drown me, but I have no choice but to sit with it. I have to stay calm for Jen. There is nothing to do except wait. I can't let her see how desperate I am. I can't let her know. I sing to her until she falls asleep and then I wait. While I wait, I research Cymevene. The words "Patients with impaired renal function are at increased risk of toxicity" send me into an even deeper panic. Clearly this is a highly potent and toxic drug, one that Paul must have thought hard about giving Jen at all.

At 8:30 pm I am visited by a statuesque woman who introduces herself, I think, as the hospital night manager. She says she is "so, so sorry", she is the bringer of bad news. They have tracked down the nurse. I was right. She did overdose Jenna.

I feel as if my legs are going to give way. I am so angry, so helpless and overcome with fear. What does this mean? How will Jen be impacted by this? Just how badly will it compromise her? I don't know; she doesn't know. She tells me that Dr Williams is on his way back to the hospital. I meet Paul in the passage. I am pacing. I don't think he has ever seen me this angry. Distraught. He doesn't know what to tell me. He has ordered a dialysis team. Jenna will be dialysed as soon as possible.

I phone Stu and then I Google "Cymevene overdose"…

Overdose symptoms
Reports of overdoses with i.e. ganciclovir, some with fatal outcomes, have been received from clinical trials and during post-marketing experience. The majority of the reports were either not associated with any adverse reactions, or included one or more of the adverse reactions listed below:
  – Haematological toxicity: myelosuppression including pancytopenia, bone marrow failure, leukopenia, neutropenia, granulocytopenia
  – Hepatotoxicity: hepatitis, liver function disorder

– Renal toxicity: worsening of haematuria in a patient with pre-existing renal impairment, acute kidney injury, elevated creatinine

– Gastrointestinal toxicity: abdominal pain, diarrhoea, vomiting

– Neurotoxicity: generalised tremor, seizure

Christ. Jenna already had most of these symptoms. What chance does she have now? My body feels weak. How much more? How much more can one young girl, one family, take?

It is midnight when the dialysis team finally arrives.

At 2 am Jen is on dialysis but at last fast asleep and being monitored very carefully. I cannot tell her she has been overdosed. She must never know, otherwise how will she trust a nurse again? I cannot keep my eyes open. Jen will be dialysed most of the night and then again tomorrow after a short break. I am filled with dread. I don't know how, but I drive home. The roads are empty.

The next day Jen's white blood cell count has plummeted. Paul starts her on Neupogen to get her count up. Neupogen is an injection that stimulates the bone marrow to increase the production of white blood cells. It is often given to patients after chemotherapy. Jen is really tired and sleeps most of the day. She is dialysed again. It's an eerily quiet day of watching and waiting.

I am filled with fear and terror that we might lose Jen. It feels like a breaking point for me. That night, when Stu is at the hospital and I am on my own at the house I phone Glynis. She answers the phone and I scream. I just scream and scream. My poor friend. She has her children in the car with her and she tells me she will call me back. Somehow I manage to pull myself together, but when Glynis calls I sob and I sob, and she listens.

Week 16 post-transplant (Wednesday, 25th March 2015)

Ali flies up from Cape Town on Wednesday. She has been up to Johannesburg many times in the past few months. When she is here, she keeps the home fires burning. She takes over the grocery shopping, sorting out the house, has business conversations with Stu about his Johannesburg clients and helps with logistics. She brings fresh energy and perspective and supports us in ways that we really need. She always visits Jen when she is here, but Ali's focus is on looking after us. Keeping us going and supporting us.

Today we have a meeting at Sun International to discuss Jen's 21st. Over 10 000 people have signed up to come to her party, which is now only six months away. If we are to deliver, which Jen insists we must, then we have to start planning now. It will be a national celebration with a live feed to each venue. Ali and her Rainbow Experiential Marketing team will co-ordinate it, Sun International will provide all the venues, Gear House is supplying all the sound plus helping to find artists – The Parlotones, GoodLuck, PJ Powers, Beatenberg and, of course, Kristi Lowe have already agreed to perform. Berry Productions will do the filming and there is a lot more exciting stuff planned.

It feels weird, though, to be planning a huge celebration when we are consumed in such an epic battle to keep our Jen alive.

When I go back to the hospital Jen is doing better. Her white blood cell count is up a little, but she has run out of her TPN feed. No one has ordered it. This kind of thing really gets my blood pressure up. The poor child is skin and bone. We wait on the pharmacy all day until the new feed comes.

Jen's temp is down, her blood pressure is good, and her white blood cell count is increasing rapidly because of the Neupogen. I wash her hair.

James and Shirley are coming up at the weekend and Kristi and Aniko arrive on Monday. It's school holidays and Kristi needs to have a laser tonsillectomy, which we are going to have done up here in Johannesburg. Doing a full tonsillectomy is not an option at this stage. Not only is it very painful, but it also requires a long recovery time and we are not in Cape Town to nurse her. I don't know who is looking after who in Cape Town but Aniko has been acting as Kristi's "au pair", which has worked out well. She drives her to school and to her extramurals. More importantly, they have become inseparable. The emotional support has been essential for Kristi.

All the same, I can't wait to have my youngest here for a full two weeks.

I visit Sandy one afternoon to sit in the stillness of her beautiful home only 10 minutes from the hospital. She cannot believe what we are dealing with. She wants to do something to help. She has spoken to some of her close girlfriends, people I don't even know but who know our story, and they are starting a cooking circle. Each week they will take turns to cook healthy meals that I can freeze for the family, and for Jen when she can eat. Plain, simple, wholesome meals. The kindness of these women will make a big difference to my life in the coming weeks.

Week 17 post-transplant (Wednesday, 1st April 2015)

Jen's breathing becomes laboured again over the weekend and on Wednesday she has another pleural tap. A procedure that once brought so much anxiety seems almost commonplace now, although it really isn't. Apart from that she is doing much better.

I leave James with Jen and drive to the other side of the city with Kristi to take her for her laser tonsillectomy. It goes well, Kristi is brave, and I have her home in Rivonia a few hours later.

For the next couple of days things are stable with Jenna. It is strangely calm. She has some nausea, but not a lot and is managing clear soups and drinking clear juices. I have even arranged a facial for her in the hospital. We sterilise all the equipment and I collect the therapist and bring her to the hospital. James and Ko-Ko are taking turns to visit Jen, and I drive between Milpark and Rivonia, where I am looking after Kristi. It is good to have some time with Kristi, but we also need to have a very difficult conversation. It has become clear to Stuart and me that she must move up to Johannesburg. There is no telling how long Jenna's recovery will take. Even if she is home next week, we will need to be close to the hospital for a minimum of six months, if not a year, post her discharge. Four months ago, when we all agreed that

Kristi would stay in Cape Town, we had hoped and believed that Jen would be out of hospital by mid-January. It hasn't turned out that way, however, and being apart from each other is too painful. We need to be together. It is not good for Kristi to be alone in Cape Town, no matter how grown up she believes she is. I have found a really good school called Redhill. It is close to our Rivonia house and they are willing to take Kristi on in the second term due to our circumstances and thanks to the influence of the fabulous Raffaella. Besides which Aniko needs to go home to Australia. She can't put her life on hold any longer.

I know it is going to be hard for Kristi ... leaving Reggie, leaving her beloved horse, starting at yet another school, leaving her friends and her home, saying goodbye to Ko-Ko ... but Stuart and I are sure it is the right decision. We also need to rent out our home in Cape Town so that we can afford to carry on living in Johannesburg.

In the days leading up to Easter, while she is recovering from her laser tonsillectomy, Stu and I broach the subject with Kristi. We are sitting in the courtyard of our Rivonia house; it is evening and the light is beautiful. I take a photograph to show Jen. Aniko and James are with her. We have lit the braai and all the candles. Candle lighting has become something of a ritual for me over the past four months. Every night when I get home from the hospital, I light candles all over the house. It started out of necessity due to rolling power outages, but then I started doing it anyway. It has become a beautiful, peaceful and symbolic way for me to hold Jen, Kristi and all our loved ones in my heart when I am not with them. It also marks the transition from hospital to home, allowing me to access a place of stillness inside me that is renewing. This place fills me up so that I can face the ward again the next day.

Initially, Kristi is resistant to the idea of moving, but in fact she has sensed that it's been coming and somewhere deep inside she knows it's the right thing. She fights against it, but I can also feel a sense of relief in her that we have taken the decision out of her hands. We explain that we will bring the dogs to Johannesburg and somehow find her a horse she can ride here. We also tell her we will fly Reggie to Johannesburg as often as we can, and that she can go back to Cape Town for holidays and stay with friends. I have arranged that tomorrow we will visit Redhill School and I will email Abbotts in Cape Town. Stuart has contacted a Cape Town estate agent to view our house and market it for rental. There are some things I need to fix up, so I will go back to Cape Town with Kristi for a few days the following week to sort them out. She won't start second term of Grade 11 there; she will start it here in Johannesburg with us. The decision is made. There are no easy choices for our family.

CHAPTER 47

An Easter full of hope

The Rivonia house is going to be full for the Easter weekend – Kristi, Aniko and James, plus Stu and I – and it is safe to say it will be an Easter full of hope. The past seven days have been good with Jen. Apart from the pleural tap on Wednesday she has only had dialysis twice, which is massive progress, and she is generally brighter. She is taking in clear liquids and being fed through a feeding tube. Her nausea, although consistent, seems a little bit more manageable if she sticks to tiny meals and hardly any solids.

Jen is thriving on the company of Kristi, Aniko and James, who visit regularly as her energy levels have increased slightly and so has her mood. They chat, share news of the outside world and show her messages from friends. The four-day-long Easter weekend is looming. Paul has suggested we work towards being able to bring Jen to Rivonia for a day visit. We are ecstatic at the news and so is Jen. She literally lights up.

This will be a first step towards leaving hospital. Her first outing in 121 days. The first time she will see Johannesburg since landing in a helicopter at Milpark Hospital on the 10th of December last year. The first time she will be in a car, see the horizon, see the home we have set up for her here. The first time we all have real hope of a proper recovery.

Paul is convinced, as are we, that the sooner we can get Jen out of the hospital, the better her chances of a full recovery will be. Now that she can go three to four days without dialysis, it is a real possibility. In order to facilitate her coming home, she will have a G-J (gastrostomy-jejunostomy) tube placed in her stomach and small intestine next week.

We cannot keep on feeding her through intravenous lines or a nasogastric tube because the risk of infection is too great, but patients can apparently be fed through a G-J tube for long periods while they recuperate enough to eat normally. I am very happy to manage feeding tubes, meds and other such complexities at home. It is far preferable to Jen staying in the hospital any longer.

Stuart and I are breathless with excitement. We rush off to buy a couch big enough for Jen to lie on that will act as a day-bed and we sterilise the house again from top to toe. I rearrange Jen's bedroom, again, making sure it is just perfect. Stuart has permission from the owners for us to heat the small pool. Now that Jen is on the verge of coming home, we have been doing our research. There is a physiotherapist just up the road, who Jen will visit regularly, but there is also loads of evidence to show that gentle aqua exercise is the best way to build muscle mass and strength, using the resistance of the water, but with little chance of injury. Jen is bordering on skeletal; she will need all the help she can get to build muscle.

The hum of excitement and hope in our home is palpable. Kristi is moving up to live with us and Jen will soon be coming home. I can feel happiness creeping up from my toes. It is warm and soft, like cashmere.

On Saturday, the 4th of April I give Jen a bath in the bathroom of her isolation ward. She looks anorexic. Her face, elbows and knees seem too large for her body and when I pick her up to put her in the bath, she is as light as a feather. Her whole body is skinny except for her cheeks. She still has a moon face from the large doses of immunosuppressant steroids that transplant patients have to take. But she can walk to the bathroom unaided, her knees no longer sway back weirdly when she walks, and her eyes have a sparkle. I wash her hair gently. It is much thinner than it was and comes out easily if I'm too firm. We plan which PJs she will wear to go home in tomorrow so that I can wash and sterilise them. She chooses the fresh green ones, the colour of life, renewal and nature. As it is Easter, the hospital carpark is empty. There is no traffic on the roads. It feels vaguely desolate. Paul visits in the afternoon. He is delighted with Jen and says tomorrow can go ahead, but he will check in on her in the morning just to be sure.

The morning of the 5th of April 2015 arrives. It is Easter Sunday and Jen is coming home for the day! I wake up with butterflies in my tummy. Stu goes off happily to the hospital to be with Jen and get her ready for the outing. He phones to tell me she had a large vomit this morning but doesn't feel bad now and is coming anyway. I stay at the house with Aniko and Kristi to do a final spring-clean and set a beautiful table. I am cooking our Sunday lunch. A clear soup for Jen and roast lamb for everyone else. James is spring-cleaning the car and sanitising every door handle. At 10 am he leaves to go and help Stu with the wheelchair, oxygen cylinder and anything else that is required. He is grinning from ear to ear as he drives out.

I am ready. Kristi and Aniko are getting dressed and music emanates from the house. It is a beautiful day, soft light and warm sun. I sit in the courtyard, the sound of trickling water from the fountain soothing my excitement as I drink a cup of coffee. Jenna is coming home. My baby is on her way home. I sit and watch the birds, as I have done for many months whenever I am at home, and I notice one I have not seen here before. A single pure white fan-tail dove – the symbol of eternal peace and the holy spirit.

Stu phones to say they are on their way. The half an hour it takes to get from the hospital to Rivonia feels like an eternity, but eventually they arrive.

Today Jen is the one wearing a face mask and the rest of us are without. It is the first time she has seen all our faces, maskless, in months. James helps her out of the car and up the steps, slowly.

She looks so small and vulnerable. She is totally overwhelmed. We have to curb our boisterous excitement and I get Ko-Ko and Kristi to turn the music down. Everything feels like an onslaught to Jen. What else did we expect? She has been through hell and the outside world is totally foreign to her. She just needs to "arrive". We get her outside into the courtyard and put a blanky on her knees and a cushion under her bottom. She is so paper thin that she shivers at even the slightest breeze. The white dove is still here, sitting in the tree, watching over us. Slowly Jen starts to settle. Her little shoulders relax, and I can see the crinkles around her eyes as she smiles under her mask. She is drinking in every minute facial expression and every detail of the gorgeous garden. I can only imagine how she must feel. We have waited for this moment for so long.

Eventually Jen is ready to see the house. We walk her around very slowly. She loves it, I knew she would, and she can't stop thanking me for her room. She opens the cupboard door and sees all her clothes, the ones she packed all those months ago on the 10th of December. Tears well up in her eyes and I hold her.

We have a long, slow lunch, taking care to savour each moment. Jen has one small bowl of clear soup and a tiny piece of crispy roast potato. I can see she wants more, but is so wary of nausea. By the time lunch is finished everyone is chatting animatedly and telling stories. Jen is happy but totally exhausted. She has a rest on the bed in her new bedroom, with James and Kristi talking to her quietly while Aniko and I clear the table and tidy up. The white dove still sits in the tree.

As it gets close to Jen's curfew time to get back to hospital, her mood starts to flag. She doesn't want to go back. None of us wants her to. I tell Jen that it will be okay, she will be home soon, and if she feels great tomorrow morning maybe Paul will let her visit again. But icicles of dread fill my stomach as they pull out of the driveway.

The white dove flies off about 10 minutes after they leave. I am overcome with sadness and exhaustion and sit in the courtyard and weep. I just want my Jen back.

On Easter Monday I am at the hospital first thing. Jen is severely nauseous and vomits all day. After the joy of yesterday, she is silent and has retreated into herself to cope. She can't eat or drink anything and has severe lung pain as well. Paul orders dialysis for the afternoon. James wants to come and say goodbye to Jen as he is flying back today, but she doesn't want him to see her like this, not after yesterday. Once again she is vomiting non-stop. I feel her brown eyes pleading with me to make it stop. Tomorrow they are inserting the G-J tube in theatre. Paul says they will do another gastroscopy while she is under to see if they can see anything to explain the vomiting. We have to get to the bottom of it.

On Tuesday I check the charts when I arrive because I missed the 7 am staff handover. The night nurse has recorded a seizure at 1 am, yet I received no call from the hospital and neither did Paul. Jen doesn't remember, which probably means it did happen; she never recalls her seizures. Paul calls for a blood test to check her Epilim levels and decides we will go ahead with surgery for the G-J tube. It must be done. He is going away tomorrow to a medical conference. By lunchtime the Epilim result still hasn't come – so much for "urgent" – and the day nurse re-orders it.

Jen has spent most of the day vomiting and at 4 pm she has another seizure. No number of seizures make them less scary and every time she has one, I seem to be alone with Jen. Sometimes I don't know if I can survive any more. If she can. But we do.

In the early evening Jen is taken into theatre to have the G-J tube placed.

Week 18 post-transplant (Wednesday, 8th April 2015)

Jen is very sleepy post-theatre and her seizure yesterday. Her white bloods are high and so is her blood pressure. She seems very "out of it". There is no nausea, though, when she is sleeping, which is a blessing. Stu takes over from me as I have loads to organise with Kristi. We are heading back to Cape Town on Friday so that I can sort out the house. I book tickets, take her to the Redhill second-hand shop to buy uniforms and drive across town to take her for a post-laser tonsillectomy check-up. All seems good.

There is no way that Stu will cope on his own with Jen, so Lizzie has agreed to come up and help nurse her while I am away.

By Friday, the 10th Jen is still very sleepy, still very "out of it". Stu and I are worried. This is not like her at all. I bring it to the attention of the stand-in doctors (Paul is still away) and we're astounded that they are not more concerned. In the afternoon she has a CT brain scan and lumbar puncture to check her cerebrospinal fluid and just before I leave for Cape Town, she is moved back into ICU.

I go to the airport with Kristi at 5:30 pm. My heart is sore and heavy. I am glad Lizzie is coming up tomorrow to help. Kristi and I sleep all the way home on the plane. Granny and Grampa fetch us. It's an odd feeling to arrive home. My house no longer feels like mine. I sit on the floor and let the dogs lick me all over – they are so happy to see us.

On Saturday morning Jen is more awake, but the minute she is, she starts vomiting again. By Monday she is still vomiting. She has another gastroscopy. The G-J tube was not in place yet.

CHAPTER 48

Moving Kristi

I spend five days in Cape Town. I pack boxes, do filing and admin, oversee a painter Sue arranged for me, sort out the garden with Mary (it was a wreck) and fix up the house. I need to get back to Jen as fast as possible, but there is a lot to be done.

Kristi has found riders to lease Riaan so that his costs are covered, and we have found a happy home for our bunnies. It was total mayhem trying to catch them, which we did with the help of about four students. I see the dentist, my GP and my therapist. I meet with our accountants and Kristi's school and arrange for Daffy's sister Demi to move in and be Kristi's au pair for the next two weeks until she moves up to Johannesburg. By Thursday morning our home is ready for rental. The agent cannot believe the difference.

On Tuesday night (the 14th) my close girlfriends arrange a surprise birthday dinner for me. It is wonderful to see everyone, but in many ways it is also extremely difficult to be out in the world. "Normality" highlights the extremity of our situation and feels surreal. I want to hide. I am not coping with the real world.

Week 19 post-transplant (Wednesday, 15th April 2015)

Kristi knows she is moving up to Johannesburg, but she has

concerns she wants to broach with me. We both think it would be a good idea for her therapist to be present because we are vulnerable and stressed. A "facilitated" space is best. The three of us meet on Thursday afternoon. Kristi asks me lots of questions and seems to be okay with the answers, but there is one question that really breaks my heart. She says she knows the trauma I deal with every day and she knows how all-consuming it is … so how, she asks, will I find the time to look after her?

Part of me wants to get defensive and say, "I'm doing the very best I can" but the other part knows that Kristi's question is a question, not a criticism. It is a very valid point. We talk it through. If Kristi comes to Johannesburg, who takes her to school? Who fetches her? Is she alone in the afternoon while I'm at the hospital until 7 pm? She doesn't know anyone there and she doesn't know the city. Practically, how is it going to work?

I realise fully then that when Kristi comes to Johannesburg, I have to commit to doing things differently. I am going to be forced to ask for help as Ian suggested. I commit there and then to dropping her at school every morning before leaving for the hospital and to spending time with her in the afternoons. I will find the right people to be with Jen in the afternoons. We can't insist Kristi moves to Johannesburg, where she knows no one, and then abandon her. I will be mindful, and I will help her with the transition.

On Friday I fly back to Johannesburg. I go straight to the hospital from the airport. Jen is still in ICU and she doesn't look good to me but she is so happy to see me. Her stomach is distended and painful and her CPR is raised, which indicates infection. Dr Williams is still away. We call the gastro specialist, who promises to visit Jen tomorrow.

When he comes on Saturday morning Jen is vomiting. She is very swollen, has severe tummy pain, her heart rate is high, and so is her blood pressure. Dialysis is difficult as her lines keep blocking. The gastro specialist insists that the nurses aspirate her G-tube every day. He demonstrates and gives instruction that 10 ml of water per hour should be put into the J-tube and every three hours the nurses must aspirate the G-tube. I watch carefully. Later that afternoon Jen's lines are changed again. It has been a shock to come back and see her like this. We have gone backwards, a lot. She is worse. The vomiting, the nausea, the pain, the dialysis; she has a catheter and a G-J tube that has yet to be used to feed her. Watching her suffer like this is extreme. It feels unbearable.

Sunday is no better. I think a gentle foot rub may help, but Jen feels too awful to even be touched. As I am rearranging the bedding to make her more comfortable I discover that her right leg is swollen. Very swollen. I call the nurse, who phones the doctor on call. It must be a clot. He orders a Doppler for Monday.

Monday is bad. High blood pressure, high heart rate, bad nausea. The Doppler shows Jen has a clot in her right leg and blood thinners are added to the mix of medications. Her stomach is still bloated and sore and the nursing handovers are lacking, to say the least. Nursing Jen is now a very complex and complicated affair. She needs consistency of nursing care and yet the nurses keep changing and the handovers are shoddy. There really should be proper handovers. Often I find the nurses making mistakes with the G-J tube. The smallest of mistakes now is compromising Jen and they happen often. I go and see the head sister to discuss my concerns. And why, I ask her, did it take me to discover Jen's swollen right leg? Is no one actually seeing Jen, "the patient", any more? It still seems crazy to me, especially for transplant patients, that the doctors don't have their own team of nursing staff. To "outsource" this level of nursing is insane.

Paul is back today. We are relieved to see him.

On Tuesday Jen has five hours of dialysis and another pleural tap. She is also given platelets. On the upside her catheter is removed. Paul has requested that the nurses start feeding her through the J-tube, very slowly at only 10 ml an hour to avoid problems. Jen is so thin. She has not eaten in weeks. She has been fed via TPN, but we need to shift from TPN to the J-tube. She has lain in ICU for 11 days now and is getting weaker, not stronger. Our morale is really taking a knock.

I have a meeting in the hospital coffee shop with a no-nonsense but gentle woman named Margy, the wife of a work colleague of Stuart's, who has very kindly offered to help. She is an ex-nurse, very experienced, and she is lovely. She has blonde hair, soft blue eyes and a kind but assured manner. I need the help. Stuart thinks we need it too. I accept.

Week 20 post-transplant (Wednesday, 22nd April 2015)

On Wednesday Jen's heart rate and BP are still high. She is dialysed but the J-tube feed is increased to 20 ml per hour and she is allowed to sip clear fluids. She is like a little baby bird.

Margy sits with her for three hours to give me a break. I go to Rosebank and sit in a coffee shop staring at the world going by. All I'm really doing is counting the hours until I can go back to the hospital. I know I need the break, but it is hard to let go.

Jen has a terrible night. On Thursday her platelets and HB are very low and she is experiencing extreme tummy pain. Severe. The G-J tubes need to be checked (this will be done by inserting colour contrast dye into the tubes); it seems the J-tube is not working. Paul stops the feed and he books Jen for a CT scan.

On Friday Jen is on TPN, she has been given platelets and her G-tube is on free drain. The physio gets her up and standing. Later she is taken down the passage in a wheelchair to Radiology. While we are waiting in the passage to go in, she tells me she was scared of her night nurse last night. The nurse shouted at her and told her she was not allowed to ask questions. The head of Radiology comes to say hello to us and takes Jen in. I am allowed in with her briefly until they have her set up and then I am sent to sit on a chair in the passage.

Jen is awake for the procedure. She is on a bed that has been tilted into a virtually standing position. When the colour contrast dye is inserted into the tubes it shows that the J-tube is in the wrong place. They call Paul. They need to try and move it with Jen awake to avoid more surgery. This is important and I know it is tough, but Jen must be fed through this tube. It is imperative for her survival that we find a way to feed her through her stomach and not via TPN so that we can avoid infection, nausea and vomiting and she can get the nutrition she so desperately needs. There is a lot riding on this.

Every now and then one of the radiologists leaves the room to catch their breath. I can see they are broken by Jen's courage and broken by the fact that they can't get it right. At one stage a young woman comes out. She has tears in her eyes. She paces up and down, her hand holding her mouth, then takes a deep breath, composes herself and goes back inside. She doesn't see me. I sit for two painstaking hours. I am willing messages of love and support to Jen through the walls. She knows I am right outside the door. She knows.

On Saturday there is no dialysis. Jen's BP and heart rate are better, her G-tube is on free drainage, but her neck lines are occluding and she has diarrhoea (which I'm told is probably from the contrast dye). James is here for the long weekend (Monday the 27th is a public holiday) and he visits for a short bit while I do a quick shop, but I swap out with him because Jen needs me. She is very flat, depressed. I have seldom seen her so sad. She tells me for the first time that she feels like there is no end in sight.

I speak to Paul. We have to do something to help Jen shift her mood.

Stuart flies down to Cape Town on Sunday morning. He will do a final pack-up of the house and fetch Kristi and the dogs to move up to Johannesburg on Thursday. James and I are on "Bean-duty" for the weekend and Lizzie will join us on Tuesday.

Today Jen's blood pressure is a little better and her platelets are up. Paul has given us permission to take Jen off the monitors for a short while and take her out of ICU in a wheelchair for some sunlight. It is amazing what some vitamin D can do. Jen's mood perks up substantially. Tomorrow I will talk to Paul about getting her out of ICU and back to Section 7. She needs to be able to see sunlight and sky.

Monday, the 27th is a better day. Jenna had a good night's sleep and in the morning she stood with the physio. She is drinking sips of clear liquids. She weighs 43 kg. Paul is going to up the TPN feed

369

and he has agreed to let Jen move back to Section 7 tomorrow.

James and I are up and down the stairs on Tuesday, moving Jen's stuff, putting her pics back up on the wall, arranging her drawers and setting up her mini-fridge and microwave. It will be so good for her to be back here.

Week 21 post-transplant (Wednesday, 29th April 2015)

Jen is so happy to wake up and be able to look out the window. She has physio in the morning and is determined to walk a few steps. When she can get to the door, we will arrange another bath. She is delighted to see Lizzie. James is going home this evening; it has been so good to have him here to help.

On Thursday I'm at the hospital at 6:30 am. I'm on morning duty today and Lizzie will do the afternoon so I can fetch Stu, Kristi, Sahara and Prince from the airport. Jen is going to theatre to have her lines removed and a Hickman line put in. Tonight my whole family, including the dogs, will be together in one city. Heaven. Jen is not on TPN because she has been prepped and is waiting for surgery. We wait and we wait. Eventually, I have to leave to go to the airport but Lizzie stays with Jen. She only goes into theatre at 4:30 pm.

At the airport Stuart, Kristi and I fly into each other's arms. This is a momentous day. We are together again. Between them they have loads of suitcases and we pile the car high and then drive to the collection point to fetch the dogs. They are confused, running around sniffing everything. Prince has literally eaten a hole through his wooden box, poor boy. We all pile into the car, dogs, humans and mountains of stuff, and drive home to Rivonia.

It is such a relief to have Kristi here. Such a relief. Sahara and Prince explore every inch of their new home and mark their territory. They keep coming back to us to lick, pant and check we are still here.

Friday, the 1st of May is Workers' Day, another public holiday, and there are hardly any cars on the road as I drive to the hospital. I can't believe it is May and Jen is still in hospital. When I get to

Milpark the physio is just leaving. Jen has managed to walk to the door and back and so it is time for the bath I promised her. The nurse and I run a warm bath. The G-J tube is waterproof but the Hickman line is not, so we must be careful not to get it wet.

The clamshell scar from the transplant is healing well. Jenna now also has a scar from the appendectomy and a whole lot of scars that look like "puncture wounds" from the many intravenous lines that have been inserted and removed over the months. Her body is still very thin, but her tummy is distended from the G-J tube, which protrudes from the middle of it. Jen says it looks sort of like a baby's dummy. But Jenna's battle-scars are the least of our problems. What really needs to be sorted is her tummy. Her lungs, her new lungs, are doing very well. Not being able to eat without nausea and vomiting is what's really hampering her recovery.

The bath exhausts Jen, but she is so grateful. We have a sneaky hug after the bath, me with my mask and gown on and her dressed in fresh PJs and smelling soapy, before I put her back in bed. It is so good to hold her.

Stuart arrives at 11 am to take over from me. Kristi and I are driving to Sun Valley. Vanessa, my incredibly resourceful and compassionate friend, has arranged for us to meet someone who is happy to let Kristi ride her horse a few times a week. There is much excitement. I haven't driven so far from the hospital before and I can't believe how pretty it is out here. Trees, greenery, rolling valleys and loads of horses. Sue is a wonderful woman. She owns a very beautiful six-year-old warmblood called Apollo. He is huge, 17 hands, and magnificent. She invites Kristi to ride him in the arena to see if they are a match for each other – they are – after which we arrange that Kristi can come out to the valley twice a week to ride him. Sue knows our circumstances and there is no charge – only kindness and compassion for Kristi, who has had to leave her stallion at home. How do you thank people like this? I don't know. We are so incredibly grateful.

I have been talking to Sandy Harper. Her daughter Lauren and Kristi used to go to school together when they were little and Sandy has come up with an idea: a "meet and greet" at our house on Monday afternoon so that Kristi can meet a few local girls before going to school on Tuesday morning. Lauren knows one or two girls at Redhill and James has a cousin, Francesca, who is in the same grade as Kristi and lives close by. We go ahead and set it up. This way at least Kristi can arrive at her new school on the first day of term and see one or two familiar faces.

On Tuesday I drop Kristi at Redhill at 7:30 in the morning. She looks cute in her little black, red and grey tartan skirt, long white socks and white shirt. I am more nervous than she is, I think. I hope like hell it goes well. Granny and Grampa are arriving today to help me with Jen in the afternoons so that I can find the time to settle Kristi into some sort of a routine. I am so relieved they are coming, I don't know how I will do this otherwise.

CHAPTER 49

Chaos and crisis

Jenna's nausea has escalated. It's worse than before – if that's possible. Apparently she vomited all night and on Tuesday she continued to vomit all day. Constant retching with nothing but clear liquid and, eventually, green bile to bring up. It is terribly upsetting.

Week 22 post-transplant (Wednesday, 6th May 2015)

Jenna's vomiting doesn't let up. It continues relentlessly. Every day.

I drop Kristi at school every morning at 7:30 am and get to the hospital by 8:15. Then I spend all day swapping silver kidney-shaped bowls. Vomit, clean bowl, swap for a second bowl. Vomit, clean bowl, swap back to first bowl. Vomit, clean bowl, swap for a second bowl. Jen has tummy pain on and off. She is becoming less and less conversant. She just endures every day. It is devastating to watch.

At about 1:30 or 2 pm, Granny and Grampa come and take over from me. They take turns: one sits at the coffee shop and one sits with Jen. By the time they get to her she is normally exhausted from vomiting and she sleeps most of the afternoon. She retches every now and then in her sleep and is nauseous when she wakes. They find it deeply upsetting, but they endure it. I am so grateful to them for enduring it. I am just so grateful. When they are there I leave and drive back to Redhill to fetch Kristi and take her to whatever extramural she has to attend that afternoon – horse-riding or singing, or just homework at home and walking the dogs. Sometimes we go to visit Jen, but Jen barely seems to notice who is there at the moment. Then either Stuart or I go back to the hospital to take over from Granny and Grampa.

I talk to Paul every day and either Stu or I see him at his morning rounds or evening rounds.

I request a meeting with him in his office. What is going on? What are the solutions for Jen? I want to know what the plan is. When the gastro surgeon first did a gastroscopy many months ago, he mentioned gastroparesis. I have done my research and all the symptoms seem to fit but I am not a doctor. What does Paul think? What can be done? I have mentioned gastroparesis to him numerous times and he has said no, he doesn't think it's that, it will come right. But now it's worse; it is getting worse still.

"Gastroparesis is a condition that affects the normal spontaneous movement of the muscles (motility) in your stomach. Ordinarily, strong muscular contractions propel food through your digestive tract. But if you have gastroparesis, your stomach's motility is slowed down or doesn't work at all, preventing your stomach from emptying properly.

Gastroparesis can interfere with normal digestion, cause nausea and vomiting, and cause problems with blood sugar levels and nutrition. The cause of gastroparesis is usually unknown. Sometimes it's a complication of diabetes, and some people develop gastroparesis after surgery.

Signs and symptoms of gastroparesis include: vomiting, nausea, a feeling of fullness after eating just a few bites, vomiting undigested food eaten a few hours earlier, acid reflux, abdominal bloating, abdominal pain, changes in blood sugar levels, lack of appetite, weight loss and malnutrition."[7]

---

7 https://www.mayoclinic.org/diseases-conditions/gastroparesis/symptoms-causes/syc-203 55787

My research tells me that the first thing for gastroparesis is "change of diet". Well, scrap that! Jen doesn't even *have* a diet. Step two if really bad is to feed via a J-tube. We have been trying that for a month. Now what? Jen is fading away in front of us and she can't handle much more.

Week 23 post-transplant (Wednesday, 13th May 2015)

Grampa goes back to Cape Town, but Granny extends her stay in Johannesburg by another week. She can see I need the help. She feels desperate for me and for my family, and mostly for Jen. And she knows that I can't bear to see that mirrored in her eyes. We plod on, putting one foot in front of the other, day by day by day.

Kristi is doing well at her new school. She seems to enjoy it and is making friends. The workload is going well too. It is a different curriculum, IEB, and she is finding it stimulating. She is bright and has been bored. We encourage her to have friends over on the weekend. I have also agreed to add to the menagerie and Kristi now has a pair of chinchilla rabbits we bought from a breeder.

Since our meeting Paul has been talking to doctors and professors and has called in the help of a paediatric professor outside of the hospital, who is coming to see Jen. Jen can't carry on like this. There is talk of a procedure called a pyloroplasty. It is used to widen the pylorus, which is the opening near the end of the stomach that allows food to flow into the duodenum, the first part of the small intestine.

The professor visits on Wednesday. He thinks he can help. Surgery to do the pyloroplasty and re-insert the J-tube into the right place in the jejunum is scheduled for Saturday, bright and early. I cannot believe my Jen has to go through yet another surgery. But we are desperate and so is she. We cannot stand by and do nothing. She will surely die of malnutrition. She is desperate for this nausea and vomiting to stop.

Early on Saturday, the 16th of May Jen is taken to theatre, again.

We have watched so many families come and go at this hospital in the past 161 days. Literally hundreds of patients have come and gone. And we are still here. I have watched people die, I have watched them heal, I have watched open heart massage in the middle of the night in ICU, I have watched families cry and rejoice, and I have watched my child suffer in indescribable ways. And still we are waiting for a miracle.

Stuart and I wait at the hospital coffee shop. Jen has fought her way back from so many challenges. Will she have it in her to do it again? She is so weak but she wants to live. She has fortitude like no one I have ever met.

The professor comes to find us. He tells us the procedure went well. Jenna is out and back in ICU. We hurry down the long passage to go and be with her. Kristi is having a few of her new friends over this evening, so Stu goes home to Rivonia to make them supper. I stay at Jenna's bedside until late in the night.

It is nearly midnight when I turn into the driveway and find the strangest thing. No one is there. Only Sahara. Stu and the girls are missing, Prince is missing. And the front door is wide open.

My heart starts pounding.

"Stu? Kristi?" I walk around the house, calling.

I can find no one. Sahara is going crazy.

I phone Stuart in a panic. I am so relieved when he answers that I shout down the phone: "Where the hell are you both?"

They are at the all-night veterinary clinic. Prince was playing around in the bushes in the garden with Sahara during the evening and was spat at by either a poisonous frog or a snake. He may lose the sight in one of his eyes. Seriously? They come home a few hours later without him. Prince needs to stay at the vet for at least a week, if not longer …

When you are going through excessive levels of stress and trauma every day there is no time for reflection. Just survival. When I get home at night, I light candles, eat and fall into an exhausted sleep. Seven hours later my eyes snap open and I can't get to the hospital fast enough. Part of me has to dissociate in order to cope. The only way I remember all of this detail, now, as I am writing this, is that every day I write up meticulous "progress" charts. I use them to keep track of her medical journey, to keep a record and to help me remember what happens each day. Otherwise each one would feel the same as the next.

When Jen is sleeping I sit and stare at the charts on the wall. It is an impossible journey. I notice that every time Jen comes out of surgery, she is nausea free for at least two days. Maybe this is due to the anaesthetic? I don't know. All I do know is that it is such a relief for her to have nausea-free days. Sometimes I wonder what we have done. This suffering is so severe, so extreme, no one would choose this. But we didn't know. There was no way to know. Transplant was, and still is, her only hope.

On Monday Kristi comes down with a bad cold. She has a sore throat and a mild temperature, but she opts to go to school anyway. She is loving Redhill. She has developed a strong bond with a new girlfriend called Ashleigh (who ended up staying over with us on Saturday night and for most of Sunday after the vet incident). Ashleigh was the one who showed Stu where to find the all-night vet.

Week 24 post-transplant (Wednesday, 20th May 2015)

After the pyloroplasty Jen has pain from the op site and has developed a bad tremor. She is still in ICU but in the back right-hand corner room. It is small and prison-like. Within a few days Paul starts feeding through the J-tube and bringing down the feed on the TPN. Ultimately this is the goal: to have no more TPN feed, only feeding through the J-tube and, eventually, real food. In a few weeks' time, once this is all working smoothly and Jenna has started gaining weight and walking, we will take her home to Rivonia.

Granny has been a godsend for two weeks, but she has gone home exhausted to Grampa in Cape Town. James is coming up on Thursday for the weekend – and so is Reggie.

Stuart and I feel we need some adult contact, some connection outside of doctors and vets to sustain us. As James will be here for the weekend, we decide to have a few special people round to braai with us on Friday night. We invite Raffaella and her husband Mike, Dean and Sarah, and James's aunt and uncle. I spend the day with Jen and hand over to Margy, who has agreed to sit with Jen from 4–8 pm so I can prep the food. I am very grateful to her. James will relieve Margy at 8 pm.

I drive away from the hospital, looking forward to having a night with friends. I need to replenish, to fill up. Stu and I do the shopping – braai meat, veggies, salads, wine, gin and tonic, and ice. We even hold hands walking around the store together. When we get home, we play some music and light the candles. I make salads.

Kristi is still not feeling well after her bad cold, but she is happy to have Reggie here. I tell her she doesn't have to join us, and I put her to bed with paracetamol and vitamin C. She and Reggie can watch a series together and I will bring them supper later. James stays for one drink with his aunt and uncle and then goes off to the hospital to relieve Margy. He phones me as instructed. Jen is doing okay. Not great, but okay. He tells us we must have a good evening.

And we do. We are having a good time. I take Kristi and Reggie some dinner, but Kristi is not hungry, so I just leave it for her. At about 9:30 pm, we are sitting at the dining room table chatting when James messages me. "Bean says she is not feeling well. She feels like she is going to have a seizure."

Shit. I go outside and phone him. Then I phone Paul, who promises to go to the hospital immediately to check on Jen. I keep checking my phone. Twenty minutes later James messages me again: "Paul has been. He says Jen seems fine."

I breathe a sigh of relief. Must be a false alarm.

We carry on chatting. Half an hour later Reggie comes through to the dining room, wide-eyed. "Gabi," he says, "you'd better come quick. Kristi needs you."

I hurry down the stairs to Kristi's bedroom. She is pale and shivering. I find a thermometer. She has a massively high temperature, 39.9°C. Raffaella is hot on my heels. "Come," she says. "We must get her to the Medi-clinic, I know the closest one." Raffaella drives and Reggie and I sit in the back with Kristi. I am trying to get her to sip water and strip down, but she is clutching a blanket tightly and is delirious. She says she is freezing. We park and race inside straight to the emergency room.

It is pretty full. People stare. Kristi is in her PJs wrapped in a blanket with mascara streaking down her face, now shaking violently. Reggie, in jeans, a T-shirt and barefoot, has his arms around her; Raffs and I, though clearly distressed, are calm. We are supposed to wait in a queue and fill in multiple forms but I walk straight up to the desk. "My daughter is in trouble," I say. "You need to look at her immediately, please." It dawns on me then from the way everyone is staring at us that they think Kristi has taken drugs of some sort. I can understand why. She is bordering on hallucinogenic and talking about how "dragonflies don't speak English" ... Reggie looks completely panicked. The admin assistant looks up at me. She is about to challenge me. I look her straight in the eyes. "Just take her temperature," I say. My tone even surprises me. She walks round the desk and takes us into a small office opposite. She puts a blood pressure pump on Kristi's arm and thermometer in her mouth. Then, immediately, "Come with me," she says. We walk round the back. A young doctor appears. Within minutes he has Kristi on a drip. Then he starts asking questions and takes bloods. Raffs is filling in the forms at the front desk.

When the bloods come back, about half an hour later, the doctor confirms there are no drugs involved and puts Kristi on an antibiotic drip. Her temperature is already coming down and the shaking has subsided, but he warns me to keep a close eye on her and get her tonsils checked again. She has a bad infection. When Kristi is out of danger, I message Stu. We are home by 3:30 am and find Stuart sitting up in the lounge, waiting. I thank Raffs profusely – this was certainly not your average dinner party. I put Kristi to bed and leave all the doors open so I can hear if she needs me. I fall into bed. I am on my knees.

James stayed with Jen that night until she fell asleep.

In the morning Kristi is still not well. Although her temperature is down, the glands in her throat are huge and she's also quite disorientated. James volunteers to go back to the hospital to be with Jen so that I can keep an eye on Kristi. He only has two days here and wants to spend as much time with Jen as possible. This means I can settle Kristi, make her some breakfast, and Stu and

I can tidy up from last night. I will relieve James at lunchtime.

From this day forward, I have no more meticulous progress charts.

As I write now, I am relying only on memory, combined with some scribbled notes in my diary, photographs on my cellphone and conversations with those who were there with me. With us.

Things get so hectic there is no time to document.

I phone James to check on how Jen is. He is sitting next to her bed but steps outside to take my call. As he does so, Jen has a seizure. He watches through the glass door as the nurses rush around helping her. I drop everything and drive to the hospital. On the way there I phone Paul. When I get to Milpark Jen is sleeping, but James is traumatised. The nurses didn't want to let him back into the room, but he insisted. Jen kept trying to get up and out of bed and they were shouting at her to stay put. James "talked her down". She was breathing rapidly and didn't know where she was. He spoke to her constantly until eventually she settled and let him hold her hand.

I feel so desperately sorry that James has seen this. I send him home. He doesn't want to leave but I insist.

I sit beside Jenna's bed. The sides have been pulled up in case she tries to get up again or tug at the tubes. Paul arrives.

Jen is totally out of it. Not herself.

I call Stu. I tell him to stay with Kristi and the kids. He must not let James come back to the hospital. I will stay here.

In the afternoon Jen has another seizure. How? She is still sedated and yet she has another one. It is too much to bear. I am heartbroken. Paul sedates her again and he sends me home. She will not wake again until tomorrow.

We have a very subdued evening in Rivonia. We try to watch a series, but I keep jumping at every sound. I am sensitive to absolutely any stimuli. Stuart runs me a bath and puts me to bed. He watches a movie with the kids.

On Sunday the ICU is quiet. I sit beside Jen but she is still sedated. She can barely wake up. She sleeps on and off all day. She groans in her sleep. She looks fragile, so very fragile. Every now and then, when she does wake, she smiles at me weakly. She keeps trying to reach her back with her left hand. I eventually get her to stay awake for long enough to tell me what is wrong. It is aching. Her lower back is aching. I roll her bony body onto her side, carefully placing just the right sized pillows between her knees and ankles so that the bones don't rub on each other. She is barely conversant. I rub her body all over, with soft cream. Dry skin stretched over her bones. When I stop, she moans. I carry on, slowly, for what feels like hours. Jenna wants the comfort. I close my eyes, willing love and healing through my hands.

Every now and then I phone home. Kristi is doing a bit better; she wants to see Jen, but I tell her she can't come anywhere near the hospital, or Jen, until she is completely well. Contact with a sick person could have dire consequences. Stu and I pass the baton in the early evening after he has dropped Reggie at the airport. I go home to be with Kristi and James.

James leaves early in the morning on Monday and I go straight to the hospital. I do my normal ritual. I wash my hands, sterilise them, put on my gown over my clothing, mask up and put a hair-net over my hair and fresh gloves before I enter Jenna's room. It used to take ages to do this; now I am quick. I do it automatically without thinking. I read her chart, which is on a table outside the glass doors, before I enter. I stand staring at my Jen. Today she barely knows I am here. I am gazing at her, a few lone tears leaking down my cheeks, when Paul comes to check on her.

While we are both in the room Jen has another seizure. A massive seizure. It is the biggest one I have witnessed. It is terrifying to see such a fragile body shake like that. I think she might break in two. Paul is right there, the nurses are right here. They inject her with Ativan almost immediately but it just doesn't stop. She has seizure after seizure after seizure. I talk to her throughout – "I am right here, Jen, it's okay, you are going to be okay. I am here. Mommy's here" – but I don't think it is. I don't think it is going to be okay. For the first time I don't think it is going to be okay. I am beside myself with fear. I don't know how much more I can take.

"Gabi!" Paul's voice breaks through my horror. "I am going to intubate Jenna and sedate her. I need you to leave the room."

"No!" I say. "I won't, I won't leave her." Even I can hear my voice is not its normal calm self; it is louder than it should be, shakey and desperate, it doesn't sound like me. It is all I can do not to break down. This is too much. This is too much.

"Come with me," Paul says. He walks me gently but firmly out of the room. "You have witnessed enough. You have witnessed more than any mother should ever have to. Go to the café and I will find you. We will take care of Jen."

I find my way down the passage but I don't go to the coffee shop. I go out into the carpark, taking in huge gulps of air. I can hear myself crying. Loud sobs. I cover my mouth with my hand to stop myself from wailing. I can't get the image of Jen's paper-thin body, with all those tubes, shaking and shaking, out of my mind. Get a grip, I tell myself. For God's sake, get a grip! Slowly I breathe deeper and deeper and calm myself down. Eventually I go back inside to the coffee shop, sit down and order coffee. I know all the staff by name, but today no one tries to chat. I wonder if anyone saw me through the window. About half an hour later Paul comes to find me. I jump up knocking my coffee over when I see him. Jen is fast asleep, he tells me, sedated and intubated. He puts both hands on my shoulders and looks me in the eyes. "Go home, Gabi," he says. "Go home and get some rest." He is going to keep her intubated and sedated for a few days. Paul is a kind man. He has become so attached to our Jen. This must be killing him too. I go back to ICU and gaze at Jenna through the glass one last time. She is fast asleep, ventilated and she looks peaceful, just like Paul said.

I go home.

Week 25 post-transplant (Wednesday, 27th May 2015)

There is nothing I can do for Jen for the next few days, she is totally sedated. I visit just to gaze at her, but she doesn't even know I am there.

Jillie is here. She has flown up from Plett to visit. She comes with me to the hospital once to see Jen. I wonder if Jen can feel that her godmother is there. I am grateful Jillie sees her looking peaceful.

For the next few days Jillie's focus is on me. I think Stuart might have asked her to keep me away from the hospital for a while. She runs me hot baths, takes me shopping, feeds me and arranges another lunch date with my Johannesburg friends Nici and Susan. It feels surreal, sitting in a shopping centre eating lunch. While they talk, I look around me and wonder how many other people are walking around with a brave face on while actually they are living in some kind of personal hell. What would the world be like if we all knew more about each other, I wonder. Would we be more compassionate if we knew each other's stories? I drift in and out of the conversation. I am acting normally, I think, but part of me wants to shout, "Help me! Somebody help me!" I don't know how much more I can take.

Jillie leaves after a few days. Stu and I have quiet visits to the hospital. Stu sits at Jen's bedside with his laptop and works. We have some recovery time while Jen is sedated and spend time with Kristi. She is getting better. Riding again and practising her singing every afternoon. She has been booked for two big paying gigs in Cape Town next weekend. One is the launch of the new Springbok rugby jersey and the other a 50th birthday. Stuart will fly down with her to be at her side for both. He will also do a final check of our home – we have a good rental starting mid-June which will help ease the ongoing financial strain.

By Thursday Jen is slightly less sedated, but she is still intubated. Paul has gone away for a few days. He will be back on Sunday. The doctors on call are following his instructions to slowly and carefully, over a period of many days, bring Jen out of full sedation.

Glynis comes up on Friday for the weekend. It is good to have her with us. She helps Stu and me talk about things that are otherwise virtually impossible to discuss. She comes with me to the hospital. We sit quietly in Jen's tiny little ICU room. She is in the back right-hand corner now. If she were more conscious she would comment quietly that this one is not a "suite". She is still intubated and can't talk but is slowly coming out of sedation. I explain to her why she is intubated and tell her not to struggle or try to talk. We communicate through small nods and eye movements.

That night Glynis convinces Stuart and me that we need to do something life-affirming outside of visiting the hospital. To our surprise we discover a beautiful river walk just 10 minutes from our house. Prince is home now so we take the dogs with us early in the morning. The light is spectacular, the river is gushing, and Sahara is running like a wild thing in and out of the water chasing the ducks. Glynis was right. Being in nature lifts our spirits.

On Saturday morning Glynis and I sit in Jen's room for a long time. I am at her side and Glynis is at the bottom of the bed. It is quiet. I rest my head on her cot side, the cold steel bar imprinting itself on my forehead. Jen lifts her right hand and places it on my head. She strokes my hair gently. I am looking down. Tears gently plop down, making a small puddle on the floor. I hope she can't see.

Paul is back on Sunday. When he walks into the room Jen's mouth stretches wide on either side of the tube. In this compromised state she is smiling at him. Tears well up instantly in his eyes before he claps his hands together and says, "Right, young lady, I think you are ready for us to remove that tube?" Jen nods. While Paul is busy Glynis and I go and wait in the coffee shop.

By the time Glynis leaves on Sunday afternoon, it is clear that as the sedative wears off, so Jen's pain and nausea have returned with a vengeance. Her stomach is sore, her lower back is sore, and she is nauseous even though she has not eaten in weeks. She must weigh about 40 kg maximum by now. Wasn't the pyloroplasty supposed to have sorted this out? We don't understand. Neither does she. This has to stop.

Stuart and I ask to meet with Paul. We talk in the passage outside ICU, on the couches that I sometimes nap on when I'm desperate. It's Sunday, 7 pm, and there is no one around. For the first time we are starting to lose hope. I can only imagine what it must feel like for Paul to be faced with these two desperate parents. "What is the plan?" we ask him. "Is there a plan?" "What is going on?" And then we ask the most difficult question of all: "Paul, do we need to be having a different conversation?" Stuart implores Paul to be honest with us. We need to know if we should be having a different conversation. A palliative conversation.

Paul is silent for a while, then he looks at us both through his glasses. "If Jenna hasn't given up," he says, "then neither will we." We nod in agreement. She has fought her way back from so much. We hope she will do it again.

But by Monday morning Jen is writhing in pain, again. She is in agony. She keeps asking me to massage her lower back, to push my thumbs firmly into the small dent between her pelvic bone, lower ribs and spine. Paul is worried she may have pancreatitis. He has tested for it before, numerous times, but fresh bloods are drawn and sent to the lab. The pancreas, a long flat organ or gland in the upper abdomen, sits tucked behind the stomach. It produces enzymes to aid digestion and hormones that help regulate the way the body processes sugar. Mild cases of pancreatitis may go away without treatment, but severe cases can cause life-threatening complications.

Ali has arrived. She is taking over. I need this. I feel like I can't do normal things any more like shop for groceries and make meals. For a long time Vanessa has been offering to come up to Johannesburg. I call her now. It's time. She must come.

Week 26 post-transplant (Wednesday, 3rd June 2015)

It's been 182 days.

On Wednesday Lizzie flies up from Cape Town and in the evening Kristi and Stu fly down. Ali has filled the fridge with fresh stuff and she makes me supper when I get home from the hospital. She puts a glass of cold wine in my hand. She is going home tomorrow and swapping out with Vanessa, who will come for the weekend because Lizzie must fly home on Friday. It is clear that I can't be alone. Vanessa will be my support. Lizzie and I are at the hospital full time. We need to be. Jen is in so much pain. Even when she is sleeping, she groans in pain. It is so difficult to see.

On Thursday I drop Ali at the Gautrain and collect Vanessa. It is really good to see her. We go straight to the hospital to relieve Lizzie. I show Vanessa how to mask up and coat up. When we go into Jen's cubicle I explain to her that Vanessa is here. She smiles at her weakly but is disorientated. We sit for a while and I rub Jen's arms and legs and brush her hair. I know Vanessa can cope. She has had many years of a very ill child and there is not much she hasn't seen. In the evening Lizzie takes over so that Vanessa and I can have supper together at the house. We warm up one of the frozen meals that Sandy's friends have made. "She will come back from this, Gabs," Vanessa says. "She will come back from this."

Just before bed Stu calls to update me on the first of Kristi's gigs. The set-up was huge and magnificent. It went so well. He sends me pictures. It feels insane, these two polar opposite worlds, and yet I am so grateful for the videos and pics. Stu sounds upbeat. I haven't heard his voice like that in a while.

Early on Friday I leave Vanessa in Rivonia and head to the hospital. Jen is curled up in a foetal position. I stare at her for hours. It feels like yesterday that she came to the Rivonia house for the day, that she was about to check out of hospital. How did we get here? She is sore and nauseous. It is hideous to witness her pain. I feel helpless. I don't see Paul today. Margy takes over in the afternoon from 2 pm and I take Lizzie back to the house so she can pack to leave. I am back at Milpark to take over from Margy at 5:30 pm. I spend the evening with Jen while Vanessa visits her good friends Mark and Jenny.

It is a difficult evening with Jen. I warm happy huggers in the microwave to alternate them on her back and tummy. Sometimes she retches and I hold silver bowls. I massage her feet and sit in silence with her. She eventually falls fast asleep.

I join Vanessa and her friends at their home close by. I've never met them before and wonder how I will cope. It's cold and raining outside. They are kind and have been well briefed by Vanessa. I am famished. I eat some food and sit at the fire. I play them some of Kristi's music that I have recorded on my phone and we chat. It is strangely comforting to be in their company. They are bright and interesting. It takes me out of my world for an hour or two.

When we get home, I have a long chat on the phone with Stu. I want to hear all about their day and how Kristi is preparing for her three-hour gig tomorrow. Stu says Kristi needs to talk to me.

When she comes on the phone Kristi is crying. She has decided to end her relationship with Reggie. She is devastated. She loves him and doesn't want to hurt him, but she is 17, totally overwhelmed by everything that is going on in her life and living in a different city. She can't cope with a serious relationship right now. She doesn't have the emotional space for it. I wish I was there to hold and comfort my baby right now. She is so sore and so brave. Most teenagers would hang on, even if just for the comfort of not being alone. We talk for a long time.

On Saturday I am up very early. I leave Vanessa at the house with the dogs and I drive to the hospital. The roads are quiet, there is no traffic.

There is a different feeling in Jenna's room today. Jen is *gatvol*. Her eyes are dead. She has retreated right into herself. I haven't seen Paul since yesterday. I don't know where he is but I am so worried about Jen. Deeply worried. She looks like a bird. Her hands are slightly curled up. She is in the foetal position squashed up against the cot side of her bed. I move her body back down to make her more comfortable and she groans and slowly works her way back up into the corner of the bed again, like a frightened animal. Her tummy is so sore she can't straighten her legs. It is awful. I stroke her body, so she knows I am there. She relaxes a bit. I don't know how much more she can take. How much more I can take. I go out the back door of the hospital and weep in among the medical waste bins. Then I compose myself and go back inside.

At 2:30 pm I hand over to Raffaella. She will sit with Jen for a few hours to give me a break. Jen knows she is there and is calm. Vanessa comes to fetch me and we eat a subdued lunch at Saigon. Then we drive to her aunt's house, where I curl up on a spare bed in one of Carrie's bedrooms, pull the covers up over my head and sleep. Vanessa takes me back to the hospital again at 5 pm. Jen has also slept all afternoon. Sweet relief.

Vanessa waits for me in the coffee shop. When Jen wakes, she seems a little better. She even talks to me a little, asking me to reshuffle her pillows and warm her happy hugger. She smiles when I tell her Sarah will be coming to spend a few hours with her this evening. At 6 pm Sarah arrives to take over from me. I kiss Jen on the forehead through my mask and tell her I will see her in the morning. She nods.

Vanessa drives us home and I phone Stu and Kristi. I want to wish her good luck for tonight. I have decided I won't tell them how bad Jen's morning was because Kristi is about to perform and they fly back tomorrow. I also don't tell them I am counting the minutes until they get back.

Stu tells me Kristi is in pieces. She broke up with Reggie earlier today. Today? Jeez, that is impossible timing. But I understand we don't always get to plan these things. Life is so messy. I remember the terrible pain of my first-ever break-up. Kristi is under extreme pressure and she has a full night of performing ahead. I'm not sure how she is going to get through it, but Stu and Shirley are there to support her. She doesn't want Stuart to put her on the phone to me in case she breaks down again. She needs to hold it together until after her gig. I know how that feels. We will talk tomorrow morning and I will see her tomorrow night in Johannesburg. Their flight is booked for early evening. They will come straight to the hospital to see Jen and then I will go home with Kristi.

Vanessa and I arrive home at about 6:30 pm and I feed the dogs, light candles and choose a meal from the deep freeze to heat up. Vanessa is a soccer freak and apparently it is the Champions League tonight. I'm less than enthusiastic but agree to be her viewing partner for a while. We eat, find the right channel and settle down to watch. Within 10 minutes my phone rings. It's Sarah.

"Gabi! Gabi, you have to come quick. Jenna is vomiting blood. They have locked me out of ICU. I am so worried. The head sister insists it's normal and she won't let me back in!" she says.

"It's not normal," I say. "Stay there. I'm coming." I grab the car keys and run.

My heart racing, I fly to the hospital. When I get there Sarah is sitting on the floor outside ICU, her head buried in her hands. She looks traumatised. She tells me breathlessly what happened. I punch the code into the ICU doors and throw them open. I wash my hands quickly but thoroughly, taking in the scene. My heart is pounding. I can see through the glass doors to Jenna's room. Her bed is in the sitting up position and there are two nurses at her side. I can see from here she is frightened.

The head sister on duty that night is walking around ICU. She approaches me, as if to stop me going in to see Jen.

"Why didn't you call me?" I say.

She suggests I go home. That's not an option. I ignore her, gown up and mask up and enter Jen's room. One of the nurses moves aside. I can see they are relieved to have me here, the nurses and Jen. I move swiftly into the ritual of rotating silver kidney-shaped bowls, holding one under Jen's chin and talking to her gently while the nurse cleans the other one. Then we swap the bowls out and do it again. This is different vomiting. This is not the usual clear liquid, white foam or bile. This is blood. Jenna vomits blood – again and again and again. I must phone Paul but there is no time to move, the blood is coming up so fast. Jen never takes her eyes off my face. The nurses and I work together. It is harrowing. After a few minutes I hand my bowl to one of the nurses and take two quick steps to the doors. I slide them open. The head sister is on the other side of ICU.

"This is not normal!" I shout at her. "Call Dr Williams immediately! Now!"

It is the first time I have raised my voice in ICU to any nurse or sister. I close the glass sliding doors again and go straight back to work, holding bowls for Jenna to vomit blood into. She can't talk. At some point I see Sarah looking through the doors. Someone has let her back in to collect her belongings, which are on the floor outside Jen's room. She looks like a deer caught in the headlights. I want to hug her and thank her, but I can't leave Jen's side. I nod at her through the glass and turn back to Jen.

When there is a small break in the vomiting, I call Paul myself. It is late on Saturday night. He answers. Yes, ICU have called him. He is away (he doesn't say where) but has made contact with an excellent doctor, who is on her way now.

The doctor arrives. Everything is a blur. She orders some tests and gives Jenna some medication, I don't know what, to slow or stop the internal bleeding. She talks on the phone, to Paul and other doctors. Jen's stomach is very distended, and she is pale, with dark rings under her eyes. Still her eyes never leave my face.

I am locked in silent communication with Jenna. There is nothing to say. I try to keep the fear from my eyes. I deduce from the doctor's calls that there are two main arteries near the pancreas and possibly one has ruptured. I don't really understand. We are there most of the night. There are tests happening and medication being administered. Slowly the vomiting subsides. The doctor sends me home at 3 am to sleep for a few hours. I don't want to leave but Jen needs to sleep and so I do.

I am back a few hours later – it is Sunday, the 7th of June – and I am there when Jen wakes. She vomits blood again. Smaller amounts. Paul is here. He must have driven through the night from wherever he was. He introduces me to a young surgeon who works at Milpark. He explains that Jen is being taken into theatre for a procedure to place a coil in the damaged artery. At least I think that's what he says. I explain to Stu some of what has been going on, and that there is a plan. We will see him tonight.

When Jen comes out of the procedure she is sleepy. Pale. I hold my breath when she wakes a few hours later. Will she vomit blood? It seems to have stopped. The relief is palpable. Doctors and nurses come in and out. All I can hear is the beep, beep, beep of the monitors. Sometimes Jen winces or groans. Otherwise there is silence. I just sit. For hours and hours, I just sit.

Stuart and Kristi are due to fly at 6:15 pm. Their flight is de-layed, they will leave in an hour. I sit. Then their flight is delayed again. They will fly at 9 pm. Stu must see Jen tonight. At 9 pm Stu phones. Their flight has now been cancelled. He is beside himself. Kristi has no idea how bad it is here at the hospital, she is overcome with sadness at her break up, so he doesn't tell her. But he knows and is desperate to get back to Johannesburg. He is so angry and frustrated. We decide he will use the credit card to book another flight, the last flight out. It is done. They will land after midnight. It will be too late to come to the hospital, but at least they will be back on Johannesburg soil and he will come tomorrow.

I fall asleep at Jen's side, the steel bar of the cot cold and hard on my forehead.

I am woken by Jen's voice. She is talking to me. She has her delicate hand on my head, and she is whispering slowly, "Thank you. Thank you, Mommy."

Someone, I don't remember who, instructs me to go home at about 11 pm. I lean down to Jen and stroke her face with my gloved hand.

"My Jen-Bean," I say, "I'm sure this is the last thing on your mind right now, but I have to go home and sleep. I will be back first thing tomorrow. I love you. I love you so much."

"No, Mommy," she whispers. She seems horrified that I said that. "It's not the last thing on my mind. You must go home and sleep. I love you, Mommy. See you tomorrow."

I leave the hospital in a daze and drive back to Rivonia. I am exhausted. I feel outside of my body. Vanessa says she will stay up and let Stu and Kristi into the house at 1:30 am. She puts me to bed.

CHAPTER 50

Monday, 8th June 2015

I'm awake. Daylight streams through the crack in the curtains. Stuart is fast asleep in the bed next to me. I rest my head on his chest for a long while. He draws me to him in his sleep. I listen to his breathing and his heartbeat and lie still, drawing strength from his body next to mine. After a while I pry myself away and pad through to the kitchen to make coffee. I check in on Kristi. She is fast asleep too. I close her door quietly. I take coffee to Stu. He wakes and we talk. I share some of the weekend and he tells me about theirs. We agree that he will come through to the hospital at lunchtime. "But before you go," he says, "you should talk to Kristi. She is really heartsore and needs her mommy."

I make Kristi some herbal tea and climb into bed next to her. We cuddle and she tells me everything. Her beautiful little face is swollen from crying but, even so, she really believes she has made the right decision. I listen and I hold her and comfort her. She is tired. I tell her to go back to sleep. She can come later with her dad to the hospital. She can go to school tomorrow. Now she must rest. She nods, thanks me and rolls over.

I am dressed and ready to leave. My adrenaline is kicking in and I need to get to the hospital. When I feel like I have been away from Jen too long I become like a woman possessed. I kiss Stu goodbye and drive to the hospital. It is 9:15 am. There is traffic, but it's moving. I will it to move faster.

Parking is a nightmare. They are still renovating. Outside the doors to ICU I take a deep breath and ring the bell. As I walk in I see the transplant psychologist walking towards me. There is something purposeful about her manner. I look over her shoulder to the top right-hand corner of the room where Jen's cubicle is. My heart stops. Jen is surrounded by nurses and doctors who look very focused. I speed up, but the psychologist stops me. "Gabi, the doctors are working on Jen," she says. "You can't go in there right now. Come with me." Someone half pulls the curtains to Jen's room and I can no longer see in. "Come with me," the psychologist says firmly. She is guiding me out of ICU and into the awful little square room next door. My adrenaline is pumping.

"What's going on?" I ask. "Why can't I see Jen? What's happening? Is she okay?"

"She's okay," she says. "Paul is with her. He is intubating her. He will tell us when we can go back in."

"Intubating her? Why?" I ask.

She tells me that Jen started bleeding again. "Paul is intubating her to make sure her respiratory system is protected."

We sit and we wait. This doesn't feel right. I ask if I should phone Stuart and tell him to come to the hospital. She says it's not necessary and we will be able to go back in soon. We wait. She is sending and receiving messages on her phone from ICU. Why is she here? I haven't seen her in ICU so early for a while. We wait some more. She suggests we go for coffee down the passage. But when we get to the coffee shop, I say I can't sit there. I need to be right next to ICU. I get a takeaway coffee and phone Stu. I tell him things don't look good. He should come to the hospital. Now.

We go back and wait in the square room. I am starting to feel desperate. A strange feeling comes over me. I can't describe it. A call. Jen is calling me. I get goosebumps from head to toe. She is calling me, I know she is. I plead urgently with the psychologist.

393

"I know what is happening," I say. "You can't hide it from me. I know what is happening. I can feel it. You have to get me in that room. You have to get me in that room now. I promised Jen she would not be alone. I promised her."

I can see she understands. She messages Paul in ICU.

At that moment Stu walks in. We hug quickly.

The psychologist's phone pings and she looks straight at me. "Come," she says. "Come now."

We go into ICU. Automatically my body moves toward the hand basin, but Stu is striding ahead of me. I look up. In that moment I know. The doors to Jenna's room are wide open. There are two nurses in the room standing aside and looking towards us, and Paul is at Jen's bedside. The whole of ICU seems to have stopped. I run into the room. It is a war zone. Equipment everywhere, blood everywhere, pipes and bags everywhere.

As I get to Jenna, I feel her leave. I feel her leave her body.

She is gone. My baby is gone.

I hear the most terrible noise and wonder where it is coming from. It is coming from me. I have thrown myself on top of her body and have my arms wrapped tightly around her and I am wailing, I am wailing so loudly. "Noo-o-oooo! Noo-o-ooo! Nooo-o-oo-oo ..." No one stops me. I don't how long I am there, wailing, hanging tightly onto her body. No one moves. Everyone else is silent.

I feel Stuart come up behind me. He puts his hands on my shoulders and gently lifts me up. He wraps me in his arms, and we sob together. Then he guides me out of the room. I don't want to leave but there is blood everywhere, pipes everywhere. Jen doesn't look like herself. Stuart wants Paul to have it cleaned up and cleared away. He asks him to remove all the pipes and make Jen look like our Jen again. I can't see. I have tunnel vision. I just see my angel.

Stuart guides me out of ICU and back to the square room. We stand clinging to each other. I pull away and look at him.

"We must phone Kristi," I say in a panic. "We have to phone Kristi."

"I will do it," says Stu. "I'll ask Vanessa to bring her to the hospital."

"You can't tell them," I say. "You can't tell them that she is gone until they get here."

"Yes," he nods. "Yes."

Paul comes to tell us we can come back in.

Jenna looks peaceful, beautiful. There is no equipment left in the room. No blood. No attachments. It's just Jen lying on the bed.

"Stay as long as you like," Paul says quietly as he closes the door.

We talk to Jenna and hold her, and then Stu asks if I would like time alone with her.

"Yes," I say. "Yes, please."

I draw the curtains and climb into the bed with my baby. I wrap my arms around her and pull her little body close to mine. I have wanted to hold her close like this for so long. To feel her soft skin on mine. Her eyes are closed, her cheeks are soft and chubby. She looks peaceful and beautiful, so beautiful. I hold her tightly and weep silently as I rock her gently back and forth, talking to her. I lie there for ages. I don't want to leave. I never want to let her go.

Eventually Stuart comes back into the room. "Come," he says. He coaxes me off the bed. "Come, Gabs, Kristi is here."

We go next door to the square room. Vanessa and Kristi are there. They stand up expectantly as we walk in. Kristi walks towards us and Stu holds out his arms. "We have lost her, Kristi," he says. "She is gone. Jen is gone." Kristi collapses into his arms. "No!" she says. "It's not supposed to be this way, it's not supposed to be this way!" She says it over and over. "I want to see her. Please can I see her?" We take her to ICU. Kristi spends a long time alone with Jen. Stu does too.

Vanessa waits in the lobby. Many hours have passed. Stuart takes over. He goes down to the isolation ward in Section 7 to start packing up Jenna's things. I join him. In silence I take the progress charts, the family photographs and our colouring-in pictures off the walls. Nurses tip-toe around us. Then we go back up to ICU and slowly begin to pack up the rest of Jenna's belongings. There is still a small smear of blood on the floor. I stand staring at it, rooted to the floor. I stare at Jen on the bed. I am stuck. Stuart steers me gently out the room. If he didn't, I might never leave.

When everything is packed I hug the nurses one by one. I hug Paul. There is nothing to say. Then the three of us – Stu, me and Kristi – walk down the long passage to the lobby, pushing our trolleys like zombies. Two silver trolleys. Piled high. One hundred and eighty-seven days' worth of stuff.

Stuart and Vanessa fetch the cars and we drive home to Rivonia in convoy.

Jesus. Who do we tell first? And how? It's an impossible task. Vanessa gives us space. We write a list and carefully divide it between the three of us. Once the first call is made the news will spread like wildfire. We must act fast. The people closest to us need to hear it from us. We delay the first call as long as possible. Once we start there will be no turning back.

At 3 pm on Monday, the 8th of June we start phoning.

Over and over again I hear myself say: "She is gone, Jen is gone, we have lost her."

By evening the house is full of loved ones. Granny and Grampa will be here tomorrow morning. So will James. Loving people take over. Everyone is doing something. I don't know what. I am just one giant pain body. I want to go back to the hospital. I want to go back to the hospital and lie with my dead child. I don't tell anyone that's what I want to do. They will think I'm mad. Maybe I am.

We gather round the table. Ali and Shirl have lit my candles and produced supper. I think other people arrive. I can't eat. Everyone is sharing stories of Jen. Stu says we must discuss important things. Coroners, paperwork, ashes … a memorial. Can this be Jen we are talking about? She is so alive inside me. Someone puts me to bed with a sleeping tablet. There is a single white feather on my bed.

Waking up is unbearable. I think my gut and heart have burst from pain. I writhe in my bed. Granny and Grampa arrive, they run to me, they hold me and we cry. They are absorbed seamlessly into the circle of people who are holding us. Everyone is doing things. Busy. I check on Kristi. She is pale as snow and silent. She won't leave her bedroom. James arrives and we cling to each other. I hold him as he cries. How can I feel so outside of my body and yet be in so much agony at the same time?

John Maytham from Cape Talk Radio has heard the news. He and Stuart speak on the phone for a long time. He cries and Stuart cries. Will we speak to the nation, John asks? They are also mourning. Stuart and I discuss it. It is important the people know that we are not bitter and twisted, that we will continue to advocate for transplant. Jen was a unique and difficult case. She had so many underlying issues and other complications. Not all transplants are like this; many have incredible results and bring decades of life and happiness. Jen would want us to be sure the nation understood that. Stuart speaks to John live on air that afternoon and I agree to do so tomorrow.

Then Ian and Nic do the unthinkable for us. They go across town to the coroner to take care of the legal part of identifying Jen's body so that Stuart and I don't have to. The light is fading. It's late afternoon when they arrive back with her ashes. Stuart brings the container to our bedroom. I stand and stare, cupping my hand firmly over my mouth to stop the cries. Stuart is saying over and over, "It's not her, my love, it's not her, these are just her ashes, Gabs, it's not Jen. She is not inside that box."

Tonight we have a gathering at the house. All those in Johannesburg who have loved and supported us are here. I barely know who, but I feel their holding. While inside I hum with pain, outside I am wrapped in love. There are messages pouring in from all over the world. People read them to me, but I don't remember.

The next morning Jenna's junior school English teacher sends me the poem Jenna wrote in Grade 7, "My Life is a Braid". I had forgotten it. I read it out loud on the radio to John later that morning. People pull their cars over on the highway and weep. The nation is mourning.

That night Stuart tells me that the family who are literally one day off moving into our home in Cape Town are willing to let go of the contract. God bless them. We can go home. I have to go home. I can't stay here.

On Thursday our little family, plus Shirl, Ali and James, drive to Milpark Hospital. The nurses have planned a gathering to honour Jenna. I stare out the window from the car. Throughout

397

Johannesburg the street poles are covered in newspaper headlines: "Organ Donor Heroine Dies".

Walking into the lobby of the hospital I am battling to breathe. I feel as though 1 000 mules have kicked me in the stomach. Stuart takes one hand and Kristi the other. As the lift doors open the sound of voices singing, wailing and ululating rises and falls. My knees go weak. Shirley holds me up from behind. We make our way into the room to loud, mournful singing. There are seats for us in the front row. Paul speaks ... nurses speak. They honour Jen and her courage, they honour our family. Somehow I speak. I thank them for their tireless care month after month after month. Then we are asked to stand in a row as each and every person comes to hug us one by one and pay tribute to Jen. They have lost her too.

We drive home.

There is packing going on all around me. I do some mindless putting of things in suitcases. Sahara doesn't leave my side. I lie down on the bed with her and stroke her soft fur. She buries her head in my neck and licks my tears.

On Saturday, the 13th of June, just five days after Jen's death, we journey home. Jonathan Ackerman has arranged a private jet to fly us back all together. We are a sorry sight. Myself, Stu, Kristi, Granny, Grampa, Shirley, James, our two dogs and Kristi's chinchillas in their large cage. When our cars pull up on the runway at Lanseria airport I imagine we look as though we are starting a pilgrimage of some sort. I've sedated the dogs, as instructed by the vet, but it hasn't touched sides. They are totally over-excited. The two pilots are kind. They don't turn a hair at the sight of this grief-stricken family overladen with stuff and animals. They manage somehow to squeeze everything in and we take off. I stare out the window.

Setting my feet on Cape Town soil breaks me. I collapse at the bottom of the aeroplane stairs and weep. We are home. One hundred and ninety-two days later we are home. Without Jen.

Epilogue

2015

I didn't think I could, or ever would, survive Jenna's death.

At first, I felt like a skinned deer. Raw. Fatally wounded. I startled at every noise, woke in a sweat at night and stumbled through my days like a ghost of my former self. Unexpected smells and sounds transported me straight back to the hospital. The pain of loss was excruciating, visceral, every minute of the day. I thought I might break in two under the weight of it.

Stuart and Ali took over and arranged a memorial fit for a heroine. We held Jen's memorial in the Sports Hall at Herschel Girls School. Gear House provided all the audio, sound and staging. Paul Sainsbury and his team who had helped with so many fundraisers took over the set-up, Ali and her team at Rainbow orchestrated the logistics and Andrea Foulkes, who had sent so many yummy dishes to my home in Cape Town when Jen was ill, did all the catering with the help of ingredients from Jonathan at Pick n Pay. Many local wine farms supplied wine thanks to the efforts of Sandy and Michael, and Jen's Angels, with help from Craig at Artlab, decorated the entire hall with the most magnificent pictures of Jen. The flowers were done by my friend Di and her daughter Monique and a literal army of others helped. Friends baked all the desserts, which Nici co-ordinated, and Steve, Mary and I created a short memorial video that will never be forgotten. The agency and Stu produced a magnificent memorial booklet and we played Jenna's favourite Disney anthems.

The Herschel girls' choir sang "Bridge Over Troubled Water" with tears pouring down their cheeks, and Kristi sang "My Heart Will Go On" from *Titanic* and did a tribute to her sister that was heartbreaking. Thousands attended. Literally. Thousands. They came from all over the world and wept together. Everyone wore "a touch of red" and brought something with them that reminded them of Jenna. I placed all their beautiful notes, poems, quotes, photographs and drawings into a large book, which I pore over when I need to remember vividly how others felt about her. It was an extraordinary day, beautiful in so many ways, deeply touching and excruciatingly painful. No one could come to terms with the fact that she was gone. How could she be? This magnificent human snatched from our lives.

For me the day went past like a whirlwind, a blur; I had to watch the memorial video to remember who was there. I do remember that Stuart was magnificent, holding the day together in the most incredible way. I don't know how he did it. Jen's friends did tributes that were astounding, and I remember that the entire hall stood up when I got up to speak. It broke me.

Straight after the memorial we did a trip, Stuart, Kristi and me, from the KwaZulu-Natal Midlands back down to the coast of the Western Cape and sprinkled Jen's ashes, "Jen-Dust", as we called it. It was the trip we had planned to do with Jen when we eventually left Johannesburg together to return to Cape Town. We visited every place we were going to go together, taking her ashes with us. Ashleigh joined us to be with Kristi for the first week. It was so painful and yet so beautiful. I felt Jen's presence so strongly throughout as we visited each of her favourite places.

Three weeks later we could suspend reality no longer. We arrived back in Cape Town to start our life without Jenna. Kristi returned to Abbotts to limp through her Grade 11 year.

Two months after Jen died, she was recognised as Lead SA's Youth Hero of the Year. It was such an honour and yet I vomited for a full day before boarding the plane at the mere thought of going back to Johannesburg. It was unbearable being back there.

Kristi fast became emotionally unreachable. Bit by bit she shut down and sank into a deep, dark hole, somehow stumbling her way through Grade 11. She swung between going out and drinking too much, drowning her sorrows, or staying in bed with the door closed and talking to no one. And she was constantly getting sick, throat infection after throat infection. For some mad reason, I think an ill-fated attempt to pretend we were okay, we held a Mexican tequila party for her 18th birthday. Predictably we all ended up crying into our margaritas at 2 am. What were we thinking? We were struggling to find our balance.

Sometimes Stu and I could cry together, but often we would end up rather "protecting" each other. It was too extreme to see the pain in each other's eyes. I believed that if I imploded or broke down, I would make it so much harder for Stu and Kristi. Part of me also felt guilty about my overwhelming grief, as if it was further injury to Kristi, who had lost so much already. It was messy and excruciating.

I don't know where the months went but the date of Jenna's "would-be" 21st birthday was upon us before we knew it. There would be no big party, no nation celebrating. But we did want to honour her life with our loved ones.

On the 28th of October 2015, we woke early and hiked Table Mountain with the dogs. Straight up past Rhodes Memorial, higher and higher. There was something fitting about pushing ourselves harder and harder until we were completely breathless. I laid a red rose on a rock with a view of Cape Town spread out before us. That day Kristi had a delicate tattoo inked on her left wrist. She designed a beautiful dragonfly with the letter J in the centre to make up the body. We did a blogpost on Jenna's Facebook group thanking the thousands who had signed up to become organ donors, and we re-launched The Jenna Lowe Trust as an NPO (not for profit) organisation that would continue working for pulmonary hypertension and organ donation awareness in South Africa in Jenna's honour.

That evening we had drinks at the river near our home with close friends and family. Ali and her team had wrapped the trunks of all the trees from our house to the river in red fabric. We tied a huge red bow around a wooden bench that Stuart had commissioned to be hand-crafted and engraved for Jen. It has a permanent home at the river so that anyone who wants to remember her can sit there, in one of her most loved places and reflect. We made a circle in her honour to sprinkle "Jen-Dust" into the river.

Two dragonflies danced between us as we read Jenna's favourite lovingkindness meditation:

> *May you be well and at ease*
> *May you be peaceful and calm*
> *May you be free of fear and self-doubt*
> *May you embrace life, and death, with an open heart*
> *Filled with lovingkindness, compassion, courage and trust.*

We strolled quietly back to our garden, filled with paper lanterns to meet the rest of our guests and a large group of Jenna's friends and together we let off 21 red and white helium balloons. We watched them float higher and higher up into the heavens until the very last one disappeared from sight. We were surrounded by love.

I saw my therapist every week. I wouldn't have coped without that safe place of refuge where I could express every tumultuous thing I was feeling. We realised that I needed additional trauma work for post-traumatic stress symptoms. The flashbacks, nausea and nightmares were debilitating and getting worse. I saw a trauma specialist, doing a process called EMDR (eye movement desensitisation and reprocessing), for three months.

There was nowhere to hide.

Sometimes therapy felt like pouring acid into a festering wound, but I also had a deep sense that the only way I was even going to begin to heal would be from deep within. A plaster is not enough to heal an infected wound. This is important. Too often in Western culture we're encouraged not to dwell on the difficult stuff, to avoid it and not to think about it – although I think that directly after a huge trauma it may be very true that one needs to access a place of denial so that you can rest. There were many times that the memories were too much for my psyche to bear. I dipped in and out of the darkness and the pain. Sometimes mind-numbing activity like watching a series or taking a sleeping tablet at night was sweet relief. But I knew that I couldn't avoid it forever. Bit by bit I would have to look at the painful memories that were locked in the darkness of my mind, because the longer I left them there, the more powerful and debilitating they became. But there was so much I couldn't talk about or share yet.

Shortly after Jen's "21st" a beloved and dear friend, Lani, took me away on a three-day silent retreat run by Sue Cooper. It was deeply painful but significantly worthwhile to do post Jenna's death. When one sits in silent reflection there is nowhere else to go but inward. Deep, deep, deep inside.

Slowly I was discovering that allowing myself to go to the places of pain became an antidote to utter hopelessness and despair. If I allowed myself to sink to the bottom of the ocean, I could find moments of stillness and calm. And in those moments, I felt a purity of Jenna's presence closer to me than ever before. I found moments of peace.

I realised while on that silent retreat that very slowly I needed to find a way to step back into hope, back into life. I was still breathing. I was still here. I was still alive. As crazy as it seemed to me, I had survived Jenna's death. I was still alive, and so were Kristi and Stu. They needed me. I needed me. And Jen needed me not to waste my life. Not to give up living. She needed me to remember to breathe, to live and to love.

On the second day of the retreat, I sat alone at a pond between meditations listening to a colony of weavers chatter and go about their business building nests and feeding babies. As I sat there a single weaver landed on a branch directly in front of me. He held a long green strand in his little beak and had chosen this spot, a beautiful willow branch hanging low over the water in the gentle dappled light, to build his nest. With fascination I watched him attach the very first strand to the branch and tie it with his beak. Back and forth he flew for the next two days, building his nest bit by little bit with meticulous care and attention. I visited him at every break and watched as the nest developed. I was captivated. On the last evening of the retreat it was done. I went to have one last look and found him perched on top of his green home singing his heart out. I spoke out loud for the first time. "It's beautiful, my boy," I whispered. That little weaver cocked his head to one side and looked me straight in the eye. We gazed at each other for a long time until eventually he lifted his head and began singing again, calling to his loved one to come and inspect his work.

As we drove home the significance of that moment really started to land. I had to rebuild my nest. Strand by strand by strand, no matter how long it took, no matter how hard it was, I had to find the pieces and rebuild my nest.

The first, most difficult and most important challenge was to emotionally fight my way back to Kristi. I was not just a grieving mother, I was also a living mother. A mother to someone I loved deeply and who desperately needed me. I carried so much guilt and pain about the fact that in many ways Kristi had been forced to "row her own boat" over the past few years. I knew she must carry so much unspeakable anger somewhere below the surface. I also had to fight my way back to Stu. We were such a strong team who were now on our knees with grief, not knowing what to do with it. In many ways it was really hard to come back from being parents at war to being a couple.

And of course, I had to find my way back to myself. I had been "in service" to Jenna for so long that I had entirely lost sight of what my own needs were. I no longer knew who I was, what I was or what I wanted. I would be forever changed, that I knew. I would never unsee what I had seen, never unlive the long, slow death of my child. Who was I now and who did I want to be? What was my heartfelt wish for my life going forward? One thing was clear. Going back to marketing glue sticks, handbags, jewellery and face cosmetics was not an option. I had to do something that mattered, something that brought a sense of purpose and meaning to my life. The work I had done thus far with The Jenna Lowe Trust brought me some of that, it was meaningful work but pro bono work and

I could not earn a living from it.

Working full time was also not an option, not yet anyway. I considered it carefully to help us relieve the financial burden. But I was still very broken, and my exhaustion levels were extreme. What should I do? Stu and I talked about options at length. I had always wished I'd studied psychology, and in fact for many years I had been considering the idea of studying to become a life coach. Until now the timing had not been right. Now it started to feel like a very good idea, one that I became more and more sure about. But very soon I would need to get back to earning money, and all the courses of any value meant at least 18 months of study. How were we going to make this work?

Stuart was convinced. He had unwavering belief in me (as always) right from the start. "You should to do it, my love," he said. "I really think you should do it. You will be the world's best life coach! We will find a way." I was worried, though. After six harrowing months in ICU I literally had cotton wool for a brain. Post the horrors of ICU concentration was a major issue for all three of us. Trauma does that to you. My memory was particularly atrocious. How was I going to study?

Stu was already back at work full time. I don't know how he did it. I had such admiration for him. He said it helped him cope, that work was the only way to be distracted from the pain. And of course, we needed to address our shocking financial state. But it was really tough. He was trying so hard to live a "normal" life.

I did my research and found an internationally accredited organisational, leadership and coaching company close to home which ran a premier 18-month Integral Practitioner Coaching programme, ICF (International Coaching Federation) accredited. I filled in the copious application forms and went for the relevant interviews. It was decided. I would start my studies in February 2016, six months after Jen's death.

About five months after Jenna's death, Max, Jenna's first boyfriend, came to visit me. He had been struck down with a debilitating, albeit temporary, form of arthritis which was making it hard for him to walk and he was in pain. He sat at my dining room table and wept. My heart broke for him. He didn't know, he didn't know what Jen was going through. How could he? My anger melted away and we hugged.

We crawled to the end of the year and in December Kristi gratefully finished Grade 11.

Kristi's Facebook post – 13th December 2015

2015 has been the hardest year of my entire life, yet also one of the most beautiful. I have made the most amazing friends and experienced the most incredible things ... and lost the person I love most in this world.

It is over six months since Jenna passed. In a way it feels like a day, and in another it feels like years. Many have said it will get easier, that time heals. But I have come to learn this is not so. In fact, as time passes the pain gets harder, and the loss is worsened. On days when I experience new things or meet new people it can become unbearable ... She will never get to do these things or meet the people who now mean so much to me. Those people will never truly know how astounding she was.

Suffering a loss such as we have can never be made right. Time will not heal that which we have endured. It doesn't get easier, you just get used to the pain ... you learn to live with the wounds. I can't begin to explain the things that Jenna went through in the months she spent in hospital, nor would anyone want to know. But I can say that I honestly cannot think of one other person who could have endured what Jenna did while maintaining such dignity and gratitude for the people she loved.

I am so grateful for the time I got to spend with my beautiful Jenna, and the bond that we shared. There are many people who will never experience that kind of love. I just wish that she wasn't taken away so soon. I can't say I am not glad this year is finally over, and I know Jen will always be with me in everything that I do.

Our first Christmas, our first holiday without Jen, was unbearable. We tried so hard to make it okay for each other, but it felt impossible. I wanted to cry most of the time and found it nearly impossible to socialise. Kristi was at the doctor every three days with recurrent tonsillitis and had no energy. And Stuart had put his back out and was in so much physical pain that he was high on anti-inflammatories, painkillers and cannabis oil on a daily basis. It was a circus really.

I understood that people grieve differently but Stu was so impossible that holiday I was convinced something else was going on too. Was our grief breaking us apart? Where was my loving rock? I was so confused. I spoke to Ian about it in confidence. He also felt he couldn't reach Stu. He was behaving weirdly and seemed to be in an altered state.

2016

In February 2015, Stuart had written an open letter to the president, just before President Zuma was due to deliver his State of the Nation Address. He posted it on social media. It was shared widely and picked up and published online by *The Daily Maverick*. It is a significant window into the heart and mind of a beautiful, brave and honest man whom I love so much and, almost a year on, a poignant reminder of how he saw – and still sees – his role as a dad.

The Cost of Being a Bad Father
by Stuart Lowe – a father and a child of South Africa
7th February 2015

I don't know much about politics but I know a little about raising a family and parenting children. I reckon there are few differences between what's required to run a harmonious, successful family and to run a harmonious successful country. So, I thought I'd list the basics here for consideration by all fathers but particularly for our president as he prepares to address us, the children of South Africa, on the state of our nation.

Be honest. There is no substitute for honesty and it's not something you can fake. You can create elaborate cover-ups, spoil your kids with little treats to conceal the truth, but they will always sense when you are being dishonest. The cost of dishonesty is high. Without honesty your statements, your actions and your leadership have no value – and it confuses the hell out of the kids. If you cannot be honest then you have no place being a father to anyone. And kids are smarter than you think – your honesty will be respected in the same measure that your dishonesty will be revealed – all of it!

Be consistent. Children watch every move their parents make and listen to every word they say and don't say. What they look for is evidence that what they think is right is consistent with what they see you do. If you have different responses to the same challenges or pressures at different times with different outcomes, then there is no way for the child to know which is correct. You cannot tell your kids not to steal if you have friends who are thieves. To be consistent you have to keep the right company. The cost of inconsistency is high – you deprive your children of their roadmap for life. They have no real guidance with their choices. The cost of inconsistency is irrelevance: "We don't know what you stand for – you are no help to me."

Be brave. Horrible things have happened in the past and horrible things will happen in the future. Parenting is a challenge in good times, but it's in bad times that it really counts. Be brave enough to call it as it is. Confront the brutal truth as it reveals itself and share the reality of it with everyone it affects. That takes bravery but you will be releasing your children from the even scarier pictures they imagine. Then paint pictures of a better future, take a deep breath and lead them to a better place. The process is the same for a kid stubbing her toe as it is for a national calamity. The cost of being a coward is high. If you hide from the truth your children will find someone else to believe, someone else to follow to a brighter place. Cowardice and dishonesty are cousins – and your children see one as clearly as the other.

Be selfless. If you can't be selfless, don't have children. Your family's needs come first and if there is food, or money or time left over – help yourself. It's a primal instinct to tend to the young.

Your job as a parent is to provide for everyone in your family. It's not easy and at times it is not even possible but that's the job. If you can't ride that bus you should not have bought the ticket. The cost of greed is high! Your children will see you put yourself first. They will hate you for it and they will shame you for it.

Be loyal. A common sense of purpose is what binds families. If it is ever questioned or threatened, your children need to see you defending that purpose – defending what the family stands for. If you have not been loyal to your own, there is no point in your children being loyal to you. The cost of betrayal is high. If you destroy your children's belief in your leadership, you will break the glue that binds you together.

Be kind. Children hate bullies. If you have to resort to fear as a tool to lead – you have already lost the battle. Fear is a terrible thing for anyone to live with, but for the vulnerable it is completely debilitating. Children cannot function when they are scared. If you are doing the right things for the right reasons then have the confidence to be a kind leader. The cost of bullying is high! People will instinctively follow firm but kind leaders, but out of fear, they will follow only instructions. That is not leadership.

Be present. The pace of life is frantic and the pressures are massive. That's why your presence is the best gift you can give your children. If you are absent too often you will try to compensate with treats and loose boundaries. Your kids will take both, but it's not what they need. They need you. The cost of absence is high. Your children will be forced to make up their own family stories, their own rules and ultimately they will find someone else to share their lives with. It's a long, lonely way back from there – so spend time with your kids.

Be sorry. Perfecting parenting is like perfecting politics – it's not possible. Things have gone wrong in the past, things will go wrong in the future – and you will make mistakes. Your children need to see your remorse for your failures, big and small. Just knowing that you know and admit that you have erred and that you are not perfect is a massive comfort to them. It gives them permission to try and to fail, and to learn and to try again. The cost of not saying you are sorry is high. Those who follow you will never know what you intended to do in the first place.

Beware. Everything has consequences and in parenting they are absolute. The way you lead your family will determine exactly what you get from them in return. You can find some comfort in possessions and distraction but if you get it wrong, you will reap what you have sown. Get it right and you will enjoy the rewards of a happy, harmonious family, confident children and the resilience to deal with whatever comes. If you get it wrong you will have long, lonely stares in the mirror knowing that your job was to lead and you failed your family, yourself and those who came before you.

Be gone. Here there is a difference between politics and fatherhood. You will never stop being a father so you are obliged to get it right. But if you have had the privilege of leading an organisation or a country and you find yourself in the unhappy place where your "family" are scared of you; if they do not respect you, cannot trust you and choose not to follow you, you should save them (and yourself) by not pretending to lead, and leave quietly.

The cost of staying is high! You will ruin your "family" and their future. You will stand in the space meant for an authentic father and not allow the true leaders to emerge. You will do no good.

The cost of being a bad father is high.

One week into January 2016 Stu packed up and drove back to Cape Town a day earlier than we had planned. He mumbled excuses about work. Something was wrong. I could feel it.

Kristi and I followed a day later. That night Stu sat me down. "Gabs, we need to talk. I don't know how to tell you this. I have cancer."

Yes, cancer.

Multiple myeloma. Bone marrow cancer.

Stuart had known for three years. Three. Whole. Years.

I was reeling. Literally reeling.

He explained to me that until now he'd been in what is called the "smouldering phase" of myeloma and didn't need treatment other than bone density infusions and blood tests every three months. There was a chance he could have stayed in the smouldering phase for decades, so he had decided not to tell us. Not to "burden" us with it. But the six months of ICU with Jen had literally kicked his cancer undeniably into the "active phase". He was now urgently in need of treatment, fast, and could no longer hide it or avoid it.

It was outrageous. A hideous and unexpected blow.

Stuart hadn't wanted Kristi or me to know, and certainly had never wanted Jenna to know. But now that he was really sick, he needed me on his team. He would start chemo in a few weeks, followed by a bone marrow transplant in August. WTF!

Kristi was about to go in for a full tonsillectomy and we knew the recovery would be painful. I made her jelly and custard and nursed her at home. Within two weeks we had no choice left but to tell Kristi. Stu was starting chemotherapy the following week. We could protect her no longer; she had to know. I watched, helpless, as she plunged headlong into a massive depression. No amount of therapy, natural remedies or antidepressants seemed to help. Kristi was fading away in front of my eyes. She would barely leave her bedroom.

When Stuart started chemo, he refused to let me, or anyone else, sit with him. "It is nothing," he would say. "Just an infusion." I started my coaching diploma the same day he started his chemo. It was crazy. I was more determined than ever to make my decision to change tack towards coaching work for us.

Then the damndest thing happened. Stuart's partners left the business, took the sales manager with them and started up in opposition. Only Brandon was left. Just Stu and Brandon limping along while Stu had treatment every month. It was astounding. Maybe I had to find a job after all? But Stu wouldn't hear of it. We would rather increase the access bond, again.

It soon became clear we that we had to take Kristi out of matric and allow her to have a year of recovery. She wasn't coping. The school work was inconsequential ... it was *life* that was hard.

While Stu was having chemo on a monthly basis, Kristi spent the better part of five months in bed.

The 8th of June 2016 was the first anniversary of Jenna's death. A whole year. It's bizarre how grief can alter your perception of time. It felt both like a lifetime since we had lost her, as well as yesterday that she put her hand on my head and said, "Thank you, Mommy."

On her first "death-aversary" I, too, had a tattoo inked onto my left wrist. A feather and Jenna's name. I was "visited" by raptors regularly and often found – still find – feathers when I most need to have a sense of Jenna around me.

Stuart's chemo made him feel crap and the steroids, a vital part of the treatment, made him grumpy, impatient and angry. Between Kristi's depression, the impact of Stu's treatment, our immense grief and the anxiety of the looming bone marrow transplant, it was not an easy time at home.

I threw myself into my studies. I was battling with concentration levels, sore shoulders, debilitating headaches and PTSD symptoms, but I loved the diploma. I loved it so much. It started to feel like a lifeline for me. Consciousness and awareness were a vital part of the learning process. Our learning was a wholehearted, whole-body experience that gave me a much-needed outlet for deep internal reflection work. Stuart was, understandably, back in survival mode and Kristi was disconnected. Any work and mourning that I needed to do felt like it needed to be internal and the course was helping me with that. Once a month I attended three-day-long modules facilitated by the best in their field. Added to that we had regular half-day learning groups, individual essays and projects, hours of readings and hours of practical. We learned the tools, models, theories, philosophies, perspectives and ways of being that are essential to coaching. Together with therapy, walking, yoga and journalling, it was helping me process my own life experiences in a deeply constructive way.

Coaching itself became life-affirming for me. I loved it. I absolutely loved it. I did three times the number of practical hours necessary for the diploma. Listening with complete attention to others helped me to develop perspective and step outside my own story. Really seeing and bearing witness to someone else is powerful medicine. Both ways.

In August 2016 Stuart had an auto-graft stem cell transplant.

A bone marrow transplant is not surgery; rather, it is a transfusion of blood and immune cells. After six months of chemo, one week prior to being admitted to isolation, some of his stem cells were harvested and sent to the lab for spinning. Then he was admitted to isolation and given what is called a "pre-lethal" dose of chemotherapy. This would totally destroy his existing bone marrow and, as you would expect, make him very sick. Then the stem cells that had been previously harvested and spun were infused back into his body. Then he had to wait and wait, getting sicker and sicker, for them to multiply and his "new" bone marrow to grow.

In some ways Stu and I took hospital and all things medical in our stride. We knew the language, we knew the equipment, we knew the environment. But emotionally it was so, so hard. I visited every day, often twice a day, but getting back into masks, gloves, coats and hair-nets was deeply triggering. My post-traumatic stress symptoms came flooding back and the only way I could do it was to dissociate. Not from Stu, but from the hospital. In all honesty I was grateful that he wouldn't allow me to sit vigil all day like I had with Jen. I wouldn't have coped, and he knew that.

Stu was so brave. His indomitable spirit and sense of humour kept the entire ward going. The nurses were sad to say goodbye to him when he left 23 days later. We had become innappropriately acclimatised to all things medical ... It is awful but true that what is a terrifying experience for others felt like a walk in the park for us. But, even so, you have never seen someone bust out of hospital so fast. We had barely packed his belongings before he was out the front door. We were given a long list of instructions on how to sterilise the house, the utensils, his food. What he could and couldn't eat. We didn't need it. We knew it backwards.

By now The Jenna Lowe Trust was involved with a Pulmonary Hypertension Clinic that Dr Greg Symons had started at Groote

Schuur Hospital. I knew Jen would be smiling down knowing that state patients now had access to diagnosis, treatment and knowledge, something that wasn't available prior to her impact. The trust supplies additional nursing support for the clinic, patient brochures, media awareness support and equipment on loan to patients who can't afford mobility devices and home oxygen.

2017

In January of 2017 Kristi went back to school to finish her matric. She was way older than the other students and most of her friends were already at university. It was a courageous thing to do. She chose an incredible, alternative co-ed school in Kenilworth called Cedar House. It "woke her up" again. I knew that there was still so much that she hadn't processed but I had a sense she was starting, millimetre by millimetre, to come up for air.

We were starting to discover that in the middle of terrible grief live moments of true joy. When it was least expected, I would be overcome with the searing pain of loss. And, when it was even less expected, the sunrise on the mountain, the light as it dances on the leaves, Kristi's smile or Stuart's laugh would warm me from the inside. Kristi was right. The grief doesn't get any easier. You don't get over it, just as much as you don't get over love. But you start to learn to live with it, all of it. Not only is it possible to feel joy in the face of pain, but the depth to which you feel the joy is as deep as the depth to which you feel the pain.

Stuart and Brandon picked up the BrandMapp business with new-found enthusiasm. Kristi focused on getting her matric and I put my head down to work on my final thesis. But before I could complete my diploma, it felt like the right time to visit my family in Australia. Craig and Tayla had been with us for the memorial, but I had not seen Margo or Nic since Jen's death and it was starting to feel weird for me. I needed to close the loop. I was longing for time with my brother and his family.

The last time I had visited Australia was when I was there with Jen during her exchange year. It was hard to go back and be in that bedroom, but visiting my family was also beautiful and healing. We cried and laughed together, and they looked after me so lovingly.

When I came home, I found the strength to go through the last of Jenna's belongings, to look in the cupboard that had haunted me for the past two years. I was also ready to re-do the family photo wall in our passage. It was a huge moment. I rearranged the photos, reframed them, had new ones printed and then put all our family photographs back up on the wall.

In May 2017 I graduated as a life coach and immediately started my practice, The Coaching Nest. Born out of the significant moment I had experienced on the silent retreat, The Coaching Nest felt like an apt name on so many levels. Significant life choices or decisions are not a linear process. We make our best choices when we consciously weave together past experience, knowledge and a multitude of perspectives with integrity, intent, our hopes and our wishes for our future. I intended to create a constructive and safe space from which my clients could make informed choices, a space from which they could launch and fly.

No one understood the paradox and complexity of choice more than Jen. When I was slowly going through all her belongings, I also read and savoured all her writings from over the years. It was then that I found this poem she had written in her final year of school:

Regret

Fickle things, choices are
Shimmering with promise,
Glistening with threat

Two choices danced before me
Twisting and rippling
Merging and diverging
Tempting and repulsive
Decide

I felt a searing line of consequence
Split me in two

In one hand a shrunken stump,
The sacrifice
In one hand a burning torch,
The chosen

Oh, the fire of choice was mine
And on that day
I lit the jagged blade which would saw me in half

Felt the burning stream divide me:
What I was
What I could have been

Laughing gleefully,
The twisting ropes of choice, opportunity, ran off

Luxury is an illusion,
Choice is a torture

I hadn't made my decision
Yet my decision had made me

...

I was swept along by repercussions
But when the river slowed and I floated on my life and
reflected,

The choices returned
More beautiful, more bright
Than before
But they brought with them a friend,
A stunning creature who smiled at me,

Compelling
And settled without hesitation in my heart

Her beautiful, terrible presence a heavy stone in my stomach
She haunted my dreams,
Leading me down corridors of lost opportunity

As I grew old, she was present
A constant ache

Long after the choices had danced away, abandoned me
She stayed
My last and constant companion

I clung to her

As my shell withers
And I am laid with dignity to rest,
She will smile her evil smile
And knowing her complete power over me,
Curl around my spine
Anchor my body to her domain
Earth
And relief will come at last as cool rain to my withered brow
I will float from my humanity,

Free at last

Jenna Lowe

By August 2017 I knew that it was time. I had to face the hardest thing and go back to Johannesburg. Other than the brief trip to collect Jen's Lead SA award, I had not been back. I had clients in Johannesburg and had been asked to speak at functions. I needed to overcome my fear of returning. Stuart had a business trip planned. We decided I would join him and stay for the weekend.

For days leading up to the trip nausea and the flashbacks set in again. Christine collected me from the Gautrain and drove me straight to her apartment. I stood in the lounge, rooted to the ground as the painful memories washed over me. That afternoon Stu and I drove the familiar suburbs, slowly and deliberately. Even though Stu had been here regularly on business trips for two years, he had managed to avoid all the suburbs surrounding Milpark. Now we drove them together, circling closer and closer to the hospital. We didn't quite manage to get there.

On Friday, I woke up and I knew. We had to see Paul. I messaged Dr Williams. Of course he would make time to see us, he said. We drove to the hospital at 4:30 pm that day in silence. Walking into the lobby of Milpark Hospital transported me back two years in an instant. I felt as if I'd been kicked in the solar plexus with great force. I couldn't breathe; I thought I might pass out. Waves of nausea threatened to engulf me. I stood dead still and breathed slowly and deliberately, in and out, until I managed to find my centre. Together Stu and I walked silently down the long passage, turning right at the end, on auto-pilot. We stood outside the doors to Surgical ICU for a while.

"I don't need to go in there," I said to Stu.

"I don't either," he said.

We turned around and walked up the stairs to the second floor, to Paul's office. It felt like there was no one there. We pushed open the double glass doors and called tentatively, "Paul?" I had not seen him since we left Johannesburg.

He walked out from his office. We stood staring at each other for a moment and then stepped towards each other and hugged and wept. He had also lost Jenna, and in a matter of minutes, he had lost us too. I wondered where, in this medical system of ours, is the emotional and psychological support for our overworked and exhausted doctors? Who do they turn to to help them process the relentless trauma they witness on a daily basis?

We talked and talked. We spoke the unspeakable and asked the burning questions that we hadn't yet been able to verbalise. Paul told us we were extremely courageous to come, but he was very grateful that we had. He told us that he had been (and he still is) deeply impacted by Jenna. As was the entire organ donation and pulmonary hypertension landscape of South Africa. We shared our impossible journey of grief with him, and the news of Stuart's diagnosis, of Kristi, of me and my studies and of The Jenna Lowe Trust.

Shortly after we returned home to Cape Town, Prof. Badesch visited from the US. He was here, as a direct result of Jen, to help Dr Williams and other pulmonary hypertension doctors complete a White Paper on the diagnosis and treatment of PH in South Africa. He, too, was devastated. It was so comforting to hear his words of encouragement. It felt crazy when he thanked us for what we had done for Jen and other South Africans with PH. It was he who had given so much of his time and expertise free of charge. He had been so compassionate. Shortly after his visit we asked Gavin Levy, Dr Symons and Dr Williams to join the board of The Jenna Lowe Trust.

As we moved towards the end of 2017, I considered writing a book. But it was way too hard, and I ended up contemplating and writing about the lessons learned from our journey instead. What was it that had enabled Jenna to be so incredibly resilient? And us as a family? What were the tools? I read more and more books on the topic of emotional resilience and thought long and hard about our own journey, what we had done to enable us to cope. Unintentionally, I started to develop a 10-step model that would become a toolkit for authentic emotional resilience. It fascinated me. Then in November I had lunch with a girlfriend, Pippa Shaper. Pippa had reached out to me and offered much-needed peer support soon after Jenna died. She understood my pain all too well. Pippa's life is a litany of loss; outrageously, she has lost two children and her first husband. We soon discovered we had more in common than death and we became firm friends. Pippa is also a life coach and works with an NPO. She, too, was navigating her way through hectic loss. Pippa loved and related to the concepts in my model. In November 2017 we joined forces to finish co-authoring our model – The Ten R's of Authentic Emotional Resilience ©.

One thing I knew for sure about resilience was that two hearts, two minds and two sets of experiences would be a whole lot better than one. Pippa and I combined our energies on the project after hours, going away on weekends to workshop our ideas, research and continue writing.

At the end of 2017 Kristi received glowing matric results and was accepted to UCT to do a Bachelor of Social Sciences degree. Then we received an unexpected email. A formal invitation to the family to attend the Sixth World Pulmonary Hypertension Symposium in Nice in February 2018. The committee was hoping that "I Need More Time" could be the theme song for the symposium and wondered if I would consider speaking at the opening ceremony to 3 000 international doctors. They invited Kristi to perform the song live. We knew it would be tough and discussed it at length. But we were deeply honoured. We could do this, we had to do this, for Jen. We decided we would go.

2018

The Coaching Nest had taken on a life of its own and January and February of 2018 were jam-packed with coaching clients, Kristi starting her first year of university, and Stuart and Brandon went in to field with a massive research survey. The end of February was upon us in no time. It was time to galvanise ourselves for the Sixth World Pulmonary Hypertension Symposium. Being thrown back into the deepest end of the world of pulmonary hypertension was harder than I could have imagined. And yet, being guests of honour at the World Symposium was also an extraordinary experience. We met the world's top experts in their field and were astounded at how many there were. We shared Jen's story and the important perspective of patients in Third World countries like South Africa with little or no access to First World treatments and expertise. We attended the sound check and rehearsal to discover the symposium was being held in a massive conference centre and 3 000 people would be at the opening. It was pretty daunting but so professionally run and organised that it was impressive.

The greatest honour – and biggest challenge – for me, though, was that I had been unwittingly seconded onto a task force with nine top-level international PH specialists and heads of PH patient associations. Before the opening I spent three days attending plenary sessions contributing towards a paper our task force was writing called "The Patient's Perspective". To be honest, in my ignorance, I had not expected or understood this process before getting to France. If I had, I might not have attended, but I'm glad I did. I learned so much! It was crazy-daunting at first, and I was very grateful that Stuart and I had had the foresight to invite nurse Lizzie, who was now living in the UK but still working with The Jenna Lowe Trust, to join us. Having her at my side gave me the confidence to do the work. Our task force, Task Force Number 13, worked day and night on the paper leading up to the start of the symposium. By the time the day of the grand opening arrived I was firmly ensconced back in the world and language of pulmonary hypertension. I needed these doctors, these experts, to understand just how difficult it is for patients who don't have access to their expertise and treatments to cope with this cruel disease. I wanted to remind them why they do what they do – for the patient. First and foremost, for the patient. It seems obvious, but it's not. For patients and patients' families, it can often feel as though these high-level experts are speaking Latin. In all their genius they need to remember to also speak the language of the patient.

On Tuesday, the 27th of February I spoke at the opening ceremony, one tiny body on this massive stage, and straight afterwards Kristi sang "I Need More Time" while the images of her music video and Jen played behind her on a huge screen. It was deeply moving. I still receive messages from various medical doctors thanking our family for reminding them why they do what they do. Stu and I had such a good giggle when a year later the paper was published: looking down the list of authors you see one impressive PH specialist after another, each with very long titles and numerous medical degrees behind their names ... and then, tacked on at the end of the list is "Gabi Lowe". Plain and simple, no title in sight. I am pretty proud, actually.

After returning from the symposium we were emotionally spent. It had definitely taken its toll. So many terrifying demons and emotional triggers had been faced. Stuart was also not feeling well and it became clear over the next few months that his myeloma markers were up again. His stem cell transplant had not been 100% effective. Stu was put onto a daily oral chemo routine, three weeks on and one week off, for the next six months. The symposium had left us all with a big fat "vulnerability hangover". I went back to the trauma specialist for a few more sessions and Kristi went back to the refuge of her bedroom for a few weeks. But we soon emerged again. The transformational work I was able to do with my clients gave me such a deep sense of purpose and kept me engaged with the world. Helping others to face their own challenges was what kept me going.

My practice was growing fast and by April of 2018 Pippa and I launched our first Authentic Emotional Resilience Workshop. Eighty people attended the first one. There is no doubt that in this ever-changing, complex and challenging world of ours emotional resilience is becoming an essential and often elusive skill. The credibility of our work and our tools lies in the fact that they are born through experience. We soon discovered that every attendee became a foot soldier for the work, and the demand for our workshops grew and grew.

The 8th of June was the third anniversary of Jenna's death. We took James, Daffy and her closest girlfriends away for the weekend. It was an incredible three days of reminiscing and sharing stories. At last it was becoming easier for the youngsters to talk about her. They were starting to discover that talking about her and their experiences was helpful.

Three short days after Jen's third "death-aversary", I did something both exciting and brave. I travelled to Greece with Denise, to the island of Lesvos, to a gorgeous little seaside village called Skala Eressos, to do a seven-day writing retreat. It was attended by a group of about 10 or 12 incredible people and writers, and led by two powerful women, Sarah Bullen and Kate Emmerson. The retreat was a transformative experience for me. It was on that beach, in that little town that the dedication for this book was written.

Once the retreat was over, I stayed on, in a beautiful medieval village called Molyvos, on my own for a further 10 days. I had found the courage to start my book, Jen's book, this book. And once I started there was no stopping. I catapulted myself into nine intensive months of writing. I didn't have the luxury of solely writing, so I eked out periods, five days, a week or 10 days at a time, when I would disappear off on my own and immerse myself in writing for 12 to 14 hours a day. I developed a ritual that every time I sat down to write, I would set out my favourite picture of Jen, light a candle, find the white feather that was always waiting for me somewhere close by, put my head down and write. I would cry, rage, reminisce, feel, remember, grieve, mourn and write and write and write.

In between these intense writing times I spent many hours coaching, running emotional resilience workshops and doing our Jenna Lowe Trust work. By now the Pulmonary Hypertension Clinic had grown to over 80 state patients and instead of running once a month, it was operating twice a month. We had also started the Jenna Lowe PH Registry, a world-class database to track patients in South Africa, hopefully Africa, so that the statistics could later be shared with medical insurances to help get this "orphan" disease firmly on the map for treatments.

In September I spoke in St George's Cathedral on Organ Donor Tribute Day to hundreds of families who had lost their loved ones and donated their organs to save the lives of others. It was a sacred space and a sacred day.

Stuart had just started another 16 weeks of triple therapy – chemo, steroids and bone density infusions – because his myeloma levels were up again. It was a huge shock that his levels had gone back up again so fast and I was feeling particularly vulnerable. Writing the book forced me to engage with every part of our pain and suffering, my grief, with no escape. It was also becoming clearer to me that the threat of loss for us was (and is) still very much in the wings. As it is for everyone in some way. The impermanence of life was truly sinking in and I was feeling particularly wobbly. One night I broke down and told Stu and Kristi that I was worried. For the first time I felt as though I wasn't coping. I was tearful, shaky, jumpy and wanted to shrink and hide from the world. I thought I might be in trouble. They were amazing, both of them, stepping up without question to love, support and help me in whatever way I needed. Allowing me to be completely vulnerable and saying they thought it was about time, I must do whatever I needed to do and take whatever time I needed to take.

That same week, on the Saturday morning Stu and I decided to take the dogs for a walk on Muizenberg beach for some gentle, healing time. We could talk, breathe in the fresh ocean air and feel the sand between our toes. We parked at Sunrise Circle and turned left onto the beach toward the river so that the dogs could run free. We love watching them bound in and out of the waves and chasing seagulls. We walked and we talked, held hands and cried. Stu was vulnerable too, not just emotionally but physically. His health was really not good. His back was incredibly sore, and he was physically weak from the chemotherapy, so we took it slowly. Eventually we reached the end and turned around to walk back to the carpark. It felt like we had the whole glorious beach to ourselves. The group ahead of us were but small figures in the distance. I was starting to breathe.

At that moment two youths dressed in jeans and hoodies appeared from behind the dunes at the top of the beach. Something about their stance and their attitude was sinister. Stu had his back to them, dragging seaweed for the dogs so he didn't notice. In a heartbeat they were upon us. One lurched for me and the other one lurched for Stu. I spun round to face my attacker, and, in that moment, I had full sight of Stu. I watched in horror as the youth threw him to his knees and pulled out a long, curved, serrated fishing knife. He started jabbing at Stu, trying to stab him. For a split second my entire body went weak. Everything was in slow motion and I felt completely outside of my body. This could not be happening! I knew that if that knife found his body just once, there was no way he would survive it. The infection alone would kill him.

I started to scream and run towards them. I was screaming and screaming, and I didn't stop. I didn't stop. I screamed and screamed and screamed. It was a voice I'd never heard before – mad, crazy, high-pitched, relentless. It seemed to awaken something in Stuart, and he started to scream too. The two of us did not stop. Spurred on by each other, our screaming became louder and louder and more and more enraged as we fought back. We fought and we fought. In the mayhem Stu rolled out of his jacket and pulled free. The youth with the knife abandoned him and came after me. He knocked me over into the water and started flailing at me with the knife. The dogs were going crazy, circling them and barking, but doing nothing. I hit the ground hard but bounced straight back up again. Instinctively, I knew that if I showed any sign of weakness I was finished. I was back up on my feet again and screaming profanities in the young man's face.

By then the group who were further down the beach in front of us had turned and were running back toward us. They were getting closer. I could feel myself tiring and I started yelling, "Help! Help us! Help us!"

For a split second I saw something shift in my attacker's eyes. He could see them closing in behind me and held up his knife again and started stabbing. Stuart grabbed a handful of wet sand and threw it straight into his eyes. It was a brilliant move. At that moment the two youths looked at each other and then half-sauntered and half-jogged brazenly backwards up the beach and disappeared into the dunes, their eyes never leaving ours.

We collapsed in the sand, heaving and heaving. It was nobody's fault, but I will never forget Stuart saying over and over, "I'm so sorry, I'm so sorry."

Neither of us could talk for days because our voices were so hoarse. It was a horrific experience and we were traumatised. But here is the thing: those two attackers gave me a gift. An unexpected gift. At my most vulnerable I discovered that I still had the will to live. More than that, I discovered that my inner lioness was very much alive and kicking. They gave me an opportunity to rage at the universe. To scream and swear and rage in a way that I never otherwise would have. They had made me fight for life, for Stuart's life and my own life.

It was a massive turning point for me and a huge lesson – often at our most vulnerable we are also our most powerful. Vulnerability is not weakness. It is about confronting all of ourselves; it is courage in spite of fear. I had been teaching this for months. Now I knew it for certain.

The last few months of 2018 were spent writing and working hard. Stu put his head down to cope with his treatment and Kristi completed her first year of university. My coaching practice flourished, and the emotional resilience work was growing exponentially. Pippa and I went into a proper partnership and started The Resilience Factory so that we could continue to grow and develop our emotional resilience work.

2019

After Jen's death I was deeply cynical about the concept of choice. It was obvious that if we as human beings had the power of choice, we would have chosen for Natalie and Jenna to live. To stay here with us on earth. Loss had made it abundantly clear to me that the idea of being "in control" is a terrible illusion. Every day bad things happen in our lives over which we have absolutely no control. But what we do have control over is the ability to choose how we are going to respond. Once I started to process my rage and stopped holding on so tightly to how I wished it had been, I was able to really start feeling again. Forcing the truth of my suffering into the deepest corners of my mind had been its very own torture.

Writing this book has been the most painful thing I've ever done other than actually living through Jenna's death. But it has truly helped me learn to embrace all aspects of life again. Through my coaching, my work on emotional resilience, the writing of this book and the cultivating of important and life-giving relationships, I have slowly, slowly found my way back to hope and joy. Pain, suffering and even devastation are an inevitable part of life. To find joy, purpose and meaning we must look inside and to each other.

Christmases and year-end holidays are a bittersweet experience for me. Every time we go back to Plett we visit all the places where we sprinkled Jen-Dust and do a beautiful hike to Jen's rock to remember and celebrate her. These are meaningful rituals that help us to honour her and feel connected. Jen's rock is high up on a mountain cliff overlooking the craggy beaches of Keurboomstrand with the Plettenberg Bay mountains in the distance. It is wild and beautiful, close to heaven and the wild ocean, a place where I feel Jen's presence so keenly. We take flowers to her rock and say a few words to pay homage to her. Then we sit in silence in wonder at the beauty of earth and of Jen and her place in our hearts. She lives inside us.

Jen, it is April 2019 and it is not insignificant that it has taken me exactly nine months to write this. As I have faced head on the searing pain of your loss, I have also shed layers and layers of trauma. The missing and the longing are savage, but I have no dark secret memories left festering inside me. I have told the whole story exactly as I remember it and for the first time in years I am able to remember all of you, Jen. The Jen before your illness as well as after it.

Thank you for the extraordinary privilege of being your mother and for all you have taught me. I will never forget.

And so, my darling Jen, with all its pain, all its joy and everything in between, I choose life. Just as you did until the moment you took your last breath, my beloved child, I choose life.

Acknowledgements and thanks

I am forever grateful to so many extraordinary people who've been an essential part of our journey and stood by us for many long years. Without them we could not have faced the impossible. In some ways Jenna became "everybody's child" and it saddens me that many of the selfless and compassionate acts of support we experienced have not made it into the pages of this book, quite simply because there were so many. But believe me when I say, we couldn't have faced this without you. Every single one of you.

Thank you to my beloved and courageous family without whom I would not be functional. Stuart, my rock, my soulmate, father of my children, my strength and the love of my life, I quite simply don't know where I would be without you. Kristi, my beautiful girl, dealt so much so young, you fill my heart with joy, love and pride every single day. A one-of-a-kind human, may you continue to blossom forever. Mom and Dad (Granny Annie and Grampa), you have stood by me, loved me and witnessed things no grandparent or parent should have to witness. Thank you for your unfailing love and belief in me. To Shirley and Alison, my intrepid sisters-in-law, who will stop at nothing to support each other, we have walked through the fire together and become true sisters, forever. To my beautiful nephews, Kola, who holds a special place in my heart, and Matt, whose quiet strength and unwavering support are both consistent and constant. And to Les, who had no idea he was marrying into such heartache, but has stood by us all through the worst of times regardless. To Craig, my beloved brother, it matters not how many geographic miles there are between us, I feel your love, support and strength daily and know I can rely on you. To Margo, beloved sister-in-law, for your unlimited kindness and loving my girls as if they were your own; and to Tayla and Nic for your constant love and fervent support from the other side of the world. To all of my, and Stuart's, cousins, nieces, nephews, aunties and uncles all over the world who have followed, watched, supported and waited in the wings to give help when it was needed.

Every day we give thanks for our incredible friends who have gone way beyond the call of duty. You have taught us the value of reaching out, of deep trust, of unstinting loyalty, of generosity of spirit and of real friendship. My trusted friends and neighbours Mary and Sue who became part of the scaffolding of my life, my "on the ground" team. I went to war with you once, and I would do it again. To Glynis, I am deeply grateful to have you as my north star, my anchor, my guide, friend and healer. Thank you to our treasured friends (and Jen's beloved godparents) Ian, Jillie and Sandy who have stood by us through hell, no matter that they hurt nearly as much as we did watching the devastation and loss. And my resourceful, compassionate brave heart of a friend Vanessa, who found ways to help when I didn't even know there were any. To Gavin and Denise for their limitless love, support and generosity. For all the high days, the sore days, the holidays, the mentorship and the safe spaces in which to write, mourn and be together. To our Wazzup couples – Sue and Haydn, James and Libby, Ian and Jillie, Dean and Sarah, and Charles and Fran – who stopped at nothing to rally the support we needed, no matter what form it had to take. And heartfelt thanks to my beloved girlfriends Nici, Tess, Lani, Justine, Pam, Elbie, Eva, Carrie, Lisa, Nicky and Lu, who have held, loved, listened, fed me wine and allowed me to cry buckets as and when I needed to. To "Jen's Angels", Karen, Carlie and Melissa, who worked tirelessly and lovingly to help me with every single fundraising event and continue to stand at my side. To Brandon for holding the fort in the office and being a fearless support and friend to Stuart throughout the good and the difficult years. And for being the talented creative director for everything we do. To Nic and Ian for being trusted mentors, sounding boards and invaluable support systems for my lion of a man throughout. To Tim and Hantie for a lifetime of friendship and offering me a safe haven in their home from which to write. And to commentator and friend extraordinaire, Matthew Pearce, who would stop at nothing to find us the support we needed in whatever way he could. To Mike and Sandy, Dean and Sarah, Mark and Christine, and Japie and Lupi for opening their homes, hearts and so much more to us in Johannesburg.

To you, James, indomitable and unwavering in your love and support, thank you for standing by Jenna through the very worst of times. Your strength, commitment and loyalty are extraordinary – you will forever remain like a son to us. Thank you, Ian and Jenny, for supporting your boy through all of this and entrusting him to us. It must have been hard. To Daffy, and his beloved family, Karen, Bob and Demi, thank you for loving Jen unconditionally and wholeheartedly for so many years. You are a treasure to us and were to her. Daffy, you too are, and will always be, a son to us.

Thank you to beautiful Nurse Lizzie: you were a godsend. Your smiling face, kind eyes, big heart and dedication to Jen made many hours of mixing and battling crises together bearable. To Margy in Johannesburg who helped me nurse Jen through some very dark hours and Sarah Holloway, who did the same, thank you for your courageous support of Jenna through some very difficult days. And Shirl for being the perfect role model of a "momcologist" and, of course, Nurse Debra from the US for sharing her expertise and teaching us how to mix.

To all the beautiful teenagers and young adults who stood by *both* my girls through the tough times. I have no doubt that the irrefutable impact of having had Jenna as your close friend will continue to play out in your lives in ways you are yet to understand. Camilla, you were an extraordinary friend to our Jen, one whom she knew she could call at any time for anything. She loved you deeply. As were you, Alex, a friend who helped her understand what real friendship is all about. Who taught her the value of unquestionable commitment. Aniko, you are a blessing and a gift to us all and a tonic for Jenna and Kristi. You have certainly earned your stripes as an honorary member of the Lowe clan. Giulietta, Celeste, Julia, Lethu, Nikita, Olivia, Shaaz, Lisa, Georgie, Abi ... you lit up Jen's life with your friendship and still light up ours. Never forget your worth, how much you matter to your girlfriends and how much they matter to you. You were part of the fabric of Jenna's life, as you will be part of each other's forever. To the "Plett boys", all of you, thank you for opening your hearts, minds and village to our Jen and becoming a loving safety net at a time when she represented the opposite of carefree, the opposite of what your life was. To the "Rondebosch boys", the "Bishops boys", in fact the myriad boys who became loyal friends throughout Jen's high school years. And to Ashleigh, who never knew Jen but became such a critical support system for Kristi in Johannesburg at a crucial time in her life. You are a loyal friend and much-loved part of our family. To Kia for the joy you brought Kristi through some difficult years, and Abigail, who came into our lives after Jen's death and did the same. Thank you, Allen, for your ongoing and dedicated friendship and support of Stuart and our family, and the Spur Foundation for your incredible dedication to the Save 7 Lives campaign.

There are many other important people for whom we have so much gratitude. The concentric circles of support, friendship and love in Cape Town, Plettenberg Bay, Johannesburg, Durban and internationally who have played a vital role in our journey ... the hundreds and hundreds, in fact thousands, of people who have followed, supported with unlimited random and not-so-random acts of kindness and compassion. I will forever be grateful to all the friends, acquaintances and colleagues in Johannesburg who opened their hearts to us, giving freely of their time and love, offering accommodation, cars, food, friendship and all sorts of other support. Special thanks to Dean and Sarah, Christine and Mark, Mike and Sandy, Gavin and Lou, Giselle, Sarah, Margy, Sue and Nicky. To Jane and Suanne and many others in the UK; and the Ferguson family, Deb and John Hornig, the Mannington family, plus many others in the US.

We will forever have limitless gratitude and respect for the incredible international doctors who were a vital part of our journey: Prof. David Badesch from UC Denver, Colorado, Dr Frank Gray from GlaxoSmithKline in the UK and Prof. Anne Keogh from Sydney, Australia for so generously giving of your time and expertise to help a patient floundering on the other side of the world with absolutely no reason to do so other than knowing you were doing the right thing. You selflessly helped a young girl fight to survive and, in doing so, made a huge difference in her world and that of many others. Your generosity and dedication are astonishing; we will never forget your kindness. Thank you, too, to our incredible team of local doctors and medical staff, many of whom went way beyond the call of duty to make new and difficult things happen as and when they were needed. Dr Williams, Prof. Wilcox, Dr Lewis, Dr Symons, Dr Calligaro and many others. Thank you for being willing to collaborate and live in the land of possibility, for putting up with my sometimes impossible demands and believing in our Jenna. Thank you, too, to all the transplant co-ordinators for their tireless and oh-so-meaningful work. May you continue to fight for the hope of all those awaiting transplant.

Thank you to all the international and local PH associations around the world; and to Sam and Jooste at the South African Organ Donor Foundation, who supported Jen wholeheartedly in her challenges and campaigning. Huge thanks to Prof. Nazzareno Galie and the committee of the Sixth World Symposium for PH for inviting the Lowe family to attend and interact with thousands of world experts. Plus a huge thank you to Kelly at Rare Diseases SA for her invaluable long-term support and friendship over the years. Thanks to the PVRI (Pulmonary Vascular Research Institute) for believing in and partnering with The Jenna Lowe Trust to further impact PH in South Africa and all the doctors on the Patient's Perspective task force who believed in me.

Thank you to the incredible education communities – teachers, lecturers and mentors – who went the extra mile (or 10): Stuart West and all at Herschel Girls School in Cape Town, Abbotts College in Cape Town, Redhill in Johannesburg, Cedar House in Cape Town and the University of Cape Town. These first-class educational institutions went out of their way to understand, accommodate and facilitate what Jenna and Kristi needed. As did the beautiful Kim at the Kim Kallie Banner Performance Academy. Thank you, Kim, for supporting Kristi through her singing journey with such love and dedication, and for being a second mommy when she really needed one.

Thank you to Discovery Health who not only shared Jenna's story with their members but found ways to support us and share the knowledge of the international doctors with local. Thank you for being open to Jenna's needs and those of other PH patients in South Africa, for listening and getting involved, for being open to re-inventing the wheel. Mostly, thank you to Raffaella for your support and friendship. You have been a blessing.

It is safe to say that I have many issues with big pharma companies, but it is also safe to say that GlaxoSmithKline, owned by Aspen, really came to the party with Flolan for Jen – thank you. Thank you, Equity Pharmaceuticals, for being so dedicated in helping us with the legalities, paperwork and importing logistics and to our very own small pharmacy, Brent and his team at Nu Pharmacy in Cavendish Square, who did everything possible to make difficult times less challenging. Thanks, too, to Mike Leathes for helping us with all the medical technology, and a huge thank you to our GP, Kathy Lewis, for her thoroughness, incredible care and support over many decades.

Then to our amazing #GetMeTo21 team – the campaign would not have been the success it was without Kirk and his creative team at Mullen Lowe, Dani at Egg Productions, Liza-Jane at Match Creative, Neal Tosefsky and Steve and Mary at Berry Productions. Your dedication to this campaign was beautiful to watch. Thank you for allowing our Jen to touch you so much, and for standing by The Jenna Lowe Trust still today in all the work we do.

A massive thank you to Jonathan Ackerman (in fact, the entire Ackerman family) and Pick n Pay for their dedicated love and support at all our fundraisers and in helping us get to and from Johannesburg in such dramatic circumstances. To Andrea and her team at Dish Food and Social who went the extra mile and then some, to support us with delicious food through hard times, hospital times, fundraisers, all my girls' birthdays and the memorial – you are literally a food angel. To Paul and his team at Venturescapes who supplied and set up everything needed for our incredible Valentine's Picnic, as well as my girls' birthday parties and Jenna's spectacular memorial. You have always come on board and helped us with so with such warmth, generosity and sheer professionalism. As did Annalise Buchanan with her spectacular feast tables at the picnic. Not least of all we could not have done any of our fundraisers without Alison, Debbie, Matt, Portia, Mandi, Carole and the entire Rainbow Experiential Marketing team; your support at every single event has been exceptional and heartfelt – thank you.

We were so fortunate throughout our epic battle to have support shown by many brands and companies over the years: Berry Productions, Sue Cooper Meditation and Retreats, Robyn and Roy at The Vineyard Hotel & Spa, the Hunter Hotel Group, The Parkwood, Southern Sun Hotels, Lauren and Neil at Relate Bracelets, Ginger & Lime, BMW Auric Auto, Cape Town Productions, The Reach For A Dream Foundation, the Baxter Theatre, Iain Banner at HQ Restaurant, Julia and Ben at GoodLuck, all at Western Province Rugby, Soccer Laduma, Europcar, King Shaka Aviation, Sabine and her team at Figaro Hair Design, the Springbok Rugby Sevens Team, Yogaway, Pathcare in Claremont, Village Skincare in Tokai, Gus and team at Constantia Glen, Sue McCallum Chiropractic Centre, Ofer and his team at Gearhouse, Nicolwood Furnishers, Michael Fridjhon Wine Academy, Luxury Brands, The Three Oaks, The Forge Web Creations, Next Music, Nuthouse Recording Studio, Tony at Ocean Blue, Carrie and David at BesterBurke, Sonic Matters, Tech

X, Art Lab, Top Copy, Johan Laas Music, Megan Carr Jewellery, Scarab, Tosca Hair Salon, Vital Aire, Ecomed, Two Oceans Vibe, the entire team at Primedia, Dream Resorts, LPH Financial Services, Wilderness Safaris, Craig at Medinformer, Shumani Mills Printers, Scenic Flights, 7films, Lovonne and Simon Burrows at Bastide Les Amis Menerbes, Sue at The Grand Café and Beach, The Fugard Theatre, Proto Trading, Rialto Foods, Makro and Derek at The Design Company.

Thank you to all the journalists, vloggers, bloggers and media who got behind Jen and the Lowe family to help us tell her story to the world, which in turn helped us to make a difference to the landscape of pulmonary hypertension in South Africa – and especially to Primedia and Lead SA who backed and supported us from the very beginning and still do.

Thank you, too, to all the #GetMeTo21 followers who signed up to be organ donors, and to those thousands who will still sign up because they are touched by Jenna's story. You are super heroes – each one of you could save seven lives one day.

Thank you to my therapist, who remains nameless for reasons of confidentiality, for being a consistent guide and mentor in my life for decades, ensuring that I always have a lifeline.

Thank you to the thousands of people who donated money, both large and small amounts, to The Jenna Lowe Trust over the years, who attended our events, who made meals, who dropped a card in the postbox, a pasta sauce or brought flowers unexpectedly. The myriad loving and kind souls who found a way, any way, to get involved and show support – you literally buoyed us up with your support and made it possible to not give up.

Thank you to all the special board members of The Jenna Lowe Trust who give selflessly and freely of their time to help continue Jenna's legacy and work: Martin Luyt, Haydn Heydenrych, Gavin Levy, Dr Paul Williams and Dr Greg Symons.

Finally, to the people who have helped me to birth this book and bring it to life. Thank you, Sarah Bullen and Kate Emmerson, for introducing me to writing on your incredible writing retreat in Greece. Not only did you get me started, you inspired me and made me believe I could do this. Thank you, Marianne Thamm, for your friendship and support over the years, for introducing me to Melinda Ferguson and for writing my beautiful foreword. You have been a significant influence in my life for which I am so grateful. Thanks to Diana Lucas for introducing me to Jacana. Melinda Ferguson of MFBooks, you are a publisher extraordinaire, filled with passion and drive. You have been a monumental support. Thank you for believing in me from the very first chapter. Thank you to all those who gave me silent, isolated, safe spaces in which to immerse myself in writing. Thank you, Shirley, for helping me edit the Natalie parts and remember painful details that trauma had snatched away from my memory. Most importantly, thank you to Alison Lowry for agreeing to edit my book and doing so with such tenderness, care and professionalism. It has been nothing but a pleasure working with you.

A heartfelt thank you to Jenna's donor family. I know that you, too, lost a loved one and have been experiencing the heartbreaking roller coaster of grief. Your courageous and selfless decision to donate your loved one's organs at exactly the time of your greatest grief and loss was truly honourable. It brought us all inordinate joy and gave us hope. You single-handedly gave our special girl a second chance, a second chance at life. Thank you does not suffice.

Mostly, a massive and heartfelt thank you to my beloved Stuart and Kristi, who have allowed me to disappear into my book for hours, days and weeks on end. Thank you for supporting me in every way possible so that I could finish this labour of love. This is not just for me, not just for Jenna, it is my gift to you so that we can put down some of the pain. So that we don't have to be the vessel that carries the traumatic memories, because they are safely and lovingly recorded here forever. Thank you for allowing me the space to write *Get Me to 21*. I love you both with all my heart.

Thank you to all of you whose names do not appear here, of whom there are very many, for being part of our journey. We invited you into our world and you came lovingly, open-heartedly and with all of yourselves. Thank you.

The Jenna Lowe Trust

www.jennalowe.org

Jenna Lowe influenced massive social change in South Africa. She fought for awareness and support of pulmonary hypertension (PH) and increased the number of organ donors by tens of thousands with her internationally acclaimed #GetMeTo21 campaign. The Jenna Lowe Trust is a not-for-profit public benefit organisation (PBO Number 930052755) which continues Jenna's inspirational work in order to honour her remarkable legacy and make a difference in the lives of others.

The objectives of the trust are as follows:

- To raise awareness of pulmonary hypertension in South Africa, to encourage and facilitate earlier diagnosis, and to provide better care for patients, caregivers and patient families.
- To increase public awareness of the shortage of organ donors in South Africa, address misconceptions and drive registration.
- To create platforms that raise funds for, and donate money

to, campaigns and projects that are directly related to pulmonary hypertension and organ transplantation in South Africa.

- To support projects and people who educate and train individuals, families and organisations in broad or specific areas of pulmonary hypertension and organ transplantation.

The financials of The Jenna Lowe Trust are freely available. It remains specifically recorded that no trustee is paid for his or her time in executing their duties as a trustee. Such time is given voluntarily, free of charge.

If you would like to donate towards this cause, purchase a Jenna Lowe Trust Relate bracelet, or read more about Jenna and see some of the incredible media coverage and videos she generated, please visit: www.jennalowe.org All support will be gratefully received.

If you would like to sign up as a South African organ donor or have any queries about organ donation, please visit either:

www.getmeto21.org or www.odf.org.za

If you would like to know more about pulmonary hypertension, please visit the PH Association of South Africa: www.phsa.org.za

Other resources for PH patients include all international PH associations:

- www.wsphassociation.org
- www.phauk.org.za
- www.phassociation.org
- www.phaeurope.org
- www.pulmonaryhypertension.in
- www.phaustralia.com
- www.rarediseases.co.za

Find Gabi Lowe at: www.thecoachingnest.co.za or www.theresiliencefactory.com